Wiebke Beushausen, Anne Brüske, Ana-Sofia Commichau,
Patrick Helber, Sinah Kloß (eds.)
Caribbean Food Cultures

Postcolonial Studies | Volume 18

Wiebke Beushausen, Anne Brüske, Ana-Sofia Commichau,
Patrick Helber, Sinah Kloss (eds.)

Caribbean Food Cultures
Culinary Practices and Consumption
in the Caribbean and Its Diasporas

[transcript]

Bibliographic information published by the Deutsche Nationalbibliothek
The Deutsche Nationalbibliothek lists this publication in the Deutsche Nationalbibliografie; detailed bibliographic data are available in the Internet at http://dnb.d-nb.de

© **2014 transcript Verlag, Bielefeld**

All rights reserved. No part of this book may be reprinted or reproduced or utilized in any form or by any electronic, mechanical, or other means, now known or hereafter invented, including photocopying and recording, or in any information storage or retrieval system, without permission in writing from the publisher.

Cover layout: Kordula Röckenhaus, Bielefeld
Cover illustration: Corinna Assmann, Heidelberg 2012, © Corinna Assmann
Printed by Majuskel Medienproduktion GmbH, Wetzlar
Print-ISBN 978-3-8376-2692-6
PDF-ISBN 978-3-8394-2692-0

Contents

Acknowledgements | 7

INTRODUCTION

The Caribbean (on the) Dining Table. Contextualizing Culinary Cultures
Wiebke Beushausen, Anne Brüske, Ana-Sofia Commichau, Patrick Helber, Sinah Kloß | 11

CULINARY AESTHETICS

The Aesthetics of Hunger and the Special Period in Cuba
Rita De Maeseneer | 27

Hotel Worlds and Culinary Encounters in Cristina García's *The Lady Matador's Hotel*
Louisa Söllner | 49

'You are what you cook.' Preparing Food, Creating Life in *Treme*
Sebastian Huber | 67

The Fierce Questioning of Fictional Caribbean Communion in Édouard Glissant's *Ormerod* **and Fortuné Chalumeau's** *Désirade, ô Serpente!*
Daniel Graziadei | 89

NEO/COLONIAL GAZE

Curiosity, Appreciation, and Old Habits. Creolization of Colonizers' Food Consumption Patterns in Three English Travelogues on the Caribbean
Ilaria Berti | 115

Representations of Caribbean Food in U.S. Popular Culture
Fabio Parasecoli | 133

CONSTRUCTIONS OF AUTHENTICITY

Cooking up a Storm. Residual Orality, Cross-Cultural Culinary Discourse, and the Construction of Tradition in the Cookery Writing of Levi Roots
Sarah Lawson Welsh | 153

The Transnational *Ajiaco*. Food Identity in the Cuban Diaspora
Ivan Darias Alfonso | 175

Reinventing Local Food Culture in an Afro-Caribbean Community in Costa Rica
Mona Nikolić | 201

CONSUMPTION AND COMMUNITIES

Barrels of Love. A Study of the Soft Goods Remittance Practices of Transnational Jamaican Households
Dwaine Plaza | 227

Hindu Ritual Food in Suriname. Women as Gatekeepers of Hindu Identity?
Elizabeth den Boer | 257

"De fuud dem produus me naa go iit it!" Rastafarian 'Culinary Identity'
Annika McPherson | 279

Notes on Contributors | 299

Acknowledgements

What had initially started as a somewhat vague conference project on transcultural exchange processes in the Caribbean back in the fall 2011, has eventually become the present volume, a compilation of thirteen articles on Caribbean Food Cultures.

But who would do Caribbean research in Germany anyway, and why?, one could ask quite provocatively.

The department of Transcultural Studies at Heidelberg University has been hosting (financed through the German governments' Excellence Initiative) the Junior Research Group "From the Caribbean to North America and Back. Transculturation Processes in Literature, Popular Culture, and New Media" since 2010. The group consists of four doctoral students, Wiebke Beushausen, Ana-Sofia Commichau, Patrick Helber, and Sinah Kloß, as well as a senior postdoc, Anne Brüske. Since then, the group's goal has been not only to contribute to research on the transatlantic Caribbean and its entanglements with North America and Europe through our individual projects, but also to spread Caribbean research within European academia. Organizing an international conference which would bring together both scholars from the Americas and Europe was the logical step to take.

The initial theoretical approach, focusing on transcultural flows and the Caribbean as a laboratory for transcultural theory, was soon discarded by the research group's think tank in favor of a more tangible and less Eurocentric focus on culinary practices and consumption cultures in the Caribbean. This leitmotiv is omnipresent, be it in Anglophone, Hispanic, or Francophone Caribbean fiction, in song lyrics, in Guyanese Hinduism and its cultural practices, as well as in the Cuban-American blogosphere, and points to the importance of research on Caribbean food cultures in a post/colonial and diasporic context. After roughly a year of preparation, the conference, entitled "Caribbean Food Cultures. Representations and Performances of Eating, Drinking, and Consumption in the Caribbean and Its Diasporas," took place from September 28 to 29 2012 at the Internationales Wissenschaftsforum Heidelberg. The conference brought together numerous scholars from both sides of the Atlantic and from disciplines as divergent as cultural anthropology, history, cultural and literary studies, soon exchanging their perspectives on the significance of food studies within the realm of Caribbean cultures.

The realization of both the conference and the publication project would not have been possible without the significant intellectual, practical, and financial contributions of numerous persons and institutions.

For the organization of the conference we are deeply indebted to the tireless assistance before, during, and after the event of, amongst others, Carmen Buschmann, Carolin Schwegler, Tjark Hecker, Ariane Müller-Guggenberger, and Lena Schondelmaier, as well as to the staff at the Internationales Wissenschaftsforum Heidelberg who provided the facilities and catering.

We would also like to express our sincere gratitude to the many people involved in the preparation and publication of the present volume: Ruel Johnson copy-edited the volume and improved it by valuable comments and meticulous proofreading. Emily Lever's bilingual expertise gave the final touch to the translations from French into English in Daniel Graziadei's contribution. Without Christina Lucas and Katharina Schöneborn, who formatted the volume and carefully checked all bibliographical references, and the support provided by our editor Anke Poppen at *transcript*, the pile of manuscripts never would have turned into a coherent book. Although you should not judge a book by its cover, we would like to thank Corinna Assmann for designing the conference poster and, subsequently, the volume's dust-jacket which encapsulates many of its topics. Of course, we are very grateful to Heidelberg University, the Excellence Initiative, and the land of Baden-Wurttemberg for funding both the conference and the publication and thus making a scholarly dream come true.

Last but not least, our greatest thanks goes to the contributors for their valuable papers, the fruitful discussions on Caribbean food studies, and the smooth cooperation throughout the whole editing process.

Introduction

The Caribbean (on the) Dining Table
Contextualizing Culinary Cultures

WIEBKE BEUSHAUSEN, ANNE BRÜSKE, ANA-SOFIA COMMICHAU,
PATRICK HELBER, SINAH KLOSS

> Food is the first of the essentials of life, the world's largest industry, our most frequently indulged pleasure, the core of our most intimate social relationships.
> WARREN BELASCO 2008: 1

CONTEXTUALIZING CARIBBEAN FOOD CULTURES

Food is at once a material good and a means of symbolic representation. Both its production and consumption can be regarded as performative acts that play a crucial role in various areas of human behavior and interaction. This involves, for example, the self-preservation of the body, the construction of ethnic, religious, and national identities, local and global commercial relationships, or the equal allocation of food and relations of production. These biological, social, economic, historic, and ethnic dimensions have taken a special turn in the Caribbean as a geographic region and for its discursive construction.[1] Forced and vol-

---

1   The Caribbean "is often defined as the island groupings of the Greater Antilles, Lesser Antilles, and the Bahamas, plus certain coastal zones of South and Central America sharing a cultural and historical relation to the island plantation societies (e.g. Suriname, Guyana, Belize)" (Sheller 2003: 5). We consider the Caribbean as a geographical and historical space as well as a sociocultural construction. In reference to Sheller,

untary migration have significantly influenced food cultures in this sociocultural space, marked by the contrast of its apparent diversity and subjacent common societal patterns. Thus, on the one hand, colonizers, enslaved Africans, indentured laborers, privateers, and refugees were social actors within specific historical relations of production, consumption, and trade. On the other hand, these different groups of people brought along social, cultural, and economic practices related to food, consumer and luxury goods such as tobacco, coffee, and sugar, which were subject to change and creolization. In the course of colonization, decolonization, migration, and tourism, the aforementioned goods, amongst many other Caribbean products and raw materials, have been circulating between the Caribbean, Europe, and North America. As B.W. Higman (2011: 97-140) and Sidney Mintz (1986) have shown, sugar has been the single most important Caribbean good. The so-called "sugar revolution" (1650-1770) brought about significant transformations of the ecosystem and society. It determined the colonies' economic and social structures by creating slaveholder societies and, subsequently, the system of indentureship. In addition, the emerging plantations, via a particular plantation architecture and extensive deforestation, visibly changed the colonies' geographical surface:

Once inscribed on the surface of the islands, sugar created a landscape that proved highly durable and a system of exploitation of land and people that was capable of withstanding social and political shocks. It was in this process and this period that the modern Caribbean was born. (Higmann 2011: 98)

In the course of the development of a highly sophisticated sugar industry, a complex interplay of production, consumption, and power structures began to dominate the relations between the European colonial powers and the Caribbean as well as within the colonies and Europe. Interestingly enough, in *Sweetness and Power,* Mintz points out the active role that colonies played in stimulating European demand for refined sugar and shaping European taste (cf. 1986: xxix). During the sugar revolution, the cultivation of sugarcane expanded on numerous islands, as e.g. Barbados, Jamaica, Guadeloupe, or Cuba. This caused a large-scale economic dependency on exportation, first to the 'motherlands' and, after decolonization, to the U.S. in many cases. For example, in Cuba, dependency shifted from Spain to the influential North American neighbor and later, during the Cold War, to the Soviet Union. In the 1990s, after the breakdown of the U.S.S.R., Cuba's political peculiarity occasioned one of the most fatal crises in

we also "think of the Caribbean as an effect, a fantasy, a set of practices, and a context" (ibid.).

Cuban economy, euphemistically called the 'Special Period in Times of Peace' (*Período Especial en Tiempos de Paz*). This epoch of extreme food shortage has left an indelible footmark on Cuban sociocultural and culinary practices, for instance instigating the population to invest in self-supply, e.g. by breeding pigs in highly urbanized areas, and the black market. Furthermore, Cubans had to adapt traditional recipes to the deteriorated nutrition conditions, involuntarily mimicking the famous socialist chef Nitza Villapol.[2] Most likely it is this combination of deprivation and inventiveness that also led to the invention of urban legends like the *bistec de frazada de piso*, or rag steak (cf. De Maeseneer in this volume).

The Cuban Special Period and the lasting effects of colonial economy referenced above are emblematic of the sociocultural aspects of culinary and consumption practices as explored in this anthology, *Caribbean Food Cultures*. It analyzes numerous facets of food cultures in the transnational and transcultural space of the Caribbean and its diasporas from the 19th to the 21st century. By taking postcolonial relations into account, it critically addresses the never tiring neo/colonial gaze and the problematic consumption of the Caribbean (cf. Sheller 2003). It further points out the historical continuity of the commodification of the region and its people, which has its origins in the sugar and banana plantations. The United Fruit Company, for instance, commodifies the Caribbean and its exotic fruit for marketing purposes of their Chiquita brand. The omnipresent icon of the 'exotic woman with fruit' sells bananas, imagines a Caribbean landscape, and also emblematizes an eroticized image of the Caribbean female body—first and famously enacted by Brazilian-Portuguese actress, dancer, and singer, Carmen Miranda (cf. Parasecoli in this volume). Thus, as Mimi Sheller rightly states, "Western European and North American publics have unceasingly consumed the natural environment, commodities, human bodies, and culture of the Caribbean over the past five hundred years" (Sheller 2003: 3). Along similar lines, Western scholarship has constructed stereotypical ideas and images of an allegedly homogeneously creolized Caribbean, reducing its complexity and diversity to symbols that fit the Western imagination. Theories of 'créolité' or 'créolisation' originated from the Caribbean and have been largely consumed by and reproduced in Western academic discourse, which either sees the Caribbean exclusively through this lens or radically decontextualizes those theories by

---

2 The famous Cuban cook Nitza Villapol (1923-1998) reached the status of a national heroine by making dishes socially presentable prepared with the few existing ingredients in these times of scarcity. She published two cookbooks, *Cocina criolla* (1954) and *Cocina al minuto* (1956), and had her own TV show. Her cuisine has been considered to be 'authentically' Cuban (cf. De Maeseneer 2012).

eliminating their sociohistorical dimension.[3] For instance, the ever so often quoted dish Callaloo[4] is held to emblematize the cultural, ethnic, and racial diversity of the Caribbean in a positive way—a stew of acculturation and transculturation, of recreation, syncretism, but also traditions (cf. Houston 2005). Publications frequently draw on this image of Callaloo-soup to illustrate these concepts.[5] Historically, however, the mixing of people and cultures has been despised as miscegenation and regarded as bastards or impure.[6] The nowadays dominant, rather romanticized imaginaries of a creolized culture, or a 'happy hybridity,' oftentimes conceal conditions and lived experience that stem from asymmetries in power structures, for example, economic exploitation within an unequal global North-South divide. Processes of consuming the ethnic and exotic 'Other' are inextricably linked to the commodification of 'Otherness.' As bell hooks affirms with regard to dominant representations and appropriations of Blackness in mass media in the majority white societies of North America and Europe,

---

3 While Bernabé, Chamoiseau, and Confiant coined the term 'créolité' to re-value a specific Antillean heritage of mixed origin, Glissant's concept of 'créolisation' insists on the process of cultural contact in a colonial context without attaching this process to a specific geographic region (cf. Glissant 1989 [1981], Bernabé and Chamoiseau 2006, Müller and Ueckmann 2013: 19-21).

4 Callaloo refers to either a specific plant used for cooking or a specific dish. According to the *Dictionary of Caribbean English Usage*, calalu (or Callaloo) is defined as "[a]ny of a number of plants with edible, succulent leaves" which is cooked as green vegetables. As a dish calalu refers to 1) a "very thick soup made of Calalu I. or Dasheen leaves and other ingredients [...] served as a main meal," 2) a "dish of solid food prepared by boiling some of the same ingredients" or 3) as a "general mixture" (Allsopp 2003: 130).

5 For example, Callaloo as a dish is referred to in Viranjini Munasinghe's study *Callaloo or Tossed Salad?* (2001), where it emblematizes creolization, the 'melting pot,' and is opposed to the image of the tossed salad. Other publications referring to Callaloo are, for instance, Aisha Khan's *Callaloo Nation* (2004).

6 The terms 'bastard' and 'hybrid' are originally racist and colonial categories, which named deviations from an assumed racial purity. They are crucial in the social construction of races and racial hierarchies and part of a discourse of social degeneration. The latter was associated with miscegenation in the eyes of the white colonizers (cf. Ha and Arndt 2011: 627). While 'bastard' maintains to date its racist content, the term 'hybrid' was picked by scholars of cultural and postcolonial studies and endued with a new and opposing meaning. It further became part of technological and postmodern capitalist discourses and is often used without any knowledge of its original racist and pejorative meaning (cf. Ha 2011: 346).

[t]he commodification of Otherness has been so successful because it is offered as a new delight, more intense, more satisfying than normal ways of doing and feeling. Within commodity culture ethnicity becomes spice, seasoning that can liven up the dull dish that is mainstream white culture. (hooks 1992: 21)

While hooks is certainly right in her critique of the exploitation of difference as commodities "offered up as new dishes to enhance the white palate" (39), the perceived and constructed 'Otherness' may also be appropriated by the 'Other' who engages in commodification processes (cf. Comaroff and Comaroff 2009: 24). In the Caribbean, chattel slavery, economic systems of exploitation, and social hierarchies based on race have favored structures that have led to the marginalization of minorities during the de- and postcolonial period until today. Consequently, the construction of the ethnic 'Other' concerns not only colonial, that is European or North American, gazes on 'non-white' Caribbean populations, but also involves processes of 'Othering' among the different groups, for instance between Indo- and Afro-Caribbean, Chinese, Lebanese, and indigenous communities.[7]

COOKING AND CONSUMING 'AUTHENTIC' FOOD

The Caribbean has traditionally been seen as a region where food was produced for export to and consumption in Europe or North America (cf. Garth 2013).[8] This perspective neglects the fact that even in the past food has been imported to the Caribbean to feed its populations, as autarchy was never achieved in post/colonial times. According to Wilson, the colonial project required the "importation of European food [...], as human factors like population increases from brutal forms of labor recruitment and geographical factors such as floods and droughts created scarcities" (Wilson 2013: 109). Non-perishable foods and products manufactured to be shipped to the Caribbean not only changed the diets of colonizers and colonized, but "became staples" (ibid.) and integral parts of

---

7 A case in point is the racialized discourse of the 'dougla' in Trinidad, referring to the offspring of mixed African and Indian ancestry. Shalini Puri comments that "anxieties around racial ambiguity are often expressed as disavowals of the dougla—either through the discursive repression of the dougla or through explicit attack on the category" (Puri 2004: 190).

8 Not only in regard to food and crops, but also concerning resources and labor, the Caribbean is often considered as a "place for extraction" (Cabezas in Garth 2013: 7).

their diets.⁹ This practice of importing foods and drinks is even (more) visible today. Not only do inter- and multinational companies such as PepsiCo Inc. and Nestlé S.A. import edible goods, but also family members and friends, who have migrated to North America or Europe, actively engage in the exchange and the sending of consumption goods to the Caribbean. The necessary infrastructure is provided by specialized shipping companies, which offer affordable shipment of boxes and barrels for individuals, families, or associations. Barrels and boxes sent from North America to the Caribbean are to a vast extent filled with food items, such as oil, pasta, instant coffee, cereals, and cookies (cf. Plaza in this volume). Caribbean people also actively engage in the consumption of goods produced abroad and defined as Western. Hence, the consumption of culturally 'othered' goods is not a one-way street. Both, in the Caribbean and abroad, branded goods that signify 'the foreign' are very popular and at times even demanded by the receivers. Through their consumption, a means to access distant places, oftentimes potential migration destinations, is created and social hierarchies are re/established on local and international levels (cf. Halstead 2002).[10]

According to Daniel Miller, consumption is a "process of objectification" meaning both "a practice in the world and a form in which we construct our understandings of ourselves in the world" (Miller 1995: 30). In other words, consumption can be defined as a performative act that not only fulfills a concrete purpose, but also serves as a medium to construct identities and to express one's position in relation to society, class, nation, religion, and culture. In many respects, food cultures are inextricably linked to symbolic and material consumption practices that are much more than simply preparing, eating, and digesting food, but include processes of appropriation, infection, exhibition as well as possession, destruction, or wasting (cf. Sheller 2003: 14). At the core of consumption lie relations that are "economic, political, cultural, social, and emotional" (ibid.). By preparing and eating *mofongo*[11] or *mangú*,[12] derived from African cul-

---

9   The majority of these goods was either smoked or salted (e.g. boxed fish and beef). Crops and food produced in the Caribbean for local markets and home consumption were "indigenous and African crops like yams, sweet potatoes, and cassava" (Wilson 2013: 109).

10 Monetary remittances have impacted the diets of people living in the Caribbean, as brands and other goods available for purchase in stores are becoming more affordable to greater parts of the population.

11 Puerto Rican dish made from pureed plantains with vegetables, seafood, or meat traditionally served with rice and beans.

12 Dominican side dish made from mashed green plantains.

inary traditions, especially in the diaspora, one nourishes oneself while at the same time revealing his or her identification as Puerto Rican or Dominican.

It is in this relation of food, consumption, and self-definitions that the social constructedness of authenticity and its importance for culinary practices come to matter. This aspect is of particular interest in the area of food studies. Changing food cultures de/construct 'authentic' Caribbeanness as well as national and diasporic identities. In this regard certain questions need to be addressed: What is the functional role of food for re/inventing and performing individual and collective identities? To what extent are Caribbean food practices and representations crucial to constructions of an authentic and stable self both for Caribbean and western communities? Particularly in migratory contexts, specific ingredients, spices, and cooking rituals help in the construction of perceived 'pure' identities. When asking how and in which contexts authenticity is constructed, oftentimes, it is "the pressure of nostalgic expatriates and authenticity-seeking travelers" (Belasco 2008: 30) that influences a culture's cuisine. Cookbooks play a fundamental role in the process of authenticating specific culinary practices and dishes by establishing written and printed standards. In "How to Make a National Cuisine" Arjun Appadurai considers the writing of cookbooks as a technique to determine a specific regional and cultural cuisine (cf. also Lawson Welsh in this volume). In doing so, Appadurai explains, "[...] what are created, exchanged, and refined are culinary stereotypes of the Other, stereotypes that are then partly standardized in the new cookbooks" (Appadurai 1988:7). Likewise, Anita Mannur underlines the impact of migration on the construction of national cuisines, clarifying that recipes in some cookbooks "strategically mobilize nostalgic memories of the past to enhance the value of the recipe for a readership hungry to consume 'authentic' difference" (Mannur 2007: 14). While this is but one example of how authenticity is negotiated, the growing influence of remittances from overseas, multinational companies, and international tourism must be taken into account. What is perceived as authentic everyday food in the Caribbean is transformed, as Wilk (1999, 2006) exemplifies in the case of Belize, which regained independence in 1981 and since then has been determining its own 'national' cuisine.

Studying Food

Food studies are not limited to a mere description, but have a clear analytical scope.[13] Their subversive potential, then, lies in their ability to transcend "disciplinary boundaries and to ask inconvenient questions" (Belasco 2008: 6). Food studies enable an enriching synthesis of historical, philosophical, anthropological, economic, political, literary, and natural-scientific research. They ask why in certain parts of the world people have foods of all kinds in abundance, while in other parts malnutrition and starvation are still a tremendous problem. The search for answers starts with the investigation of the origins and routes of food. These inquiries inevitably raise new questions concerning hunger, inequality, neo-colonialism, and their connection to global capitalism in general (cf. ibid.). Food studies therefore always display a complex system of exploitation based on a variety of power relations between the global North and the countries in the South.

As "intrinsically interdisciplinary" (Parasecoli 2008: 11), the emerging academic field of food studies includes a multitude of perspectives and areas of interest, such as nutrition and health, food chain and production, food security, religious usages of food, culinary practices and identities, and many more (cf. Mintz and Du Bois 2002, Belasco 2008). Journals like *Gastronomica* or *Food, Culture and Society* offer multidisciplinary platforms for this diverse research area where they enable discussions on the history, literature, as well as on the social and cultural impact of food. Interestingly enough, the contributions often reach beyond the scope of academia by including works of culinary professionals and artists.

Publications on food, its production and consumption in the Caribbean and its diasporas are scarce which is all the more intriguing given that food and crops have always been of high significance in the region. The few existing studies have mainly been conducted in the disciplines of history, social and cultural an-

---

13 Roland Barthes identified the symbolic value of food as a "system of communication" (Barthes 1997 [1961]: 29). The usage of specific ingredients and different methods of preparation are, then, part of a "system of differences in signification" that enables a "communication by way of food" (30). Claude Lévi-Strauss even attempted to provide cultural categorizations of dietary customs by analyzing specific food preparation habits. His highly controversial concept of the culinary triangle opposes three food conditions: the raw, the cooked, and the rotted. Therein, the angles are divided according to the required cultural impact, since "the cooked is a cultural transformation of the raw, whereas the rotted is a natural transformation" (Lévi-Strauss 1997 [1966]:37).

thropology (Ortiz 1940; Mintz 1986; Miller 1995; Sheller 2003; Higman 2008; Garth 2013), agricultural sciences (Ganpat and Isaac 2012), cultural studies (Cooper 2004; Dreisinger 2010; Hope 2010), and literary criticism (Mehta 2005; De Maeseneer and Collard 2010; Mannur 2010; Loichot 2013). Several recurring key topics discussed in these works include issues of ethnicity and authenticity, the significance of national dishes, their symbolism for the nation and national identity, and how the local and the global meet over kitchen talk. They furthermore show that food often serves as a medium to translate memory, longing, and nostalgia. Culinary practices are aestheticized in advertisements, fictional literature, film, and visual arts. Here, they represent 'ethnic food' or function as metaphors or symbols, depicting gender norms, (normative or 'deviant') sexualities, and constructions of the body.

The present volume fills this evident gap in food studies dedicated to the Caribbean and its diasporas from the perspective of social anthropology, cultural studies, social and behavioral sciences. The essays of this volume are methodologically diverse. They explore food, consumption and related practices, performances and aesthetics in religious contexts, popular culture, new media, and literature concentrating on a variety of key aspects. For example, they consider how food-related practices and discourses in colonial, postcolonial, and transnational Caribbean spaces de/construct ethnic, gender and class identity, as well as alterity. Moreover, the contributions demonstrate to what extent consumption, power constellations, and human exploitation have been interrelated in their historical continuity. Food discourses and practices have subversive potential to counter hegemonic structures and neo/colonial discourses. Following this lead, the contributions take into consideration perspectives that are critical of gender biases and social hierarchies. The authors focus on the geographical locations of the Caribbean diaspora in the U.S. and the U.K. as well as on various Caribbean nation states, such as Cuba, Jamaica, Suriname, and Martinique. Furthermore, the interdisciplinary anthology draws extensively from source material as diverse as TV shows, cookbooks, travelogues, novels, advertising, and commercials as well as quantitative and qualitative observation.

MENU, DISHES, AND INGREDIENTS

Now, in what way does this anthology serve the academic dining table with a Caribbean and diasporic menu? If not literally then certainly intellectually nourishing, the collection offers a rich and tasty four-course meal made up of Caribbean food and consumption cultures. What are the major dishes? Which theoretical and methodological spices flavor this interdisciplinary stew? The twelve contributors selected and cooked up the best ingredients. They focus on medial representations of food cultures, neo/colonial perspectives, the pungent question of authenticity, as well as community-building through consumption practices.

The chapters of the first course "Culinary Aesthetics" pay attention to the aestheticization of food practices in various medial genres. Food and its consumption are represented artistically in literature, film, or television, conveying a significant role in the construction of (culinary) identities. In the first article, Rita De Maeseneer examines different strategies in novels and films that refer to the so-called *Período Especial en Tiempos de Paz* in Cuba. These strategies are applied to convey hunger as an artistic expression. Louisa Söllner focuses on Cristina García's novel *The Lady Matador's Hotel* (2010), in which the Cuban-American author refers to food as indicator for social and political conflict. Söllner highlights food as a medium of resistance that is more than just a nostalgic practice. Sebastian Huber analyzes the U.S. American TV series *Treme*, which takes place in the eponymous New Orleans neighborhood after the devastating hurricane Katrina in 2005. On the basis of the TV show, Huber demonstrates how cinematic representations of cooking produce social relations which resist biopolitics. Daniel Graziadei takes a closer look at Fortuné Chalumeau's novel *Désirade, ô Serpente!* (2006) as well as at the poetical afterword of Édouard Glissant's novel *Ormerod* (2003). Emphasizing how realist representations of food and food practices have primarily metafictional functions, Graziadei puts his analytical focus on the female cooks and reads the two novels as a critique of exoticising and euphemistic images of the Caribbean.

This aspect of 'Othering' by constructing an exotic image of the Caribbean takes center stage in the second course, "Neo/Colonial Gaze." Both articles focus not only on historical, but also on contemporary representations of the Caribbean through images and descriptions of food in literature and popular culture, thus arguing for the existence of a colonial and neocolonial gaze on the Caribbean. Accordingly, Ilaria Berti applies the notion of creolization to food practices and consumption in order to reflect the relationship between colonizers and colonized. Berti illustrates how the contrast of 'our' and 'their' food is overcome in three British travelogues from the 19th century. Moreover, Fabio Parasecoli explores, in the context of U.S. popular culture, how the Caribbean is produced and reproduced as a real and imaginary space. Parasecoli demonstrates how specific representations of food and fruits, such as the banana, are utilized to construct and exploit the Caribbean as a means to fantasize and escape.

The notion of authenticity as well as specific items that are perceived as authentic vary within different cultural and socio-historical contexts, and are influenced in the course of migration. The third course, "Constructions of Authenticity," highlights and analyzes different ways of how authenticity is constructed, transformed, and promoted. Sarah Lawson Welsh offers an analysis of how authenticity is negotiated on the basis of specific food, recipes, and cookery books in the Caribbean diaspora in the U.K. Based on the case of Jamaican-British cook Levi Roots, the paper focuses on the influence of economics and marketing of cultural products as authentic, and how the idea of authenticity is continuously addressed, questioned, and reconstituted. Further, it addresses how the diasporic context influences and constructs a culinary version of the Caribbean. Ivan Darias Alfonso elaborates on the construction of Cuban identity and a sense of belonging through food and eating in London. The study describes how perceptions of 'authentic' Cuban cuisine are revised in diasporic contexts. The link between authenticity and cultural difference is discussed by Mona Nikolić in reference to tourism in Costa Rica. Nikolić' analysis focuses on the transformation of Afro-Caribbean cuisine and how relevant social actors, such as tourists, influence the notion of authenticity in the local Afro-Caribbean culinary culture.

The consumption of food can be interpreted as a process of transformation and re/construction, rather than merely an act of destruction. Similarly, the exchange of food items as well as practices of grocery shopping, preparing food, eating, and drinking can be interpreted as acts of constitution and creation. Eating and drinking nourish an individual, but also serve as a means to reconstruct communities and identities through, for example, communal meals. Therefore, the fourth and last course, "Consumption and Communities," approaches the creative aspect of consumption in regard to social relations and the construction of community. It additionally emphasizes the significance of abstinence from certain foods and drinks as well as strategies that evolve in the course of food shortages and unavailability of specific products. Dwaine Plaza examines the material exchange of food by Caribbean migrants focusing on the practice of barrel-sending from Canada to Jamaica. The analysis of these practices highlights how food items are among the most important items sent in "barrels of love" to friends and (fictive) kin at 'home' as gifts and / or remittances, hence maintaining and recreating social relations within families and accordingly transnational social fields. Plaza further argues that the practice of barrel-sending is a gendered ritual, in which women usually shop for and pack groceries to be sent. Elizabeth den Boer discusses how especially women are regarded as transmitters and keepers of culture and religion through the act of cooking and preparing Hindu ritual food in Suriname. Drawing on the examples of part-time vegetarianism and fasting, den Boer further elaborates how these practices of abstinence are a means to establish, maintain, and influence social relations. Practices of not-eating and the existence of food taboos are also discussed in Annika McPherson's analysis of Rastafarian culinary identity. The Rastafarian concept of Ital food restricts the consumption of certain types of food to counteract Euro-American hegemonic influences. McPherson theorizes Ital food as decolonial practice and demonstrates how the consumption and non-consumption of certain foods create and facilitate means of resistance and means to create identity.

Caribbean Food Cultures thus brings into dialogue different disciplinary and thematic approaches to food practices and discourses in the Caribbean. The collection restructures and decolonizes the production of theoretical knowledge by overcoming neo-colonial gazes on the Caribbean. It offers a promising theoretical framework which enables a comprehensive study of food-related research. With its strong interdisciplinary approach, it allows for new insights into the importance of transnational food and consumption practices for the shaping and the re/invention of Caribbean as well as Western identities in the wake of colonial history, decolonization, and globalization.

BIBLIOGRAPHY

Allsopp, Richard 2003. *Dictionary of Caribbean English Usage*. Kingston: University Press of the West Indies.

Appadurai, Arjun 1988. "How to Make a National Cuisine. Cookbooks in Contemporary India." *Comparative Studies in Society and History* 30.1: 3-24.

Barthes, Roland 2008 [1967]. "Toward a Psychosociology of Contemporary Food Consumption." *Food and Culture. A Reader*. Eds. Carole Counihan and Penny van Esterik. New York / London: Routledge, 28-35.

Belasco, Warren 2008. *Food. The Key Concepts*. New York: Berg.

Bernabé, Jean, Patrick Chamoiseau, and Raphaël Confiant 2006. *Éloge De La Créolité. Édition Bilingue Français / Anglais*. Paris: Gallimard.

Comaroff, John L. and Jean Comaroff 2009. *Ehnicity, Inc.* Chicago / London: University of Chicago Press.

Cooper, Carolyn 2004. *Sound Clash. Jamaican Dancehall Culture at Large*. New York: Palgrave.

De Maeseneer, Rita and Patrick Collard 2010. *Saberes y Sabores en México y el Caribe*. Amsterdam: Rodopi.

De Maeseneer, Rita 2012. *Devorando a lo Cubano. Una Aproximación Gastrocrítica a Textos Relacionados con el Siglo XIX y el Período Especial*. Madrid: Iberoamericana / Frankfurt a. M.: Vervuert.

Dreisinger, Baz 2010. "Is Reggae Rum? Caribbean Sounds and the American Music Trade." *Jamaica Journal* 32.3: 38-45.
Ganpat, Wayne G. and Wendy-Ann Isaac, eds. 2012. *Sustainable Food Production Practices in the Caribbean*. Kingston: Ian Randle Publishers.
Garth, Hanna, ed. 2013. *Food and Identity in the Caribbean*. London / New York: Bloomsbury.
Glissant, Édouard 1989 [1981]. *Le Discours Antillais*. Paris: Ed. du Seuil.
Ha, Kien Nghi 2011. "Hybrid / Hybridität." *Wie Rassismus aus Wörtern spricht. (K)Erben des Kolonialismus im Wissensarchiv Deutsche Sprache. Ein kritisches Nachschlagewerk*. Eds. Susan Arndt and Nadja Ofuatey-Alazard. Münster: Unrast Verlag, 342-46.
Ha, Kien Nghi and Susan Arndt 2011. "Bastard." *Wie Rassismus aus Wörtern spricht. (K)Erben des Kolonialismus im Wissensarchiv Deutsche Sprache. Ein kritisches Nachschlagewerk*. Eds. Susan Arndt and Nadja Ofuatey-Alazard. Münster: Unrast Verlag, 624-28.
Halstead, Narmala 2002. "Branding 'Perfection.' Foreign as Self; Self as 'Foreign-Foreign'." *Journal of Material Culture* 7: 273-93.
Higman, Barry W. 2008. *Jamaican Food. History, Biology, Culture*. Kingston: University of the West Indies Press.
—. 2011. *A Concise History of the Caribbean*. Cambridge: Cambridge University Press.
hooks, bell 1992. *Black Looks. Race and Representation*. Cambridge: South End Press.
Hope, Donna P. 2010. *Man Vibes. Masculinities in the Jamaican Dancehall*. Kingston: Ian Randle Publishers.
Houston, Lynn Marie 2005. *Food Culture in the Caribbean*. Westport: Greenwood Press.
Khan, Aisha 2004. *Callaloo Nation. Metaphors of Race and Religious Identity Among South Asians in Trinidad*. Durham: Duke University Press.
Lévi-Strauss, Claude 1997 [1966]: "The Culinary Triangle." *Food and Culture. A Reader*. Eds. Carole Counihan and Penny van Esterik. New York / London: Routledge, 36-44.
Loichot, Valérie 2013. *The Tropics Bite Back. Culinary Coups in Caribbean Literature*. Minneapolis: University of Minnesota Press.
Mannur, Anita 2010. *Culinary Fictions. Food in South Asian Diasporic Culture*. Philadelphia: Temple University Press.
—. 2007. "Culinary Nostalgia. Authenticity, Nationalism, and Diaspora." *MELUS* 32.4: 11-31.

Mehta, Brinda 2005. "Culinary Diasporas. Identity and the Language of Food in Gisèle Pineau's *Un Papillon dans la Cité* and *L'Exil Selon Julia*." *International Journal of Francophone Studies* 8.1: 23-51.

Miller, Daniel 1995. *Acknowledging Consumption. A Review of New Studies*. London / New York: Routledge.

Mintz, Sidney Wilfred 1986. *Sweetness and Power. The Place of Sugar in Modern History*. Harmondsworth: Penguin Books.

Mintz, Sidney W. and Christine Du Bois 2002. "The Anthropology of Food and Eating." *Annual Review of Anthropology* 31: 99-119.

Müller, Gesine and Natascha Ueckmann, eds. 2013. *Kreolisierung Revisited. Debatten um ein weltweites Kulturkonzept*. Bielefeld: Transcript.

Munasinghe, Viranjini 2001. *East Indians and the Cultural Politics of Identity in Trinidad*. Ithaca: Cornell University Press.

Ortiz, Fernando 1940. *Contrapunteo Cubano del Tabaco y el Azúcar*. La Habana: Jesús Montero.

Parasecoli, Fabio 2008. *Bite Me. Food in Popular Culture*. New York: Berg.

Puri, Shalini 2004. *The Caribbean Postcolonial. Social Equality, Post-Nationalism and Cultural Hybridity*. New York / Houndmills: Palgrave Macmillan.

Sheller, Mimi 2003. *Consuming the Caribbean. From Arawaks to Zombies*. International Library of Sociology. London et al.: Routledge.

Wilk, Richard 1999. "'Real Belizean Food.' Building Local Identity in the Transnational Caribbean." *American Anthropologist, New Series* 101.2: 244-255.

—. 2006. *Home Cooking in the Global Village. Caribbean Food from Buccaneers to Ecotourists*. Oxford: Berg.

Wilson, Marisa 2013. "From Colonial Dependency to Finger-Lickin' Values. Food, Commoditization, and Identity in Trinidad." *Food and Identity in the Caribbean*. Ed. Hanna Garth. London / New York: Bloomsbury, 107-20.

Culinary Aesthetics

The Aesthetics of Hunger and the Special Period in Cuba

RITA DE MAESENEER

In one of his foundational essays, "Problemática de la actual novela latinoamericana," published in 1964, the Cuban writer Alejo Carpentier reflects on the contexts necessary for writing novels: among other ideas, he describes the importance of cultural, political, racial, economic, ideological, spatial, and culinary contexts. His definition of what he terms the culinary contexts is particularly interesting:

[Los contextos culinarios t]ienen una importancia en cuanto a sus particulares contextos históricos. El ajiaco cubano, por ejemplo, plato nacional de la cocina criolla, reúne, en una misma cazuela, la cocina de los españoles—la que traía Colón en sus naves—, con productos (las "viandas" llaman todavía a eso) de la primera tierra avistada por los descubridores. Después la cocina española se llamó el *bucán* porque unos aventureros franceses, por ello llamados *bucaneros*, se dieron a sistematizar en Cuba la industria elemental consistente en solear, ahumar y salar carnes de venado y de cerdos jíbaros. (Carpentier 1987: 22)[1]

---

1 "[The culinary contexts] are important for their particular historical contexts. For example, the Cuban 'ajiaco' (stew), the national dish of the creole (Cuban) cuisine, combines, in a single pot, the Spaniards' ingredients—introduced via Columbus' boats—with the edible roots (still called 'viandas') found on the first land that the explorers discovered. Later, the Spanish cuisine was called *bucán*, because a group of French adventurers called *bucaneros* (buccaneers) started to use one method rather systematically in Cuba. This was a simple method which involved hanging up meat from game and wild pigs in the sun, before smoking and salting it" (Carpentier 1987: 22; my translation).

Carpentier refers to a number of areas that are important to the study of food. He begins, for example, by emphasizing its diachronic nature. Since the French *Ecole des Annales* of the interwar period put forward event-based historical analysis, historians have effectively been studying subaltern modes of life and pursuing their interest in culinary habits and customs. Next, Carpentier focuses on the identitarian aspect. Caribbean identity is often characterized by racial miscegenation, as symbolized by Cuban anthropologist Fernando Ortiz's *ajiaco*, a stew using ingredients from different continents, thus conveying ethnic diversity. In the extract above, Carpentier refers only to a mix of Spanish and indigenous ingredients, but it is well known that African and Chinese influences were also significant. Moreover, race is often associated with class. Sociological works such as Michel de Certeau's *L'invention du quotidien* (1994) have underscored the opposition between quantity and quality in order to distinguish social classes. Moreover, in *La distinction: Critique sociale du jugement* (1979) Bourdieu demonstrates the importance of food as an aspect not only of economic but also cultural capital. Cultural capital, not unlike economic capital, can be either inherited from the family or acquired through some type of education. It is revealed both by what is consumed and how products are consumed. For example, cookery is a structure of consumption that reveals differences either inherited or acquired. So food is culturally shaped and socially controlled. In his description of how game and wild pigs were prepared, Carpentier seems to echo the ideas expressed by anthropologist Claude Lévi-Strauss, who links degrees of civilization to means of preparing food. This theory is expounded in what he terms the culinary triangle:

> To conclude, let us return to our culinary triangle. Within it we traced another triangle representing recipes, at least the most elementary ones: roasting, boiling and smoking. The smoked and the boiled are opposed as to the nature of the intermediate element between fire and food, which is either air or water. The smoked and the roasted are opposed by the smaller or larger place given to the element air; and the roasted and the boiled by the presence or absence of water. The boundary between nature and culture, which one can imagine as parallel to either the axis of air or the axis of water, puts the roasted and the smoked on the side of nature, the boiled on the side of culture as to means; or, as to results, the smoked on the side of culture, the roasted and the boiled on the side of nature:

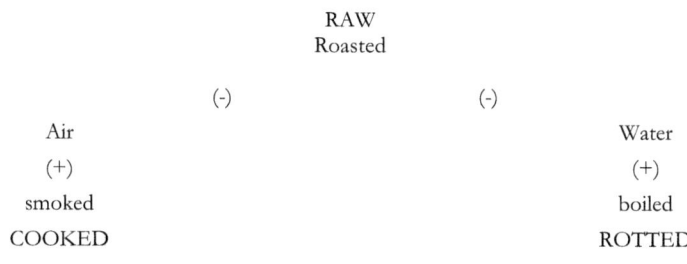

(Lévi-Strauss 1997: 34)

The distinction between nature and culture is particularly relevant for the Caribbean (and Latin America as a whole), because in colonial discourses based on binary oppositions the islands have often been considered as 'natural,' even barbaric, in opposition to the civilized West. So Carpentier seems to have been aware of the multiple connotations that food references engender and therefore indicates that various areas of the human sciences are necessary for the study of culinary contexts.

Although no theoretical framework as such currently exists in the literary field, many case studies have been published, for example on Lezama Lima (Teja 1992, 1993), Carpentier (De Maeseneer 2003) and Sarduy (Vadillo 1996), to name some examples relevant to the Cuban context. Generally, scholars refer in their studies to Barthes, who formulated a number of interesting ideas in "Lecture de Brillat Savarin," his introduction to a republication of *Physiologie du goût* (*Physiology of Taste*), an 1825 text by gastronome Brillat Savarin. *Physiologie du goût* was one of the first attempts to reflect 'scientifically' on food. In "Lecture de Brillat Savarin," Barthes meditates on issues such as the relationships between food and the mother, food and eroticism, food and social class, eating and talking as two related phenomena, the importance of sensation and hedonism, the liquid versus the solid, and their cultural implications. Similarly, *L'œuvre de François Rabelais et la culture populaire au Moyen Age et sous la Renaissance* (1970) by Bakhtine also serves as an important background text for researchers' analysis in its commentary on the abundance of food at feasts as a celebration of life and work, a triumph of life over death, and an emphasis on the body and sexuality.

In 1990, Ronald Tobin, a scholar specializing in French literature of the *Ancien Régime*, coined the term gastrocriticism as a subcategory of sociocriticism in his book, *Tarte à la crème. Comedy and Gastronomy in Molière's Theater* (1990). In an essay of 2002, "Qu'est-ce que la gastrocritique?", he clarifies how the gastrocritical approach consists of detecting the multiple connotations of food and drink in relation to social, racial, geographical, identitarian, historical, sexual, anthropological, religious, philosophical, medical, cultural, psychological, ideological-political, gender, and linguistic issues. In fact, his definition bears some comparison to Carpentier's reflections:

> Cette méthode suppose une vaste entreprise de recherche dans les sciences humaines qui explore les liens entre l'alimentation et l'art. Elle appartient et fait appel à l'histoire—histoire culturelle, histoire économique, histoire des mentalités et de la vie quotidienne, et histoire de l'art—, à la sociologie, à la civilité et la galanterie, à l'alimentation et les livres de cuisine, à la médecine, la nutrition et les questions diététiques et de santé, à la critique littéraire et la sémiotique, à la psychanalyse et la philosophie, aux études de la femme et, surtout à l'anthropologie. La gastrocritique est conçue pour mettre en relief le fait que le poète et le cuisinier travaillent tous deux à créer la métamorphose et l'illusion. (Tobin 2002: 624-5)[2]

What interests me most about Tobin's definition of gastrocriticism is the last sentence, he insists on the metafictional function of food. He affirms that a poet or writer is like a cook: both create an illusion. Writing and cooking are effectively two similar operations. García Márquez once stated in an interview: "I know exactly how *Leaf Storms* went straight from my guts onto the paper. The others also came from my guts but I had served my apprenticeship... I worked on them, I *cooked* them, I *added salt and pepper*" (in Guibert 1973: 326; emphasis added). The writer has a "cuisine of writing," "una cocina de la escritura," to quote a famous essay by Puerto Rican writer Rosario Ferré (1985). Furthermore, it is clear that the representation of food, one of the 'real' elements of fiction, points to the conflict between the text as a referential entity ('mimesis') and the text as an autonomous and auto-referential entity ('imitatio'). In other words, *les mets ne sont pas les mots*[3] (Jeanneret 1987) and the word is not the world. It is therefore not sufficient to present a screening of the multiple connotations suggested by food, the gastrocritical approach must be interpreted within the broader context of the writer's poetics.

---

2 "This method presupposes a vast undertaking of research in human sciences that explores the connections between alimentation and art. It belongs and appeals to history—cultural history, economic history, history of mentalities and of daily life, and history of art—, sociology, civilty and gallantry, alimentation and cookbooks, medicine, nutrition and dietary questions and health, literary criticism and semiotics, psychoanalysis and philosophy, gender studies, and, particularly anthropology. Gastrocriticism serves to underscore the fact that the poet and the cook work both to create a metamorphosis and an illusion" (Tobin 2002: 624-5; my translation).

3 The dishes are not the words.

Before applying gastrocriticism to a specific area of the Caribbean and to a concrete period, I wish to make two remarks. First, it should be kept in mind that the study of food discourse as a starting point for analysis inevitably limits the selection of works, because a fictional character does not have to eat or refer to food in order to exist in an artistic expression. In fact, food scenes in novels are often only included in extreme situations: lack or abundance, fast or feast. In films, on the other hand, food scenes of all types are much more frequent. The genre known as Food Films is well established, and extends beyond great classics such as *La grande bouffe* (Marco Ferreri 1973), *Le festin de Babette* (Gabriel Axel 1987), *Como agua para chocolate* (Alfonso Arau 1992) and *Eat Drink Man Woman* (Ang Lee 1994).

Second, some doubts have been raised as to the seriousness of gastrocriticism and it has occasionally been referred to as "scholarship lite" (Ruark 1999: n.p.). This attitude can perhaps be explained by the fact that the gastrocritical approach has often been employed in relation to a certain type of literature: food is increasingly being used as a central element of subversion in a (proto)feminist / feminine approach.[4] Since the overwhelming success of *Como agua para chocolate* (1989) by Mexican writer Laura Esquivel, and the film of the same name released in 1992, using food references as a means of expressing their characters' struggles against patriarchy has become very marketable for women writers. Esquivel exploited the theme later in her *Íntimas suculencias. Tratado filosófico de cocina* (2007). And Isabel Allende also wrote a bestseller containing aphrodisiac recipes, entitled *Afrodita* (1997). Moreover many Chicana and Latina writers (also from the Caribbean) have used food reminiscences to emphasize a nostalgic return to the homeland. This can be evidenced, for example, by the longing for Puerto Rican food in *When I Was a Puerto Rican* (1994) by Esmeralda Santiago, and by Julia Alvarez's protagonist arriving in the Dominican Republic and immediately wanting to eat wild guavas in *How the García Girls Lost their Accent* (1991).

Many eponymous novels by women writers fail to elaborate on the issue of food beyond the parallel between food and woman as sexual object, nostalgic remembrance of the homeland through food and rebellion by means of cooking in the kitchen "as a self-empowering site" to quote a part of André's book title

---

4   For an overview, cf. "Mimesis and Metaphor. Food Imagery in International Twentieth-Century Women's Writing" (2004) by Harriett Blodgett. To quote two interesting examples: in Margaret Atwood's *The Edible Woman* (1969) the female protagonist serves a cake in the shape of a woman to be eaten by her partner, and in the short story "Lección de cocina" (1971) by Mexican writer Rosario Castellanos, the narrator compares the preparation of a steak to her relationship with her husband.

(2001). And in the case of some Latina writers they use their gastronomic imagery to market the margins in a kind of postcolonial exotic (cf. Huggan 2001). Because of the interpretation of these novels as a kind of marketing, then, and some deceiving results, the gastrocritical approach has been somewhat disapproved. In what follows, however, I attempt to demonstrate the variety of interesting ways in which food references can be studied, regardless of the fact that they are written by men or women.

Taking into account these remarks and my understanding of gastrocriticism, I provide a gastrocritical commentary on certain literary and cinematographic expressions from the last two decades (1990-2010) that evoke the 1990s either to a greater or lesser extent in Cuba, and more specifically in Havana, often considered rightly or wrongly as the metonymy for the Cuban situation.

Since Columbus' diaries, the islands of the Caribbean and Cuba have been described in terms of their supposed abundance, though scarcity was often closer to reality. Cuba was associated with sugar and sweetness (for both its produce [cf. Mintz 2003] and its population); edible roots such as manioc and sweet potato; meat, especially pork and chicken; and finally tropical fruits—"the fundamental element in the imagination of the Cuban community" (Calvo Peña 2005: 80; my translation)—such as *guanábana, mamey, caimito*, and the queen of fruits since the colonial period, the pineapple (*piña*). At the beginning of the 1990s, however, the Cuban economy was plunged into severe crisis. An economic disaster loomed, partly due to the disappearance of the aid from the Soviet Union. The Cuban authorities were struggling to guarantee sustenance for a population used to receiving a minimal food basket thanks to the *libreta* food rationing system. The government was not able to cope with the scarcity of energy, food, and transportation. Castro invented the euphemism "Special Period in times of peace" (*Período Especial en Tiempos de Paz*), a war economy during times of peace, to justify the shortages. The beginning of the 1990s was particularly harsh and one of the most painful moments of this period was the *balsero* (rafter) crisis of August 1994. Cubans had become so desperate due to the shortages that they were attempting to flee the island by crossing the Florida Straits in rickety boats or on precarious rafts made of tires. In order to calm the protest in the streets, Castro opened the Cuban borders and announced that any Cuban wanting to take to the sea could do so without fear of reprisal. Many Cubans were successful in their attempts to flee, but many also died. In *Cuban Palimpsests*, José Quiroga inverts the traditional association between Cuba and sweetness by asserting that "bitterness was the 'mood' that best seemed to encapsulate Cuba then" (Quiroga 2005: 16).

In order to overcome this unsustainable situation, a number of new systems were introduced including private initiatives, a parallel dollar economy, which generated inequality of access to consumer goods, and incentives for international tourism, which engendered tourist-geared prostitution. The scarcity underscored the gaps in the supposed socialist egalitarian system and even brought to the surface racial differences, because the black population often couldn't rely on the remittances sent from abroad. In the second half of the decade, the situation improved slightly (for some Cubans). For writers, the shortage of paper made publication very difficult, but as of November 1993 Cuban authors residing on the island were permitted to publish abroad. Similarly, filmmakers were permitted to make co-productions. Nonetheless, the struggle for daily life continued; many Cubans were and are *en la lucha*. Two verbs summarize their situation: *resolver* (resolve) and *inventar* (invent). Cubans had to resolve / *resolver*: this entailed the day-to-day scraping together of staples such as cooking oil, milk, meat, and soap which couldn't be found in Cuban *peso* stores. At the same time, they also had to invent / *inventar:* this entailed improvising with creative solutions to everyday problems. Where food was concerned, this often meant replacing a certain product with an *ersatz* version. Although the end of the Special Period has never been announced officially, the decade of the nineties is usually designated as the crucial reference.

Cubans had endured suffering and deprivation before the 1990s, but never to the same extent. It is therefore interesting to note how *Alicia en el Pueblo de Maravillas*, a film made by Daniel Díaz Torres between 1988 and 1991—as economic collapse loomed—appears to anticipate the coming scarcity in certain food scenes. The film is a satire of Cuban bureaucracy, depicting the inhabitants of Maravillas' acceptance of all of the senseless rules that are imposed by the authorities. This controversial film was initially banned, but following protests by Díaz Torres' colleagues it was eventually released. Although food is not the film's central issue, the food-related sections are particularly relevant, even visionary. For example, in a restaurant scene set in Maravillas, the film announces the implementation of a double economy and the segregation of tourists and Cubans. Cubans may only eat spaghetti and eggs, while tourists are served rich, sumptuous dishes. Similarly, the Cubans' cutlery is chained to the table in order to prevent its being stolen; some of the chains are too short. Moreover, the waitress wears an apron bearing a print of fried eggs. This print is a visual leitmotiv in the film, which we could interpret as a reference to scarcity: fried eggs are cheap meals that are almost always available, even in times of hardship.

Many books written in Spanish or English by authors residing on the island, in political exile or in diaspora since the 1990s seem to have integrated the referential context of hunger out of an apparent need to bear witness to the problems caused by the Special Period. I analyzed an important corpus of narrative (1990-2010) situated in the Special Period and concentrated on Havana in order to study the ways in which the referential starting point of scarcity was translated into artistic expressions. I found different forms of coping with this referential ground which I call strategies. In what follows, I comment on five main strategies that move progressively further away from the referential ground of food and hunger, namely stereotype, contrast, metonymy, relegation, and metaphor. My aim is to demonstrate with only one or two of the most significant examples for each strategy how it supports specific objectives in terms of ethics, poetics, and aesthetics of hunger. For some strategies, I draw a parallel with films made in the Special Period or related to it, in order to corroborate and widen the scope of my findings.

The first means of evoking the Special Period and the food problems is through the introduction of certain spectacular manifestations of scarcity, which have become stereotypes. In "Literatura versus lechuguitas" ("Literature versus hard currency [dollars]"),[5] Ena Lucía Portela, a writer living on the island, explains how editors from Spain and the United States recommended to develop her work around what was considered the Cuban reality. This reality was supposed to include elements such as "the Special Period, blackouts, misery, soy meat (minced soy as a substitute for meat), boat people (*balseros*), prostitutes (*jineteras*), witchcraft, punks (*rockeros*), Angola wars, etc." (Portela 1999: 73; my translation). Portela criticizes the fact that the market demands the *couleur locale* of the 'Cuban reality' which she defines as a folkloric aesthetics of scarcity.

Numerous literary expressions, mostly by authors living outside Cuba, employ culinary imagery that selects and privileges certain (auto)exotic topics from that period. They create a "Special Period Exotic," a construction of the other, mainly based on the outsiders' perceptions, desires and appropriations (cf. Whitfield 2008: 20). It is a kind of postcolonial exotic that markets the margins, in the sense of Huggan. For example, Daína Chaviano, who went into exile in 1991, introduces these clichés in *El hombre, la hembra, el hambre* (1998), a novel completely situated in Havana during the Special Period. The protagonist, Claudia, educated in art history, decides to become a prostitute in order to overcome the difficulties of the Special Period and to feed her son. Although Sonia Behar argues in her study that the novel reflects on different types of hunger (physical, spiritual, and affective hunger, cf. Behar 2009: 80-6), in my view *El hombre, la*

---

5   *Lechuguitas* are American dollars or 'greenbacks,' referred to as pieces of lettuce, and representing hard currency.

hembra, el hambre fails to go beyond general observations and provides only a very stereotyped representation of the alimentary issue during the Special Period. One of the multiple examples of such stereotyping is that Claudia has a relationship with an economist who has become a butcher's assistant, a far more lucrative profession. Her lover is aware of his attractiveness: he can exchange meat for sex.

As I mentioned, meat is an important foodstuff for Cubans and the clandestine commerce of this commodity was very prosperous in the 1990s. Above all, the inhabitants of Havana appear keen to procure pork in order to prepare the quintessential roast pig for Christmas. Some inhabitants were so anxious to succeed in this that they began to rear pigs in their apartments. A number of texts evoke this reality, for example the short story entitled "César" (2002) by Nancy Alonso, a writer who lives on the island, and "Macho Grande en el balcón" (2009) by René Vázquez Díaz, an author who is in exile in Sweden since 1975. In both texts, the story evolves in the same way: the pig becomes a part of the family, is humanized and even given a name (César, Macho Grande). At the end of the story, the animal is never slaughtered. These stories of "pig-o-philia" are another example of the Special Period (auto)exotic. The domestication of a pig appears also frequently in films, even in the well-known *Fresa y chocolate* (1993), situated in the seventies, but with brief allusions to the nineties: the film includes a short fragment where a pig is carried into an apartment on the first floor.

As described above, in times of shortage populations attempt to imitate or recreate the taste of their most identitarian foods, they invent. One of the most weird examples is the rag steak *(bistec de frazada de piso)*, which is probably an invention of the urban mythology. The rag steak is incorporated in numerous novels, mostly published outside of Cuba. For example, it is a real leitmotiv in *Ruins* (2009), by Cuban-American writer Achy Obejas, who left Cuba in 1961 at the age of six. In the summer of 1994, the protagonist's wife earns a living preparing this kind of food. On YouTube[6] a video shows a supposed cook explaining the preparation of the *bistec de frazada de piso* in a parody of the official cooking program "Cocina al minuto" on Cuban television, presented by Nitza Villapol.[7]

Besides the use of stereotypes, another successful strategy for depicting the Special Period consists in the use of contrast, also combined with exaggeration.

---

6 "Cocina al minuto—Bistec de frazada de piso"
[http://www.youtube.com/watch?v=5Ljla4YbS5Q (retrieved: 8 July 2013)].

7 I return to this famous woman, both despised and adored throughout Cuba, later in this text.

Te di la vida entera (1996) by Zoé Valdés is a good example for illustrating this tendency. Valdés is considered to be the pioneer of what Esther Whitfield terms "Special Period Fiction" (2008). Valdés was born in 1959 and left Cuba in 1995, when she became outspokenly anti-Castro. In *Te di la vida entera* (1996) she evokes the life of Caridad [Cuca] Martínez and part of the book is situated in the 1990s. Cuca was born before the Cuban Revolution and spends her life waiting for mafioso Juan Pérez, the One (Uan). Juan had disappeared after giving her a child, María Regla, born in 1959 at the beginning of the Cuban Revolution. The story is a mix of melodrama and dirty realism, humor, and crude language. It is a virulent critique of Castro's regime, in which the leader is referred to as XXL or the Comedian-in-chief instead of the Commander-in-chief.

One of the ways in which Valdés attacks the regime is by comparing dishes before and after the Revolution. Nostalgic gazing at alleged prerevolutionary abundance is contrasted with the scarcity experienced during the Revolution and, particularly, in the 1990s. For example, in the second chapter, the protagonist remembers delicious food from before the Revolution. In what seems to be a kind of ironic allusion to the typical strategies of feminist writers, such as Laura Esquivel in *Como agua para chocolate*, Zoé Valdés devotes two pages to detailed recipes of certain identitarian dishes, such as black beans "a lo Valdés Fauly."[8] It is interesting to see that the description of this recipe in Zoé Valdés' book imitates almost exactly the prerevolutionary cookbooks written by Cuba's most renowned cook, Nitza Villapol. Nitza Villapol became famous in the 1950s when she published a number of cookbooks, such as *Cocina al minuto* (1956) and *Cocina criolla* (1954). After the Cuban Revolution, her television cookery program made her an icon of the regime. She adapted Cuban dishes to the changing circumstances, for example when Cubans became obliged to use Soviet products e.g. peaches in syrup. She was "one of the principal Maria Auxiliatrix of the Revolution" in the words of Catalan writer Manuel Vázquez Montalbán (2008: 46; my translation). In the Special Period, Villapol invented recipes that did not contain meat, a shock for meat-loving Cubans, and suggested avoiding the question "what are we going to prepare today?" in favor of "which products are available to cook?" (Ponte 2012: n.p.). Villapol continued to publish versions of her cookbooks, but eliminated all references to American products and a series of dishes. For example, I was unable to locate the recipe for black beans "a lo Valdés Fauly" in any post-1959 versions. In quoting recipes from Nitza Villapol's prerevolutionary books, the metonymy of the Castro regime, Zoé Valdés executes a pointed attack.

---

8   Valdés Fauly was the name of an important Cuban family.

As evidence for the contrastive method, I can also refer to the detective stories by Leonardo Padura Fuentes, who lives in Cuba and publishes both abroad and on the island. Of particular interest is his cycle of four novels set in 1989, each in a different season, namely *Pasado perfecto* (1991), *Vientos de Cuaresma* (1994), *Máscaras* (1995), and *Paisaje de otoño* (1998). Although the four books are set on the boundary of the Special Period, they demonstrate a clear opposition between hunger and abundance (cf. Collard 2010). Sumptuous dishes inspired by prerevolutionary recipes are prepared by Jose(fina), the mother of detective Mario Conde's best friend and a kind of counterfigure to Villapol. Nonetheless, Padura Fuentes' critique of the regime is much more moderate than in Zoé Valdés' work, he insists on the economic rather than on the political failure of the system (cf. Song 2009). What is more, scarcity in Padura implies a deeper sense of loss; it has ontological resonances. Wilkinson states that "[t]he conflict between the individual (Conde) and his world (Havana in the 1990s) represents a wider conflict between personal freedom and collective coercion" (2006: 288).

As in Padura's case, other writers go beyond the contrastive-hyperbolic approach to hunger and marketable stereotypes. Scarcity, even when expressed in a stereotyped way, can be used as a kind of metonymy for ontological and / or philosophical questions. Ronaldo Menéndez, who lives in Madrid since 2004, used the stereotype of the rearing of a pig by a professor of art philosophy in the Special Period as a starting point for a more thorough reflection on the implications of hunger and food in *Las bestias* (2006). As in the short stories mentioned above, the pig in this story is sometimes humanized. More often than not, however, the opposite is true: many characters are animalized. The professor, for example, is compared to a "biped without feathers" (Menéndez 2006: 62; my translation). And when the professor discovers that he is to be killed, he succeeds in capturing one of the supposed murderers, nicknamed Bill. He locks up the man, whom he calls Lo Negro, and treats him as an object. Bill, Lo Negro, has to share the bathroom with the pig, often indicated by another reifying expression—"la máquina de devorar todo lo que no sea su propio cuerpo." In this way, Bill is constantly threatened by the pig. In order to make Bill confess to the crime, the professor subjects him to sadistic torture: first, Bill has to share the pig's food, and ultimately, due to the shortage of food, the pig devours Bill. Redruello describes accurately how Menéndez creates an "animal community" (Redruello 2011: 241) in this text. Food is not an anodyne theme, it generates profound questions, raised also from an anthropological or philosophical point of view. The pretext of food supply and the rearing of a pig become means of reflecting on good and evil, racism, the boundary between human and animal, and civilization and barbarism.

Another, perhaps surprising, example of metonymy can be found in Pedro Juan Gutiérrez's famous novels. The author lives in Cuba and publishes abroad, although some of his works are also released on the island. Gutiérrez wrote a series of texts that many foreign readers saw as the ultimate representation of the Special Period. In many books from his cycle on Centro Habana, a poor neighborhood of the capital, the protagonist evokes in a very provocative and dirty realistic way numerous sex scenes, often with *mulatas*, so often related to eroticism in the cultural construction of the Caribbean. The protagonist lives as if there is no tomorrow, unencumbered by the big utopias and dreams that characterize the Cuban Revolution. Some critics, for example Guillermina de Ferrari (2007), have interpreted the abjection and eschatological constancy in the books as a metaphor for the degradation of Havana and as a means of protest against the Cuban system and hunger: sex is the only thing the Cuban characters can get for free. In order to go beyond this political and referential interpretation, I propose to concentrate my analysis on *El Rey de La Habana* (1999). The protagonist is a young boy, Reynaldo (Rey), whose life and death are clearly situated within the Special Period context. Rey is accused unfairly of having killed his mother and is brought to a detention center for young criminals. Having escaped, Rey survives, sometimes stealing but essentially because of his sexual relationships with women, often prostitutes, who maintain him. The protagonist is an outcast; his story could have unfolded at the margins of any system and not only in the Cuban context of the Special Period, though this period is addressed obliquely in the text.

This novel also contains an abundance of sex, dirt, violence, and the abject, evoked in a very simple style. There seems to be no moral dimension. Rey even has sex with the dead body of his favorite woman, Magda, having just beaten her to death. His life is a struggle for survival. Quintero Herencia calls it a "tropical darwinism" (Quintero Herencia 2005: 23). The book raises the question of where the border lies between human and animal behavior. This also applies to the food scenes. Rey eats like an animal: he devores the things he finds on the streets, as well as food given to a pig. He is not familiar with the etiquette of eating at a table, he doesn't possess this cultural capital.

Although the unabashedly sexual exploits are omnipresent, I noticed that in *El Rey de La Habana* the word hunger is as frequent as the sexual isotope. Hunger is not described in terms of its physical or psychological effects; there is only the obsessive repetition of the word. This recalls the picaresque novel, and especially *Lazarillo*, first published in 1554, where the word *hambre* (hunger) recurs frequently.[9] For example, it is repeated 33 times in the third chapter. Effectively, Rey could be considered a *pícaro*. Like Lazarillo de Tormes, he goes from one master to another, but here the master is a mistress. His stomach is his criterion, the satisfaction of his basic needs drives him. It is hunger and not sexual desire that incites Rey to move from one woman to another. The sequence is not the usual 'food as a prelude to sex': sex is a means of obtaining food. Sex is transacted for meals; Rey doesn't pay with money, but with his *pinga de oro*. The veiled sexual allusions of the picaresque novel become explicit and sordid in Gutiérrez's work.

Unlike in the picaresque novel, hunger does not imply a metaphorical search for the father here, but we can assert that a search for the mother is evident in *El Rey de La Habana*. The various women who maintain Rey are surrogate mothers. The word hunger itself is also related to his biological mother in the narrative. Rey remembers two occasions when his mother told him to ignore the hunger and he recalls her words in order to overcome his appetite in the present. For Rey, then, his mother is associated with absence, with the lack of food, and not with mother's milk, a metonymy for protection. In the novel, breast milk is replaced by Rey's milk, his *leche*, a vulgar term for semen. His *leche* is his symbol of masculinity and his means of obtaining food rather than generating offspring.

In my view, then, *El Rey de La Habana* is more than a play on stereotypes. It is undeniable that the novel contains erotic *mulatas*, sex scenes, and scenes of magic and sorcery, all of which are items mentioned by Ena Lucía Portela as examples of stereotypes. However, the book also invites the reader to reflect on the ontological and philosophical implications of hunger. It poses questions on how hunger should be represented and how one can survive at the margin. It blurs the borders of good manners and good taste and questions the limits to abjection and between human and animal. Hunger and lack of food is then much more than a circumstantial issue due to the Special Period. The intertextuality between this novel and the picaresque genre also intensifies the broader dimensions of this book.

Dara Goldman briefly compares *El Rey de La Habana* to the film / documentary *Suite Habana* (2003) by Cuban cineaste Fernando Pérez. According to Goldman, both works reveal the hidden side of daily life in Cuba, invisible to tourists, without denouncing the system. *Suite Habana* covers one day, from sunrise to bedtime, in the life of real people living in deprivation in Havana. There is no dialogue except for a number of stray phrases picked out in a back-

---

9   The picaresque novel could be defined as a popular sub-genre of prose fiction which is usually satirical and depicts, in realistic and often humorous detail, the adventures of a roguish hero of low social class who lives by his wits in a corrupt society.

ground mix of street sounds and music and one classroom scene. *Suite Habana* has an untimely dimension and could have been situated in the Special Period (cf. Serra 2006: 99), although the leitmotiv of John Lennon's statue, unveiled in December 2000, sets the film in the 21st century. The film interweaves fragment scenes and alternates among the individual protagonists as they move through the day. There are sustained close-ups of their physical actions, for example the preparation of the peanuts by retired textile worker Amanda or the repairs by the shoe-mender Julio. Captions identify them by name and age. In an epilogue, stills with captions outline the characters' dreams for the future. These dreams are always related to artistic achievements and have already been suggested by the double lives that most of the protagonists live, for example, the shoemaker Julio frequents the Benny Moré dancing-hall. The film goes beyond evoking hardship in a specific period and focuses on ontological and ethical questions on behalf of man's destiny, his dreams, the meaning of life, the fulfillment of wishes, the relationship between material and corporal needs and spiritual or artistic aspirations.

Vicky Unruh describes the film as an example of Pérez's "aesthetic of the fragment" (2009: 203) and it is certainly true that the film turns the spotlight upon daily acts in a poetic way. In the culinary aspect, the different times for eating (breakfast, lunch, and dinner) provide the film with a certain rhythm. The preparation and eating of rather sober dishes—picking through grains of uncooked rice (*escoger el arroz* in Cuban), preparing peanuts, chopping an onion, and so on—become rituals of aesthetic beauty. Poverty and scarcity are presented without any denunciation of the system; it is simply a subtle recording of misery with dignity, sometimes combined with nostalgic overtones. For example, while Amanda and her husband eat a frugal dinner, the camera focuses on a photograph of the young couple cutting a wedding cake. This nostalgic image of better times is underscored by the melancholic ballad "Mariposas," by Silvio Rodríguez, icon of the Cuban Revolution, playing on television in the background.

It is as if Pérez has proposed an ethical approach to scarcity and some critics even identify an ideological and political message in it: 'in spite of the crisis, we still can.' The highly crafted composition of the suite, the well-chosen music, the uncomfortable close-ups, and the sepia tones of the images at the end of the film all serve to embellish the poverty and make it less severe. We could state that instead of an aesthetics of hunger there is rather a cosmetics of hunger. I follow here Ivana Bentes' (2003) ideas on recent Brazilian films in opposition to Glauber Rocha's theory concerning the aesthetics of hunger. In the sixties Rocha called for a Third World Cinema or Cinema Novo, one which would inspire revolution and accurately reflect the impoverished lives of those living in Latin America. Third World Cinema would reject the glossy conventions of Hollywood cinema in favor of a raw, hitting, and anti-imperialist approach. Rocha insisted on the ethical dimension of filmmaking and saw violence as an expression of hunger. Bentes argues that more recent films like *Cidade de Deus* are closer to what she coins in a wordplay with Rocha a cosmetics of hunger, a desire to hide the rawness, to simulate the real, and to glamorize poverty producing more pleasing images. These ideas can be applied to *Suite Habana*. Although there still is an ethical vindication from below in concordance with Rocha's ideas, violence is very subliminal in *Suite Habana*. More in Bentes' line, there is almost a celebration of poverty and dearth in certain fragments. Hardship is covered up into a spectacle and glamorized. Third World Cinema becomes in this case a kind of more digestible World Cinema.[10] Whereas poverty and hunger are related to abjection in Gutiérrez's book, Pérez embellishes poverty. Both cases obviously provoke philosophical, meta-artistic, and aesthetic questions about how poverty should be represented.

Besides stereotypes, contrast, and the metonymical use of food as a starting point for broader reflections, we can also identify a fourth strategy, which consists in almost omitting the theme relegating it to the background. I identified this strategy of relegation primarily among writers who live or at least are published in Cuba. They apply to their work a kind of obliviousness to the food problems, and treat the issue tangentially. The *Bildungsroman Silencios* (1999), written by Karla Suárez before she left the island in 1999, portrays the coming of age of a young girl, la Flaca (Skinny), in the 1980s and early 1990s (up until 1994). Her nickname, la Flaca, perhaps suggests that her major concern is not food. Instead, she is concerned with finding the meaning of her life. She reflects on the importance of lies, means of expression, betrayal, and friendship (because all of her friends leave the island). She is not interested in the problems that surround her. The few culinary references are mostly made to the alcoholic drinks that may help her and her friends find their way. And the fact that she has only rice and chickpeas to eat when the Special Period begins does not appear to affect her significantly. At the end of the novel, when all of her friends have left the island, she locks herself up in her house with her cat, waiting for nothing.

It is striking that in one of her reflections, the protagonist criticizes the marketing of the Special Period and the lack of literary concern:

---

10 World Cinema is usually defined as films of non-English speaking countries, not distributed by the major companies, less determined by Hollywood commercialism and characterized by more artistic values. For a discussion, cf. Chanan (2011).

No sé si sería la carencia de un periodismo verdadero, pero se me antojaba que los escritores hacían periodismo. Nadie contaba historias. Todos decían lo que yo podía ver con sólo asomar las narices fuera de mis paredes. Hablaban de gente fugándose en balsa de la isla, jineteras en las noches de La Habana, el dólar que subía y subía, la esperanza que bajaba y bajaba. Resultaba aburrido. (Suárez 2008: 244)[11]

The same existential search and escape from the context for personal reasons lie at the core of *Madagascar,* by Fernando Pérez, a film made in 1994, the most difficult year of the Special Period. While the setting of the film in Havana's dilapidated buildings clearly refers to the Special Period (Havana in ruins is another successful cliché), the film avoids the problems of shortage in the 1990s. The central issue is the conflict between a mother, Laura, who still believes in the Revolution, and her daughter, Laurita, who is obsessed with the idea of travelling to Madagascar, an island that represents the spiritual side of the human being. Laurita attempts to escape from her monotonous and materialist life. She wishes to eschew an automatized life, as symbolized at the end of the film in an oneiric scene in which people eat slowly and without enthusiasm plates of rice at a table with large amounts of cabbage. This indirect reference to the difficulties of the Special Period may not affect her ontological quest.

Another Cuban writer living on the island, Ena Lucía Portela, also pays little attention to food in *La sombra del caminante* (*The Shadow of the Walker*), though the story is set at the end of the 1990s on the so-called diabolical island (Cuba). This very complicated novel in terms of narrative and content is a kind of failed thriller, and is also a reflection on race, literature, gender, guilt, violence, and evil. The referential dimension is largely absent. Nonetheless, there are a number of brief remarks and certain facts that indirectly highlight the scarcity of the Special Period. The protagonist is a vegetarian and the eating of hibiscus flowers functions as a leitmotiv. This seems to be a critique of the meaty Cuban diet and an indirect allusion to the island's food problems. Another subtle way in which the deprivation is referred to is the narrator's description of Cuban spectators' reaction to a well-known food scene in Ingmar Bergman's film *Fanny and Alexander*: they start to laugh, because "Cubans laugh at everything that is related to *food*" (Portela 2001: 94; original emphasis; my translation). The nar-

---

11 "I ignore if it is the lack of real journalism, but it seemed to me that in Cuba, writers were journalists. Nobody told stories. Everyone wrote about what I could see if I just looked out of my window. They talked about people who fled the island in rafts, prostitutes in the Havana night, the dollar that went up and up, the hope that went down and down. It was boring" (Súarez 2008: 244; my translation).

rator refers to the typical Cuban means of defense, their *choteo*: they make fun of their problems.

The last example I wish to comment on both encompasses and goes beyond the various strategies of stereotype, contrast, metonymy, and relegation that I have discussed so far. I describe it as a metaphorical approach to food. In order to demonstrate this strategy, I refer to an essay by a writer who has been in exile since 2007, Antonio José Ponte, entitled *Las comidas profundas*. Ponte wrote this short text in 1996 and it was published in France. It comprises a meditation in seven chapters on the desire for food in a context of shortage. The opening scene depicts the narrator writing on a table covered by a tablecloth that is decorated with "fruit, roasted meat and glasses and bottles, all things that I don't have" (Ponte 1997: 7; my translation). Unlike Gutiérrez's *El Rey de La Habana*, the word hunger is almost entirely absent from Ponte's text. The narrator links together very heterogeneous meditations based on personal memories or literary references in which food is described in terms of its absence. Although the last chapter consists of one noun phrase, "Una mesa en La Habana" (81), the author does not restrict his meditations to Cuba and proceeds to expand the text in time and space. He describes King Charles V's desire for a pineapple that he did not eat but only smelled, or he reproduces a food-related fragment from Virginia Woolf's diary at the time of the Second World War.

That said, Ponte does not avoid references to the Special Period and the Cuban context. His meditations sometimes originate from evocations of identitarian commodities such as pineapple, edible roots, and the famous *ajiaco* (stew). The usual connotations are present: pineapple and its sensuality, edible roots as an identitarian expression, and *ajiaco* as a symbol of racial miscegenation, following Fernando Ortiz. Even *bistec de frazada de piso* is mentioned in the text. However, the narrator juxtaposes the story of the steak with two stories about suitors eating the cooked shoes of the women they adore, stories told by Apollinaire in his book *Les diables amoureux*. The narrator concludes that "the two stories by Apollinaire substitute, they equal, that is, they metaphorize"; "the history of the false meat also evokes the search for metaphors by means of food"; and "despair causes the metaphors to increase" (28; 29; 30; my translation).

For the narrator, writing about food is like a *château en Espagne*, a chimera. In a metafictional sense, the fundamental idea could be that in the absence of food, writing can only be performed using metaphors and quoting other texts, words that have lost their referential dimension. Ponte's poetics is based on the word, with its endless associations, its metonymical and metaphorical implications, and its search for the lost origin. This origin will always be absent, and food is a metaphor for it. The absence, the void, and the emptiness provoke a linguistic abundance and the baroque, an element widely present in the Caribbean arts. Abundance and scarcity are complementary: the narrator "has an empty stomach and the hunger helps him to consider that every dish is substitutive, that to eat is to metaphorize, to build bridges" (Ponte 1997: 31; my translation). This is essentially what Ponte achieves: he builds linguistic bridges between texts and words, *puente* in Spanish, which is very close to his last name, Ponte.

The aim of this essay was to give a brief overview of five key strategies employed by artists in their expression of food during the Cuban Special Period. Evidently, further research is required to provide deeper insights into these texts and the theme in general. However, the examples I provide here of how food is used as stereotype, by contrast, metonymy, relegation, and metaphor, demonstrate that the study of food references and hunger goes beyond a mere summary of its well-known connotations. The identitarian approach is present, but does not explain it all: the idiosyncratic desire for meat goes beyond some original inventions and poses profound questions. We also see that hunger and scarcity in a Cuban context cannot be explained only by a social interpretation: Menéndez's professor and Gutiérrez's outcast Rey are confronted to the same problems of sustenance in a context were social classes are supposed to be abolished. Neither the political interpretation is sufficient: hunger is not always associated to the political regime. Stereotyping, for example, cannot be related only to ideology, often associated to an inside-outside dichotomy in the Cuban case: writers residing inside and outside the island play with the pig stereotype. In other words gastrocriticism is more than Castro-criticism, to use a rather obvious wordplay. Gastrocriticism is in fact a question of poetics, aesthetics, and ethics. Be it hunger or abundance, the poetics of the writer will necessarily influence the way of approaching it. Exaggerated contrasts concerning food serve well Valdés' sarcastic style; the hidden layers of hunger give more depth to Gutiérrez's dirty realism; the use of a pig as a pretext for abuse suits Menéndez's interest for the crime novel and its implied questions on evil; the negation of food scenes matches with Suárez's introspective research; the *choteo* concerning food is very appropriate for Portela's profound scepticism and Ponte's poetic-essayistic-neobaroque attitude influences the oblique ways that he copes with hunger. As far as ethics is concerned, the gastrocritical approach leads us to reflect on essential questions of good and evil, real life and dreams, and the boundaries between animal and human. In terms of aesthetics, food discourse poses the question of how writing should be performed, and how the materiality of everyday realities of food and eating should be expressed. The five strategies I commented on show, on the one hand, rather predictable methods that are frequently applied to food references. Culinary fragments represent often extreme situations: fast or feast, hunger or abundance. The exaggeration that leads to stereotypes or the contrast between the two extremes are frequent ways to introduce the gastronomic theme. On the other hand, the apparent oblivion of the subject as well as the metonymical strategies present a more ambiguous approach. In what I call the metaphorical approach the subject is still more fictionalized and questions profoundly the function of fiction in relation to the material world.

Bibliography

Alonso, Nancy 2002. "César." *Cerrado por Reparación*. La Habana: Ediciones Unión, 12-20.
Allende, Isabel 1997. *Afrodita. Cuentos, Recetas y otros Afrodisíacos*. New York: Harper Collins.
Álvarez, Julia 1991. *How The García Girls Lost Their Accent*. Chapel Hill: Algonquin Books.
André, María Claudia 2001. *Chicanas and Latin-American Women Writers. Exploring the Realm of the Kitchen as Self-Empowering Site*. Lewiston: Edwin Mellen Press.
Anonymous 1977 [1554]. *Lazarillo de Tormes*. Buenos Aires: Editorial Francisco de Aguirre.
Apollinaire, Guillaume 1977. *Oeuvres en Prose Complètes*. Bibliothèque de la Pléiade III. Paris: Gallimard.
Atwood, Margaret 1980. *The Edible Woman*. London: Virago.
Bakhtine, Mikhail 1970. *L'Oeuvre de François Rabelais et la Culture Populaire au Moyen Age et sous la Renaissance*. Paris: Gallimard.
Barthes, Roland 1984. "Lecture de Brillat-Savarin." *Essais Critiques IV*. Paris: Ed. du Seuil, 303-26.
Behar, Sonia 2009. *La Caída del Hombre Nuevo. Narrativa Cubana del Período Especial*. New York: Peter Lang.
Bentes, Ivana 2003. "Cidade de Deus Promove Turismo no Inferno." [http://www.consciencia.net/2003/08/09/ivana.html (retrieved 8 October 2013)].
Blodgett, Harriett 2004. "Mimesis and Metaphor. Food Imagery in International Twentieth-Century Women's Writing." *Papers on Language and Literature* 40.3: 260-295.
Bourdieu, Pierre 1979. *La Distinction. Critique Sociale du Jugement*. Paris: Minuit.
Brillat-Savarin, Anthelme 1975. *Physiologie du Goût*. Paris: Hermann.

Calvo Peña, Beatriz 2005. "Cocina Criolla. Recetas de Identidad en la Cuba Independentista." *Catauro. Revista Cubana de Antropología* XII.7: 76-84.

Carpentier, Alejo 1987. "Problemática de la Actual Novela Latinoamericana." *Tientos y Diferencias*. Barcelona: Plaza y Janés, 7-28.

Castellanos, Rosario 1989. *Obras I. Narrativa*. México: Fondo de Cultura Económica.

Certeau, Michel de, Luce Giard, and Pierre Mayol 1994. *L'Invention du Quotidien. 2. Habiter, Cuisiner*. Paris: Folio.

Chaviano, Daína 1998. *El Hombre, la Hembra y el Hambre*. Barcelona: Planeta.

Chanan, Michael 2011. "Who's for 'World Cinema'?" [http://www.mchanan.com/wp-content/uploads/2010/08/Reflections-on-World-Cinema.pdf (retrieved 24 October 2013)].

Collard, Patrick 2010. "El Conde en la Cocina de Jose." *Saberes y Sabores en México y el Caribe*. Eds. Rita De Maeseneer and Patrick Collard. Amsterdam / New York: Rodopi, 335-349.

"Cocina al Minuto—Bistec de Frazada de Piso," YouTube Video, 8:51, posted by Carlos Cobas, 13 June 2010 [http://www.youtube.com/watch?v=5Ljla4YbS5Q (retrieved: 8 July 2013)].

Díaz Torres, Daniel 1991. *Alicia en el Pueblo de Maravillas*. ICAIC. DVD.

Esquivel, Laura 1989. *Como Agua para Chocolate*. Barcelona: Mondadori.

—. 2007. *Íntimas Suculencias. Tratado Filosófico de Cocina*. Madrid: Ollero & Ramos Editores.

Ferrari, Guillermina de 2007. *Vulnerable States. Bodies of Memory in Contemporary Caribbean Fiction*. Charlottesville / London: University of Virginia Press.

Ferré, Rosario 1985. "La Cocina de la Escritura." *La Sartén por el Mango. Encuentro de Escritoras Latinoamericanas*. Eds. Patricia Elena González and Eliana Ortega. Río Piedras: Ediciones Huracán, 137-54.

Goldman, Dara 2008. "Urban Desires. Melancholia and Fernando Pérez's Portrayal of Havana." *Bulletin of Hispanic Studies* 85: 867-81.

Guibert, Rita 1973. *Seven Latin American Writers Talk to Rita Guibert*. New York: Alfred Knopf.

Gutiérrez, Pedro Juan 1999. *El Rey de La Habana*. Barcelona: Anagrama.

Gutiérrez Alea, Tomás, Tabío Hernández, and Juan Carlos 1993. *Fresa y Chocolate*. ICAIC. DVD.

Huggan, Graham 2001. *Postcolonial Exotic. Marketing the Margins*. London: Routledge.

Jeanneret, Michel 1987. *Des Mets et des Mots. Banquets et Propos de Table à la Renaissance*. Paris: José Corti.

Lévi-Strauss, Claude 1997. "The Culinary Triangle." *Food and Culture. A Reader*. Eds. Carole Counihan and Penny van Esterik. London: Routledge, 28-35.

Maeseneer, Rita De 2003. *El Festín de Alejo Carpentier. Una Lectura Culinario-Intertextual*. Genève: Droz.

Menéndez, Ronaldo 2006. *Las Bestias*. Madrid: Lengua de Trapo.

Mintz, Sidney W. 2003. *Sabor a Comida, Sabor a Libertad*. México: Ediciones de la Reina Roja.

Obejas, Achy 2009. *Ruins*. New York: Akaschic.

Ortiz, Fernando 1998. "Los Factores Humanos de la Cubanidad." *La Isla Infinita de Fernando Ortiz*. Ed. Antonio Fernández Ferrer. Alicante: Instituto de Cultura "Juan Gil-Albert," 187-207.

Padura Fuentes, Leonardo 2000. *Pasado Perfecto*. Barcelona: Tusquets.

—. 2001. *Máscaras*. Barcelona: Tusquets.

—. 2006. *Paisaje de Otoño*. Barcelona: Tusquets.

—. 2007. *Vientos de Cuaresma*. Barcelona: Tusquets.

Pérez, Fernando 1994. *Madagascar*. Wanda Vision & ICAIC. DVD.

—. 2003. *Suite Habana*. Wanda Vision & ICAIC. DVD.

Ponte, Antonio José 1997. *Las Comidas Profundas*. Angers: Deleatur.

—. 2012. "¿Quién Va a Comerse lo que esta Mujer Cocina?" *Diario de Cuba*, 2 de marzo [http://www.diariodecuba.com/cultura/1330677346_1206.html (retrieved 8 October 2013)].

Portela, Ena Lucía 1999. "Literatura versus Lechuguitas." *Voces para Cerrar un Siglo* I. Ed. René Vázquez Díaz. Stockholm: Skogs Grafiska, 70-9.

—. 2001. *La Sombra del Caminante*. La Habana: Ediciones Unión.

Quintero Herencia, Juan Carlos 2005. "No Es lo Mismo Llamar al Cimarrón, que Verlo Huir." *La Torre* 10.35: 1-28.

Quiroga, José 2005. *Cuban Palimpsests*. Minneapolis: University of Minnesota Press.

Redruello, Laura 2011. "Touring Havana in the Work of Ronaldo Menéndez." *Havana Beyond the Ruins. Cultural Mappings After 1989*. Eds. Anke Birkenmaier and Esther Whitfield. Durham / London: Duke University Press, 229-45.

Rocha, Glauber 1965. "Uma Estética da Fome." *Revista da Civilização Brasileira* 3: 165-70.

Ruark, Jennifer 1999. "A Place at the Table." *The Chronicle and Research Publishing* 9: A.17 [http://chronicle.com/free/v45/i44/44a00101.htm (retrieved 2 July 2008)].

Santiago, Esmeralda 1994. *When I Was Puerto Rican*. New York: Vintage Books.

Serra, Ana 2006. "La Habana Cotidiana. Espacio Urbano en el Cine de Fernando Pérez." *Chasqui* 35.1: 88-105.
Song, H. Rosi 2009. "Hard-Boiled for Hard Times in Leonardo Padura Fuentes's Detective Fiction." *Hispania* 92.2: 234-243.
Suárez, Karla 2008. *Silencios*. Madrid: Santillana Ediciones.
Teja, Ada 1992. "El Banquete, la Muerte y la Comedia." *Codici del Gusto*. Ed. Maria Grazia Profeti. Milano: Francoangeli, 466-86.
—. 1993. "Bajtín y los Banquetes de Lezama." *Revista de Literatura Cubana* XI.21: 78-99.
Tobin, Ronald W. 1990. *Tarte à la Crème. Comedy and Gastronomy in Molière's Theater*. Columbus: Ohio State University Press.
—. 2002. "Qu'est-ce que la Gastrocritique?" *XVIIe Siècle* 217.4: 621-30.
Unruh, Vicky 2009. "All in a Day's Work. Ruins Dwellers in Havana." *Telling Ruins in Latin America*. Eds. Michael Lazzara and Vicky Unruh. New York: Palgrave-Macmillan, 197-209.
Vadillo, Alicia 1996. *The Culinary Text as Constructive Strategy in the Work of Three Contemporary Writers. Severo Sarduy, José Lezama Lima, and Alejo Carpentier*. PhD University of Syracuse. Michigan: Ann Arbor.
Valdés, Zoé 1997. *Te di la Vida Entera*. Barcelona: Planeta.
Vázquez Díaz, René 2009. *El Pez Sabe que la Lombriz Oculta un Anzuelo*. Barcelona: Icaria.
Vázquez Montalbán, Manuel 2008. "Las Comidas Profundas." *El País Semanal* 1634 (23 de marzo): 46-48.
Whitfield, Esther 2008. *Cuban Currency. The Dollar and 'Special Period' Fiction*. Minneapolis: Minnesota Press.
Wilkinson, Stephen 2006. *Detective Fiction in Cuban Society and Culture*. Bern: Peter Lang.

Hotel Worlds and Culinary Encounters in Cristina García's *The Lady Matador's Hotel*

Louisa Söllner

> Mirrors on the ceiling,
> The pink champagne on ice
> And she said 'We are all just prisoners here, of
> our own device'
> And in the master's chambers,
> They gathered for the feast
> They stab it with their steely knives,
> But they just can't kill the beast
>
> Last thing I remember, I was
> Running for the door
> I had to find the passage back
> To the place I was before
> 'Relax,' said the night man,
> 'We are programmed to receive.
> You can check-out any time you like,
> But you can never leave!'
> THE EAGLES, HOTEL CALIFORNIA

This essay explores how the expressive potential of food is regulated through spatial arrangement in the sphere of the 'hotel world.'[1] The core part will be ded-

---

1 The expression is borrowed from Henry James' remarks on the Waldorf-Astoria that will play an important role in the following observations on modern and postmodern approaches to hotel space (cf. James 1993).

icated to Cuban-American author Cristina García's novel, *The Lady Matador's Hotel* (2010). Spontaneous thoughts about hotel spaces expose a set of contradictory associations: on the one hand, chance encounters, and notions of travel and transition come to mind; on the other hand, one might think of the high level of organization that links the hotel to the outside world, while at the same time enabling its functioning as a seemingly independent microcosm. In order to achieve a better understanding of spatial arrangements in hotels, I revisit two, by now, canonical texts: Henry James' comments on the Waldorf-Astoria in *The American Scene* (1907), and Fredric Jameson's descriptions of the Westin Bonaventure in *Postmodernism, or The Cultural Logic of Late Capitalism* (1984). This detour will prove useful for an understanding of the critical propositions García's text has to offer. In my reading, I show how García turns the Central American hotel that provides the setting for her novel into a space in which problems of dislocation and global communication are negotiated through culinary practices. García's novel thus embodies a trend that becomes tangible in much diasporic writing: a turning away from the construction (or productive deconstruction) of ethnic identities, and towards more complex images of globalization.

While the focus on political tensions in a global context might be a recent occurrence in García's fiction, some of the strategies that surface in *The Lady Matador's Hotel* are no novelty to her readers: García's preceding works are similarly marked by an engagement with food as a site of critical revisions and the novelist constantly seeks to expose the more subtle implications of food as a language. Roland Barthes, in "Toward a Psychosociology of Contemporary Food Consumption," explains the transformation of eating practices into systems of communication with the following words: "Substances, techniques of preparation, habits, all become a system of differences in signification; and as soon as this happens, we have communication by way of food" (Barthes 1997: 22). Barthes introduces examples that show how eating habits are indicative of class, sentiments of national belonging, and gender. These observations demonstrate that food is not only language individuals can employ in order to communicate a sense of belonging; in reverse, it also hints at the manner in which the conventions that determine the meaning of food potentially limit individual choices. García, from her early fiction onwards, has proven herself highly perceptive of the restrictive dimensions in culinary discourse. One might even argue that the need of situating her work in the context of Cuban-American writing has sharpened García's ability to critically deal with the ways in which food produces meaning.

'COMMUNICATION BY WAY OF FOOD' IN CUBAN AMERICA: GARCÍA'S EARLY FICTION

A short introduction into the strategies that are frequently used in representations of food in the context of Cuban-American literature can help in demonstrating what is special about García's culinary language. Gustavo Pérez Firmat, one of the spokesmen for 'Cuban-America' (Pérez Firmat 1994), in his autobiography *Next Year in Cuba* (1995), stylizes palatal pleasures as pendants to a Proustian *mémoire involontaire*: "Proust has his madeleines; I have my mangoes" (Pérez Firmat 2005: 24). The Proustian rhetoric that is employed here apparently guarantees for the authenticity of memories: the past re-awakened through a physical sensation, through the taste of a fruit that is associated with a long lost childhood. Readers are thus presented with the illusion that communication through food (or fruit) is spontaneous and, to a certain degree, uncontrollable. The scene Pérez Firmat so fondly remembers is how, as a small boy, he watched one of his family's servants picking mangoes. Pérez Firmat describes how he made use of the opportunity to peek under Aselia's skirt and informs us that "[t]o this day I cannot bite into the pulp of this juicy fruit without thinking of Aselia's undies" (ibid.). For Pérez Firmat, eating mangoes constitutes not only an act of remembering but also a small gesture of resistance against the erasure of his family's Cuban past: in this respect, we are not dealing with a personal memory here, but instead with one many of Pérez Firmat's readers, particularly those who feel a comparable resentment about the loss of their former home country, will be able to identify with. Pérez Firmat, however, fails to see that the harmless thrill of boyish voyeurism he describes is indicative of the privileges he enjoyed in Cuba and, beyond this, points to the inflexible preservation of class and gender categories that marked the island's social structures in pre-revolutionary times. His text evokes a Cuban past through a language in which food not only transports memories of a protected childhood, but simultaneously carries certain ideological connotations. Instead of the illusion that food mediates memories in a personal and spontaneous manner, it turns out that Pérez Firmat's mangoes are highly codified. In the context of Cuban-American literature, representations of food are often inscribed with similar layers of meaning. On the surface level, the wistful evocation of traditional Cuban dishes (or as in Pérez Firmat, fruit) comforts nostalgic longings for a lost home; but on a deeper level such desires are also imbued with a political amnesia.[2] This might account for the need that emerges,

---

2 Karen Christian's essay "Sexual Stereotype and Ethnic Pastiche in Cuban American Fiction" (1993) explores literary representations of traditional gender codes, fashion,

particularly for female authors, such as García, to rethink the structures that link food to memory.

In García's literary debut, *Dreaming in Cuban* (1992), we encounter a Cuban exile who attempts to forge a new life for herself as a bakery owner in Brooklyn. We are introduced to the ambitions that accompany this new self-invention through the sceptical eyes of Lourdes' daughter, Pilar: "She [Lourdes] bought a second bakery and plans to sell tricolor cupcakes and Uncle Sam marzipan. Apple pie, too. She is convinced she can fight communism from behind her bakery counter" (García 1992: 136). Rather than fondly remembering pre-revolutionary Cuba, García's character engages in a personal battle against expropriation through a language of food. Cupcakes, apple pie, and mangoes, in the context of Cuban-American literature, are much more than a sensual temptation; they constitute ingredients of a heavily politicized language. Different from Pérez Firmat's fantasies about mangoes, García refuses to gloss over this political dimension, and instead spells it out for her readers. Lourdes' aggressive politics of forgetting contrast with the soothing memories of "mangoes" and "undies" Pérez Firmat shares with us.

In her second novel, *The Agüero Sisters* (1997), García uncovers new nuances of the Proustian rhetoric I have introduced above. The novelist initially has her protagonist Constancia go through an experience that resembles the one described by Pérez Firmat: "At the best bodega in Little Havana, two dozen varieties of bananas are sold. There are pyramids of juicy mangoes, soursops, custard apples, and papayas. In a flash, they'll make her a milk shake that tastes of her past" (García 1997: 44). But this scenario is only called upon in order to examine how desires for similar experiences are exploited in consumption culture: Constancia launches a line of cosmetic products that are based on precisely the tropical fruit that were also ingredients of the milk-shake she tasted in Little Havana's *bodegas*. This strategy is highly successful: "Already Constancia has received dozens of letters from women who confess that they feel more *cubana* after using her products, that they recall long forgotten details of their childhoods" (130). What Constancia's customers experience is, of course, not the authentic memory Proust describes when he stages the tasting of the *madeleine*, but rather a form of codified and collectively shared nostalgia: the sentiment Pérez Firmat also seeks to make use of when writing about mangoes.

Susan Stewart, in her essay on Proust's memory concepts, demonstrates how, once the evocation of memories enters into a system of representation, we are no longer dealing with involuntary memory, but instead with the form of voluntary

---

music, and food in Cuban-American fiction as strategies for establishing a sense of cultural belonging and soothing sentiments of nostalgia.

memory that is labelled as "nostalgia." Stewart explains the effects of this sentiment with the following words: "Voluntary memory creates generations, reinforces bonds, produces retrospective conformity, and molds social forms of ego ideals" (Stewart 1999: 81). These observations aptly describe the mechanisms that are at play in many Cuban-American literary texts. García, by contrast, stages her narrative in a way that uncovers the manner in which codes of nostalgia are established and spread instead of simply reproducing this language. Nostalgia, here, is not stylized as an individual sentiment of longing, but explicitly exposed as a codified and collective experience. García's culinary conjugations thus serve the double-edged purpose of participating in the evocation of a lost homeland, while simultaneously unsettling the structures that allow for such fantasies. *The Lady Matador's Hotel*, it will turn out, makes use of a comparable critical awareness. García's fifth novel transcends the earlier Cuban-America-centered books as it introduces a wider vision of global politics. The method of staging unease with social structures through culinary discourse gains new dimensions in the context of this book, but still remains recognizable to readers of García's early fiction.

DISORIENTING HOTEL WORLDS: (POST-)MODERN ANXIETIES AND A CENTRAL AMERICAN HOTEL

The Lady Matador's Hotel displaces García's readers into Central American geographies. In spite of the marginal position the country holds in the context of international politics (it remains unidentified throughout the narrative), the hotel Miraflor, where most of the novel is set, is a site of multinational communication: it not only hosts a press conference for García's eponymous 'lady matador,' but also a hemispheric military conference. This is the space, where the fates of characters from various backgrounds intersect: hotel visitors, figures who supposedly play leading parts in local politics and the country's economy, and a character who enters the stage quite inconspicuously as a waitress. The hotel setting García selects for her novel turns out to be much more than a backdrop for juxtaposed narratives but instead constitutes a space that is symbolically charged and reflects the social tensions and imbalances that are also embodied by the novel's heterogeneous cast of characters. In order to gain a better idea of how García constructs the space of her hotel, I shortly introduce the aforementioned texts on hotel worlds by Henry James and Fredric Jameson. Both texts help in formulating criteria for the hotel's potential as narrative space, with both writers emphasizing the way in which hotels function as spaces that are emblematic for social change on a wider scale.

Henry James, in *The American Scene*, muses that the Waldorf-Astoria represents "a social, indeed positively aesthetic ideal;" "a synonym for civilization, for the capture of conceived manners themselves" (James 1993: 440). The hotel experience, in his text, is conceptualized as a new model of sociality in which individual action melts into the homogenizing form of what James labels as "publicity," and, in a more detailed description, depicts as machinery of busy "promiscuity":

> It sat there, it walked and talked, and ate and drank, and listened and danced to music, and otherwise revelled and roamed, and bought and sold, and came and went there, all on its own splendid terms and with an encompassing material splendour, a wealth and variety of constituted picture and background, that might well feed it with the finest illusions about itself. (441)

James perceives the hotel world as a spectacle of faceless activity: visitors participate in the production of a shared dreamscape without noticing the more nightmarish aspects of public culture. Instead of achieving a sense of individual importance and agency, the visitor is drawn into the larger composition that does not allow for any idiosyncratic chords: "Such was my impression of the perfection of the concert that, for fear of its being spoiled by some chance false note, I never went into the place again" (444).

While James accentuates on the public spectacle for which the hotel becomes much more than stage and inspiration, Fredric Jameson offers a detailed analysis of the architecture designed by John C. Portman that turns the Westin Bonaventure into an emblem of "postmodern hyperspace" (Jameson 1991: 44). The different focus however hardly belies that Jameson is equally troubled by the individual's loss of autonomy. On the one hand, Jameson foregrounds the manner in which the Bonaventure displaces visitors into a narrative whose development they are no longer able to control. Pondering the hotel's system of connection between seemingly disparate levels and areas, he notes that "[h]ere the narrative stroll has been underscored, symbolized, reified, and replaced by a transportation machine" (42). On the other hand, Jameson attributes much importance to the hotel's "disjunction from the surrounding city" (41), its aspiration of functioning as "a total space, a complete world, a kind of miniature city" (40). He visualizes this detachment through a description of the "glass skin," which "achieves a peculiar and placeless disassociation of the Bonaventure from its neighborhood" (42). Jameson explicitly sets the Bonaventure's disinterested "aggressivity" (ibid.) apart from modernist "Utopian space" that "fan[s] out and eventually transform[s] its surroundings" (41). Henry James, however, states about the Waldorf-Astoria that she "is reduced to confessing, with a strained smile, across the traffic and the danger, how little, outside her mere swing-door, she can do for you" (James 1993: 440). There is no trace of interference here, but a sense of detachment very similar to the one Jameson describes.

This collection of text passages has demonstrated how both Henry James and Fredric Jameson struggle with transformations in social structures. Jameson repeatedly articulates his conviction that the postmodern experience of hyperspace takes place on a scale that remains incomparable to architectural provocation in the modernist era. Both texts stress, however, a profound sense of disorientation when confronting the intricate interiors of their respective object of analysis. And both rely on the trope of a narrative machine in which the individual body turns into a passive entity. These parallels are interesting, as they mitigate Jameson's claims about the novelty of the experience he depicts.

Similar doubts become tangible in Homi Bhabha's comments on Jameson's text, which particularly respond to Jameson's central claim that the hyperspace of the Westin Bonaventure "can [...] stand as the symbol and analogon of that even sharper dilemma which is the incapacity of our minds [...] to map the great global multinational and decentered communicational network in which we find ourselves caught as individual subjects" (Jameson 1991: 44). Drawing parallels, not to Henry James and the fears public culture awakens, but to Joseph Conrad, Bhabha suggests that Jameson's problems with the global communication structures are, in fact, related to the modernist fears of the "incomprehensible" Conrad stages in his literary masterpiece: "The Horror! The Horror! Almost a century after *Heart of Darkness* we have returned to that act of living in the midst of the 'incomprehensible' that Conrad associated with the production of transcultural narratives in the colonial world" (Bhabha 1994: 308). The dialogue with Conrad's novel uncovers new dimensions in Jameson's concern with disorientation. Jameson laments the "incapacity of our minds [...] to map the great global multinational and decentered communicational network in which we find ourselves caught as individual subjects" (Jameson 1991: 44). However, considering Bhabha's comments, one might feel tempted to think twice about the adequacy of "mapping" as an approach. Bhabha underlines this by juxtaposing Jameson's remarks about the unmasterable dimension in postmodern communication networks with the multiple geographies "borderline existences" inhabit: "Hybrid hyphenations emphasize the incommensurable—the stubborn chunks—as the basis of cultural identification" (Bhabha 1994: 312-13). Diasporic subjects, Bhabha suggests, construct unmarked in-between spaces as realms of identification.

The question I want to pursue is whether García can contribute anything to the debate. Let me first introduce the international cast of her most recent novel in more detail. Apart from Suki Palacios, the Japanese-Mexican-American *matadora*, there are characters from various cultural backgrounds: Gertrudis Stüber, a lawyer of German origin, has selected the hotel in order to conduct her own 'export' business with babies that are specifically 'bred' for the purpose of being 'adopted' by U.S.-American parents; the 'adoption' business lures Ricardo Morán, a Cuban-exile and poet, who left the island during the Mariel boatlift, and his American wife Sarah, a pastry chef, to the hotel; we also encounter Won Kim, a depressive Korean businessman who owns a local textile manufactory; while his workers are on strike, and the press carries out xenophobic campaigns against him, his pregnant teenage mistress Berta waits in the Miraflor's honeymoon suite. The two characters, whose destinies are most closely linked to the unnamed country, and simultaneously to each other, are Aura Estrada, a waitress and vengeful ex-guerrilla, and Colonel Martín Abel, the organizer of the hemispheric military conference the hotel hosts. As it turns out, Colonel Abel is the person who was responsible for Aura's younger brother's violent death during a recent civil war. The histories of rupture and dislocation that García assembles in her novel visualize the complex intersections of global communication networks: her hotel is populated by characters that, while often following their own agendas, lose sight of the role they play within the larger context. Similar, although not quite comparable, to the way James and Jameson use the hotel spaces as an emblem for larger social transformations, García's Miraflor is thus conceived as a symbol for asymmetries in global interactions.

SEDUCTION AND COOPERATION: NARRATIVE SPACE IN *THE LADY MATADOR'S HOTEL*

The preceding discussion can productively inform a reading of García's text on two levels. On the one hand, we are offered two traits that determine the functioning of hotels as narrative space: the detachment from the surrounding environment and the imposition of a system of communication that limits the movements of individual actors to a certain degree. On the other hand, the question emerges whether there is any potential for a rewriting of the hotel space: can the narrative that hotel spaces coerce visitors to participate in be unsettled through individual intervention? Some passages from the initial sections of García's novel offer readers their first glimpses of the Miraflor and, at the same time, introduce Suki Palacios, the 'Lady Matador':

Suki Palacios has come a long way to this spired hotel in the tropics, to this wedge of forgotten land between continents, to this place of hurricanes, violence and calculated erasures. She arrived yesterday from Los Angeles, trading the moody squalor of on city for another, the broken Spanish for one more lyrical. In a week she will compete in the first Battle of the Lady Matadors in the Americas. By the time the other *matadoras* arrive in the capital, its citizens will be clamoring for blood. (LMH: 4)

Suki's temporary residence at the Hotel Miraflor is the result of a sudden and yet strategic displacement. Her early arrival for the bullfighting championship is not caused by her desire to explore the "forgotten land" that hosts the event, but instead by the intention of securing an audience for her own show. Some readers might note the cynical dimension in Suki's wish to have the capital of a civil war-shaken country "clamoring for blood." Considering this somewhat solipsistic interest in marketing her own persona, it is hardly surprising that the hotel Suki selects for her stay constitutes a well-protected space:

Every window of the hotel looks inward to a crosshatch of courtyards and fountains, banyans and Madeira palms. The pool is visible beneath Suki's window, a glazed and artificial blue. A cascade of bougainvillea brightens the patio. Aviaries with raucous jungle parrots outmatch the mariachis in volume and plumage. (LMH: 4)

Instead of urban splendor and avant-garde architecture, which James' and Jameson's texts respectively explore, García's paints visions of nature and tropical comfort. Yet the implications resemble the previously introduced analysis of hotel spaces. The most striking feature of this description is the choice to have the hotel's windows open towards the patios and gardens instead of revealing a view of the cityscape: visitors are blinded and, perhaps, instilled with dreams of invulnerability through the exclusion of the outside. Bhabha labels Jameson's textually modelled Westin Bonaventure as a "postmodern panopticon" (Bhabha 1994: 311). A comparable impression is evoked here; the pool figuring as an oversized, but blind, eye in the midst of its lush surroundings. The pleasant illusion of security and wellbeing the hotel conveys thus remains tainted by a sense of artificiality. The contrast between paradisiacal luxuries the Miraflor offers to its visitors and the atrocities that permeate the unnamed country's history are obvious. Visitors find themselves in a shielded microcosm and are lured into succumbing to a narrative that is carefully planned out for them. Suki, as we learn, longs to "submit to the hotel's shielding niceties, to ignore the afternoon torpor awaiting her in the ring" (LMH: 4). Here, a subtle irony becomes visible:

Suki enters the hotel with the intention of leaving an impact and transforming the space that surrounds her. Instead, we witness how the space that surrounds her exerts a kind of lulling effect on these original desires.

While Suki allows herself the fantasy of indulging in the hotel's extravagancies without giving a second thought to inward-looking windows, some of the other characters experience the hotel space as a limiting and inadequate housing for their narratives. Aura suffers from the stasis her waitressing job imposes on her—the country's ex-dictator is one of the candidates in the ongoing elections, and Aura "is convinced that the entire country has succumbed to a collective amnesia" (LMH: 9). As Suki's initial reactions show, the Miraflor appears as an emblem of such "amnesia": it invites visitors to dwell in a dream of untarnished nature, and is stylized as a paradise in which all one's needs are tended to. Unable to express her fury, Aura "smoothes her pink and white apron" (LMH: 8) and "wills her hands to stop trembling" (LMH: 7), when she serves pork chops to her brother's murderer. The manner in which the hotel space restricts its visitors' movements is mirrored by the set of rules Ricardo and Sarah have to face because of the "adoption" business. Here, the reader is introduced to a strategy of manipulation that does not rely on the gentle hypnotism Suki is so susceptible to, but instead to a form of blackmailing. Gertrudis, we learn, has a "mutually lucrative" agreement with the Miraflor's director, which, for the American couple, signifies: "no leaving the hotel with the baby; meals must be eaten at the hotel; formula and baby supplied must be purchased at the hotels sundries shop" (LMH: 16). Ricardo and Sarah are forced to limit their movements to the hotel, thus, not only helping in covering up the illegal adoption business, but also leaving their money within the well-guarded hotel walls instead of distributing it in the city. The uncannily magnetic force the hotel exerts is, moreover, exhibited through the difficulties characters face, whenever they choose to leave in one way or another. Ricardo, on a stroll during the adjacent streets, is mugged and immediately transported to another secluded space, a hospital, before once again entering the world of the hotel (LMH: 64-9; 129-34). Won Kim, by contrast, attempts to leave not only the hotel but also the entire world of failed business and awkward love by jumping off the hotel's roof. This form "exit" from the stage is, however, prevented by Aura, the ex-guerrillera and hotel employee (LMH: 153-4).

It is the strand of the narrative that focuses on Won Kim and his mistress Berta—a former embroiderer from the factory—that especially illustrates frictions between the hotel space and the characters it accommodates. The discrepancies are rendered tangible in Berta's attempts at transforming her surroundings. Berta embroiders the hotel's cushions, "her fancy handiwork will cost him a fortune" (LMH: 18), Won Kim reflects; breaks porcelain; and performs other seemingly futile acts of resistance: "Berta has thrown soap off the balcony, taped toilet stationary to the toilet seat. He cannot guess what might be next. If he strung her nonsensical utterances together, Won Kim wonders, would they constitute a manifesto of sorts?" (LMH: 19). García's hotel world displaces the characters into a narrative of amnesia. Desires for self-expression and resistance, in such a context, apparently cannot assume any form other than "nonsensical utterances": "'Scars in the heaven,'" Berta comments after smashing a porcelain cup, which, in Won Kim's eyes, resembles a "minuscule skull" (LMH: 19). While both, Berta and Won Kim, experience the hotel space as threatening and devoid of meaning, only Berta attempts to communicate her frustration. For readers who are familiar with Henry James and Fredric Jameson's observations on hotel spaces, Berta's actions translate into a rejection of the manner in which the Miraflor's "shielding niceties" gloss over her own history. In this light, they, in fact, constitute "a manifesto of sorts": Berta seeks to 'scar' the seemingly intact hotel space, to inscribe it with new meaning and transform it into a site of expression rather than silencing. She will not remain the only character who seeks to intervene into the hotel space. In the following section of my reading, I turn to one specific aspect of communication in the hotel: food and culinary practices. It is this aspect which allows García to make her own contributions to the debates about hotel spaces. Food is an essential factor in the hotel world: "it ate and drank," James writes. But can eating and drinking in the hotel world also follow a different grammar than the impersonal forms James suggests?

RITUAL AND REWRITINGS: 'COMMUNICATION BY WAY OF FOOD' IN THE MIRAFLOR

For the reading of food and eating representations in García's most recent book, it is useful to remember the ways in which her previous novels characterize and critique food as a language that favors the expression of collective fantasies over individual histories. In the Miraflor, the distribution of food is well-organized: hotel employees provide a room service that attends to customers' every need; additionally there are bars, and most importantly, Aura's workplace, the Garden Restaurant. Through the eyes of Aura, readers are introduced to diverse groups who use food as a site for producing a sense of community. One of these is the assembly of the "adoptive mothers" who cultivate what Aura labels "their mid-morning ritual" (LMH: 81). These women order pastries and coffee, and discuss childcare. A striking contrast to this gathering is provided by the participants of the military conference, who adjust their choices of drink and food to those of the most powerful member of the group, the representative of the American army; this means Bloody Maries and pork chops for everyone. In Aura's perception, the instinctive alignment accounts for much of the pain she, her family, and country experienced through the hands of some of these men: "It's no wonder these officers commit the atrocities they do. Not a single one has a mind of his own" (LMH: 11). Ordering Bloody Mary and pork chops, the military men, in fact, stage a collective performance of masculinity and invulnerability. This becomes most obvious, when one of the generals uses the food Aura serves to him as an opportunity for lubricious remarks:

One of the generals sent his [pork chops] back, complaining that they were too tough. '*A sus órdenes*,' Aura said, taking his plate. She noticed him noticing her as she walked. When the pork chops are ready, Aura discreetly spits on them, working in the saliva until they gleam. [...]
'Now they are extra juicy,' he says, giving her a wink.
'*Algo más, General?*'
'Save me some of your most delicious dessert.' The snub-nosed general says this loud enough for the neighbouring tables to hear. Everyone brays on cue. (LMH: 7-8)

The general's words are placed in slippery territory that metonymically links Aura's body to the food she serves: they indicate that Aura is an as desirable object of consumption as the pork chops on the plate she carries. Aura's small gesture of resistance (spitting on the pork chops) somewhat re-stabilizes the imbalance, the general seeks to establish; but her private revenge remains impotent against the collective reaction of approval that greets his crude sexism.

At this point, it is useful to remember the initial observations about food, and particularly Barthes' analysis of the social coding that items of consumption are subjected to. As suggested earlier, these forms of social coding provide not only opportunities of self-performance (from which characters such as the general can benefit) but also assume a more oppressive dimension. Passages such as the one discussed here demonstrate how García stages hierarchies of gender and ethnicity through culinary encounters. The two groups Aura serves, the adoptive mothers and the participants of the military conference, are characterized by a clearly gendered selection of food; and, particularly in the case of the military men, sharing food enforces sentiments towards unassailable collective strength. The novel, however, also introduces uses of food that transcend such tendencies of uninspired adaptation. In my analysis of food as a medium of resistance in *The Lady Matador's Hotel*, I would like to concentrate on two of García's characters,

Suki and Aura, whose stories are constructed in a complementary fashion. While Suki enters the stage as self-empowered character, and for a long time remains under the impression that she can easily control her environment, Aura is initially shown in a position of helpless exposure. As the novel evolves, this dynamic is twisted and turned around.

Born in Los Angeles to a Japanese mother and Mexican father, Suki situates herself in a web of multicultural identifications. In the initial section of her novel, García uncovers the strategies through which her protagonist establishes coherence in her otherwise restless existence:

The lady matador devours the sliced pear she ordered, at great expense, from the room service. [...] Ritual is everything. Her father a professional dancer taught her this. [...] One sliced pear. For extra luck, silent sex with a stranger two nights before a fight. [...] Then in the shadowed moment before she steps into the ring, Suki repeats three words in Spanish and Japanese: *arrogance, honor, death*. (LMH: 5)

Suki's rituals are noteworthy in several respects: they are her own creations and indicative of her hybrid cultural heritage as well as her ability to transcend an inflexible understanding of gender roles. Encompassing diverse elements, namely food, sex, and language, Suki's rituals appear as a reversal of the 'juicy' comments Aura is forced to listen to at the Garden Restaurant. While the general uses the conjunction of food, sex, and language in order to participate in an unimaginative collective performance, Suki's rituals are private and designed to overcome communication routines: the sex is silent, and the words, ritualistically spoken before her fights, are pronounced in two languages. Bhabha's comments on Jameson's text, and the indication that transcultural spaces allow for a rewriting of the poetics of homogenization and disorientation the Bonaventure's spatial arrangements represent, are helpful here. Most of García's characters do not engage in forms of rewriting that visualize the productive aspects of cultural encounters, but Suki is a notable exception. Her rituals celebrate displacement and simultaneously endow Suki with a sense of immunity against personal fracture: the ritual always remains the same, even if the pear costs a small fortune.

It is interesting to note that Suki's handling of the sex aspect in her rituals emulates the male sexism Aura experiences. The lady matador is intent on maintaining an imbalance between herself and her lovers: she "knows what works best for her: a simple man, not too intelligent, grateful and discreet" (LMH: 44). In the Miraflor, her choice falls on a waiter, "skinny, clean-shaven, a bit pale for her taste": one of the employees who provide the hotel's impeccable room service. The encounter, however, jumbles Suki's expectations; once again she succumbs to charms of the Miraflor and loses control of the situation. After having given in to the waiter's erotic expertise, Suki is left with assurance that: "It has been an honor to serve you, señorita" (LMH: 46). While Suki enjoys the incident, her inability to exert control over her lover also announces a fiasco in her next bullfight. Suki is injured, and while still combating in the finale of the championship, she enters this last fight in physically unstable condition. Anxieties of being pressed into a narrative system that she cannot transform, surface for the first time, when Suki imagines that the audience is "willing her to fail because for a woman to fail reinforces tradition" (LMH: 208). At the same time Suki acknowledges her helplessness in confrontation with well-established routines: "Suki is a novelty, a passing phenomenon, like the hurricane that never quite arrived. It doesn't matter how spectacular or perilous her performance. Tomorrow, business will return to the maddening usual, to more changeless seasons" (LMH: 208). Readers leave Suki in the moment of suspense, in which it still remains uncertain, whether she will be able to kill her last bull.

Aura, the waitress, also utilizes food as a private language of ritual and resistance, but her treatment is intricately knit into the hotel's eating arrangements. Readers accompany Aura on several secret trips to the hotel's roof, where she brings offerings to her dead brother's ghost: "Her pink-and-white uniform provides the necessary camouflage. No one will question her carrying this tray of sugar buns and tea" (LMH: 47). Communication through food, in these scenarios, transcends limits of time, space, and social order: Julio's ghost identifies his murderer and leaves Aura with the task of revenge. The journey into a space that lies beyond the well-organized hotel routine, thus, also signals another passage: Aura, the waitress, turns into Aura, the guerrillera again, and starts a silent operation that undermines the elaborate narrative system of the hotel. As this strand of the story develops food becomes part of new practices; the colonel is psychologically tortured through anonymous gifts of chocolate cakes (LMH: 97), orange juice, coffee, bread, and muffins (LMH: 115). The chocolate cake is a particularly perfidious instrument of creating unease, as it comes with an ambiguous letter; the second one the colonel receives. The first one runs: "*My dearest colonel, Soon you will be mine...*" (LMH: 93). The message that accompanies the cake is: "*Our time is growing closer*" (LMH: 97). These little notes transform the conventional games in which female bodies are conquered through a language of gifts and sweets. They therefore are explicitly designed in order to attack the colonel's exaggerated performances of masculinity.

Some of the culinary gifts are, in fact, poisoned, but instead of proving fatal, they increase the colonel's suspicions and anxieties. It is important to note here, that Aura's actions follow a language of resistance that has been established among the hotel employees: in the initial sections, readers not only witness how Aura spits on the general's pork chops, but are also informed that the bartender put "stool hardener in the Americans' drink" (LMH: 11). The hotel employees thus use the visitors' exposure to the hotel's services and narrative systems in order to stage acts of retaliation. After the game with the culinary gifts has gone on for a while, the colonel is still alive, but so ravaged that when Aura sneaks into his room, he is unable to defend himself against his execution:

Aura is tempted to kill the colonel with his own pistol, make the world think he took his life. This is the ultimate humiliation for a military man. Instead she brought a knife from the hotel kitchen. She removes it now from her satchel. It's eight inches long and slightly curved, used for butchering beef and lamb. But the colonel isn't a lamb. He's a killer of children, of brothers and lovers, a destroyer of lives. (LMH: 192)

Once again, Aura uses the hotel's equipment in order to unmake the protected system of the Miraflor. Using a kitchen knife, she also rewrites the connection between food and violence, which she first draws in the Garden Restaurant, when confronting the cohort of generals ordering Bloody Mariess in accordance with the American's choices (LMH: 11). In reverse to the initial comparison of Aura's body to a piece of meat; it is now the colonel's body, which is put in this position with fatal consequences. The knife not only serves as an instrument of severance, but also as a connection between different parts of García's narrative. It most importantly re-enforces the parallels between Aura and Suki who, as a *matadora*, kills with a sword. Aura's last thought, in fact, sounds like an answer to Suki's final doubts: "The last word in history, she fears, must be fought for again and again" (LMH: 193).

CONCLUSION: A DIFFERENT HOTEL WORLD

Aura's rewriting of the hotel's food routine exposes how food is not only a site that cements social hierarchies but also a site of vulnerability. Aura's terrorist actions 'by way of food' certainly constitute a more transgressive form of self-assertion than the projects characters in García's earlier fictions undertake. While characters such as Lourdes, in *Dreaming in Cuban*, or Constancia, in *The Agüero Sisters*, act in accordance with the system in order to exploit its weak spots, Aura deliberately perverts the hotel's system of communication. Yet *The Lady Matador's Hotel* is linked to the earlier books by a thread of continuity as it similarly exposes the oppressive dimensions in culinary discourse and demonstrates how characters transform eating routines in order to stage a form of social critique.

The context of social instability García depicts contrasts with the initially discussed reflections on distinctively U.S.-American hotel worlds. Both Henry James and Fredric Jameson present the hotel as a disorienting, and at the same time, rigidly organized microcosm that endangers a sense of personal agency. García's text exploits both aspects and rephrases them in order to expose a new set of problems. Rather than depicting the Miraflor as a space of complete homogenization, García's hotel world produces its glamorous surface in order to gloss over social and political imbalances. Under illusion of tropical splendor, the tensions live on. And it is precisely the Miraflor's functioning as mirror of political asymmetries that undermines its aspirations of shielding visitors from the outside.

Through interventions from the inside, the Miraflor is eventually turned into a space that hemorrhages into the open rather than remaining the self-contained entity it aspires to represent. While many visitors might indeed be unaware of the political tensions that they are surrounded by, and eager to submit to the hotel's comforting sense of amnesia, there are traces of those tensions in the hotel, culminating in the end with a dead body. The Miraflor is thus presented a space that resembles Gloria Anzaldúa's "Borderlands": cultural encounter is not only a sphere of inspired rewritings but also of wounding confrontations. García's transformation of the hotel world, one should conclusively note, takes place in a decade, in which the primary concern that permeates political and media discussions is not so much the pressure impenetrable systems impose on individuals, but rather the anxieties the newly discovered vulnerability of such systems awaken. García's book, thus, offers a daring narrative of political asymmetries and terrorism through the depiction of a new hotel world.

BIBLIOGRAPHY

Anzaldúa, Gloria 1987. *Borderlands / La Frontera. The New Mestiza.* San Francisco: Aunt Lute Books.

Barthes, Roland 1997. "Toward a Psychosociology of Contemporary Food Consumption." *Food and Culture. A Reader.* Eds. Carole Counihan and Penny van Esterik. London: Routledge, 20-27.

Bhabha, Homi K. 1994. "How Newness Enters the World. Postmodern Space, Postcolonial Times and the Trials of Cultural Translation." *The Location of Culture.* Ed. Homi K. Bhabha. London / New York: Routledge, 302-337.

Christian, Karen 1993. "Sexual Stereotype and Ethnic Pastiche in Cuban-American Fiction." *Gender, Self, and Society*. Ed. Renate von Barderleben. Frankfurt a. M. et al.: Peter Lang, 171-189.

García, Cristina 1992. *Dreaming in Cuban*. New York: Alfred A. Knopf.

—. 1997. *The Agüero Sisters*. New York: Alfred A. Knopf.

—. 2003. *Monkey Hunting*. New York: Alfred A. Knopf.

—. 2010. *The Lady Matador's Hotel*. New York et al.: Scribner.

James, Henry 1993. *Collected Travel Writings. Great Britain and America: English Hours, the American Scene, Other Travels*. New York: The Library of America.

Jameson, Fredric 1991. *Postmodernism, or, the Cultural Logic of Late Capitalism*. Durham: Duke University Press.

Pérez-Firmat, Gustavo 1994. *Life on the Hyphen. The Cuban-American Way*. Austin: University of Texas Press.

—. 2005. *Next Year in Cuba. A Cubano's Coming of Age in America* (revised edition). Houston: Scrivenery Press.

Stewart, Susan 1999. "Proust's Turn from Nostalgia." *Raritan* 19.2: 77-94.

'You are what you cook'

Preparing Food, Creating Life in *Treme*

SEBASTIAN HUBER

> That's the great thing about New Orleans:
> at some time or other, everybody becomes one.
> The food prevails.
> LEAH CHASE, *TREME*

> There is no need to fear or hope,
> but only to look for new weapons
> GILLES DELEUZE 1992: 4

THE BIO-LOGICS OF FOOD

Although it should nowadays certainly not be taken for granted that food is biological, I want to begin this essay with the thesis, which will guide the overall argument of my paper, that food is *bio-logical*. This is not to say that food—by which I mean a very general notion of edible and inedible materials, practices involved in its cultivation, killing, preparation, consumption, digestion, and excretion, as well as the discourses involved in its narrative and anti-narrative, pictorial, sensual, etc. constitution as well as the actors who are in some way or other involved in these processes[1]—has something specifically to do with a very

---

1 It seems striking that in considering the research on 'food,' one hardly ever gets a cogent definition of what is being talked about. While one explanation might certainly lie in the fact that food is so omnipresent and all-encompassing, in very much the same way as language (cf. Barthes 1997: 21), another reason might be that despite its apparent universality (cf. Lévi-Strauss 1997: 28) it is so heterogenous that in talking

problematic notion of nature.² Rather, I insist that food is necessarily concerned with the bios and, as a consequence, offers its own logic thereof. In relating food to 'life' I address the quite obvious fact that life is existentially dependent on food. However, in assuming a more differentiated notion of 'life,' namely as bios, what Giorgio Agamben shows has a history of implying "the form or way of living proper to an individual or a group" (Agamben 1998: 1), also appertains to a fundamentally political, in fact, bio-political context. In this sense, this essay reveals two levels of the aphoristic dictum, "You are what you eat," that is slightly altered in the title of this article. 'You are what you cook' points in this context, on the one hand, to the essentially ontological ramifications of food and particularly of its preparation. If compared to the processes of internalization that are latent in the more popular saying according to which 'one is what one eats,' and which crucially affect our notion of identity through the mechanisms of culinary consumption, I emphasize the productive means that cooking involves as a practice that is directed to an 'outside': quite simplistically, one might say that eating involves, at least physically, the consumption from outside into inside, whereas cooking could be said to reverberate with notions of creation as when I cook a gumbo that can then be consumed by others. Without stretching the opposition between eating as a process of internalization and cooking as a mode of externalization, I would nevertheless like to uphold a certain conceptual distinction between the two acts that assume a crucial role when we talk about food and how it influences our 'being.'

By the same token, another contrast between eating and cooking, the former defined by a somewhat solipsistic focus on the self, the latter often by a tendency to involve a variety of people, segues into the second realm that the first part of my title suggests.³ 'You are what you cook,' thus also reflects on an ethical di-

---

about it, the subject matter incessantly slips away. In this sense, I can only ascribe to an as encompassing a definition of food as possible in order to perpetuate its critical study and reject the assumption that "food connotes triviality" (Barthes 1997: 21).

2 My argument that food is biological does therefore point into a different direction than Sidney Mintz's observation that "[f]or us humans, then, eating is never a 'purely biological' activity (whatever 'purely biological' means). The foods eaten have histories associated with the pasts of those who eat them; the techniques employed to find, process, prepare, serve, and consume the foods are all culturally variable, with histories of their own" (Mintz 1996: 7).

3 One may obviously again point to the instability of this binary, since eating is, arguably, primarily a social act. Despite the inexorably collective setting of consumption, I rather suggest an understanding of eating that is as social as sexual intercourse is for Lacan. Lacan's famous "il n'y a pas de rapport sexuel" (Lacan 1991: 134) thus ad-

mension, precisely the constitution of a bios, a common political / ethical life that constructs a collectivity to the extent that one should rather say 'We are what we cook.' Particularly when faced with the increasing presence of dispositifs that assume to control the bios of a nation's (or Empire's) citizens, this essay underlines the highly subversive form of resistance that so ubiquitous and quotidian a custom as cooking may embody.

More specifically, I argue that cooking, as it is represented in David Simon and Eric Overmyer's HBO-series *Treme* (2010-),[4] functions as a technique that antagonizes biopower by the creation of its own form of 'life' that undermines the hegemony of the state.[5] Michael Hardt and Antonio Negri's much discussed (and not exactly unproblematic) notion of 'biopolitical production,' which "creates not only material goods, but also relationships, and ultimately social life itself" (Hardt amd Negri 2004: 109) serves as a theoretical concept to grasp the workings of cooking and its potential to unsettle the current system of biopolitics. By extension, this paper thus suggests that food and cooking, in *Treme,* implies its own bios-logic that spatially, sociologically, and cinematographically resists the homogenizing and regulating mechanisms of biopower.

---

dresses the impossibility of a relation between the sexes in a sexual act. Just like this most intimate, but simultaneously most 'social' experience fails to create a relation to the other and cannot escape its solipsistic undercurrents, I see eating caught up in a similar pseudo-communality.

4   This paper focuses to a large extent on the two first seasons of the show, although the third has also been aired by the time this essay was written. In the following, I cite the show by referring to the various episode titles.

5   To this extent, I fundamentally reject Wade Rathke's analysis that *Treme* upholds a "steadfast refusal to deal with the issues and dynamics of power" (Rathke 2012: 262), as will be depicted in the following. Moreover, I will show that Rathke's argument that "Treme only really cares about the experience of the 'eaters,' the tourists, and not the New Orleans of workers and whatnot, no matter how many high-end kitchen b-rolls we see" (264) needs some re-evaluation in the context of cooking as biopolitical production.

We won't bow down, on nobody's ground

HBO's 2010 series *Treme*, which is named after a particularly vibrant and economically underpriviliged black neighborhood in New Orleans,[6] tells the story of the city's post-Katrina struggle to get back on its feet. In a similar manner as in Simon and Overmyer's enormously popular and critically acclaimed *The Wire* (2002-2008) the show geographically dissects the Crescent City as in a realist novel, juxtaposing various segments of society both in terms of class and race, and interweaves these portfolios in order to arrive at a complex image of the 'whole.'[7] While there are a variety of different cultural alcoves and social professions depicted—from John Goodman as a university professor to Clarke Peters' highly complex role as a Mardi Gras Indian chief to Khandi Alexander's work as a local bar owner—it is music that is sketched as the most prominent and most productive form of cultural production. Yet among the range of musical success stories and narratives of failure, there is also a plot line that follows Janette Desautel (played by Kim Dickens) who together with her Caribbean sous-chef Jacques Jhoni (Ntare Guma Mbaho Mwine) runs a restaurant, Desautel's, that is initially flourishing, but can ultimately not avoid insolvency due to increasing repair costs that Hurricane Katrina caused.

Despite its minor role within the cultural, economic, and political milieu that the show conjures, I want to emphasize the crucial function that Desautel's cooking plays as a counter-narrative to a heightened form of control that makes itself felt in New Orleans. Before showing the potential of resistance that cooking conveys in *Treme*, it is, however, necessary to begin with the regime of biopower that suppresses and surveills the city's inhabitants, since New Orleans, Louisiana (NOLA), as depicted in the show, combines mechanisms of discipline and of control. While Foucault's historical account of disciplinary societies, in which, as Hardt and Negri observe, "social command is constructed through a diffuse

---

6 The Tremé was, in fact, the first community that was settled by free black people, which foreshadows its counterpointal position within the United States. "Built by free people of color in the early 1800s," as Helen Morgan Parmett (2012:193) notes, the Tremé is certainly the synecdoche for a radical counter-site to the United States' race policy.

7 The problematic question of authenticity that was already a stylistic dominant in *The Wire* is equally put to the test in *Treme*. See especially Courtney George's "Keeping it 'Reals'" (2012), Rathke's "*Treme* for Tourists" (2012), or Joy V. Fuqua's "'In New Orleans, We Might Say It Like This …'" (2012) for their varying discussions of the show's 'authenticity.'

network of dispositifs or apparatuses that produce and regulate customs, habits, and productive practices" (Hardt and Negri 2000: 23) is followed by an epistemological break that establishes societies of control "in which mechanisms of command become ever more 'democratic,' ever more immanent to the social field, distributed throughout the brains and bodies of the citizens" (ibid.), *Treme*'s NOLA seems to conflate these two modes of governmentality.

On the one hand, disciplinary mechanisms manifest themselves in the show's persistent representation of institutional settings that aim at the regulation and containment of New Orleans' inhabitants. In Episode Three ("Right Place, Wrong Time") of the first season, Wendell Pierce's character Antoine Batiste, for instance, gets incarcerated for accidentally running into a police car. This not only results in an exaggerated form of violence that damages the musician's front teeth that are indispensable for being able to play his trombone, as well as his confinement; most symbolically, the police officers break Batiste's instrument, what he calls his 'bone,' which carries not only economical repercussions, but also implies a more fundamental attack on his body and its creative capabilities. As a consequence, the assault has unmistakable physical consequences that are tied to economic dispositions in that it literally disables Batiste's ability to perform; to this extent, this incisive infringement on the musician's corporeal and identitarian integrity negatively affects his very mode of life.

In another crucial plotline, bar owner Ladonna Batiste-Williams' brother Daymo ends up in prison, what Deleuze, in following Foucault, terms "the model site of confinement" (Deleuze 1990: 177), without having done anything wrong. In a similar manner as *The Wire* unmasks the malfunctioning system of the police (amongst other institutions), *Treme* unravels the bureaucratic confusions that initiate a contingent cause of events and lead ultimately to Daymo's death. In fact, this arbitrary execution of power over life is framed within the political context of the series' production. Since, on their search for Daymo, Ladonna and her lawyer inspect video footage that surveillance cameras in the prison yard shot just after Katrina. The iconography of these images, which depict masses of mostly black inmates, some in their orange prison garment, others bare-chested, crumbling on the floor, are reminiscent of the media coverage of Guantanamo Bay and Abu Ghraib.[8] Although not as explicitly vivid, the use of

---

8   Through the place's analogy with such sites of Guantanamo Bay or Abu Ghraib, there lies a particular parallel to Agamben's diagnosis of Nazi concentration camps, which for him are the epitome of biopolitics (Agamben 1998: 166 ff). Agamben goes on to say that "if the essence of the camp consists in the materialization of the state and in the subsequent creation of a space in which bare life and the juridical rule enter into a threshold of indistinction, then we must admit that we find ourselves virtually in the

camera footage that portrays the brute conditions of the Louisiana disciplinary institutions evokes a cultural imagery (and imaginary space) that is essentially embedded in a paradigm of corporeal domination. In fact, the biopolitical mechanisms latent in these processes of incarceration conform to Agamben's notion of the homo sacer. Agamben shows to what extent sovereign power and its declaration of a state of emergency has always been contingent upon the exclusive inclusion of a homo sacer.[9] In Agamben's historical extension of biopolitics, the sovereign only establishes his power by constituting a sacred man, a being who has been deprived of its political life (bios) and is reduced to a more fundamental form of living (zoē), what Agamben calls 'bare life.' As Agamben goes on to show, the processes conducted by the national government thus "separate zoē and bios in another man and [...] isolate in him something like a bare life that may be killed" (Agamben 1998: 42). The transformation of Daymo into a sacred man suspends the concept of murder as a juridical concept and renders his killing para-legal. In this win-win-situation for the state, Daymo's murderers avoid persecution, while this act concomitantly resuscitates the nation's sovereignty.

Treme thereby shows the extent to which the state of emergency that a natural catastrophe caused was appropriated by the U.S. government to reinstate its sovereign power. In the series' first episode "Do You Know What It Means" Goodman's character Creighton Bernette accordingly insists in an interview that "what hit the Mississippi Gulf Coast was a natural disaster, a hurricane, pure and simple. The flooding of New Orleans was a man-made catastrophe, a federal fuck-up of epic proportions and decades in the making" (00:17:16). While

---

    presence of a camp every time such a structure is created, independent of the kinds of crime that are committed there and whatever its denomination and specific topography" (174). However, Agamben insists that "[a]s the absolute space of exception the camp is topologically different from a simple space of confinement" (20) such as disciplinary institutions.

9   For Agamben, the process of sovereign legitimation is pointedly an inclusive exclusion, for only through the exclusion of a 'sacred man' can the sovereign order ground its state of exception. Its founding is thus inevitably dependent on the inclusion of the exception. Agamben thereby shows that Carl Schmitt's notion of sovereignty, according to which he is sovereign "who decides on the state of exception" (Schmitt in Agamben 1998: 11), has to be viewed in the light of processes that only create the liminal figure of the homo sacer. In this context, the homo sacer is not simply an exclusion necessary for the constitution of political orders, but rather constitutes, like the sovereign, the very foundations of every form of politics as bio-politics. The sacrality of this liminal figure thus implies his simultaneous position inside and outside of the political order, which allows to sacrifice him without fear of legal consequences.

Bernette's nature-culture binary certainly does not hold, he nevertheless addresses to what extent the governmental state of exception was supposed to bring the city back into the control of the American nation. Due to the fact that New Orleans has historically always been a thorn in the side of the United States and its foundational ideologies of economic and ethnic motivation,[10] the show makes a case that the government co-opted this 'natural' state of exception and transformed it into a political one in order to resuscitate its territorial sovereignty. One may easily glimpse the need for the United States' attempt in reaffirming its grip on New Orleans in the city's aberrational status within the nation. As Berndt Ostendorf so comprehensively argues, there are a variety of factors playing into its peripheral location, in more than merely geographical terms. Ostendorf posits that New Orleans, being "situated on the margin of European colonial powers, Spain, France and England" (Ostendorf 2003a: 100), marks a site of convergence of various conflicting ideologies, particularly religious and ethnic ones. The annexation of Louisiana within United States jurisdiction that was conducted relatively late in the nation's history as well as New Orleans' geographical location virtually made it an outpost to the Caribbean: its "marginality has given [it] the role of an urban, Catholic, and hedonistic counterpoint to the ruling North-American standards of negative nutrition and dietary NoNos" (100-101) that Ostendorf comments on with a specific focus on the Crescent City's status as a culinary enclave. "As a creolizing oikoumene on the periphery" Ostendorf further elaborates, "it profited from negligence which translated into a lack of norms imposed from the center" (100), which the United States government, in the show, intends to correct.

Treme's very first scene neatly characterizes its spatial and historical setting and evokes specific tropes that relate to the "Great Southern Babylon," to borrow the title of Alecia P. Long's homonymous book from 2004, which conveys the city's alleged sinfulness. The opening sequence fades in, accompanied by background noise of trumpets rehearsing and people laughing, to a fast-paced set of extreme close-ups: amongst other things, one sees musicians tuning their instruments, a tattooed arm, the feathers of a Native American headwear fluttering in the wind, empty liquor bottles, a burning cigarette in a man's hand, two youngsters lighting up a joint, the young and old dancing in the street. It is emblematic for the show's introduction to and rendering of New Orleans that the initial sequence is almost exclusively inhabited by Black people.[11] It seems thus notewor-

---

10 Cf. Ostendorf 2003a: 100.

11 Herman Gray notes that "black themed shows like *The Wire*, *Treme*, and documentaries now appeal to a specific market niche, lifestyle, and aesthetic sensibility" (Gray 2012: 274). One might well read this cultural phenomenon with Eric Lott's analysis of

thy in the context of the show's reception that it sets in with a mosaic panorama of 'non-whites,' which even for HBO's standards seems to take its toll on its viewers and subscribes to a narrative of ostensible authenticity that, as Lynnell L. Thomas argues, perpetuates the commodification of New Orleans under the viewer's "tourist gaze" (Thomas 2012: 214).[12] While, on the one hand, one should not be color-blind to subliminal marketing strategies according to which "media coverage of Hurricane Katrina and its aftermath shifted the focus of national discourse onto African Americans" (216) in an exoticist manner, one should equally not neglect the unsettling reverberations that this exposure lets loose on its audience.

Moreover, showing the consumption of various drugs in broad daylight, or the gathering in the open street to make music and dance, clearly works against various prevailing ideological convictions of the American nation. In this sense, *Treme* instantaneously characterizes New Orleans within a semantics of illegality. Next to the obvious fact that the consumption of alcohol and drugs in the public sphere runs against the grain of national jurisdiction and the American sacralization of privacy, the show's audience is also immediately confronted with an incessant stereotype against NOLA's inhabitants in an economic sense. For in depicting the city's celebrating residents right after the white letters "New Orleans, Louisiana, Three Months After" on black background to introduce the audience to the spatio-temporal setting, the show confronts two clashing narratives that construct New Orleans. The juxtaposition of the introductory text that approaches the viewer in a neutral and withdrawn, almost documentary-like manner and the chaotic in medias res of the Crescent City as the show fades in on the first close-up frames thus coalesces two different narratives and reflects on the

---

blackface minstrelsy and wonder whether this exposure to the black body is "less the incarnation of an age-old racism than an emergent social semantic figure highly responsive to the emotional demands and troubled fantasies of its audiences" (Lott 1993: 6). While Gray, for instance, argues that the exaggerated presentation of black people in the show "is all very much in keeping with the entrepreneurial neoliberal project of branding and marketing blackness as quality television" (Gray 2012: 276), I would rather opt for an inherent "mixed erotic economy of celebration and exploitation" (Lott 1993: 6) that Lott diagnoses.

12 Thomas observes that "recent case studies of New Orleans tourism have demonstrated, tourist evocations of authenticity historically have relied on the interdependent allure of black expressive culture and containment of black cultural producers and their communities. In this way, blackness has been used to titillate and entertain tourists while validating, and even exacerbating, systemic racial and class inequities" (Thomas 2012: 214).

public's prefabricated assumptions. Instead of answering the audience' expectations that the textual signifiers certainly evoke in the nation's cultural memory, the show refrains from opting for a melodramatic depiction of the city's inhabitants in a wretched condition of existential precarity. Similarly, the series' very first set of images avoids all too familiar patriotic scenes of reconstructing the city that are framed within a larger national symbolic rite that has pervaded the iconography of other catastrophes, particularly 9/11. While the representation of the preparation for the first Second Line parade after Katrina certainly fits the show's overall inclination to emphasize the various coping strategies with the catastrophe, I would argue that the beginning also conjures a very specific image of New Orleans and its inhabitants. Simultaneously, it seems as if *Treme* borrows common stereotypes that were conventionally employed when imagining the city, while in the same breath appropriating these narratives in order to illustrate New Orleans' form of resistance. For, next to the 'won't bow down' mentality, the show also characterizes the residents by resorting to the prevailing rhetoric of their unproductivity. Instead of being productive, working towards a specific teleological goal such as the reconstruction of the city, NOLA's inhabitants drink, smoke, and loiter in the street. In the vein of the city's lack of an "industrial base" (Ostendorf 2003a: 106) and the resulting emphasis on non-industrial forms of labor that do not merit a similarly comparable net product, New Orleans as a city of aesthetic, culinary, and cultural productivity is often denounced for its resistance to neo-liberal dispositions that the show tunes in from the very start. This results not only in common clichés according to which its inhabitants are "choosing sensuality over seriousness" (Long 2004: 1), but also has more severe repercussions.[13]

While the opening sequence also hints at the dialectics between New Orleans and the rest of America by constantly shifting the images' focus, thereby indicating the difficulty of arriving at a lucid understanding of the city and its inhabitants, the cinematographic presentation also implies another layer. Besides the extreme close-ups of NOLA's residents, *Treme* intersperses medium shots of police officers and state soldiers patrolling the city. The difference in camera angle might not only suggest a self-reflexive comment upon Simon and Overmyer's

---

13 A telling example of this internalization of the neo-liberal mode of productivity is Rathke's argument that "tourism in New Orleans is somewhere between big business and the only business in town" from which he concludes: "We need the business in New Orleans" (Rathke 2012: 262), by which he means a different, more productive kind of business. Moreover, he goes on to criticize the show for, amongst other things, simply caricaturing its musical characters such as Antoine Baptiste: "This is a show about lazy and not that kind of hard work" (265).

oeuvre, to the extent that they now focus in on New Orleans while keeping up some distance to an interrogation of institutional dispositifs that were at the heart of *The Wire*; the different proximities that differentiate between locals and state representatives at the same time also create an environment that is evocative of surveillance. The police officers and soldiers overlooking the Second Line preparations, along with the crosscutting of the two diegetical levels mirroring the two positions of power by cinematically confronting them, thereby manifests the extent to which New Orleans is also the site of more transparent modes of regulation. In accord with a shift to more ubiquitous forms of biopower that are no longer confined to institutional settings, the Crescent City is thus also part of a control society. To this extent, mechanisms of surveillance emanate outside of the confines of specific institutions. On the one hand, this interpersonal form of control is transported by police officers and soldiers assuming a withdrawn position from which they oversee the inhabitants in the public sphere. On the other, the 'democratic' dimension of this new mode of government also incorporates the audience in this network of supervising the show's bodies. The subliminal breach of the fourth wall thereby indicates to what extent the new governmentality is not restricted to the diegetic realm of the show, but inevitably spreads to affect the viewers by creating a complex structure of panoptical scope. Next to the self-reflexive commentaries on the audience' expectations, the show also integrates structures of surveillance by means of such characters as the construction worker Arnie, who is "from the state of Texas" and condemns the New Orleansian "defective work ethic" (Season One, Episode Nine "Wish Someone Would Care": 00:29:40). Both diegetically and extradiegetically, *Treme* meditates on these internalized narratives that stipulate a specific norm of neo-liberal productivity that plays into the hands of a biopolitical world order, which focuses according to Hardt and Negri on the "production and reproduction of life itself" (Hardt and Negri 2000: 23-24).

MISE-EN-PLACE

However, while the omnipresence of modes of control perpetuates a very concrete form of life that is a cog in the neo-liberal system, *Treme* simultaneously portrays the preparation of food as a valid form of resistance, since it produces its own form of life. By this, Hardt and Negri conceive of a "shift from biopower to biopolitical production" (Hardt and Negri 2004: 95), which formulates a strategy of undermining the sovereignty of the society of control. The difference between biopower and biopolitical production is explained by Hardt and Negri as such:

Both of them engage social life in its entirety—hence the common prefix bio—but they do so in very different ways. Biopower stands above society, transcendent, as a sovereign authority and imposes its order. Biopolitical production, in contrast, is immanent to society and creates social relationships and forms through collaborative forms of labor. (ibid.)

While there are certain points of divergence between Hardt and Negri's notion of biopolitical production and the setting of *Treme*, I still want to insist upon the productivity of relating the practice of cooking to a political form of resistance. Since, while Hardt and Negri are concerned with a global regime of biopower, perceiving the agent of resistance in a swarm-like multitude, and necessarily grounding their notion of biopolitical production within postindustrial society, it seems as if *Treme*'s focus lies on national biopower, with the show's cooks assuming a special place in defying the hegemonic rule by a form of labor that is neither exactly industrial nor post-industrial.[14] Yet given the structures of control that palpably affect New Orleans' inhabitants, it is specifically cooking that creates social relationships through collaborative forms of labor and thereby undermines the predominant system from within.

When the pilot episode introduces the plotline of Janette Desautel's upscale restaurant, the first impressions that are transmitted evoke a dark and chaotic setting. Janette's kitchen, which is right in the midst of evening shift bustle, is depicted as an extremely gloomy place that metaphorically hints at the restaurant's looming bankruptcy. Paradoxically, the reason behind the restaurant's shutdown lies in Janette's inability to settle the debts that the repair costs due to Katrina put on her. It is in fact ironic that her highly successful establishment that is "busy [...] every night" ("Do you know what it means": 00:46:39) has to be closed down because of the insurance's failure to pay her off in time. Irrespective of Janette's economic failure, her abilities as a cook make her not only take the credit of a group of experts in her metier;[15] she also succeeds in producing excel-

---

14 Hardt and Negri clarify that their notion of post-industrial production is not a quantitative assessment, but a qualitative one (Hardt and Negri 2004: 112). In this sense, they do not argue that post-industrial production makes up the largest part of the world's economy, but that it affects all other forms of labor. Still one wonders what the actual product of cooking is, since it is neither strictly material nor immaterial.

15 In Episode Five "Shame, Shame, Shame," of Season One, a group of highly renowned chefs eat at their restaurant (with cameos by Wylie Dufresne, David Chang, Eric Ripert, and Tom Colicchio), which Jacques comments upon as: "you killed those

lent food, as well as a particular form of life through her cooking that is democratic, ad hoc, socially productive, and located in smooth space.

The incessant democratic impetus of her kitchen is thus conveyed by her relationship to her Caribbean sous-chef, Jacques. While Janette is the head of the kitchen, her interaction with Jacques attests to a fundamentally anti-hierarchic mode of production. Particularly if compared to Janette's later position in the New York restaurant Brulard, led by an eccentric head chef who permanently instills terror in his staff, the relation to Jacques is marked by mutual respect and horizontal power-relations. Whereas one of the kitchen staff in New York remarks that they "try not to look at the guy, never directly, right, 'cause the eyes is like his way in, is how he gets you, is how he gets inside, he looks at you and then he crawls up in your brain and takes a dump on it" (Season Two, Episode One: "Accentuate the Positive": 00:07:52), which neatly summarizes the psychological and identitarian repercussions that the patriarchically led restaurant engenders, Janette leads her kitchen in a way that cherishes the opinions of her coworkers. In fact, if there are any black kitchen members in the Brulard, they are relegated to errand boys; Desautel's kitchen, in contrast, does not adhere to any form of racial stereotyping or discrimination.

The particular way of life that Desautel's cooking generates is not only democratic, but also ad hoc and creative. When Janette has to come up with a menu for the aforementioned chefs who come to her restaurant on short notice, she tells Jacques to think "about what the hell [they]'re gonna cook these guys" ("Shame, Shame, Shame": 00:33:22). However, while he suggests "smoked salmon around caviar. Seafood truffle stew, fingerlings, then the lamb off the menu," Janette interjects that they

> lowball 'em. We start with the sweet potato, andouille shrimp soup. Then we get the rabbit kidneys out the freezer. They're tiny, they'll thaw fast. We skewer them with some lardons of the Benton's bacon. Then we hit 'em with sweetbreads and crawfish over grits. (00:34:32)

For the last plate, she considers the "braised lamb neck from the staff meal" (00:34:38).

For one thing, Janette's approach to cook for the acclaimed chefs employs ingredients that do not immediately appear fit for their spoiled palates. The frozen kidneys, in particular, as well as the remnants of the staff meal would ordinarily seem below the standards of the metropolitan chefs des cuisines, yet

---

chefs" ("Shallow Water, Oh Mama": 00:24:39), thereby implying in a metaphorical way how Janette's cooking affects the bios of others.

Janette employs her cooking knowledge and creativity in preparing an ad hoc menu that undermines specific class structures. Her serving of kidneys instead of caviar thereby marks a particular choice that opts for an ingredient that rejects an economically entrenched haute cuisine that simply conforms to streamlined standards of extravagant products. In serving kidneys, she addresses the cooks' expertise in offering a dish that is not as commonly appreciated, in fact often derided, by bourgeois statutes.[16] Moreover, ostensible class boundaries are undermined, since she puts a meal on the table that was initially prepared for her staff. While this implies that she, on the one hand, does not distinguish in her cooking for customers or crew, it simultaneously fashions a way of cooking that is irrespective of income level or social status. In a sense, one might say that Desautel's cooking, in this instance, performs a form of 'basse cuisine' and undermines the class hierarchies that affect gastronomical life.

By the same token, Janette's proposed menu also rejects the cosmopolitan appeal of Jacques' suggestion. Her remark that they "can't out-New York a bunch of New York chefs" ("Shame, Shame, Shame": 00:33:25) thereby addresses a site-specific form of cooking that dismisses a faceless and homogenized cuisine of globalization by insisting on the local yet flexible ingredients and traditions of their surroundings. Instead of trying to create an 'authentic' meal that insists upon its roots within New Orleans, Janette employs 'Creole' ingredients such as Andouille sausage and fuses it with 'American' Benton bacon to arrive at a hybrid dish that thwarts any local essentialisms of food. Without adhering to the fixed concepts of a particular kind of cuisine, she combines the dominant forms of New Orleans kitchen, namely "Creole, Cajun, and New Orleans" (Ostendorf 2003a: 97) and thereby undermines the distinction between "family-based cooking and restaurant-based cuisines" (ibid.) that Ostendorf separates out. In so doing, she furnishes a creolizing practice that unsettles the various identity constructions that prove to be unsustainable, especially when it comes to food.[17] However, despite the hybrid movements that undergo her cooking procedures, she nevertheless situates her food in an unstable, but specific locale without letting it diffuse into a globalized system of interchangeability.

---

16 One might speculate on the interconnection between the bourgeoise repulsion by innards as ostensibly 'unclean' products and the spreading discourse on hygiene that propels a specific form of cleanliness that also pertains to matters of eating in Western spheres. While this is certainly grounded in religious practice, one might again see biopolitical mechanisms within secular history as a dominant driving force behind the 'abjection' of specific food products.
17 This also recalls Doris Witt's (1999) analysis of the construction of 'Soul Food' in her *Black Hunger*.

Although one could cast doubts about the positive dimensions of her creolizing form of cooking, and either see it as an attempt to meet the exoticist desires of the chefs as culinary sightseers in order "to perform [her] authenticity" (Fuqua 2012: 240), or as a white imposition over Jacques' Franco-Caribbean 'authentic' expertise, I would argue that her culinary practice essentially undermines the concept of authenticity. For Janette does not simply present the chefs with a strictly New Orleansian, or Cajun, or Creole cuisine that would evoke an existing narrative of a culinary tradition and thereby meet the stereotypical expectations that the cooks maintain of New Orleansian food. Her combination of various ingredients that do not lose their particularity as in an Ortizean abominable melting pot—for the chefs can single out the ingredients within the meals—but rather combine in a dish that upholds the various local particularities, creates a productive means of undermining the streamlined form of bios that the American nation wants to uphold.[18] To a similar extent, Janette also does not merely perform a problematic act of Oriental re-presentation in the sense that she knows the culinary techniques of the Creole cuisine better than the natives. Instead of viewing her rejection of Jacques' menu as a patronizing act that is embedded in racist ideologies, her fashioning of a New Orleansian culinary bios viewed in terms of an antagonistic practice of resistance rather illustrates her bio-political struggle. Without being color-blind, I would still argue that Janette's cooking plays its part to "reimagine New Orleans" and fosters, as Gray observes, "[n]ot the pre-

---

18 Thomas (2012) and Faisst (2013) both interrogate the image of the 'gumbo' as a valid metaphor for cultural constellations. Thomas thus writes that "Treme's creators and writers often promote a type of tourist-driven 'gumbo pot' history that reprises de Crevecoeur's 'melting pot' in the context of post-civil rights era notions of diversity, multiculturalism, and postracialism and that minimizes the material reality and continuing legacy of white racial privilege" (Thomas 2012: 219). Faisst elaborates on Thomas' thoughts that "[t]his kind of stew would not discriminate its varied—yet divisive—ingredients. As a metaphor, the 'gumbo pot' comprises notions of multiculturalism, diversity, and post-racialism, suggesting that" (Faisst 2013: 447) the result of this cultural contact zone fashions a homogenized and un-differentiable as well as undifferentiated mass that can be grasped in Leah Chase's epigraph. Ostendorf, however, shows to what extent the gumbo, among the various culinary metaphors for cultural exchange, inhabits the best potential as a societal metaphor, even though it certainly also runs into some problems. I would also argue that Janette's cooking is not a simple form of exoticist fusion kitchen that combines two seemingly oppositional culinary contexts for the sake of a desire of otherness. Her merging of various cultural culinary realms simultaneously undermines any rigid forms of identity constructions without ending up with abominable paste.

Katrina conditions of racism and poverty but a more dialogic, equitable, open, and democratic New Orleans" (Gray 2012: 276).[19]

While Desautel's produces a counter-hegemonic form of life in its kitchen, the restaurant as a whole also functions as a production site of such a bios. If again compared to the gastronomical setting at the Brulard in New York, New Orleans' restaurant fundamentally undermines the clear separation between workplace and site of consumption. In the Brulard, the diegetic representation solely depicts the modes of production in the kitchen without once showing the dining room.[20] Through this spatial hermeticism, *Treme* renders the New York kitchen another site of disciplinary confinement. In contrast, Janette's restaurant repeatedly breaks the strict boundary between kitchen and seating area, as she moves from one into the other. Unlike the container-like factory setting of the Brulard, Janette functions as a literal mediator between the site of culinary production and consumption. However, the dining room constitutes more than a mere place of consuming food; Janette not only feeds her diners as customers, but essentially fosters social relationships with them, thereby questioning the exclusively dietary dimension of food. In stark contrast to the industrial metaphysics of food, which is so neatly articulated by Henry Ford's dictum "Food is fuel" (qtd. in Ostendorf 2003b: 42), Desautel's cherishes a holistic approach in which food implies a more encompassing bios instead of merely an energetic stimulus to perpetuate capitalist production. To this extent, Janette not only serves the food to her customers, but also engages in conversation, exchanging personal problems and concentrates on her clientele's needs. Creighton Bernette summarizes this combination as a constellation of "good food, companionship, community" ("Do you know what it means": 00:31:58) and thereby comprehensively expresses the alternate bios-logic of food in *Treme*. For Creighton's enumeration is not structured as a list of bourgeoise values, but rather constitutes a reciprocal network in which food is inevitably related to companionship and community—

---

19 To this extent, I would not see Janette as a heroic white character that Thomas points to: "By normalizing progressive racial and economic attitudes and practices among its white characters, Treme elides the deep-seated racial and class tensions that persist in the wake of Hurricane Katrina. As a result, white characters' acts of heroism or bravado often seem beyond the realm of possibility, or at least credibility" (Thomas 2012: 216). Instead, I would see her white identity as anything but stable or fixed.

20 One of the exceptions of the spatial representation combines Janette's literal escape from Brulard's kitchen with her attack on a restaurant critic who wrote a devastating review on New Orleans' culinary standards that proved to have severe economical consequences for the city, which was already on its knees after Hurricane Katrina.

in short, an ethical form of life. The interaction between Janette and her customers thereby biopolitically produces affects: for Hardt and Negri, it is a form of

> labor that produces or manipulates affects such as a feeling of ease, well-being, satisfaction, excitement, or passion. One can recognize affective labor, for example, in the work of legal assistants, flight attendants, and fast food workers (service with a smile). (Hardt and Negri 2004: 108)

In questioning the very concept of the 'customer' by exchanging it for a more intimate relationship with her guests she moves beyond the mere transaction of monetary values and tends to her diners by blurring "the traditional distinctions between the economic, the political, the social and the cultural" (109). To this extent, Janette also undermines the very concept of haute cuisine gastronomy in serving Cleighton a Hubig's[21] for dessert that she gives Jacques to "dress it up, baby. Drizzle something on it" ("Do you know what it means": 00:45:44). Instead of complying with the gastronomical code of conduct, which certainly would eye the serving of a plastic-wrapped pie suspiciously, Janette prefers the values of social interaction to an overweening high-class cuisine that has lost its contact to its guests. Even though she thus parenthesizes food to the cravings of her clientele, she nevertheless embeds the Hubig's as an alien, since ostensibly mass-produced, item in her kitchen, and within her ad hoc culinary practice by letting Jacques embellish it to fit the food that Desautel's puts out. Indeed, Hubig's pies, which are a cornerstone of New Orleans' culinary capital, what Fuqua regards as one of many "place-specific signifiers" (2012: 237), evokes the narrative of a Warholian culture of consumption. With the baked pies being covered in plastic wrapping that shows the company's mascot Savory Simon, an obese white man carrying a Hubig's drawn in a 50s pop design, Janette again retorts to a specifically local food and simultaneously undermines the high- and low-brow dichotomy in a gastronomical context. Faced with various discursive regulations that seem to impose their mechanisms of how to behave in this particular sociological milieu, Janette incessantly undermines these various conceptualizations by her cooking and the consequent production of a bios that resists these apparatuses.

---

21 Hubig's Pies is an American bakery that has been present in New Orleans for over hundred years. Interestingly, the only establishment that survived the Great Depression was the New Orleans location, which might thus be telling for both, Desautel's economic conundrums and, at the same time, NOLA's potential to perpetuate business despite national crises.

I want to conclude this essay by emphasizing a last point in which Janette's culinary biopolitical production manifests itself by focussing once more on the show's negotiation of space. While space has been discussed in respect of the show to some extent,[22] the space of the kitchen has been neglected from these readings, by and large. To this extent, I want to propose that in reading Desautel's kitchen as a form of what Gilles Deleuze and Félix Guattari term a 'smooth space,' one may glimpse the antagonistic impetus that this particular social site inhabits and understand the role of cooking in this bio-political endeavor. In their 1980 magnus opus, *A Thousand Plateaus*, Deleuze and Guattari introduce their topological understanding of space that oscillates between smooth and striated space.[23] In their distinction between two kinds of spatial textures, the concept of striated space refers to spaces that have been ordered, put into grids, systematized and consequently homogenized. Smooth space, in contrast, is characterized by the exact opposite, defying homogenization, structure, the logos, embracing heterogeneity and the nomos.[24] "Smooth space," they declare,

> has no homogeneity, except between infinitely proximate points [...]. It is a space of contact, of small tactile or manual actions of contact, rather than a visual space like Euclid's striated space. Smooth space is a field without conduits or channels. A field, a heterogeneous smooth space, is wedded to a very particular type of multiplicity: nonmetric, acentered, rhizomatic multiplicities that occupy space without "counting" it and can "be explored only by legwork." (Deleuze and Guattari 1987: 371)

Deleuze and Guattari's notion of smooth space neatly complies with Janette and Jacques' kitchen. The lack of order that defines smooth spaces is thus not only

---

22 See, for instance, Faisst's "Rebuilding the Neighborhood" (2013), or Parmett's "Space, Place, and New Orleans on Television. From Frank's Place to *Treme*" (2012).

23 Deleuze and Guattari acknowledge Pierre Boulez to be the inventor of the two "concepts and words in the field of music" (Deleuze and Guattari 1987: 477). The two plateaus that are most concerned with smooth and striated space are plateaus 12 "Treatise on Nomadology" and 14 "1440: The Smooth and the Striated."

24 Deleuze and Guattari write that "[t]he smooth is a nomos, whereas the striated always has a logos" (Deleuze and Guattari 1987: 478). Furthermore, they explain that "[w]hen the ancient Greeks speak of the open space of the nomos- nondelimited, unpartitioned; the preurban countryside; mountainside, plateau, steppe- they oppose it not to cultivation, which may actually be part of it, but to the polis, the city, the town" (481). Edward Casey highlights how the words 'nomad' and 'nomos' share the etymological root of "nem-, a root that signifies distribution rather than allocation" (Casey 1998: 464).

conveyed by their ad hoc assemblage of food that might to some appear chaotic; moreover, their seemingly hectic style of cooking, which is drastically different from the precise and almost ceremonial movements in the New York kitchen, equally indicates a specific movement in smooth space that is not linear or steady. Cinematographically, this structural fuzziness is also transported by the dark lighting that predominates in the New Orleans kitchen, which starkly contradicts the luminescent white aesthetic of the Brulard. By means of its lighting, the Brulard's kitchen indeed figures as a striated space whose inclination to order makes it a metonymic extension of the state apparatus. Both are "hierarchical organisms that [...] enjoy a monopoly over a power of function" (Deleuze and Guattari 1987: 366) and thereby enact biopolitical control. This is specifically amplified in the New York kitchen's chef, whose eccentric execution of power has already been commented upon, and which renders the gastronomical space an industrial site of production. As in a factory, working life in the Brulard is, on the one hand, guided by the supervising head of the kitchen who controls the various processes of production which are separated into rationalized posts—Janette, for example, assumes the position of entremetier at the assembly line. Whereas the camera furthermore pans in straight and steady motions through the symmetrical architecture of the New York cuisine, Desautel's is depicted through shaky shots of a hand-held camera. Unlike the orderly stability of the Brulard that is fashioned like a Euclidean coordinate system, the space of Janette's kitchen is increasingly smooth and thereby counteracts the homogenizing processes of streamlining its food as well its inhabitants according to a specific form of life.

    Janette's active role in unsettling the 'metric, centered, and rootlike' spaces of biopolitical control is thus part of her implication in smooth space. Since smooth space can only be "explored by legwork" the cook assumes this potential of resistance and becomes a nomad. When, in Season One, her restaurant has to shut down, Janette, for one thing, rents a mobile barbecue to cater various locations, which makes her abandon even her sedentary cuisine for the sake of an entirely detached culinary practice; after quitting the Brulard in Season Two, she moreover moves to two different kitchens on her "tale of a journey in three kitchens," as real-life chef Anthony Bourdain puts it in the *New York Times* article on *Treme*'s food by Kathryn Shattuck (2011). As a matter of fact, by means of her roaming through the culinary sphere of New York, she takes on the nomad's antagonistic praxis in unsettling the striated spaces from within. Unlike a straightforward defiance of the biopolitical State, the nomad, has as its object not war but the drawing of a creative line of flight, the composition of a smooth space and of the movement of people in that space. At this other pole, the machine does indeed encounter war, but as its supplementary or synthetic object, now directed against the State and against the worldwide axiomatic expressed by States. (Deleuze and Guattari 1987: 422)

In the vein of a subliminal pattern of resistance, Janette thus draws lines of flight that destabilize the reign of biopower as spread by striated spaces by working from within its territory. In confronting the global "axiomatic" that biopower expresses, Janette, as a nomad, changes positions—both between restaurants and inside the positions of these restaurant—which ascribes to her production of an alternative mode of bios that rejects remaining fixed at all costs. The last station in her journey makes her find herself in David Chang's Lucky Peach, which combines both the real-life homonymous food magazine with Chang's existing restaurants "Momofuku Ko and Ssäm Bar" (Shattuck 2011: n.p.). Here, Janette's production of a culinary *bios* allows her to instill her New Orleansian culinary identity at the presumed center of gastronomical life of the United States. In Episode Ten of the second season, "That's What Lovers Do," in which she teams up with Chang, who equally tries to undermine the conventions of both cooking and consumption, Janette is allowed to create a New Orleans-style dish on the menu, since her Asian interpretation of chicken and waffles "is right in Dave's happy place" (00:26:15). Once more, her "Chinese fried chicken and waffles" (00:36:38) adapts a New Orleansian dish by integrating Asian ingredients with neither losing the distinctness of the various elements nor assuming a stable identity of these products. However, now Chang's concession that she cooks "southern food, New Orleans food," but with her "own take on it, our own take on it" (00:36:54) undermines the culinary order from the very core of the metropolis and fashions a collective *we* that Chang articulates. While Janette's moving to New York might suggest that she retorts to an escapist strategy when confronted with the increasing manifestations of economic discouragement in the Crescent City, I would argue that she embodies a crucial form of resistance by traveling to the heart of the nation (culinarily speaking, if not politically). When read as a culinary nomad, her active struggle to unshackle from the constraints of biopower makes her work as a mole that deterritorializes the State from underneath, if one wants to employ Deleuze and Guattari's jargon. Or, in Hardt and Negri's words, Janette becomes part of

these dangerous classes [that] continually disrupt the ontological constitution of Empire: at each intersection of lines of creativity or lines of flight the social subjectivities become more hybrid, mixed, and miscegenated, further escaping the fusional powers of control. (Hardt and Negri 2004: 137)

However, while her resistance is thus not precisely "a questioning of hierarchy," in the sense of a "perpetual blackmail by abandonment or betrayal, and a very volatile sense of honor, all of which, once again, impedes the formation of the State" (Deleuze and Guattari 1987: 358), her fashioning of a bios through her cooking well adds to the conceptual frameworks of Deleuze and Guattari as well as Hardt and Negri. She has thus 'found a new weapon,' to refer to the Deleuzian epigraph of this article, by orchestrating the fundamentally bio-logical dimensions of food that neither of the theoreticians have in mind: food and its preparation thereby constitutes a site of resistance to the regime of control that *Treme* shows at work in post-Katrina New Orleans.

The cinematographic representation of cooking in *Treme* thereby mediates both, the dimensions of biopower as showcased in the Brulard, as well as Desautel's potential for defying this particular order. In contrast to the New York kitchen's unilateral tendencies that are marked by hierarchical formations, Janette fashions a culinary practice that is essentially based on exchange: not only is she exchanging knowledge and opinions with her co-workers; her ad hoc approach also swaps ingredients between container-like cultural domains and thereby undermines these repositories without acknowledging their various conditions of storage. Janette, however, also modifies the concept of exchange that is predominant in the capitalist framework of food by altering the relations to her customers. Her active production of social relations, and ultimately, social life itself constitutes a counter-hegemonic site that produces not only its own kind of food, but, as this article hoped to show, also its own kind of life.

If one may thus wonder about the biological, i.e. organic / ecological modes of production of the food that Janette uses in her dishes, this essay elucidated the inevitable logics of life that food and its preparation may entail. If this particular kind of "food prevails" as Leah Chase has it, the 'body without organs' that Deleuze and Guattari conceptualize and Hardt and Negri assume as the antagonistic political body of biopolitical production might not have a stomach to process food; however, it certainly has a mouth and tongue to taste voluptuously.

BIBLIOGRAPHY

Agamben, Giorgio 1998 [1995]. *Homo Sacer. Sovereign Power and Bare Life*. Trans. Daniel Heller-Roazen. Stanford: Stanford University Press.

Barthes, Roland 1997. "Toward a Psychosociology of Contemporary Food Consumption." *Food and Culture. A Reader*. Eds. Carole Counihan and Penny van Esterik. London: Routledge, 20-27.

Casey, Edward 1998. *The Fate of Place. A Philosophical History*. Berkeley: University of California Press.

Deleuze, Gilles 1990. "Control and Becoming. Gilles Deleuze in Conversation with Antonio Negri." *L'Autre Journal* 1: 169-182.

Deleuze, Gilles 1992. "Postscript on the Societies of Control." *October*: 3-7.

Deleuze, Gilles and Félix Guattari 1987. *A Thousand Plateaus. Capitalism and Shizophrenia*. Trans. Brian Massumi. Minneapolis: University of Minnesota Press.

Faisst, Julia 2013. "Rebuilding the Neighborhood. Race, Property, and Urban Renewal in Tremé." *American Lives*. Ed. Alfred Hornung. Heidelberg: Universitätsverlag Winter, 443-463.

Fuqua, Joy V. 2012. "'In New Orleans, We Might Say It Like This...'. Authenticity, Place, and HBO's *Treme*." *Television & New Media* 13.3: 235-242.

George, Courtney 2012. "Keeping it 'Reals.' Narratives of New Orleans Jazz History as Represented in HBO's *Treme*." *Television & New Media* 13.3: 225-234.

Gray, Herman 2012. "Recovered, Reinvented, Reimagined. *Treme*, Television Studies and Writing New Orleans." *Television & New Media* 13.3: 268-278.

Hardt, Michael and Antonio Negri 2000. *Empire*. Cambridge, MA / London: Harvard University Press.

—. 2004. *Multitude. War and Democracy in the Age of Empire*. New York: Penguin Press.

Lacan, Jacques 1991. *Le Séminaire. Livre XVII. L'Envers de la Psychanalyse, 1969-70*. Ed. Jacques-Alain Miller. Paris: Ed. du Seuil.

Lévi-Strauss, Claude 1997. "The Culinary Triangle." *Food and Culture. A Reader*. Eds. Carole Counihan and Penny van Esterik. London: Routledge: 28-35.

Long, Alecia P. 2004. *The Great Southern Babylon. Sex, Race, and Respectability in New Orleans, 1865-1920*. Baton Rouge: Louisiana State University Press.

Lott, Eric 1993. *Love & Theft. Blackface Minstrelsy and the American Working Class*. New York / Oxford: Oxford University Press.

Mintz, Sidney W. 1996. *Tasting Food, Tasting Freedom. Excursions into Eating, Culture, and the Past*. Boston: Beacon Press.

Ostendorf, Berndt 2003a. "Eating New Orleans Style." *Erlesenes Essen. Literatur- und Kulturwissenschaftliche Beiträge zu Hunger, Sattheit und Genuss*. Tübingen: Gunther Narr, 96-108.

—. 2003b. "Melting Pot, Salad Bowl, and Gumbo. Die Neue Welt und ihre Küchen. Nationale, regionale oder ethnische?" *IAKE* 11: 26-47.

Parmett, Helen Morgan 2012. "Space, Place, and New Orleans on Television. From Frank's Place to *Treme*." *Television & New Media* 13.3: 193-212.

Rathke, Wade 2012. "*Treme* for Tourists. The Music of the City without the Power." *Television & New Media* 13.3: 261-267.

Shattuck, Kathryn 2011. "'*Treme*' Sharpens Its Focus on Food." *New York Times* 3 June 2011.
[http://www.nytimes.com/2011/06/05/arts/television/treme-on-hbo-focuses-on-food.html?_r=0>. (retrieved 13 May 2013)].

Thomas, Lynnell L. 2012. "'People Want to See What Happened.' *Treme*, Televisual Tourism, and the Racial Remapping of Post-Katrina New Orleans. *Television & New Media* 13.3: 213-224.

Treme. Writ. David Simon and Eric Overmyer. HBO. 2010-. Season 1-2. Television (first broadcast 11 April-20 June 2011 and 24 April-3 July 2012).

Witt, Doris 1999. *Black Hunger. Food and the Politics of U.S. Identity*. New York / Oxford: Oxford University Press.

Sapho's *Blaff de poisson* Followed by *Flan au coco* and a Bit of Slaver's Rum
The Fierce Questioning of the Purpose and Power of Fictional Caribbean Communion in Édouard Glissant's *Ormerod* and Fortuné Chalumeau's *Désirade, ô Serpente!*

DANIEL GRAZIADEI

The literary depictions of food, its preparation, and consumption in works that fall under the label 'Caribbean' can be read as references to the oldest example of creolization, which—according to José G. Guerrero—was of neither cultural nor sexual but of culinary nature, and began right with the first recorded 'contact,' 'invention,' or 'touch' in 1492.[1] Obviously, the literary staging of Creole

---

1 By proposing three alternatives to the still haunting fallacy of naming the successful search for a Western seaway to the easternmost Indies 'the discovery of the West Indies' I do not simply want to question the Eurocentric narrative of Columbus 'discovering' established continents and cultures as well as the geographical nonsense of referring to the region of contact in the aforementioned way, but I also seek to highlight Edmundo O'Gorman's (1985) argument that Colón invented according to his worldview and readings as well as Patrick Chamoiseau's proposal that they did not even enter into contact, but were merely able to touch the Other: "[C]ela me permet non d'entrer en *contact* mais de *toucher aux Autres*, juste toucher—seulement ça" (Chamoiseau 1997: 110). Consequently, the first creolization is neither to be found in the first instances of mistranslations and the subsequent birth of pidgin and Creole languages, nor the (forced) sexual mixing and reproduction, but what José G. Guerrero calls 'an early culinary fusion': "La fusión temprana de las culinarias antecedió a la hibridación de la gente y la cultura. En carta a los Reyes entre 1498-1500, Colón fun-

cuisine mainly concerns a later and more sophisticated stage of mixing and stirring a predominantly transatlantic but global array of products, techniques, and tastes. Depictions of pre-industrialized cuisine have often been interpreted as cultural markers that create or promote Caribbean cultural identity in texts. Richard Wilk confirms this for individual and collective identity construction, but points out that "much less well understood is how such a stable pillar of identity can also be so fluid and changeable," especially as a "group's unique dietary practices and habits can be maintained, while diets, recipes, and cuisines are in a constant state of flux" (Wilk 1999: 244).

The following pages will use this line of argument as a backdrop, but highlight another argument: literary food does not necessarily have to be interpreted as a nodal point for direct interaction between nature and culture or as a reference for geographical placing and social standing, culinary traditions, table rules and rites, agricultural and environmental practices, commercial relations, and the importance of food intake for the protagonists or narrator. Graham Huggan's critical perspective on the troubling mechanisms of the consuming eye of the armchair traveller and the continued impact of imperialist nostalgia warns that the analysis should not succumb to "Marketing the Margins" via the exhibition of an always and everywhere easily-consumable "Postcolonial Exotic" (cf. Huggan 2001).[2] Accordingly one should ask: what further implications are generated by a literary staging of Caribbean food, its preparations, and consumption?

One very simple answer could be: it makes us hungry; it stimulates an appetite for preferred, (well-)known, exoticized, or unfamiliar dishes whilst impeding direct satisfaction on a corporeal level. This points towards the limits of the literary depiction of food and its inherent metafictional qualities.[3] Since this 'papery' food excludes writers, external narrators, and readers as potentially hungry spectators, the visibility of fictional construction rises. In such a line of argument the

---

    daba el éxito de la colonización en una mezcla de carbohidratos y proteínas aportados por alimentos europeos y aborígenes [...]" (Guerrero 2010: 186).

2   "Late twentieth-century exoticisms are the products [...] of a worldwide market—exoticism has shifted, that is, from a more or less privileged mode of aesthetic perception to an increasingly global mode of mass-market consumption. The massification of exotic merchandise implies a new generic form of exoticism, 'suitable for all markets and at the limits of its own semantic dispersion' [...]. These 'new' exotic products [...] are characterised, not by remoteness but by *proximity* [...]" (Huggan 2001: 15).

3   As Patricia Waugh defined in 1984, it is "a term given to fictional writing which self-consciously and systematically draws attention to its status as an artefact in order to pose questions about the relationship between fiction and reality" (Waugh 1996: 2-3).

staging of local food can not only be interpreted as a part of the unnecessary extras to the storyline which allow a successful implementation of realist modes of narration that accentuate and promote Caribbean cultures. On the contrary, a highlighting of narrative techniques or even a rupture of the fictional pact seems to be implicitly at play as well. Therefore, no matter what interpretation the single reading is drawn towards—be it informed by a personal knowledge about its taste, its cultural role, and its various recipes, be it led by complete ignorance that may even be compensated by generalizing and exoticist ideas about tropical food—the chance of an exposure of the fiction as fiction, that is to say a certain metafictional potential, should be taken into account when focusing on the paradox of a simultaneous presence and absence of literary food (cf. De Maeseneer in this volume). This poses a certain challenge to any intent of interpreting the literary staging of Caribbean food cultures as realist representations without taking the discursive nature and imaginative power of fiction into account.[4] In the following examples, the matter is further aggravated due to the recurrent stress on the (transmedial) staging and commercialization of traditional Creole food production as well as consumption. Furthermore, elements of metafiction can be seen as crucial indicators of the continued self-reflexivity of the contemporary (Caribbean) novel—strategies that are said to be typical for at least one definition of postmodernism and neo/avant-garde poetics.[5]

Following this lead, the next few pages will be dedicated to the analysis of two contemporary literary representations of traditional food, female cooks, and small restaurants in and from the French Caribbean. The first part features Man-Joliba, the chef of a famed traditional Creole restaurant *Chez Joliba* in the con-

---

[4] As Waugh says: "The metafictionist is highly conscious of a basic dilemma: if he or she sets out to 'represent' the world, he or she realizes fairly soon that the world, as such, cannot be 'represented.' In literary fiction it is, in fact, possibly only to 'represent' the *discourses* of that world" (Waugh 1996: 3). The difference to the realist mode is also passionately highlighted by Raymond Federman when defining his similar term *surfiction*: "[T]he kind of fiction that constantly renews our faith in man's imagination and not in man's distorted vision of reality—that reveals man's irrationality rather than reality [...] I call SURFICTION [...] not because it imitates reality, but because it exposes the fictionality [...]" (Federman 1981: 7).

[5] Waugh writes about the "absence of a clearly defined avant-garde 'movement'" in 1984 (Waugh 1996: 10), but this may not be upheld after the appearance of three neo-avantgardist groups in the Americas in the last decade of the twentieth century, McOndo, el grupo del Crack, and Avantpop, all of which share the same metafictional strategy (cf. Graziadei 2008: 45-52).

temporary novel, *Désirade, ô Serpente!* (2006) by Fortuné Chalumeau.[6] The second part of the article concerns Madame Sapho, the owner of *Le canari d'antan* in the literary Martinique of Édouard Glissant's *Ormerod* (2003).

The women central to this task are comparable due to a series of similarities. Both cook traditional Creole dishes that make various phases of creolization palpable or, rather, readable. Both own a small restaurant on an island of the French Caribbean and in both cases cooking, serving, and eating are portrayed as a special and valuable form of nurture, connected to strong cultural markers and signifiers.[7] Their service is furthermore depicted as consumable tradition based on nostalgia and exoticism, but may at the same time be interpreted as literarily enacted cultural memory, resistance, and preservation in times of processed fast food by global brands. The traditional costumes in which both Man-Joliba and Madame Sapho dress at work allow to expand on this point. Like the recipes, the ingredients, and the religious and cultural systems attached, these robes show the representation of post/colonial tradition, the staging of folklore, and ultimately the marketing of an earlier (globalized colonial) phase of creolization as exotica *and* tradition.[8] These far-travelled and locally incorporated cloths can furthermore be understood as a faint reference to what Erika Greber called 'textile texting,' the interweaving of fictional threads and which on a formal level structure the storyline of Chalumeau's spy novel as much as the highly complex relational

---

6 As the nickname of her husband—Baba-Joliba—shows, "Man" stands for "manman" and is a show of respect for older women as Amabelle Désir explains to Mimi in Edwidge Danticat's *The Farming of Bones*: "You call them 'Man' even though they're not your mother" (Danticat 1998: 64).

7 One can therefore agree with Roland Barthes' answer to his own rhetorical question "For what is food? It is not only a collection of products that can be used for statistical or nutritional studies. It is also, and at the same time, a system of communication, a body of images, a protocol of usages, situations, and behavior" (Barthes 2009: 29).

8 Pointing towards Frantz Fanon's allusion to a popular Creole song ("Adieu foulard, adieu madras") in *Peau noire, masques blancs* (1952), David Macey writes: "The song itself is part of a network of signifiers that all signify 'Martinique'. Women dressed in 'foulards' and 'madras' [which he defines as "a checked cotton dress"] are key signifiers in the exoticism that surrounds so many images of Martinique in both literature and promotional material addressed to potential tourists. Fanon's allusion to the song is also a farewell to the literature of 'doudouism', a form of exoticism that celebrates the beauty of both the 'île des fleurs' and its female population [...]" (Macey 2005: 13).

writing in Glissant's transhistorical novel.[9] It is however within the thoughts and memories of the madams wearing the cloth in the text that the truly significant questioning occurs.

MAN-JOLIBA AND TELEVISION: HOW TO SATISFY BOTH THE LOCAL AND THE METROPOLITAN TASTES

In Fortuné Chalumeau's *Désirade, ô Serpente!*, the role of commercialized French-Caribbean traditional Creole food culture[10] is rather obvious: due to her restaurant and her cooking, Man-Joliba is the most prominent citizen of the island. The present of the narrated time finds her at the beginning of the novel as a retired old widow who recalls her whole career as a chef and restaurant owner with special glee towards her fifteen minutes of fame when becoming part of a French television program. Her thoughts span from the opening of the restaurant to the end of her enterprise when pressed by the competition of another traditional Creole restaurant owned by a younger and more hospitable woman, Flora Deshauteur. The brutal death of Man-Joliba and the presence of Flora furthermore form nodal points within the larger storyline of this spy- and detective-novel that puts the island Désirade into multiple relations with the surrounding archipelagos, the U.S., and France as well as international criminal activity.[11] Here various instances of the global and the local are intrinsically connected and

---

9   The dresses call for the inclusion of the attention for the weaving, knitting, braiding, and felting metaphors, and operations in "self-reflective literary texts" and "metatexts by writers" (Greber 2002: 8) that Erika Greber analyzes in *Textile Texte*.

10 The relevance of traditional Creole food preparation by a female chef and owner in a traditional garb in the coastal area of an island belonging to an archipelago in the French *Départements d'Outre-Mer* of the so-called Lesser Antilles allows specification of the focus on Caribbean food cultures. Creole would in this sense be closer to a fixed set of traditional practices and tastes as well as nostalgic icons of *creolité* rather than the ongoing processes of *créolisation*. As the dishes are the products of restaurants and integrated into their marketing strategies, one cannot simply write about food, but about a commercialized French-Caribbean food culture.

11 In the personal geography of the islanders, "la proche Guadeloupe" are not two bridged islands but the "Continent" (Chalumeau 2006: 27); to speak of archipelagos is therefore true and false at the same time. However, whilst the Caribbean archipelago has no geographical, cultural, or political center, the archipelago of Guadeloupe has—in this fictional world—two continental ones, the main island(s) and France.

mobilized; they show the historical fusion and creolization that allow the meals offered by the restaurant owners to be read as part of a continuing process of interaction. This becomes especially clear in Man-Joliba's most cherished moment in life, when "manman-télé, celle de la France lointaine" (Chalumeau 2006: 30)—"mother-television from faraway France"—comes to feature her in "Magies et Gastronomie de la Désirade" (34), an episode of Micky Bruckbader's televised culinary travelogue from around the world. The show appears to be designed for European francophone popular mass entertainment without any postcolonial reservations and stages the island, its biosphere, and its culinary heights in a paradisiacal space outside of globalized contemporaneity whilst simultaneously proving its accessibility.[12]

The exoticized and partial depiction of the island's beauties, treasures, and wonders stresses edenic, antediluvian, pre-mechanic, small, and parochial attributes while omitting all negative elements such as "ugliness, waste mismanagement and the island's historical usage as a leper colony."[13] Albeit the obvious perpetuation of exoticist narratives, a win-win situation seems to be at hand. Due to the popularity of French television on the islands, the colonial subjects not only eagerly comply with the needs of televised reality, but also are overjoyed to be at the center of transatlantic attention. This is especially true for the featured chef Man-Joliba, for whom this episode turns into an unforgettable moment of fame:

Jusqu'à son souffle ultime, Man-Joliba, et toutes les îles d'alentour, à dire la vérité vraie, devait se souvenir du tournage en compagnie du célébrissime présentateur et vedette,

---

12 Wonderful beaches and lagoons are being shown in magicorealist terms: "les plages au sable mordoré [...] les lagons si azurés [...]; les *souffleurs* des cayes proches pareils à des dragons lanceurs de flammes [...]" (Chalumeau 2006: 32) and the program ends the episode with a 'sensational sunset' that sublimely 'reminds the spectator of the intimate proximity of the gentle inhabitants to the primodial forces of creation': "L'écran se referma sur un sensationnel coucher du soleil dont les couleurs, en un époustouflant dégradé qu'appuyaient les accents majestueux d'une ouverture wagnérienne, rappelèrent à chaque téléspectateur combien, ici à la Désirade des Antilles, les doux habitants se trouvaient proches des éléments naturels de la Création" (34).

13 The narrative voice highlights that the TV star talked even about the crabs, but forgot to cite and show all the ugly things that would not go down well with the food to be served: "[I]l est juste de dire qu'il oublia de citer les laideurs et de montrer la masse de saletés qui, ici et là, maculent le paysage. Il ne pipa mot de la léproserie [...]. Il faut admettre que l'évocation des croûtes rosâtres et des nez mangés par la terrifiante vérolade n'eût point fait bon mélange avec les bons petits plats de chez Joliba!" (Chalumeau 2006: 32).

Micky Bruckbader en chair et en os, oui et oui! Pour la personne visée, ce moment fut comme une entrée au Paradis [...]. Tout avait été agencé par la technicité débarquée de métropole. (Chalumeau 2006: 31)[14]

The account of the making of the show suggests that paradise may not exist, but paradise may be constantly created via carefully arranged staging and (audiovisual) narration. It can be enjoyed both locally during the recording and later globally in an emphasized orchestration and multiplication on millions of screens. The picturesque scenery and setting, the overabundance of edible props, the presence of celebrity, and the eulogistic *mise-en-scène* are remindful of a "gigantic advertisement": "Reconnaissons-le tout net: en ce rivage des Épices apprêté pour la célébrité, on se serait cru devant le décor mythique d'une giga-publicité pour crèmes glacées de l'opulente Amérique" (ibid.).[15] There is, however, a fundamental difference between the insular and the 'metropolitan' motivation for the auditive and visual construction of this desirable paradise: the islanders seem concerned with a decent and proud representation in a contemporary mass communication channel that broadcasts directly from the French metropolitan center to all corners of the francophone world—the director of the show seems to stress colonial continuity when recurring to the exoticist imaginary of the tropical island paradise in the French Caribbean.[16] Therefore Man-Joliba cooks not only in front of the camera but *in-between* differing desires and intentions.

---

14 "Until her last breath, Man-Joliba, and, to tell you the truth, all the surrounding islands, would remember the shoot featuring the glamorous host and star, Micky Bruckbader in living color, yes indeed! For the person filmed, this moment was like entering Paradise [...]. It had all been conducted by the expertise disembarked from the motherland."
  N.B. If not stated otherwise, the translations of Chalumeau's and Glissant's novels are provided by the author, Daniel Graziadei, and Emily Lever. The editors would like to thank Emily Lever for her support and advice on the respective quotes.
15 "Let us be honest: on this shore of Spices, adorned by the celebrity, one could have thought oneself in front of the mythic decoration for a gigantic ice-cream advertisement from the opulent Americas."
16 Thereby the *mise-en-scène* inserts itself into a repetitious imagination and narrative of the Caribbean "as a tropical paradise in which the land, plants, resources, bodies, and cultures of its inhabitants are open to be invaded, occupied, bought, moved, used, viewed, and consumed in various ways. It is represented as a perpetual Garden of Eden in which visitors can indulge all their desires and find a haven for relaxation, rejuvenation, and sensuous abandon" (Sheller 2003: 13).

En réponse aux questions du présentateur, elle répondit en vaillance d'âme, roulant les *r* à l'espagnole et ânonnant avec un détonnant naturel les spiritualités qu'un membre de l'équipe lui avait fait répéter. Puis, au bénéfice des millions d'admirateurs télévisés [...] elle fit la démonstration de son savoir-faire centenaire non sans épicer le tout de ses commentaires kiakiaseurs. (Chalumeau 2006: 33)[17]

Even if Man-Joliba seems complacent to reveal and "demonstrate centuries-old culinary knowledge for the benefit of millions of television spectators," the detailed account of the making of the show allows discernment of instances of deliberate and forced acting. This is especially serious when Man-Joliba—in compliance with the producer's expectations—spices her talk and cooking with (fake) vodou incantations, popular sayings, as well as secret Creole wisdom. Tellingly, the race-conscious narrator attributes to her appearance "the air of a Zulu idol," stressing the transatlantic connection to Africa and hinting at a primitivist masquerade.[18] Arguably the process of transmediation that allows the novel's narrator to "re-transcribe" (33) the episode of the television program has an implicit metafictional quality due to its disclosure of the media as well as the act of narrating and writing. Thus the critique of the exoticist elements of the scripted reality affects the narrative voice itself. This is especially true for the single instance when Man-Joliba does not act within her TV role, but swears spontaneously and in a crude way after her robe is spoiled by one of the assistants: the narrator, seemingly obliged to observe the classicist principle of *bienséance*, does not reproduce the swearing.[19] In the dissimilar reaction of the two sets of spectators, the divide between the faraway mainland French and the local Caribbean perspective become obvious:

---

17 "In response to the host's questions, she answered with stout heart, rolling the *r* the Spanish way and stumbling with jarring fluency through the quips that a member of the crew had had her rehearse. Then, for the benefit of millions of admiring viewers [...] she gave a demonstration of her hundred-year-old know-how, spicing everything with her twittery comments."

18 "[...] Man-Joliba, l'air d'une idole zouloue droit issue de la glorieuse tribu de l'impérial Chaka, rayonnait telle une Vénus barbare née d'une coquille cuite et recuite au charbon de bois" (Chalumeau 2006: 31).

19 "[G]este épouvantable qui fit lâcher à Man-Joliba, et cela d'un ton de courroux terminal, une bordée d'injures sommaches que seuls la bienséance, et le respect dû au lecteur, nous interdisent, nonanvolant, de retranscrire" (Chalumeau 2006: 33). By upholding 17th century *doctrine classique*, the narrator proceeds highly anachronistically. This can either be read as satire or as a *translatio/n* (Italiano and Rössner 2012: 11-12) of comic elements from the criticized local gossip to himself as the narrative instance.

Précisons que si les gens de la France hexagonale ne virent dans cette épisode rien que gazouillis de parler local (oh, la gentillesse innée du téléspectateur de Notre-Maman la France-mère lorsqu'il s'agit de ses fils et filles à peau chocolatée de l'outre-mer!), la chose, point coupée dans son exposé prit ici des proportions épouvantables. Autant énoncer que les langues vipérines des amies ma-cocotte et d'une tiaulée impitoyable de vieux ma-commères allèrent un train d'enfer, toutes personnes fort jalouses du succès de la télévisée que ses consœurs de l'île voire de l'archipel ne portaient point dans le cœur. Cette troupe bêlante et éructante de rhumipèdes et de mâchemerdes crut de bon ton d'y aller de ses bémols—cela, au bénéfice de la dame qualifiée de "négresse primitive," mais aussi de "grosse malpropre" qui fabriquait ses mets à l'équidistance de son langage "ordurier et très crapuleux." (Chalumeau 2006: 33-34)[20]

Interestingly enough it is not her taking up the role of the "primitive Negress" or telling a supposedly secret recipe to millions of spectators that instigates the scandal, but her breach of post/colonial etiquette, her linguistic impropriety.[21] The local spectators—described in crude and inventive ways of free indirect speech—are not amused by her loss of countenance. They want to see themselves represented in the best of lights and from the best angle and would gladly take over Man-Joliba's role, making amends to stereotyping and exoticizing in order to fit the supposed expectation of the media and its metropolitan public, sporting a "sound colonial education" as one could say by citing Shabine on

---

20 "To be clear, if people from continental France saw in this accident nothing more than the babble of local patois (oh, the innate kindness of the television spectator from Our-Mama France-mother when it comes to her chocolate-skinned sons and daughters overseas!), the thing, aired uncut, took on terrible proportions over here. Needless to say, the vicious tongues of the mother-hen friends and the pitiless piping by the old mother-gossips spread like wildfire, all of them very jealous of the success of the interviewee, who was not thought fondly of by her sisters throughout the island or even the archipelago [...]. This bleating and belching troop of rum-legs and shit-chewers thought it appropriate to let loose with its jibes for the benefit of a lady described as 'primitive negress' but also as 'big filthy one' who concocted her dishes like her 'lewd and heinous' language."

21 One can try to explain this with Chris Bongie's argument for a nonlinear and continued relation within the "post/colonial" condition. The "state of propinquity" (Bongie 1998: 17) between the departmental phase and the colonial one would therefore allow the local public to perceive Man-Joliba's choice of words as scandalous within a colonizing, civilizing, and proselytizing framework whilst overlooking the Eurocentric exoticism and Othering of the *mise-en-scène*.

"The Schooner *Flight*."[22] The hexagonal (i.e. French metropolitan) spectators do not perceive the breach as such, for it is—as the narrator explains in highly ironic and / or problematically racist brackets—"oh, the innate kindness of the television spectator from Our-Mama France-mother when it comes to her chocolate-skinned sons and daughters overseas!"[23]

The diverging reactions towards the same instance call for the reader's reflections on the staging and perception of Caribbean food cultures in the media. Due to the metafictional or "metadiegetic" effect of transmediation and the explicit reference to it, the question does not remain limited to the televised representation or "diegetic narrative" (Seager 1991: 24-25). On the contrary, it calls for more general questions about the literary depiction of Caribbean produce, cooks, and food, but especially about our interpretations of these. Recalling / telling / writing the televised staging of Caribbean food cultures provokes an enhanced visibility of the different media involved in this transmedial de- and recontextualization.[24] This enhanced metafiction of food in *Désirade, ô Serpente!* generates such a disruptive force that it surpasses and implicitly criticizes the narrator's very own explanatory compliance to the metropolitan gaze. In this way the re-transcription of the filming at Man-Joliba's does not only show that the (re)presentation of Caribbean food cultures always has an angle, a lighting, and a focus, but puts itself into question due to its compliance with canonical aesthetics and commercialized knowledge.

As the second example will show, the critique of the susceptibility to nostalgic and exoticist reductions of (Caribbean) food culture and its severe questioning is not limited to the work of a somewhat marginalized author, but can also be found in the last novel by the most established and possibly central author of contemporary French Caribbean literature.

---

22 The famous lines from Derek Walcott's long poem read: "I'm just a red nigger who love the sea, [/] I had a sound colonial education, [/] I have Dutch, nigger, and English in me, [/] and either I am nobody or I'm a nation" (Walcott 1992: 346).

23 Interestingly enough, of the three mothers in play—France, television, and Man-Joliba—none is a biological one; all three seem to be named as such out of respect, thus accepting the continuing power of the colonial system, the neo-imperial propaganda as well as the traditional matriarchal power structures.

24 For a theory of cultural *translatio/n* as a process and negotiation of de- and recontextualisation in accordance with Homi Bhabha cf. Italiano/Rössner (2012:11-12). Arguably transmedial processes can also be seen as *translatio/n*.

MADAME SAPHO BETWEEN TRADITIONAL ORNAMENT AND CURRENT PROBLEMS

A short but decisive critique of the literary exhibition of dying-out traditions can be found in Madame Sapho's thoughts at the end of Édouard Glissant's last novel *Ormerod*, published at the famous Parisian publishing house Gallimard in 2003. As Elena Pessini argues, it is quite impossible to subsume this fragmented and multi-layered novel which can be connected to the latest philosophical and cultural theories that the author defines six years later in his *Philosophie de la Relation* (2009) and to the foregoing thoughts about a process of creolizing globalization, *Tout-monde* (1997) (cf. Pessini 2004: 116).[25] I will desist from the temptation of subsuming a novel that has fragmented but intertwined storylines; these depict similar actions on different islands of the same archipelago in different times and do not give orientation, but stress similarities and relations. Instead I will simply repeat what Pessini highlights as the main *chronotopoi* of the novel after focusing on the complexity of the geographical and intertextual schemes that lie at the heart of the text (cf. 111-118). One is situated during the revolutionary events on St. Lucia at the end of the 18th century under the impact of the French Revolution and the imperial warfare between Britain and France and, most importantly, a local maroon army—"Brigands des Bois" under the guidance of "Flore Bois Gaillard" (Glissant 2003: 49)—that fights in guerrilla style from the mountainous woods. This war refers into the past and can be seen as a repetition of Amerindian warfare and animist enhancements of fighting power. At the same time, it refers into a later time and another place that the strange title vaguely refers to: Grenada between 1981 and 1983, which means leftist local politics versus the U.S. backyard intervention as part of the Cold War's bloc policies.[26] The questions posed at the beginning of this paper do not lead into these war-, revolution-, and history-packed parts of the three main chapters. Nevertheless, I would like to point out one underlying parallel of existential dimensions between the French Revolution and slave revolutions, as well

---

25 It is not necessary to split the *Tout-Monde*-phase into two because the basic message "Le monde se créolise" (Glissant 1996: 15) remains valid when relation comes into play. It is however an interesting mind-game to accept the *Philosophie de la Relation* as a further step that does not need 'all' and 'world,' but relates anything to everything.

26 In the first place the title refers to the Jamaican-Australian francophone literary scholar Beverley Ormerod (cf. the acknowledgements Glissant 2003: 362) and also to the explicit reference within the novel (203-208).

as enslaved people taking to the high hills and the remnants of tropical forest in an act of *marronage*: hunger. As Sidney Mintz has argued, the absence of proper nourishment is one of the core reasons for uprisings next to extreme violence and injustice. For the questions at stake, however, it is less helpful to focus on the absence or scarcity of food and the alternative (mal)nourishment of the guerrilla in the woods who has to rely—for practical and strategic reasons—on techniques that Claude Lévi-Strauss subsumes under "the raw."[27] On the contrary, in order to answer this paper's question about the metafictional quality of food, it is imperative to focus on "the cooked" and a few pages of the "Annexes et Affluents" which are numbered with "5."[28] This part consists of the same amount of pages as its number foretells, and it directly connects the afterwords with the two forewords that tell the volcanic emergence and fluvial submergence of the fictional archipelago.[29] These introductory and closing parts of the novel can thus be perceived as a metafictional frame, albeit one with plurivocal and multi-perspective fractures.[30] Whilst the two pretexts imagine, tell, and expose the creation and end of the Caribbean archipelago, the fifth annex arguably questions the utility of the narrative creation of islands in revolt whenever the protest prose remains historical and does not touch present problems.

The pages concerned construct a here-and-now, they position in contemporaneity and explicitly name both time and location of the literary enunciation.[31] The action is situated in the late 1990s on the western fringes of Martinique, somewhere on the territory of its second largest commune, Le Lamentin.[32] Thus

---

27 Guerilla tactics do not always allow for open fires and time-consuming practices of food refinement. Furthermore tropical fruits, roots, and herbs do not necessarily need cooking, roasting, or fermentation to be edible.

28 "Annexes et Affluents" (Glissant 2003: 337-361) and "5" (352-356).

29 Cf. the "Deux Prétextes" (Glissant 2003: 13-16).

30 I will expand on contemporary Caribbean nissopoetics, the creation of islands in the archipelago of Caribbean literature, in a forthcoming monograph with the title *Insel(n) im Archipel*.

31 "Par la côté d'ici, ainsi disent les vieilles paroles, pour nous c'est au Lamentin de Martinique, nous en parlions fin des années 1990, la rivière et la mangrove, du temps qu'elles étaient vives et qu'elles débordaient, aimaient et attiraient Nestor'o, lequel a dévalé sa plage beaucoup plus tard [...]. C'est pour lui un haut plaisir que de s'entendre apostropher en 'vous', signe d'amitié, par Apocal, l'archéologue de la rivière Lézarde desséchée, conservateur en chef de l'esprit de la mangrove et gardien de ce vieux Lamentin [...]" (Glissant 2003: 352).

32 Even if that location seems to point towards the Aéroport International Martinique Aimé Césaire, within Glissant's writing it connects with his first novel *La Lézarde*

place and time are set for a *mise-en-scène* of Caribbean food culture as an authenticating and identifying gesture, even as a collective re-enactment of cultural heritage: Twice a week the two old friends Nestor'o and Apocal, who address each other with the slightly antiquated polite form, meet at their regulars' table at the traditional Martinican Creole restaurant *Au Canari d'Antan*. For the informed reader, the name of the *resto* pays tribute to the traditional earthenware vessels of different sizes.[33] For a reader who is not acquainted with the history of local ceramics the name of the restaurant does not necessarily point towards pottery but to its homophone, a non-endemic canary bird from some imprecise old days of transatlantic seafaring.[34]

Madame Sapho, chez laquelle ils réservent au mercredi midi le blaff de poisson et le flan au coco et au samedi soir le colombo de cabri, mais léger et diététique, suivi d'un blanc-manger au maracudja et au citron vert, fait mine à chaque déclamation des deux amis d'arranger les nappes des autres tables de son petit restaurant, *Au Canari d'Antan,* puis n'y tenant plus elle se plante à côté d'eux et elle boit la parole, les yeux au plafond et la

---

and the ecocritical as well as culinary part of the definition of *pensée archipelique* in his last philosophical essay *Philosophie de la Relation*. There he visualizes the thinking in minuscule and interrelated details to local rivers and its crayfish, not only for the sake of the comparison, but "for pleasure, everyone knows about their tastiness": "Par la pensée archipélique, nous connaissons les roches des rivières, les plus petites assurément, qu'elles ouvrent et recouvrent, où les *zabitans* (d'eau douce, il s'agit de ces écrevisses bleues et grises, menacées de pollution), en Martinique, et qui sont appelées *ouassous* en Guadeloupe (noms de fonds, noms d'appartenance), (je les désigne par résolu plaisir, chacun connaît leur succulence), s'abritent encore" (Glissant 2009: 45-46). For Glissant and *Ormerod* within archipelagic island literature, cf. Lestringant (2008).

33 The traditional clay vessel which is homophone to the famous yellow bird from the archipelago at the other side of the colonial triangle is possibly a local Pre-Columbian invention or of West-African origin. As Patricia J. Fay argues, actual production on the former British Isles still retains "ceramic technologies from Africa, India and Europe" (Fay 2008). According to Hauser, there exists archeological evidence of production and commerce of "local coarse earthenwares" in Jamaica—its local generic name being *yabba*—during slavery (Hauser 2011: 171).

34 Arguably this could be read as a highly ironic way of referring to the so-called discovery by an island hop(ing) by three ships that came from La Gomera and changed course due to the flight of birds. For *island hopping* and *island hoping* cf. Depraetere and Dahl (2007: 84-94). For the colonization and extermination of the Canaries as prequel to the Caribbean enterprise cf. Grove (1995:30).

bouche en rond. Elle balance en toupie mabial quand Apocal déroule la phrase, elle l'entraîne dans les périodes oratoires au rythme des larges robes créoles qu'elle fait valser autour d'elle. (Glissant 2003: 353)[35]

Each Wednesday at midday, Nestor'o and Apocal eat chopped fish that was boiled in a stew of spices, followed by a sweet made from milk, eggs, and the fruit of the iconic tropical palm-tree: the coconut.[36] On Saturday evening, they eat goat meat seasoned with "[t]he best-known French Caribbean spice mix" *Colombo* (Mandelblatt 2011: 209).[37] This main course of red meat is described as being light and dietetic, thus enhancing the realist mode and stressing the possibility of the old men enjoying it every Saturday evening. It is followed by a sweet, the "blanc-manger," a jelly that nowadays is usually made of gelatin, sugar, and milk. The tropical version of this medieval Lenten food usually also contains coconut (cf. Désormeaux 1977: 120). In this literary case, the two accompanying sauces are based on lime and passion fruit. If one focuses on the composition of the menu, one notices drastic differences in the social background of the single dishes. The set meal combines the results of the needs and tricks of enslaved workers' food preparations that had to achieve a rich, locally grown nourishment, with the pompous and exuberant technical finesses and extravagances of French cuisine. These transculinary mixes bring one fundamental change to the forefront that José Guerrero called the first culinary revolution since the Neolithic Age, namely the birth of most European, African, and American national dishes *after* the global exchange of plants and animals in the wake of 1492 (cf.

---

35 "Madame Sapho—at whose restaurant they order in advance the fish stew as well as the coconut flan on Wednesday midday, and on Saturday evening the light, healthful kid colombo, followed by passion fruit and lime blancmanger—pretends during each utterance of her two friends to arrange the napkins on the other tables of her little restaurant, *Au Canari d'Antan*, and when she can't stand it no more she stands next to them and drinks their words, eyes towards the ceiling and mouth agape. She sways like a spinning top as Apocal unwinds his sentences, sweeps him along in oratory periods to the rhythm of the ample Creole frocks that waltz about her."

36 "The palm would go on to become a key symbolic icon representing the entire Caribbean region" (Sheller 2003: 40).

37 Colombo "contains *curcuma* (turmeric), cumin, coriander, fenugreek, pepper, cloves, mustard and ginger; cardamon, saffron, fennel seed, and anise are other spices that can be added. This spice mix is directly related to the Indian populations of the islands, particularly on Guadeloupe, and it is used in the preparation of several classic dishes such as colombo au poulet (stewed chicken with Colombo powder) or riz jaune (yellow rice)" (Mandelblatt 2011: 209).

Guerrero 2010: 187). Furthermore, the introduction of tropical fruits (coconut, passion fruit, and lime) into both desserts can be read as a point for Mintz' assertion that food meant a certain extent of freedom (of culinary expression) and power (over their masters' food staples) for enslaved people and especially cooks in the Caribbean colonies. Mintz points out that the enslaved cooks were the ones who actually invented and created Caribbean food culture: "Those who caught or grew the food, who prepared and cooked it, who contributed most of all to the creation of the cuisine, were the slaves themselves" (Mintz 1993: 259). The freedom that Mintz ascribes to the planting, breading, processing, and feeding cycle is a highly creative, self-serving, and emancipating *bricolage* in the sense of Lévi-Strauss, that gives a certain power to the enslaved over the enslaving.[38] Knowledge, practice, and means of feeding seem slave-centered, while their owners are completely detached and unable to feed themselves. This constitutes a limited but highly interesting power inversion within the Caribbean societies during the four centuries of slavery and may be an additional explanation for the recurring presence of food, cooking, and eating in Caribbean texts: it repeats a gesture of emancipation. A traditional postcolonial analysis of this fifth part of "Annexes & Affluents" could therefore read the repeated meetings with their recurring menus of typical dishes as a strong representation of lived cultural memory. The local garb of the host with the significant name "Madame Sapho"[39] and the oratory style of the two old men could be used as further proof to read this evocation of culinary and poetic tradition as a serious tool for literary identity construction out of the creolization between West-African, Mediterranean, Arawak, and Taíno cultures. In this line of argument, the restaurant's name (*Le canari d'antan*) acknowledges and pays a strong tribute to the traditional arti-

---

38 "The origins of particular crops and food items may seem to matter little in the total picture of slavery. Yet it mattered much in regard to the way that new cuisines were built up over time. In this as much else, a kind of *bricolage*—a French word for 'patching together' made famous by the great French anthropologist Claude Lévi Strauss—occurred" (Mintz 1996: 40). For *bricolage* cf. Lévi-Strauss (1966: 16-17).

39 "Madame Sapho" points towards highly repudiated, original, and partially lost female poetry as well as towards an open concept of love that is not confined into heterosexual binaries. She appears to form—together with the main character of the St. Lucian thread of the novel—a decisive alternative to the dominating male protagonists of the earlier novels, which were criticized repeatedly (cf. Pessini 2004: 122). Interestingly, both Madame Sapho and Man-Joliba (after becoming a widow) can be seen distributing their love to more than one man only. All two women can be read as successfully living an independent, public, and autonomous lifestyle, one in line with the central educational pillars of the Sapphic school, rather than the sexual one.

facts for mixing the intra- and inter-island as well as transatlantic connections of traditional Caribbean food culture into a nutritious and tasty meal. These are, however,—together with the renowned Martiniquan rum—the physically altering and coloring parts of a greater *mise-en-scène* of Creole traditional taste, at whose center the oral invention and subsequent praise of the islands on the Caribbean rim are situated.

Le goût est d'inventer d'abord, de vanter ensuite, les îles déposées en arc dans cette Caraïbe par cette ravine primordiale, qui est l'occasion de leurs délires les plus gros. Le relent du vezou y plane, combien séducteur, c'est-à-dire, aux rares endroits où vous imaginez qu'il s'élève encore. "Vous n'y résistez pas...," dit Apocal, "alors que vous auriez dû haïr ce rhum esclavagiste...." (Glissant 2003: 354)[40]

Here it becomes obvious that "the pleasure of inventing first and boasting later" is being recounted at the expense of a detailed realist depiction of the preparation and consumption of the actual meals and drinks. Apocal's critical position further complicates and differentiates the paradoxical identity politics of the two characters, as they are enjoying what they should hate in the name of postcolonial political correctness: all these products of slavery, and especially the slaver's rum, which directly leads back to sugar plantations and the most important reason for the slave trade as such (cf. Mintz 1993: 260). The whole dilemma of postcolonial reconciliation and conscious consumerism becomes apparent in Apocal's stress on the failing resistance in front of slaver's rum. And, in accordance with the first example in this article, one could further argue that in the same way in which tradition and nostalgia are stronger than consumer's historio-political consciousness, they challenge the analytical possibilities.

It is therefore only sensible to focus as well on the antithesis to the argument that the depiction of traditional French-Caribbean Creole food cultures in postcolonial novels constructs identity and resistance: Just like the transmedial presence of television in Chalumeau's novel, the repeated live sessions of Creole oratory during the meals in this afterword of Glissant's novel can be read as questioning the larger project of staging cultural authenticity and its consump-

---

40 "The pleasure is to invent first and subsequently praise the islands sprinkled in an arc within that Caribbean by that primordial gully, which is the subject of their grandest ravings. How seductive is the stench of the sugarcane juice in the plain, that is to say, in the rare places where you imagine it still wafts. 'You cannot resist...,' says Apocal, 'though you should have hated this slaver's rum....'"

tion.[41] There is a set of demystifying strategies to be encountered within the text that seem to support this: firstly, the establishment is portrayed as commercializing its traditional dishes via nostalgia and a mistress in local garb. The traditional Creole dress of Madame Sapho —be it "[t]he more formal *la grande robe*," *la douillette* as "all-in-one gown," or *la titane* (formerly reserved for courtesans)— is "a veritable Creole invention" (Franco 2004: 65; cf. also Buckridge 2004: 60). Arguably, these kinds of dresses are not worn on a daily basis any more, only in highly commercial and touristic settings. Therefore, the stress lies on the role and presence of capitalism, international and local tourism, as well as a tendency towards nostalgic regression and a consumerist gaze onto this staged authenticity. Needless to say, her dishes show not only traces of the creolization of local and global food staples over various centuries, but also ingredients for the construction of the icon of a sexualized and consumable tropical island paradise (e.g. the phallic palm, the ample coconut, the alluring passion fruit), as well as the visible part of a whole variety of creolization processes. In the same line, the two fierce word-battling protagonists are at this very end of the novel reduced from their primordial and 'geopoetical' role as creators or storytellers and private archeologists of little histories to a routinely observable curiosity and nostalgic remnant of Creole orality in the semi-public space of Sapho's restaurant.[42] Even if this is not an eatery for mass tourism but a regular's restaurant, the painstakingly hidden eavesdropping by the local crowd receives a lot of attention and detailed description by the narrating voice.[43] It marks the truncated relationship between tradition and contemporaneity, between the old men and other inhabitants of the island and hides the most astonishing absence within this depiction of Caribbean food cultures: no single word is reserved for the actual process of cooking, serving or smelling, tasting, and judging. Some are named, but none is

---

41 For a theory of "Consuming the Caribbean," cf. Mimi Sheller's monograph with the corresponding title (Sheller 2003: 3-37); for "Consuming Traditions" and "Selling Authenticity," cf. Outka (2009: 3-8).

42 The terms *geopoetics* and *géopoétique* were coined by Kenneth White and denominate a transdisciplinary theory-practice that tries to re-establish and enrich the relationship between humanity and the earth (cf. White 1989). Federico Italiano took up the term for its poietic and landscaping qualities within fictional worlds. In order to analyze the geopoetics of a text with a predominant poetic function he translated the system of *geospheres* from geography to literary studies (cf. Italiano 2009: 11-27). For "Geopoetics of the Island," cf. Graziadei (2011).

43 "Les autres clients, tous des habitués, participent de cette fête de la parole. Ils entretiennent juste le remuement de bruit qu'il faut pour ne pas sembler écouter les échanges des deux amis […]" (Glissant 2003: 352).

shown: all the depictions and actions within the restaurant and the chapter circle around narrating, listening, thinking, and cleaning. The absence of the actual physical communion would obviously offer itself to a psychoanalytical or theological reading that could focus on the evasion of a depiction of death, a plate full of food that is, if one follows one of the many interesting thoughts of Norman Wirzba in *Food & Faith* (2011).[44]

This leads towards a second opposition to the affirmative interpretation of this literary depiction of a traditional meal in a traditional restaurant with a matron in a traditional garb. This second antithesis lies only slightly hidden within the text and activates...

...THE FIERCE QUESTIONING OF THE PURPOSE AND POWER OF FICTIONAL CARIBBEAN COMMUNION

Arguably this short depiction of two storytelling, poieticizing, world-inventing, fiercely arguing, and word-battling old men with powerful and ornate rhetorical styles at repeating lunch and dinner tables questions the purpose and power of representations of traditional cuisine and eating habits. Food—its provenience, preparation, taste, or consumption—is not the central reason for the scene at Madame Sapho's restaurant; oratory is. The fierce questioning consists of a parody of the reiteration of cultural stereotypes and the staging of identity politics through an ironic take on the possibilities and mechanisms of Caribbean *oraliterature* or writing in general. Here the strategic function of a staged banquet in the plot is not primarily the siting, development, and realization of human, biopolitical, and ecological interaction or community. Not food and possibly not even sex but discussion seems to be the first reason for this scene of word-battling at the regulars' table. The accentuation of the fictionalized table scene—that is said to be recurring, but is metonymically shown only once—as *mise-en-scène* of Creole oratory shows and questions the supposed authenticity of setting and action.

Similar to the challenge that the depiction of food poses to the reading process when reminding us of something quite crucial on a corporeal level, the private thoughts of Madame Sapho remind us of present-day problems, point to-

---

44 "Eating is the daily reminder of creaturely mortality. We eat to live, knowing that without food we will starve and die. But to eat we must also kill, realizing that without the deaths of others—microbes, insects, plants, animals—we can have no food" (Wirzba 2011: 110-111).

wards global relations, and destroy any exoticist removal to a remote island paradise. The metafictional reference is quite obvious in the afterwords and starts as a strong connection to orality with the opening words of part five ("Par la côté d'ici, ainsi disent les vieilles paroles," Glissant 2003: 356), when the situating *anacrusis* "On this side" is cut off or followed by the interjection "so say the old words."[45] This interjection after the upbeat of the first sentence does not simply interrupt the beginning of a *histoire* in order to specify word usage and form, but to give credit to the tradition of the *récit* via the self-referential definition as oral intertextuality. Thereby it instantly raises metafictional awareness. Fiction that is conscious and explicit about its fictionality confronts us—according to Chris Bongie—"with a world of images, alerting us to the *produced* and *producing* status of the ideas and identities it presents, and thus situating us at a point from which their authority can be put into question, but also, and inevitably, reproducing that authority and its effects" (Bongie 1998: 178). Ten years later, Bongie expressly differentiates the earlier *Tout-Monde*-phase, with its more decidedly metafictional take on authority, from "the novels produced by 'late Glissant,' *Sartorius* (1999) and *Ormerod* (2003)—novels in which I find little of the 'post/modern' tension" (Bongie 2008: 366). While one may agree on a substantial late development or concluding relational phase in Glissant's work, the focus of this paper seems irreconcilably opposed to Bongie's assertion that the reduced metafiction of the last novels "serves to pre-empt any reflection upon the possible inadequacy of 'the authoritative ideological claims and posturings' of his most recent, post-political works of theory" (369).[46] In line with Madame Sapho's reflections about a successful rhetorical strategy within Creole oratory

---

45 Certainly, "paroles" point towards the affinity of French Caribbean to Creole orality. This is especially true for Glissant, who writes at the beginning of *Le discours antillais*: "Le cri du monde devient parole" (Glissant 1981: 14) in order to schematize a history of the poetic voice from the individual and collective cry into poetic utterance. As Glissant mentions elsewhere, tales from various West African tribes were recounted by enslaved people during their only free time—after eating at nightfall at the end of a long and hard working day—and were pronounced in the only communal languages available to them, the creolized languages of their imperial tormentors (cf. Glissant 2004: 5-12).

46 "The difference between the use of metafiction [...] is that this strategy no longer signals Glissant's quarrel with himself' but merely his 'quarrel with others' [...]. Instead of 'poetry' we have [...] mere 'rhetoric': metafiction becomes one expression among many [...] which serves to pre-empt any reflection upon the possible inadequacy of 'the authoritative ideological claims and posturings' of his most recent, post-political works of theory" (Bongie 2008: 369).

and its highly political content one could argue that decisive moments of implicit metafictionality not only point towards the "inadequacy […] of theory" (ibid.), but also towards the subtleties of a literary construction of Caribbean authenticity and identity.

The afterthoughts of Madame Sapho in the fifth part of the afterword "Annexes et Affluents" lead to a profound questioning of the offerings and consumptions of any kind of Caribbean *nissopoetics* and literary conviviality.[47] This questioning can be interpreted as especially fierce as it touches the relevance of the old generation's Creole oratory and thus, via metafictional abstraction, the novel's strictly historical treatment of resistance, revolt, and revolution. Madame Sapho's afterthoughts trigger a highly critical metafictional stance, which questions the whole purpose of staging Caribbean food culture without references to contemporary social, economic, and consumerist problems "that nobody would want to discuss, at least not seriously" (cf. Glissant 2003: 356). Apparently only the ornate oratory of the old "friendly enemies" in competition covers social problems and negative changes from a local, compassionate perspective with a conservative stance towards global influences. This becomes especially tangible as their word-battling is not transcribed; the reader of Glissant's last novel is not able to read the position concerning the pressing questions that "nobody wants to discuss seriously."

Madame Sapho dessert les tables, tranquille, son champion du jour a calé la dernière parade, même si elle n'est pas très fulgurante. L'important est de frapper sans recours, que l'amical ennemi trop fatigué ne puisse répondre et laisse aller. Combats de parole qui couvrent ce dont personne ne voudrait discuter, du moins sérieusement, le chômage en épidémie, les saisissements des jeunes gens dans le vide autour d'eux, les agressions en pagaille comme partout dans le monde, les tentations des grands magasins, toutes les modes adoptées d'entrain, et le reste, qui babille, se tait, roule en cancans. (Glissant 2003: 356)[48]

---

47 As the next citation will show, Madame Sapho thinks in highly political and transatlantic terms, thus working against isolation and exotization. The questions of Caribbean *nissopoetics* and *conviviality* are central to my doctoral thesis. There I try to analyze how contemporary texts from the anglo-, franco- and hispanophone literatures of the Caribbean construct islands (nissopoetics). Furthermore, instead of focusing on the exposure of cultural signifiers as an act of identity construction I concentrate on the ways fictional characters interact with themselves and the island, thereby following to a certain degree Ottmar Ette's pledge for "Literary Studies as Science for Living" (2010).

48 "Madame Sapho clears the tables tranquilly: her hero of the day has choked on the last pass, though it was hardly lively. The important thing is to strike without quarter, so

The protagonists of this part of the afterwords and / or the narrating voice seem to situate 'serious' discussions in opposition to the old men's "word battles." Ironically, the first do not evade pressing topics whilst the second very apparently does so by evading to show or transcribe the arguments, but pointing towards a serious and contemporary political potential to be found in a passionate debate in traditional style and language. A further ironic twist is to be found in the fact that the so-called non-serious word-battles are not to be won with the better argument, but by having the better stamina. These appear to be especially stark metafictional hints which amount to self-criticism at the end of a postcolonial novel that stages two wars between revolutionary and imperial forces on two islands in differing centuries.

Apart from the very novel, many other works from contemporary (francophone) Caribbean literature appear to comply to this attitude of not wanting "to discuss, at least not seriously," actual political, spiritual, economic, and social problems. If read as a political and ethical literary critique, these lines seriously question the depictions and assertions of any kind of local tradition, socio-historical and cultural background that propagate a fixed label of *Créolité* (cf. Bernabé 2002) without including the ongoing changes or latest visibility of the process of *créolisation* (cf. Glissant 1997: 37).

The cited silence after the babble would allow a performative finale to this paper, but the reference to the furiously galloping and revealing cancan dance leads from exoticism to eroticism, to the instigation of consumers' desires, to bananas and passion fruits. These fruits are, as the dishes in the Creole restaurants of the two novels, complex and conflicting signifiers between local traditions and global marketing schemes, between creation and consumption, nurture and value, symbol and icon, life and death, always much more than just plain (literary) decoration. As the narrative voices in *Ormerod* and *Désirade, ô Serpente!* give special attention and visibility to the *mise-en-scène* of Caribbean Creole food cultures via the metafictional as well as transmedial aspect of the relevant scenes, they allow and foster a revealing insight into its mediated constructedness for more than one public and more than one objective.

---

that the friendly enemy is too tired to answer and lets it go. Battles of words that deal with what nobody wants to discuss, at least not seriously: rampant unemployment, young people thrashing in the emptiness around them, massive violence like everywhere else in the world, the temptations of upscale department stores, all the trends adopted enthusiastically, and everything else, babbling, falling silent, churning out gossip."

Bibliography

Barthes, Roland 2009. "Toward a Psychosociology of Contemporary Food Consumption." *Food and Culture. A Reader*. Eds. Carole Counihan and Penny van Esterik. 2nd ed. New York: Routledge, 28-35.

Bernabé, Jean, Patrick Chamoiseau, and Raphaël Confiant 2002. *Éloge de la Créolité. Éd. Bilingue Français / Anglais*. Paris: Gallimard.

Bongie, Chris 1998. *Islands and Exiles. The Creole Identities of Post/Colonial Literature*. Stanford: Stanford University Press.

—. 2008. *Friends and Enemies. The Scribal Politics of Post/Colonial Literature*. Liverpool: Liverpool University Press.

Buckridge, Steeve O. 2004. *The Language of Dress. Resistance and Accommodation in Jamaica, 1760-1890*. Mona / Kingston: University of the West Indies Press.

Chalumeau, Fortuné 2006. *Désirade, ô Serpente!* Paris: Hoëbeke.

Chamoiseau, Patrick 1997. *Écrire en Pays Dominé*. Paris: Gallimard.

Danticat, Edwidge 1998. *The Farming of Bones*. New York: Soho Press.

Depraetere, Christian and Arthur L. Dahl 2007. "Island Locations and Classifications." *A World of Islands. An Island Studies Reader*. Ed. Godfrey Baldacchino. Charlottetown: Island Studies, 57-105.

Désormeaux, Emile 1977. *La Cuisine Créole Traditionnelle*. Fort de France: Desormeaux.

Ette, Ottmar 2010. "Literature as Knowledge for Living, Literary Studies as Science for Living." *PMLA* CXXV.4: 977-93.

Fay, Patricia J. 2008. "Coalpot and Canawi. Traditional Creole Pottery in the Contemporary Commonwealth Caribbean." *Interpreting Ceramics* 10 [http://www.interpretingceramics.com/issue010/articles/05.htm (retrieved 30 January 2014)].

Federman, Raymond 1981. *Surfiction. Fiction Now and Tomorrow*. Chicago: Swallow Press.

Franco, Pamela R. 2004. "The Martinican. Dress and Politics in Nineteenth-Century Trinidad Carnival." *Carnival. Culture in Action. The Trinidad Experience*. Ed. Milla Cozart Riggio. New York: Routledge, 64-75.

Glissant, Édouard 1958. *La Lézarde. Roman*. Paris: Éd. du Seuil.

—. 1981. *Le Discours Antillais*. Paris: Éd. du Seuil.

—. 1993. *Tout-Monde. Roman*. Paris: Gallimard.

—. 1996. *Introduction à une Poétique du Divers*. Paris: Gallimard.

—. 1997. *Traité du Tout-Monde*. Paris: Gallimard.

—. 2003. *Ormerod. Roman*. Paris: Gallimard.

—. 2004. "Ouverture." *Paradis Brisé. Nouvelles des Caraïbe*. Eds. Édouard Glissant and Roland Brival. Paris: Hoëbeke, 5-12.
—. 2009. *Philosophie de la Relation. Poésie en Étendue*. Paris: Gallimard.
Graziadei, Daniel 2008. *McOndo, Crack und Avant-Pop. Neueste Entwicklungen der spanischsprachigen und englischsprachigen Literatur der Americas*. Saarbrücken: VDM.
—. 2011. "Geopoetics of the Island." *Tra Paesaggio e Geopoetica. Studi di Geografia*. Eds. Marco Mastronunzio and Federico Italiano. Milano: Unicopli, 163-182.
Greber, Erika 2002. *Textile Texte. Poetologische Metaphorik und Literaturtheorie. Studien zur Tradition des Wortflechtens und der Kombinatorik*. Köln et.al.: Böhlau Verlag.
Grove, Richard H. 1995. *Green Imperialism. Colonial Expansion, Tropical Island Edens and the Origins of Environmentalism 1600-1860*. New York: Cambridge University Press.
Guerrero, José G. 2010. "La Culinaria Colonial de América y Santo Domingo." *Saberes y Sabores en México y el Caribe*. Eds. Rita de Maeseneer and Patrick Collard. Amsterdam et al.: Rodopi, 183-233.
Hauser, Mark W. 2011. "Of Earth and Clay. Locating Colonial Economies and Local Ceramics." *Out of Many, One People. The Historical Archaeology of Colonial Jamaica*. Eds. Douglas V. Armstrong, James A. Delle, and Mark W. Hauser. Tuscaloosa: University of Alabama Press, 163-84.
Huggan, Graham 2001. *The Postcolonial Exotic. Marketing the Margins*. London: Routledge.
Italiano, Federico and Michael Rössner 2012. "Translatio/n. An Introduction." *Translatio/n. Narration, Media and the Staging of Differences*. Eds. Federico Italiano and Michael Rössner. Bielefeld: transcript, 9-16.
Italiano, Federico 2009. *Tra Miele e Pietra. Aspetti di Geopoetica in Montale e Celan*. Milano: Mimesis.
Lestringant, Frank 2008. "Insulaires en Mouvement. Saint-Exupéry, Michaux, Calvino, Glissant." *Des Îles en Archipel. Flottements Autour du Thème Insulaire en Hommage à Carminella Biondi*. Ed. Carmelina Imbroscio. Bern: Peter Lang, 215-34.
Lévi-Strauss, Claude 1964. *Le Cru et le Cuit*. Paris: Plon.
—. 1966. *Savage Mind*. Translated by John Weightman. Chicago: University of Chicago Press.
Macey, David 2005. "Adieu Foulard. Adieu Madras." *Frantz Fanon's* Black Skin, White Masks. *New Interdisciplinary Essays*. Ed. Maxim Silverman. Manchester: Manchester University Press, 12-31.

Mandelblatt, Bernie 2011. "Martinique and Guadeloupe." *Food Cultures of the World Encyclopedia*. Ed. Ken Albala. Santa Barbara: ABC-CLIO, 209-216.

Mintz, Sidney W. 1993. "Tasting Food, Tasting Freedom." *Slavery in the Americas*. Ed. Wolfgang Binder. Würzburg: Könighausen und Neumann, 257-276.

O'Gorman, Edmundo 1993 [1985]. *La Invención de América. Investigación Acerca de la Estructura Histórica del Nuevo Mundo y del Sentido de Su Devenir*. 2nd ed. México: Fondo de Cultura Económica.

Outka, Elizabeth 2009. *Consuming Traditions. Modernity, Modernism, and the Commodified Authentic*. Oxford: Oxford University Press.

Pessini, Elena 2004. "Ormerod ou les Embûches de la Lecture." *Rêver le Monde Écrire le Monde. Théorie et Narrations d'Édouard Glissant*. Eds. Carminella Biondi and Elena Pessini. Bologna: Clueb.

Seager, Dennis L. 1991. *Stories Within Stories. An Ecosystematic Theory of Metadiegetic Narrative*. New York et al.: Peter Lang.

Sheller, Mimi B. 2003. *Consuming the Caribbean. From Arawaks to Zombies*. London: Routledge.

Walcott, Derek 1992. "The Schooner *Flight*." *Collected Poems. 1948 - 1984*. London: Faber & Faber, 345-61.

Waugh, Patricia 1996 [1984]. *Metafiction. The Theory and Practice of Self-Conscious Fiction*. London: Routledge.

White, Kenneth 1989. "What is Geopoetics?" *Scottish Centre for Geopoetics* 28 April [http://geopoetics.org.uk/page3/what-is-geopoetics.html (retrieved 13 January 2014)].

Wilk, Richard R. 1999. "'Real Belizean Food.' Building Local Identity in the Transnational Caribbean." *American Anthropologist* 101.2: 244-55.

Wirzba, Norman 2011. *Food and Faith. A Theology of Eating*. Cambridge: Cambridge University Press.

Neo/Colonial Gaze

Curiosity, Appreciation, and Old Habits
Creolization of Colonizers' Food Consumption Patterns in
Three English Travelogues on the Caribbean

ILARIA BERTI

INTRODUCTION

Following on from a growing group of anthropologists, sociologists, and, more recently, historians, I am convinced that food and cuisine could and should be an excellent vantage point from which to explore wider processes of social and cultural change.[1] A focus on food can help the understanding of the historical genesis of cultural patterns and formations and thus shed new light on our own contemporary food habits by seeing them in connection to their past. It also allows us to comprehend the various ways in which food, its preparation, and its consumption connect people who belong to different cultures.

This paper focuses on the process of food creolization as a lens through which to examine the relationship between colonizers and colonized in the Caribbean in the first half of the 19th century. By 'food creolization,' I mean a process of cultural response to colonial encounters that leads to the development of a new food consumption pattern that features elements belonging to different cultures, but modified into something significantly different from the original cultures. According to Sidney Mintz, the concept of food creolization can be usefully employed to investigate the connections between food and self-identification, the reasons behind food choices, food as a form of communica-

---

1   Cf. Flandrin and Montanari (2003); Scholliers (2001); Wilson (2006); Counihan (2000); Gabaccia (1998); Nutzenadel and Trentmann (2008); Pilcher (1998); Leong-Salobir (2011).

tion, emulation of food consumption patterns, and the cultural meaning underlying eating practices (cf. Mintz 1996: 36).

The academic debate on creolization in the Caribbean began between the 1940s and 1960s, during the phase of decolonization and independence of most of the Caribbean islands. Bolland argues that the concept of creolization was *invented* in this period to promote social cohesion and to create an *imagined community* (cf. Bolland 2002: 15-46).[2]

A significant part of the discussion on creolization focuses on how many of the African traditions were retained in the Afro-Caribbean and also Afro-American culture of the 1940s. The debate revolved around whether the experience of slavery had been so devastating that it completely obliterated the African roots in favor of the emulation of the European culture, or, instead, Afro-American cultures were still influenced, under the surface, by African traditions (cf. Crahan and Knight 1979; for the U.S. context cf. also Herskovitz 1990; Frazier 1939). Also, the historians Crahan and Knight described the process of creolization and its results, stating:

The confluence of a variety of African cultures, plus the consistent input of European and Amerindian elements, produced through the centuries a striking amalgam of linguistic, religious, dietary, familial, literary, and artistic currents that resulted in a uniquely rich, diverse, and dynamic Afro-Caribbean culture. Such a culture was neither static nor homogeneous across the Caribbean. (Crahan and Knight 1979: vi)

The "confluence" and "amalgam" of various cultures will also be a central theme of this paper. In my view, creolization is something more than a process of mixing and re-assembling pre-existing cultures—it is rather a process of synthesis, leading to the birth of a new culture. Already in 1938 C.L.R. James expressed this concept pointing out that Caribbean culture was native, being neither European nor African nor American nor indigenous, but typically West Indian (cf. James 1968: 321).

Even if neither James nor Derek Walcott used the term creolization explicitly, Walcott's description in his Nobel Prize speech is useful to explain what I mean by "creolization" in this paper:

Break a vase, and the love that reassembles the fragments is stronger than that love which took its symmetry for granted when it was whole. The glue that fits the pieces is the sealing of its original shape. It is such a love that reassembles our African and Asiatic frag-

---

2 For an in-depth analysis of the debate on the meaning of creolization, cf. also Mintz and Price (1976); Mintz (1985); Ortiz (2007); Brathwaite (1971); Burton (1997).

ments, the cracked heirlooms whose restoration shows its white scars. This gathering of broken pieces is the care and pain of the Antilles, and if the pieces are disparate, ill-fitting, they contain more pain than their original sculpture, those icons and sacred vessels taken for granted in their ancestral places. Antillean art is this restoration of our shattered histories, our shards of vocabulary, our archipelago becoming a synonym for pieces broken off from the original continent. (Walcott 1992 n.p.)

The Caribbean region is described by Walcott as a broken and reassembled vase —despite its scars, it is exactly because of these fractures that the multifaceted Creole Caribbean exists. Some more recent ideas on the meaning of the term creolization were developed by Swedish anthropologist Ulf Hannerz. His monograph *Transnational Connection. Culture, People, Places* (2001) is an analysis of various cultural traits and their redefinition under colonialism as a result of the encounter and the amalgam between different populations. Creolization is a multifaceted process, in which differences as well as interactions and innovations all play a part; it is a complex interplay of cultures, in which the origins of each population, as well as the signs of a past marked by colonialism, slavery, and racial hierarchies are still visible (cf. Hannerz 2001: 108-109).

More specifically, in this paper the term 'creolization' is used to describe the blending of various food cultures and consumption patterns in the Caribbean context. It should also be underlined that creolization[3] as a process began with the arrival of the first Europeans in the Americas and thus emerged well before being described by the historical documents from the 19th century the present study is based on. At the same time, in the eyes of those who moved from Europe to the Caribbean at this point of time, creolization was a completely new phenomenon.

The encounter with a large number of culinary traditions and the associated food consumption patterns is far from simply a matter of food: it is an important example of a wider process of creolization. In his well-known work on sugar consumption, Sidney Mintz argues that "[o]ne could *become* different by *consuming* differently" (Mintz 1985: 185). Taking the cue from Mintz' reflection on food and identity, in this paper the focus on food is used as an analytical tool to understand a broader process of creolization of cultures, with the aim of highlighting that through such colonial food encounters, every social actor involved in the process is transformed, or at least perceived to modify their previous habits.

---

3 From my point of view, creolization is a process that belongs to what historian Fernand Braudel defined as part of the "longue durée" (cf. Braudel 1966: 52-54).

The food consumption patterns of Europeans in the American colonies have been the subject of a number of studies, including among others Dunn's work (2000) on Caribbean colonizers during the 17th and 18th centuries and Earle's study (2010) on 16th- and 17th-centuries Spanish America. The general trend, which is formulated in those works, is a rejection of local food by colonizers; such rejection may enhance their desire to go back to their home country and to stop eating "strange food" (Dunn 2000: XVI). Dunn also explains that the consumption of familiar food helped the colonizers in the unknown and threatening Caribbean environment and contributed to underlining the hierarchical order the colonizers wanted to maintain (cf. 263). In fact, both Dunn and Earle argue that, since the beginning of the Caribbean colonization, colonizers preferred to import English preserved and salted food instead of eating fresh local food, the exception being fruit. According to Earle, the colonists were afraid that "without access to European food, Spaniards would sooner or later turn into Indians" (Earle 2010: 708).

On the basis of an examination of a group of 19th-century egodocumentary sources,[4] however, a rather different picture emerges, in which dynamics of contamination, cross-cultural communication, and food creolization can be observed in the West Indies, a context deeply marked by uneven power structures, racial hierarchies, and asymmetrical policies. Whereas in the previous centuries of colonization local food was viewed with suspicion, during the 19th century mistrust was replaced by curiosity and interest, bringing about the processes of food creolization that will be the subject of this paper.

Towards this objective, the main sources through which the process of food creolization will be discussed here are the travel diaries of three British colonizers[5] of the first half of the 19th century and the first published Jamaican cookbook (1893). However, it should be underlined that all the documents used in this paper were produced by the white colonial elite. European and American colonizers were the only population groups who extensively produced written documents in the 19th-century Caribbean, while there are very few documents

---

4   Even though the use of the term egodocuments became widespread during the 1990s only, the word was coined by the Dutch historian Jacques Presser in the 1950s. He defined an egodocument as a source where the self with its feeling, thoughts and actions are present (cf. Presser 1958: 208-10; Dekker 2002a: 7-20 and 2002b 13-37).

5   Even if the authors of travelogues used in this paper describe the process of food creolization, in their notes, mainly in Bayley's and Lewis', they do not give an exact definition of what they mean when using the term creole.

written by slaves and non-whites in general.[6] Subsequently, my analysis will focus mainly on how the European elites perceived and described food creolization, and their feelings about this process.

The first travelogue to be analyzed is Mrs. Carmichael's (1833). Relatively little is known about her, except that she was a Scottish gentlewoman who lived with her family in St. Vincent and Trinidad for five years from 1820 to 1825.[7] In her diary she was very meticulous[8] in the descriptions of daily life in the Caribbean: in fact, as she wrote, "man, rather than nature, is my object" (Carmichael 1833: I, 3). The second source I will use was written by Frederic William Naylor Bayley (1808-53). On the day of his eighteenth birthday, Bayley, the son of a British officer, was told that he had to move to the British colonies of the West Indies with his father. During the second half of the 1820s he lived mainly on the island of Barbados and also visited St. Lucia, St. Vincent, Trinidad, Anguilla, Barbuda, and Montserrat. The main purpose of his travelogue was to shed new light on the condition of slaves (cf. Bayley 1833: 3-5). The third travelogue to be examined in order to discuss if and how the European colonizers creolized their food consumption patterns is Matthew Lewis' (1775-1818) (cf. Lewis 1999). After his father bequeathed to him two sugarcane plantations, Cornwall and Hordley, Lewis travelled twice to Jamaica. During his trips, he lived mainly at Cornwall plantation in the Westmoreland parish of Southwestern Jamaica, where he stayed for four months in 1816 and six months in 1817-18. While in Jamaica, Lewis wrote a very detailed diary on many aspects of the colonizers' life.

These travel diaries are extremely useful to reconstruct and to understand how the colonizers adapted their food consumption habits to the new environment and to illustrate how their food consumption patterns contributed to a change in the previous foodways. My analysis of the travelogues revolves around the issue of how eating is represented and whether and how the colonizers' accounts describe a process of food creolization. I set out to investigate how the colonizers reacted to the encounter with foreign food; if they maintained their previous food culture or if they accustomed themselves to the new food; what strategies they employed to settle in the new food environment; and finally how the colonizers portrayed and perceived the phenomenon of food creolization.

---

6 Cf. Morgan (1999: 42-78); McWilliam (2005: 43-53); Fox-Genovese (1988: 32-33); O'Callaghan (2004: 1-16).
7 There is very little information on Carmichael's life. Cf., for example, Williamson (2008: 1-17).
8 She described her attitude as "attentive observation" (Carmichael 1833: I, vi).

A First Taste of the New Foods: Drawing Analogies with the Homeland

Many European colonizers in the Caribbean tried to maintain their previous eating habits. The colonizers' attempts to cling to their familiar eating customs might be explained by the fact that, as Jack Goody noted, "[t]he hierarchy between ranks and classes takes a culinary form" (Goody 1982: 113). Despite the desire and the imperial need to emphasize a colonial hierarchical order, however, the colonizers only managed to arrive at a synthesis between their own habits and the local ones.

This process is well illustrated in Carmichael's diary, in which she stressed her resolve to follow her old eating customs after her arrival in the Caribbean island of St. Vincent. On the very first day in the Caribbean, she wrote that she and her family had spent the evening "in the same way as in England, drinking tea between seven and eight" (Carmichael 1833: I, 12). A few days later she was invited to a dinner "at five in the afternoon" (I, 33). This was the customary time of the evening meal, already described by Dunn in his work on the 17th and 18th centuries as "a very hot time of the day for heavy eating in the West Indies" (Dunn 2000: 279). But this dinner, even though it was scheduled as in England at five in the afternoon, was a fusion between the familiar and the unknown. As Carmichael wrote, although the banquet she was invited to was given at the customary British time, "the dinner was like all West Indian dinners;" a huge amount of food was served, to the point that, as she noted, "I instinctively drew my feet from under the table, in case it should be borne to the ground" (Carmichael 1833: I, 34). Even the drinks served at this dinner were a mixture between the familiar and the unknown: they had London porter, for example, a traditional British dark beer that, in her view, in the Caribbean weather "acquires a degree of mildness and flavor far beyond that which it ever attains in Britain" (I, 37). In particular, Carmichael criticized the Caribbean cooking for the lack of desserts; on the rare occasion they were prepared, they were too expensive and did not live up to the excellent British style (cf. I, 51-53). In her opinion, shared by the majority of European travellers, the reason for the lack of good desserts was the scarcity of suitable ingredients. For example, she found that the local gooseberry was too acidic and "unfit for use unless when baked in tarts, when it serves as a humble imitation of the English gooseberry" (I, 11).

In Carmichael's view, the scarcity of familiar food very often forced the colonizers to use local food as a substitute for English ingredients not existing in the West Indies. This absence of 'their' food compelled the colonists to reconsider the value and the significance of the 'new' food, which instead was widely available. Despite her opinion on the inferiority of the Caribbean gooseberry cited above, she did believe that in the Caribbean islands one could find good alternatives for English food. For example, she wrote that "the guava bush is indigenous to most of the islands [...] when stewed with sugar, are not unlike the flavor of a strawberry" and the fruit of the guava bush was often cooked "into jelly by coloured free women" from which she "regularly" bought (Carmichael 1833: 177-86). Moreover, she found an excellent alternative for her "apple fritters" in the local "fried [...] ripe plantains" (ibid.).

This strategy of looking for imitations of familiar food is widely described by Lewis as well. He defined a vegetable called "calalue" as "a species of spinach" (Lewis 1999: 68); he noted that a local rat called "Cane-piece Cat [...] might have been mistaken for a very good game-soup" only when cooked in a "high seasoned stew [...] with negro pepper and salt" (147).

In a similar way, Bayley's travelogue also uses the similarities and comparisons to describe local food. His diary shows a young man who not only seemed to really appreciate local food and dishes (cf. Berti 2013a), but also noted that a good number of Caribbean vegetables resembled and were used as a replacement for well-known colonizers' ingredients. In his description of the vegetables grown by slaves, he wrote:

The plantain or yams are to the negro, what the potatoe [sic] are to the lower classes in Britain. [...] Yams are planted by cutting, in the same way as the English potatoe. [...] Tania is a root something of the size of a potatoe. The sweet cassada [sic] is a farinaceous root resembling the carrot only in shape, for in colour and taste is more like the yam. (Bayley 1833: 161-73)

However, it should be added that the vast majority of writers used this kind of comparative similarity (and dissimilarity) as a literary trope to help their readers understand what they were writing about. More generally, looking for similarities and dissimilarities was and still is part of a wider human tendency to enhance our understanding by drawing analogies; in fact, such a tendency to look for analogies had already become established as a typical European way to represent the 'new world' during the first centuries of colonization of the Americas (cf. Earle 2010).

THE ROLE OF THE "NEGROES": COOKS, RETAILERS, AND PEASANTS

In her diary, Carmichael explained the clashes between the familiar and the unknown, the encounter between old and new food, and the related search for resemblances in just one word: according to her, it all depended on the cook. It was because of the cook, usually a Creole[9] or an African man, that "a West Indian kitchen is so different from an English one" (Carmichael 1833: I, 114-15). Even though "the likings and dislikings of negroes are very different from those of a European [...] a negro cookery is by no means so despicable as some suppose" (II, 169). It was a female slave, or usually a man according to Carmichael's accounts, that selected the food to be bought and the dishes to be served in the families belonging to the local elite.

The crucial role played by cooks is also highlighted in the diary of Frederika Bremer (1801-65), a Swedish feminist novelist who visited Cuba in 1851. Her diary is a collection of the correspondence between her and her sister in which she recorded "that which I saw and found in the New World" (Bremer 1853: I, vii). In writing about Cuba and the Creole population who lived on the island, Bremer pointed out that "the ladies in this country have very light house-keeping care" (II, 280) because of the help they received from their cook. The people in charge of the kitchen in the Cuban houses are described in very similar, racial terms to the cook in Carmichael's diary. According to Bremer:

> The cook, always a negro woman, and if a man, a negro also, receives a certain sum of money weekly, with which to provide the family dinners. She goes to market and makes purchases, and selects that which seems best to her, or what she likes. The lady of the house frequently does not know what the family will have for dinner until it is on the table; and I can only wonder that the mistress can, with such perfect security, leave these matter to the cooks, and that all should succeed so well: but the faculty for, and the pleasure in all that concerns serving the table, is said to be universal among the negroes, and they compromise their honour if they do not serve a good dinner. (ibid.)

As shown in Bremer's *Impressions*, in Cuba the phenomenon of food creolization was already well established in 1851, when she visited the island. In Bremer's writings there is no mention of the "likings or dislikings" of the fami-

---

9 "As the term Creole is often in England understood to imply a Mulatto, it is best to explain that the word Creole means a native of a West India colony, whether he be white, black, or of the coloured population" (Carmichael 1833: II, 17).

lies who employed a "negro woman" as a cook in their kitchen. Bremer's only statement concerns the good reputation of the cooks, "their honour [sic] if they do not serve a good dinner." As is evident from both Carmichael's and Bremer's accounts and impressions of the diet of the colonist elite, the food that they consumed was in the process of being creolized as a direct result of the cross-cultural relationships between the Caribbean-born cooks and the people who ate the food which they chose and prepared. Notably, slaves also played an active role in other aspects of the establishment of a colonists' creolized diet: in fact, the great majority of the available food was also raised, fished, hunted, farmed, and sold by Africans and Afro-Creoles.[10]

ENJOYING CREOLE FOOD

British colonists were not simply forced to eat creolized food—they also learnt how to appreciate it. Lewis, for example, was convinced that one of the best ways to eat food in the West Indies was to season and to cook it in the Creole style. He especially praised the immense variety of soups cooked in the "Creole" way (Lewis 1999: 68). In a similar fashion, Carmichael pointed out that "the creole soups are [...] much liked" and that she "never met with an European who did not relish all the different creole soups or, as they are often called, negro pot" (Carmichael 1833: I, 51, 53). According to the colonists, these soups were commonly eaten by all the different social and ethnic groups of the West Indies population. "Calialou[11] [...] is a favourite vegetable with white, coloured, and black [...] and a soup cooked with a root called eddoe, [...] This soup is excellent, [...] and palatable to all – creoles, white, free, coloured or slave" (I, 161-73 and II, 68). This excerpt from Carmichael's diary allows to examine how colonizers represented the food habits of those living in the Caribbean, including slaves: she claimed that all those living in the Caribbean, "creoles, white, free, coloured or slave," at least for their everyday meals, had the same type of food and dishes.

Even if Carmichael tried to cling as much as she could to her British food and foodways, she was also affected by the process of food creolization among "white people" (I, 51) who lived in the Caribbean islands. In her diary, she pro-

---

10 Cf. for example, Carmichael 1833: I, 177-186. In another entry Carmichael also wrote: "in town I was regularly supplied with all the fruits, roots, vegetables, poultry, eggs, pork, and also goat and kid, by the negro slaves" (Carmichael 1833: II, 286).

11 Lewis too describes callaloo: "Calalue (a species of spinach) is a principal article in their pepper-pots" (Lewis 1999: 68).

vided a wealth of useful information on the colonizers' food habits. Seafood was said to be their "chief food" to which they added fowl, pork, beef, a stew called Irish mess, salted meat, and fish (I, 51-3). An example of creolization of the colonists' food consumption patterns can be seen from this list of the different proteins eaten by the "white people" (ibid.). Even if they maintained part of their eating habits by consuming beef, Irish mess, and sometimes pudding,[12] the daily diet of the colonists described by Carmichael was going through a process of creolization. Not only were the colonists used to have salted meat and fish, which were usually consumed by the slaves as well, but they also consumed "fried jack-fish [...with] a roasted plantain, or yam" (I, 51-4)—a typical Creole dish today too. Carmichael's careful description of jack-fish is also revealing of an ongoing change in her diet: "The jack-fish is indeed an excellent fish, resembling the herring in size, and somewhat in flavour also" (I, 51-4). The theme of resemblance emerges once more; apparently, jack-fish is similar to a herring.

If Carmichael felt the need to compare jack-fish to a familiar fish and in a very exact way, one may assume that the Britons who did not live in the Caribbean colonies did not commonly eat jack-fish and, moreover, that its consumption in the colonies was part of a wider process of food creolization. She wrote directly about this process in an excerpt that is worth quoting in full:

Those who have been long settled, and who are accustomed to this style of living, take it very contentedly, and ask their intimate friends to come and eat a fish with them; but they know this is not the style of living in England, and it is not before a considerable lapse of time that they consider you sufficiently creolized [sic], to invite you and eat fish, and when they do, it is a sure sign that they consider you no longer as a ceremonious visiter [sic]. (I, 51-3)

The use of the term "accustomed," the contrast drawn between "this style of living" and "the style of living in England" and between "visiter" and "long settled" clearly indicate that Carmichael perceived the existence of a widespread phenomenon of food creolization. In her own words, colonists never invited newcomers to have fish but they preferred to wait a long time, until they could "consider you sufficiently creolized" (I, 53).

Lewis also frequently mentioned dishes cooked in the Creole style. On January 14 1816, he invited a few guests, described as "white people," for a dinner at his plantation house (Lewis 1999: 66). The menu included a great variety of dishes, among which at least two recipes were autochthonous to the West Indies:

---

12 Cf. Carmichael 1833, I, 52 where she wrote on pudding: "Pudding and sweet dishes of any kind are little used in families except rare occasions."

barbecued pork and pepperpot. Pepperpot was, and still is, a Caribbean stew cooked with meat or fish. Lewis described it as a soup cooked with at least salted fish and callaloo—apparently, common ingredients in the meals given to the slaves working in the sugarcane plantations (cf. 68, 117). In the aforementioned journal entry there is no trace of negative comments on the food served at his table or any indication that his guests did not like it. Since in his diary Lewis proves to be a very skilful observer, it is not difficult to imagine that, if his guests' impressions on the meal had been negative, he would have noticed it, and modified the menu to be served on future occasions.

In fact, two weeks later, on January 29, Lewis invited again a few "gentlemen" to dinner at his house. The creole food was still on the menu. As he wrote:

We had a barbecued pig, [...] the best and richest dishes that I ever tasted; [...] which was dressed in the true maroon fashion, [...] I have eaten several other good Jamaica dishes, but none so excellent as this. (94-5)[13]

When comparing this dinner with the previous one, the strong number of 'indigenous' dishes, that is dishes 'invented' in the Caribbean, with a strong African influence strikes even more.

Again, on February 25 he wrote that his "water-mill did not work properly" because there was a "large alligator" which was clogging the mill's grating. As soon as Lewis realized that he could take the opportunity to taste the alligator's flavor, he "ordered it to be broiled for dinner." He asked for it to be dressed in the Creole style, with pepper, salt, and onion sauce "and [declared] the dish to be a very good one" (119-20). What is evident here is a habit of consuming local food products and cooking techniques that he insistently labelled as "Creole." Of course, the episode of the alligator could also be interpreted as the result of Lewis' desire to show off his open-mindedness and his bravery in eating 'strange' food. An analytical reading of the diary, however, shows that open-mindedness and bravery were not always peculiar characteristics of his personality. One of the first food descriptions in the diary concerns a "black pilot" who offers watermelon to those travelling between St. Christopher and Jamaica. Lewis' diary entries about food do not depict him as particularly interested in culinary experiences—he refuses this fruit and describes it as bled and with a taste of raw flesh (cf. 35; cf. Berti 2013b). They rather demonstrate that food creolization, as in Carmichael's writings, was a widespread process in the Caribbean islands during

---

13 The maroons were groups of fugitive slaves who fought guerrilla wars against the British colonizers and sought refuge in Jamaica's mountainous area.

the 19th century. Moreover, in addition to creolization, the analysis of Lewis' journal highlights another important aspect: the fascination of novelty.

THE IMPORTANCE OF NOVELTY IN PROMOTING A CREOLE DIET

In her article on the emergence of a European consumer culture, Maxine Berg sheds light on the pivotal role played by novelties (cf. Berg 1999). According to Berg, novelty was one of the fundamental factors that encouraged the growth of the consumer culture, as we know it today. Between the 17th and the 19th century, the increased consumption of exotic goods such as sugar,[14] coffee, tea, and chocolate was mostly due to their newness; it was the same desire for novelties that fostered consumption. A craving for new products also influenced the eating habits of European colonists in the Caribbean: it was such a desire for novelty that led Lewis to taste and to frequently eat local food even though he was not familiar with it and its cooking techniques.

If in Lewis' travelogue the attention paid to novelties and the desire to experiment with 'bizarre' food could be seen as extreme,[15] Bayley's diary offers a more balanced view, in which the appreciation of new recipes is linked with the feeling of homesickness for his food. Nonetheless, a close reading of both Lewis' and Bayley's accounts shows that their desire and their willingness to taste exotic foods was deeply connected with the novelty of the latter, even though in their diaries they never provide any information on the reasons why they were so fascinated by food novelties. In Lewis' diary, this appreciation for new food mainly emerges in the entries devoted to the food and its preparation. Bayley's travelogue instead is imbued with an intense desire to taste different foods, arguably to a degree that could be considered gourmandizing (cf. Berti 2013a). In almost all his visits to sugarcane plantation owners, there is a sense of expectation about the new foods that he will have a chance to taste. When, after four months in Barbados, he was scheduled to leave, Bayley wrote that he would spend four months more there because "I have eaten of the best soups and drunk of the best wines" (Bayley 1833: 144). Although he was nostalgic for mutton,

---

14 In *Sweetness and Power*, Sidney Mintz underlines that the consumption of sugar was a widespread habit among the middle classes and laborers in the 19th century (cf. Mintz 1985).

15 In addition to alligator, Lewis also tasted manatee, iguana and rat (cf. Berti 2013b).

lamb, beef, and veal of good quality,[16] the appreciation of the new food can be seen in his description of the local fish, which he praised as "delicacies which creole cooks dress better than my readers wot of" (148).[17] The food, its seasoning, and the Creole cooking techniques were all regarded by Bayley as delicacies. His enthusiasm about local food seems to suggest that, similarly to what was happening in Europe, the desire for newness was one of the forces that contributed to the diffusion of a Creole diet among the colonizers.

AN ESTABLISHED PROCESS OF FOOD CREOLIZATION

An excellent example of the outcomes of the process of food creolization is shown in the first Jamaican cookbook, *The Jamaica Cookery Book*, published in 1893 by Caroline Sullivan, the governess of a sugarcane plantation.[18] Although in the book there is no information about the intended readership, every time historians use cookbooks as a source they should underline to whom the books were addressed. In the Caribbean of the late 19th century, the number of people able to read was quite limited.[19] One could therefore argue that the recipients of cookbooks published in Jamaica and in the West Indies at the end of the 19th century were mainly the local Creole or European elite women. White women in the Caribbean did not have to do the actual cooking (they employed their own cooks), but were still able to appreciate Jamaican cuisine.[20] Moreover, recipe books were also bought as status symbols and "mirrored the life" (Neuhaus 2003: 2) of the people who bought them. Therefore, cookbooks of the past can also be used to investigate the economic and social aspirations of their buyers.[21]

---

16 He wrote that they "are not to be compared to any thing [sic] we get in England" (Bayley 1833: 148).

17 Wot is an archaism, the past form of the verb "to wit" that means "to know."

18 For a study on Caribbean cookbooks from the end of 19th century to the end of 20th century, cf. Higman (1998: 77–95).

19 Even if there is no exact data on literacy rates in the West Indies, Knight and Palmer point out that primary school became compulsory only in the 20th century (cf. Knight and Palmer 1989: 10).

20 Cf. Inness (2006: 3-7); Neuhaus (2003: 1); Leonardi (1989: 340-347); Teophano (2002: 6, 14).

21 Cf. Neuhaus (2003) as well as Mennell (1985). Mennell observed the connection between cookbooks and status symbol pointing out that cookbooks were amongst the earliest printed books "associated [...] with the symbolism required of aristocratic

The Jamaica Cookery Book shows that by the end of the 19th century the colonizers had completely changed their food consumption patterns, eating in a new way that may be defined as creole. Sullivan's recipes show that practices such as the adaptation, substitution, incorporation, and indigenization of ingredients and methods of preparation had eventually become part of the standard Jamaican cuisine.[22] In her codification of the local cuisine, Sullivan included butter and the traditional British sauces, Worcester or Harvey, with Jamaican pepper; she used Porto, a common drink of the British colonizers, to prepare patties; and in her "cool drink" section she suggested squeezing lime, a tropical citrus fruit, instead of lemon, more common in Great Britain (cf. Sullivan 1893: 24-36, 151–160).

Not only were British and European foods introduced in the Jamaican cuisine, but also the same symbolic meaning of certain food was modified. For instance, Sullivan wrote that, while in England salted fish was usually eaten as a "penitential dish," in Jamaica it was widely consumed by all social and ethnic groups: "there is hardly a more popular dish [...]. Here it is almost daily, and certainly the favourite [sic], food of the people generally, and cooked as they cook it cannot fail to please the most fastidious" (Sullivan 1893: 37-43). The examination of the ingredients and recipes in Sullivan's cookbook allows to understand that the kitchen can be regarded as a site of creolization in which a food-based identity emerges from the encounter of various eating cultures.

When Bayley lived in the Caribbean, he noted a process of food creolization, exemplified by a simple observation about yam: "The yam is a very fine vegetable and when roasted and eaten with butter is deemed by many superior to the English potatoe [sic]" (Bayley 1833: 553-4). Of course, he did not write that he preferred yam to potatoes, even if he usually had a creole breakfast that included "flying fish and roasted yam, with a good cup of coffee" (66-7). He simply observed that many colonizers preferred yam to potato, but they were said to consume yam exactly in the same way as they ate potatoes in Europe, seasoning them with butter. Perhaps this preference was due to economic (cf. Carmichael 1833: I, 51–53) or practical (cf. Lewis 1999: 131) reasons, but, in my view, what Bayley wanted to communicate to his readers was that British people were now used to eat yam in the same way as they once had eaten potato—a prime example of food creolization.

---

feasting" (Mennell 1985: 65). Furthermore, historian Carol Gold notes that only a minority of people who buy cookbooks "uses very many of the recipes" (Gold 2007: 11). These books are mainly bought because of their portrayal of a lifestyle one possibly aspires to.

22 In my view, it is not accurate to use the term "cuisine" prior to its codification that occurs with the writing or the publishing of a cookbook.

CONCLUSION

My analysis of these three colonial diaries allows to assert that Europeans in the Caribbean changed their habits and that the kitchen was, at least, one of the sites where the process of creolization occurred. On the one hand, consumption of familiar food made (and still makes) those living abroad feel protected; on the other hand, however, in the 19th century Caribbean, an exact replication of the colonizers' customary diet was impossible and unhealthy. The sources discussed in this paper show that during the 19th century the consumption of local food, even if it was not the only food eaten, was a common habit among the colonizers. These food habits not only gave rise to new eating practices but also created dynamic spaces of creolization, spaces that originated from the food and the cuisine. The sources produced by the white colonial elite, suggest that the Europeans who lived in the 19th-century Caribbean perceived that they shared the same food consumption pattern as the blacks and the Creoles—that is to say, creolized food. The Caribbean area is therefore one of the best examples of a process of food rejection, adaptation, and re-elaboration. Maura Franchi, an Italian sociologist, has written that *"consumando, costruiamo il nostro mondo"* (Franchi 2007: xi). This can be translated to "by consuming, we construct our world." Applying this sentence to the 19th-century colonists' food consumption patterns, by consuming and mixing different foods, the Europeans in the Caribbean contributed to the development of the Creole cuisine as we know it today (cf. Pilcher 2000).

BIBLIOGRAPHY

Bayley, Frederic William Naylor 1833. *Four Years' Residence in the West Indies during the Years 1826, 7, 8, and 9*. London: William Kidd.

Berg, Maxine 1999. "New Commodities, Luxuries and their Consumers in Eighteenth Century England." *Consumers and Luxury. Consumer Culture in Europe, 1650-1850*. Eds. Maxine Berg and Helen Clifford. Manchester: Manchester University Press, 63-85.

Berti, Ilaria 2013a. "Turisti Gourmet e Promozione Enogastronomica del Cibo Caraibico Durante l'Ottocento." *Miscellanea di Storia delle Esplorazioni* 38: 97-106.

—. 2013b. "Reinvenzione e Creolizzazione. Il Consumo Alimentare dei Colonizzatori Britannici ai Caraibi nel Diario di Matthew Lewis." *Acta Iassyensia Comparationis* 11.1: 65-70.

Bolland, O. Nigel 2002. "Creolisation and Creole Societies. A Cultural Nationalist View of Caribbean Social History." *Questioning Creole. Creolisation Discourses in Caribbean Culture.* Eds. Verene A. Shepherd and Glen R. Richards. Kingston: Ian Randle Publishers, 15-46.

Brathwaite, Kamau 1971. *The Development of a Creole Society in Jamaica, 1770-1820.* Oxford: Clarendon Press.

Braudel, Fernand 1966. *Il Mondo Attuale.* Turin: Einaudi.

Bremer, Frederika 1853. *The Houses of the New World. Impressions of America.* Vols. 1-2. New York: Harper & Brothers Publishers.

Burton, Richard D.E. 1997. *Afro-Creole. Power, Opposition, and Play in the Caribbean.* Ithaca / London: Cornell University Press.

Mrs. Carmichael 1833. *Domestic Manners and Social Condition of the Coloured, and Negro Population of the West Indies.* Vols. 1-2. London: Whittaker, Treacher, and Co.

Counihan, Carole 2000. *Food in the USA. A Reader.* New York: Routledge.

Crahan, Margaret E. and Franklin W. Knight, eds. 1979. *Africa in the Caribbean. The Legacies of a Link.* Baltimore / London: The Johns Hopkins University Press.

Dekker, Rudolf 2002a. "Introduction." *Egodocuments and History. Autobiographical Writings in Its Social Context Since the Middle Ages.* Ed. Rudolf Dekker. Hilversum: Verloren, 7-20.

—. 2002b. "Jacques Presser Heritage. Egodocuments in the Study of History." *Memoria y Civilización* 5: 13-37.

Dunn, Richard 2000 [1972]. *Sugar and Slaves. The Rise of the Planters' Class in the British West Indies, 1624-1713.* Chapel Hill: The University of North Carolina Press.

Earle, Rebecca 2010. "'If You Eat Their Food....' Diets and Bodies in Early Colonial Spanish America." *The American Historical Review* 115.3: 688-713.

Flandrin, Jean-Louis and Massimo Montanari, eds. 2003 [1996]. *Storia dell'Alimentazione.* Rome / Bari: Laterza.

Fox-Genovese, Elizabeth 1988. *Within the Plantation Household. Black and White Women of the South.* Chapel Hill: The University of North Carolina Press.

Franchi, Maura 2007. *Il Senso del Consumo.* Milan: Pearson Paravia Bruno Mondadori.

Frazier, Franklin E. 1939. *The Negro Family in the United States.* Chicago: University of Chicago Press.

Gabaccia, Donna 1998. *We Are What We Eat. Food and the Making of the Americas.* Cambridge, MA: Harvard University Press.

Gold, Carol 2007. *Danish Cookbooks. Domesticity and National Identity, 1616-1901.* Seattle: The University of Washington Press.
Goody, Jack 1982. *Cooking, Cuisine and Class. A Study in Comparative Sociology.* New York: Cambridge University Press.
Hannerz, Ulf 2001 [1996]. *La Diversità Culturale.* Bologna: Il Mulino.
Herskovitz, Melville Jean 1990 [1941]. *The Myth of the Negro Past.* Boston: Beacon Press.
Higman, Barry W. 1998. "Cookbooks and Caribbean Cultural Identity. An English-Language Hors d'Oeuvre." *New West Indian Guide / Nieuwe West-Indische Gids* 72: 1-2.
James, Cyril Lionel Robert 1968 [1938]. *I Giacobini Neri. La Prima Rivolta contro l'Uomo Bianco.* Milan: Feltrinelli.
Knight, Franklin and Colin Palmer 1989. "The Caribbean. A Regional Overview." *The Modern Caribbean.* Eds. Franklin Knight and Colin Palmer. Chapel Hill: The University of North Carolina Press: 1-20.
Inness, Sherrie 2006. *Secret Ingredients. Race, Gender and Class at the Dinner Table.* Basingstoke: Palgrave Macmillan.
Leonardi, Susan J. 1989. "Recipes for Reading. Summer Pasta, Lobster à la Riseholme and Key Lime Pie." *PMLA* 104.3: 340-347.
Leong-Salobir, Cecilia 2011. *Food Culture in Colonial Asia. A Taste of Empire.* Abingdon: Routledge.
Lewis, Matthew 1999 [1834]. *Journal of a West Indian Proprietor During a Residence in the Island of Jamaica.* Oxford: Oxford University Press.
McWilliam, James 2005. *A Revolution in Eating. How the Quest for Food Shaped Americas.* New York: Columbia University Press.
Mennell, Stephen 1985. *All Manners of Food. Eating and Taste in England and France from the Middle Ages to the Present.* Urbana: University of Illinois Press.
Mintz, Sidney and Richard Price 1976. *An Anthropological Approach to the Afro-American Past. A Caribbean Perspective.* Philadelphia: Institute for the Study of Human Issues.
—. 1985. *Sweetness and Power. The Place of Sugar in Modern History.* New York: Viking-Penguin.
—. 1996. *Tasting Food, Tasting Freedom. Excursions into Eating, Culture, and the Past.* Boston: Beacon Press.
Morgan, Philip 1999. "Encounters Between British and 'Indigenous' People, c. 1500-1800." *Empire and Others. British Encounters with Indigenous People, 1600-1850.* Eds. Martin Daunton and Rick Halpern. Philadelphia: The University of Pennsylvania Press, 42-78.

Neuhaus, Jessamyn 2003. *Manly Meals and Mom's Home Cooking. Cookbooks and Gender in Modern America.* Baltimore / London: The Johns Hopkins University Press.

Nutzenadel, Alexander and Frank Trentmann, eds. 2008. *Food and Globalization. Consumption, Markets and Politics in the Modern World.* Oxford / New York: Berg.

O'Callaghan, Evelyn 2004. *Women's Writing in the West Indies, 1804-1939. 'A Hot Place Belonging to Us.'* London / New York: Routledge.

Ortiz, Fernando 2007. *Contrappunto Cubano del Tabacco e dello Zucchero.* Troina: Città Aperta Edizioni.

Pilcher, Jeffrey M. 1998. *¡Que Vivan los Tamales! Food and the Making of Mexican Identity.* Albu-querque: University of New Mexico Press.

—. 2000. "The Caribbean from 1492 to Present." *The Cambridge World History of Food.* Vol. 2. Eds. Kenneth F. Kiple and Kriemhild Coneè Ornelas. Cambridge: Cambridge University Press, 1278-88.

Presser, Jacques 1958. "Memoires als Geschiedbron." *Winkler Prins Encyclopedie.* Vol. 8. Amsterdam / Brussels: Elsevier, 208-10.

Scholliers, Peter, ed. 2001. *Food, Drink and Identity. Cooking, Eating, Drinking in Europe since the Middle Ages.* Oxford: Berg.

Sullivan, Caroline 1893. *The Jamaican Cookery Book. Three Hundred and Twelve Recipes and Household Hints.* Kingston: Gardner.

Teophano, Janet 2002. *Eat my Words. Reading Women Lives through the Book they Wrote.* Basingstoke: Palgrave Macmillan.

Walcott, Derek 1992. Walcott's Nobel Prize lecture, "The Antilles: Fragments of Epic Memory." [http://www.nobelprize.org/nobel_prizes/literature/laureates/1992/walcott-lecture.html (retrieved 31 October 2013)].

Williamson, Karina 2008. "Mrs. Carmichael. A Scotswoman in the West Indies, 1820-26." *International Journal of Scottish Literature* 4: 1-17.

Wilson, Thomas, ed. 2006. "Food, Drink and Identity in Europe." Special Issue of *European Studies* 22.

Representations of Caribbean Food in U.S. Popular Culture

FABIO PARASECOLI

The Western imagination has historically perceived the Caribbean as a contested space of escape, fantasy, exploitation, as well as race and class contamination. As the presence of the United States in the region was closely associated with sugarcane and fruit production, it was inevitable that food and eating played an important role in the way Americans have represented and experienced the Caribbean.

However, at times the Caribbean is too close for comfort for its northern neighbors, especially when the massive presence of its diasporic communities on American soil turns the inhabitants of the islands from exotic Others to neighbors in everyday life. When I invited a Lukumi priest to talk to my classes about the food norms and practices in his religion, and how those elements have been adapted to foreign urban environments, students appeared to be utterly surprised and slightly troubled by the discovery of the vitality of Afro-Caribbean religions in their own backyard. American history and cultures are more connected with the Caribbean world than many would care to admit. In fact, when talking about food, it can be argued that the Caribbean spans from South Carolina to Salvador de Bahia, as the work of culinary historians suggests (cf. Carney and Rosomoff 2009; Harris 2003: 1-17; Schiebinger and Swan 2005).

Popular culture, a simmering cauldron in which we are all steeped, provides interesting material to attempt a reflective analysis on the cultural perceptions of the Caribbean in the U.S. Practices, objects, and representations in U.S. popular culture, including movies, music, tourism, advertising, and food marketing, serve to reproduce, question, or reinforce cultural assumptions about the Caribbean. They offer a unique gateway to investigate the ambivalence of desire and fear, pleasure and abjection that have informed social and political negotiations around the construction of the islands as a real and imaginary space. In particular, I will focus on bananas and their use in the construction of colonial subjects who are excluded from society's power structures and whose existence is perceived in connection with the entertainment and the satisfaction of white audiences in the North. These elements have gained widespread visibility in the global exchanges and fluxes of communication, objects, visual material, norms, values, and behaviors that constitute contemporary popular culture.

In this chapter, I will also build on these examples to raise more general pedagogical and methodological questions about the use of popular culture in the study of food, and the use of food in the study of popular culture. Food constitutes an important site of social practice whose relevance cannot be ignored. Eating is a realm of personal and social experience that is usually considered a mere expression of 'natural' instincts and biological needs and that, precisely for this reason, is not politically and culturally sensitive. However, food production and consumption are far from being simply natural: culturally and socially constructed, they are determined by economic and political dynamics and as such they are submitted to change. These dynamics constitute the engine of the historical developments that we witness in material and popular culture. Food's apparently neutral and often uncontested normality can reveal aspects of cultural and social tensions that are otherwise concealed, offering a privileged point of view to look at the encompassing, worldwide webs of meaning established by the global network of popular culture.

Even the most cursory glance at how representations and practices around Caribbean food shape and are shaped by perceptions, social structures, and economic relationships indicates how the stakes are higher than they might seem. Nothing would appear more natural and normal than eating fruit, an important element in human diets all over the world and in all historical periods; however, there can be enormous differences in what fruits are eaten, how, where, and by whom they are grown, harvested, transported, distributed, marketed, and consumed.

The bananas, probably first domesticated in South East Asia and today's Papua-New Guinea, did not make their appearance in the Caribbean until the arrival of the Europeans, who had already introduced them in Brazil from the West African coast. The fruit became a staple crop, mostly grown in small quantities for self-sufficiency, an important source of starch for slave populations, and a buffer among harvests of commercial crops such as pepper, cacao, and coffee (cf. Langdon 1993).

Larger scale production of bananas was not established until the early 1830s, when the crisis of the plantation complex based on slavery and the explosion of beet sugar production affected the economic viability of sugarcane cultivations. Shortly after the Civil War, Americans in cities on the Northeastern seaboard began consuming bananas, but only on a small scale as difficulties in transportation kept prices quite high (cf. Koeppel 2008: 51-53). The expansion of faster transportation networks based on steamships and railroads, together with the development of refrigeration technology and the diffusion of the sturdy Gros Michel banana variety, allowed the fruit to be exported in increasingly larger quantities to North America (cf. Soluri 2003). From the 1880s, low marshlands were drained and forests were cleared to grow bananas in Central America, where large foreign companies adopted intense monoculture systems and vertical integration. The United Fruit Company, founded in 1899, and the Standard Fruit Company, launched in 1924, soon emerged as the biggest players, heavily influencing politics and economic policy in the Caribbean and Central America (cf. Tucker 2000; Wiley 2008).

As bananas became cheaper, Americans started consuming them in great quantities and images related to the tropical fruit production began to appear in North America (cf. Jenkins 2000)—photography, a relatively new medium by the last decades of the nineteenth century, was already permeating U.S. popular culture. In 1888, the commercialization of George Eastman's Kodak Camera made photos easy and available. Photos of manual work in Caribbean and Central American banana plantations deserve great attention. Although they were sometimes commissioned and paid for by fruit companies as a way to document the oversea operations, we cannot avoid wondering if the images also served other functions. Were there other recipients besides the companies' management and stockholders? What circulation did they have outside the companies' archives? How were they received? And also within the fruit companies, what kinds of perceptions did they generate, reinforce, or question about the far-away places where the products were grown and the people that cultivated them? As the collection at the Washington Banana Museum in Auburn, Washington, indicates, scenes of the banana industry were also represented in images that were to be enjoyed through a special device known as a stereoscope. It involved the simultaneous viewing of a pair of slightly differing two-dimensional images—known as stereoviews—to give the illusion of three dimensions. All the phases of production, from harvest to cultivation and transportation, are illustrated in stereoviews, pointing to the interest of the public at large in this fruit and the world it came from.

The nature and content of these representations contest the supposed neutrality of visual media such as photography and later video. The very decision of taking a picture, selecting subjects, and framing them in a specific way, identify objects or practices as worthy of interest, defining them as self-standing phenomena while somehow detaching them from the surrounding flow of reality that is considered irrelevant for the author of the image and his or her audience. These choices are inevitably influenced by cultural and ideological factors. In discussing the way images inherently encode aspects of history and how photography acquired dominance among other kinds of images due to its alleged capacity to "capture the moment," visual scholars Lynn Hunt and Vanessa R. Schwartz comment:

Images have a deeply ambivalent relationship to time. The single image appears to freeze it, capture it, and memorialize it, and in doing so works against the flow of duration. Yet images are also resolutely historical since they incorporate within their very material a history of their making: a long history of techniques, preferences for subjects, and expectations about viewers. (Hunt and Schwartz 2010: 259)

Scholar Robert Burgoyne argues that, through photography, historical events become experiences that shape individual viewers and generate new kind of "experiential collective memories," whose constructed and mass-mediated nature inspired Alison Landsberg's reference to photographs as "prosthetic memories" (cf. Burgoyne 2003; Landsberg 2003).

Photos from plantations illustrate various phases of cultivation, collection, and transportation of bananas. The fruit could not be extricated from manual work, usually carried out by individuals who were clearly identifiable as lower class labor, even when they temporarily interrupted their activities to have their pictures taken. Their demeanor and clothing differentiated them from the overseers and other characters that seem to be in charge of the operations. Although apparently purely denotative, these pictures reinforced the perception of plantation workers as subaltern subjects whose presence is closely connected—if not justified—by their function as food producers for the companies, and indirectly for the upper class and foreign consumers.

These representations might have been important at a time when bananas were a little-known crop making its appearance in the relatively developed U.S. market from an area perceived as beyond the physical borders and outside the national project. Images can mediate fears—or at least suspicions—about the ingestion of a fruit that was unfamiliar and connected with cultures often interpreted as marginal and underdeveloped, but for that very reason ready for the taking by a superior civilization. As sociologist Claude Fischler has observed, humans are always torn between *neophilia*, the desire to try new foods that could become sources of nutrition and energy, and *neophobia*, the awareness that those foods could also be damaging, poisonous, or even fatal (cf. Fischler 1980 and 1988). In the case of bananas and exotic fruits, emphasizing the superiority of consumers and their complete detachment from producers may have assuaged anxieties about unknown substances. Furthermore, buyers were reminded that other foreigners guaranteed quality and safety by controlling production. "In the context of nineteenth-century United States," as literary critic Kyla Wazana Tompkins points out, "[e]ating threatened the foundational fantasy of a contained autonomous self—the 'free' Liberal self—because, as a function of its basic mechanics, eating transcended the gap between self and other, blurring the line between subject and object" (Tompkins 2012: 3). Tompkins also notices that between the Louisiana Purchase and the Civil War, whiteness had become the "dominant racial position" in American society, projected also onto outside spaces that could be included in the United States' "imperial and civilizing agenda" (72). At the same time, the act of looking at photos sets viewers in a privileged and dominant position, as the objects of their gaze can neither look back nor offer any other form of resistance. The subjects of the pictures were made available for the inspection and scrutiny of actors in the U.S., whatever their position may have been in the production chain.

Caribbean bananas became the theme of other kinds of visual representations besides photos, from posters to postcards and trade cards. A prevalent element was the cleanliness of the clothes of the workers. Although engaged in manual and tiring work, both men and women working in plantations or transporting fruits are frequently depicted as wearing simple but otherwise immaculate clothes, often white. This element may have been meant to underline the product's purity and healthiness, a necessity due to the dubious origin of the fruit. At the same time, the tidiness of workers could also be interpreted as a form of cultural erasure of the harsh working conditions in the plantations, an aspect that transpired more directly from photos and stereoviews. Visual representations in popular culture succeeded in establishing and solidifying ideas and expectations about banana production, exotic workers in faraway lands, and the proper relationship between them and the more advanced and civilized consumers. In turn, these perceptions were enmeshed in discourses, practices, and institutional structures that encompassed transportation, hygiene, trade, legislation, marketing, consumption, etc.

These first observations require a clarification of popular culture as a field of research, which due to its ever-changing and disparate objects, its varied actors, and its constant expansion, comes across as slippery and hard to delimit. In this context, we can regard popular culture as the totality of ideas, values, embodied experiences, representations, discourses, material items, practices, social relations, organizations, and institutions that are conceived, produced, distributed, and consumed within environments influenced by market and consumption, with or without the specific economic goal of reaping a profit. Considered as such, popular culture includes the mainstream and all possible alternative or oppositional subcultures, as well as the evolving dynamics through which the mainstream is constantly defined, reinforced, and resisted. From the methodological point of view, this kind of research requires a productive dialogue with various disciplines (anthropology, sociology, political sciences, economics, cultural studies, media and communication) and fields (food, gender, ethnicity studies).

While it is impossible to look at the whole of popular culture due to its complexity, pervasiveness, and breadth—we must keep popular culture in its totality in the background of research, so that we can follow connections and ramifications, including to unexpected places. However, for practical reasons it is more efficient to define and limit the primary object that we are looking at, both in terms of time and space. In our case, we are exploring popular culture representations and practices connected with Caribbean food, bananas in particular. Yet we have to remember that as focused as our research might be, these representations often have global implications, as since their inception they have been enmeshed in transnational networks of production, trade, consumption, practices, and discourse. At the same time, we need to distinguish between the contemporary dynamics of globalized popular culture and previous forms of exchange of information, media, and behaviors.

An important implication of this historical approach to popular culture is that it uncovers its evolving characteristics and impact, urging us to interpret contexts to highlight differences and explore the social and cultural environment in which a communication took place or an object was created. Looking at the beginning of banana consumption in the U.S., what distinguished turn of the twentieth century popular culture from similar phenomena from previous periods should be understood in terms of speed and intensity of change, heralded by increasingly rapid technological advances in food production, transportation, and distribution. As we will see, the budding globalization of ideas, people, goods, and money allowed popular cultures in different parts of the world to interact and, to a certain extent, share some elements. Ripples traveled faster and wider in the global 'meaning pond' while objects, practices, and representations took on new connotations, sometimes even denotations, when adopted and used in different contexts, a phenomenon that Arjun Appadurai and Igor Kopytoff aptly defined as "the social life" and "the cultural biography" of things (cf. Appadurai 1986, Kopytoff 1986).

In North America, at the turn of the twentieth century, bananas were still considered as novelties, interesting enough to be featured in photos meant to constitute mementos of special occasions. Among the material collected by the Washington Banana Museum in Auburn,[1] several photos depict groups of people in nice clothes that seem to enjoy different kinds of social activities, from picnics to outings in the countryside to car rides. The collection also includes a tintype showing two well-dressed men and women against a painted background—probably a memento for family and friends—with the men holding a big bunch of bananas, prominently displayed in the foreground. In another picture, the five members of a female theater troupe from Chicago, elegantly dressed in all white and wearing elaborated hats, all hold bananas, whole in various stages of peeling, in their hands. What would seem to present-day viewers an incongruous presence might be explained by the status of the banana as a relatively recent novelty. Since their price was still considerable, the bananas were displayed as symbols of modernity, hipness, and conspicuous consumption.

Already in the 1910s, the fruit had become commonplace enough to be consumed as a snack during work breaks or for a stop on the road. By the time the Great Depression hit the United States, the fruit had lost its exotic appeal and was solidly integrated into the American diet. Bananas were appreciated for their nutritional value and, in a period concerned with disease and disease transmission, for their perceived sterility, supposedly ensured by the peel. In previous decades, the country had already revealed its obsession with diet as a tool for agendas that not only promoted health but also propriety, civilization, and citizenship (cf. Levenstein 2012). In Sylvester Graham's writings from the 1830s (which maintained a certain popularity until the 1880s), exotic foods like sugar, coffee, spices, and wine were considered, due to their excessively stimulating nature, as potentially threatening not only for the body of American citizens, but also for the political body of the United States and its position vis-à-vis the space from where these products came. In Tompkins' words, "foreign excitants threaten to become the totality of the consumer, concretizing diet as a central term in the imperial metonymy between body, home, and nation" (Tompkins 2012: 81).

Bananas' perceived healthiness made them a good food with children. Advertisers built on this aspect to promote the fruit among mothers and doctors. By so doing, they also created a built-in market, with consumers used to consuming bananas since their childhood, and for that reason potentially more devoted to the product. Unlike other tropical items from the Caribbean, bananas were not stimulants. Products like Banana-Nutro, launched as a coffee substitute, could

---

[1] Available online at: Banana Museum [http://www.bananamuseum.com/ (retrieved 31 October 2013)].

avoid the "constipation and indigestions" that stimulants could cause, as a contemporary advertisement claims. Banana-Nutro was made with banana flour, embracing the use of the fruit as a staple, just like in its lands of origin.

Nevertheless, unlike wheat and other cereals, bananas could not be construed as a civilized and essential staple, a perception that ran against the strategies of producing companies. At most, they could "make every fruit and cereal better," bringing out the flavor of other products. Furthermore, consumers were constantly reminded of the provenance of bananas, which maintained some exotic allure while reaffirming their colonial nature. Images of tropical landscapes and of plantation labor were often displayed in advertising and editorial pages in magazines, closely associating bananas with a distinct colonial identity that underlined its subaltern character. From this point of view, bananas shared the same place in the American diet as coconuts, another tropical product. The fruit could not aspire to become a staple-like element in civilized meals, but was kept on their margins as a snack or in desserts, such as the popular banana split.[2]

Lore locates the invention of the banana split either in 1904 in Latrobe, Pennsylvania, or in 1907 in Wilmington, Ohio. Latrobe celebrated the 100th anniversary in 2004, the year that the National Ice Cream Retailers Association (NICRA) certified the city as its birthplace. However, Wilmington organizes a Banana Split Festival every June, and supports its claim with a picture supposedly taken in 1907 at Hazard's, a restaurant indicated as the dessert's birthplace, where the banana split is listed on what seems like a menu or advertising board above the counter. Whatever its origin, the immediate popularity of the dessert points to the relevance of the fruit in the leisure practices of the period, which increasingly placed aspects of food consumption at their core. The banana split could be consumed at soda fountains, in cafes, and in restaurants, providing a relatively affordable indulgence.

The close connection with colonial production was never totally erased, and it was frequently made visible in an array of marketing media and objects used to boost sales. Banana workers were often featured, always smiling and happy to provide American consumers with the delightful treat. This element appears particularly relevant at a time when the political power of American fruit companies was so pervasive in Central America that the expression "banana republic," coined by the American writer O. Henry in *Cabbages and Kings* (1904), came to

---

2   The banana split is a dessert, usually served in a narrow oblong dish (called a "boat"). It is composed of a banana split in two lengthwise and ice cream scoops (usually chocolate, vanilla, and strawberry), topped with whipped cream and often a maraschino cherry.

indicate corrupt and politically unstable countries where the State operated to the advantage of private profit, both domestic and foreign.

Bananas and tropical fruits appeared constantly in advertising for Caribbean cruises, which were organized and made profitable by the same companies that grew and sold bananas, like United Fruit Company and Standard Fruit Company. On cruises, affluent American consumers could enjoy the sights and the flavors of the Caribbean without getting too close or through very controlled excursions that limited the actual interaction with the locals and their environments. In visual representations, cruise guests are often represented looking at the coast from afar, "living the past in present day comfort," as United Fruit cruise posters proclaimed. The islands were explicitly represented as spaces rooted in the past and as cultural leftovers in the history of progress, where white actors played the leading role. Locals were often depicted as providers of fruit to the ships' guests, underlining their subaltern role and their dependence from American consumers for their survival. The Caribbean cruises in the first decades of the twentieth century mark the beginning of what is now sometimes referred to as the "tourist bubble," where visitors are shepherded through a set of pre-organized activities and spaces that do not allow any real contact with the local culture (cf. Jaakson 2004). This set-up is particularly troublesome because it limits any positive impact of cruises on the coastal economies, especially when it comes to food procurement. Oftentimes, the dishes and specialties offered by local restaurants and stalls are depicted by cruise organizers as unhygienic, potentially harmful, and served in unsafe areas that tourists should avoid.

A small aside is necessary to briefly comment on the pervasiveness of the use of banana peels as a comic device in printed cartoons and films from the period. These representations probably reflected the actual presence of banana peels on the streets due to increased consumption, while allowing for movement and action in silent movies and graphic art, where physical comedy had to make up for the absence of dialogues. At the same time, they seem to suggest resistance and rebelliousness, as though the naughty fruit was taking its vengeance against proper and civilized individuals. Later on, this performative element was also often included in animated cartoons, which were initially mostly geared towards adult audiences. Could this be interpreted as an expression of anxiety toward the colonial—hence potentially unruly—origin of the fruit? Could the peel symbolize the potential danger of bananas as the result of colonial labor?

Representations and practices around bananas are so ramified that it can be daunting to follow all the connections across different fields of research, often the domain of specific disciplines with well-defined methodologies. How can we deal with this enormous amount of material? It can be useful to approach the very diverse aspects of popular culture as expressions of a single "code," in the sense introduced by film theorist Kaja Silverman:

A code represents a sort of bridge between texts. Its presence within one text involves a simultaneous reference to all of the other texts in which it appears, as to the cultural reality which it helps to define – i.e. to a particular symbolic order... The codes which manifest themselves through connotation function endlessly to repeat what has been written in other books and portrayed in other films, and so to reproduce the existing cultural order. Repetition does the same thing for that order as constant re-interpellation does for the subject. It creates the illusion of stability and continuity. (Silverman 1983: 239)

This understanding of communicative codes reflects the provocative proposition put forward by Roland Barthes that texts—in their traditional interpretation as individual 'works'—are actually a cultural illusion. In the famous 1968 essay, "The Death of the Author," often read as a precursor of poststructuralist theory and a founding text for cultural studies, he stated:

The birth of the reader must be at the cost of the death of the author and that as a matter of fact there is no author speaking, but just language. A text consists of multiple writings, proceeding from several cultures and entering into dialogue, into parody, into contestation; but there is a site where this multiplicity is collected, and this site is not the author, as has hitherto been claimed, but the reader: the reader is the very space in which are inscribed, without any of them being lost, all the citations out of which a writing is made; the unity of a text is not in its origin but in its destination, but this destination can no longer be personal: the reader is a man without history, without biography, without psychology; he is only that someone who holds collected into one and the same field all of the traces from which writing is constituted. (Barthes 1986: 54)

As a consequence, single works must be distinguished from texts. While the work "is a fragment of substance, it occupies a portion of the spaces of books (for example, in a library), the text is a methodological field" (57). It is evident that the concept can be applied also to the study of popular culture. We can look at our object of interest as a text whose fragments appear in diverse media, discourses, practices, and institutions. In examining popular culture, we try to identify what Michel Foucault called a "discursive formation" in his 1969 *Archaeology of Knowledge*: a regularity in terms of order, development, correlations, positions, and functioning among concepts, modality of enunciation, and thematic choices that identify otherwise invisible patterns. These formations take place within a discourse field, determined by systems of norms, economic and social dynamics, techniques, and ideas that constitute the preconditions of their very existence (cf. Foucault 1972). I would also include objects and practices, as popular culture tends to blur clear boundaries between representational and material elements.

While it is crucial to fully understand the historical aspects in the analysis of popular culture, which allows for the exploration of change and transformation, it is also relevant to apply a synchronic analysis that takes space and distance into consideration. Already in the period we have been exploring, North American representations, practices, and institutions around bananas were not isolated from similar phenomena in the rest of the world. When talking about this fruit, we cannot avoid discussing the towering figure of Josephine Baker. Born Freda Josephine McDonald in St. Louis, Missouri, on June 3, 1906, the artist started performing in the U.S. in 1919, enjoying some popularity at the Plantation Club in New York City. Fame came to her in 1925 when she performed her famous *Dance Sauvage* as an act of *La Revue Nègre* in Paris, where she played on exotic themes and introduced bold and sensual movements. Bananas were later integrated into her performance during her shows at the Folies-Bergère, in the form of a skimpy skirt made exclusively from the fruit. Her success in France was echoed in the U.S. by the admiration of jazz musicians and expatriate artists such as Langston Hughes, Ernest Hemingway, and F. Scott Fitzgerald. Of course, such performances could not have taken place in the United States, but precisely for that reason visual elements connected to her dance became iconic in popular culture.

Through her banana skirts, Baker allowed viewers to metonymically consume the exotic fruit and her own body, exposed to their gaze for entertainment's sake. It was the most explicit expression to date of a theme that had haunted American popular culture since colonial times: the black body perceived and described not only as a source of nourishment, due to its involvement in food production and preparation, but as an edible substance in itself. The topic is made even more intricate by a strong ambivalent element of sexual attraction and repulsion, danger and fascination towards black women. In her study of early British colonial writing, historian Jennifer Morgan (1997) pointed out that white men, feeling both desire and repulsion, often perceived black female sexuality as dangerous and consuming, almost cannibalistic, as opposed to the white female body, which is normalized and subsumed in the patriarchal order. Josephine Baker's daring performance flaunted the fascinating black female body in a more direct way compared to the contemporary blues divas, who used allusive eroticism to publicly articulate sexual desire, employing not only their voices, but also their physical persona. Often hefty and fleshy, brown- or dark-skinned, they flaunted their fully dressed bodies in front of eager audiences, emphasizing their voluptuous forms with provocative costumes and flashy jewelry.

The blues diva's provocation was more visibly expressed in Baker's performance, through its focus on a colonial product, the banana, which functioned as a symbol of white viewers' and consumers' often ambivalent and frequently unexpressed longing. Baker's very essence was somehow identified with the wild nature that white civilization was trying to tame. The artist took several photographs together with stuffed animals such as leopards, tigers, and elephants, symbols of danger and exoticism. Conveying lack of fear and familiarity with the beasts, these images reveal the intentional play on the perception of the black woman as a wild, barely controlled force of nature. It is unclear to what extent Baker was aware of these meanings, but later in her career she used her fame not only to her professional advantage, but also to assume an important role in supporting the Civil Rights Movement in the 1950s.

The theme of the banana as ornament and metonymical invitation to the consumption of exotic women resurfaces with a vengeance in the performances of Carmen Miranda (cf. Enloe 1990). The Portuguese-born Brazilian actress became famous in the U.S. as the "Brazilian Bombshell." After meeting her at a White House dinner in 1939, President Franklin Delano Roosevelt coopted her as the public relations face for the Good Neighbor policy, aimed at reinforcing U.S. ties with Latin American countries during a period that saw the rise of Nazism and World War II (cf. Grandin 2006).

Bananas are featured prominently in Carmen Miranda's number "The Lady in the Tutti Frutti Hat" in the 1943 movie *The Gang Is All Here*. Designed in the fictional narrative as a night club number, the sequence transports the viewers into a non-specified Latin country where bananas are produced, bare-chested male workers pull carts full of fruits, and scantily clad women dance to entertain the night club guests. Bananas are not only included in Miranda's famous hat, but they are also used as musical instruments and props, constituting a relevant motif in the whole *mise-en-scène*. As if the metaphor of the spicy Latina woman as consumable as the fruits from her land of origin were not clear enough, in the end Miranda's hat turns into an enormous 'explosion' of bananas suspended over the stage. The complete lack of references to specific Caribbean and Centro-American cultures and nationalities is noticeable. In the dreamlike land of bananas, ethnic characters become undifferentiated, their function determined by their relationship with the night club audience, which in this case stands for all the consumers of fruit from the exotic Tropics.

Carmen Miranda and her fruit hat claimed a visible space in the American imagination in the following years, indicating that it had touched on a culturally relevant issue. In Disney's 1942 *Saludos Amigos*, a movie commissioned by the United States Department of State, we see Donald Duck dancing the samba with a woman whose silhouette reminds viewers of Miranda and her hat. In the 1943 *Baby Puss*, a Merry Melodies animated cartoon, a cat in drag, wearing a hat containing fruit, sings "Mamãe Eu Quero," a popular Miranda's song from the 1940 movie *Down Argentina Way*. The performance and its contrivance acquired a sort of Caribbean blackface flavor when in the 1947 movie *Ladies' Man* actress Cass Daley sang "Mamãe Eu Quero" in a comedic tone, with her oversized hat and sleeves comically falling off, eventually closing the number by morphing the tune into "My Mommy," Al Jolson's hit in 1927's *The Jazz Singer*. The connection between tropical characters and the historical Other for white Americans could not have been more explicit.

Slick Hare (1947), a cartoon developed as a parody of the Mocambo Club in Los Angeles, later included a performance of Carmen Miranda and Bugs Bunny hiding in her fruit hat, peeling and eating a banana. In *What's Up Doc* (1950) the rabbit goes a step further when he uses the bananas—fruits and vegetables thrown at him on stage as a result of a bad performance—to create a Carmen Miranda-like costume. As late as 1951, in an episode of *I Love Lucy*, comedian Lucy Ball imitates Carmen Miranda on the soundtrack of her by-then hyper-popular "Mamãe Eu Quero." Besides Miranda's colorful dress, the skit includes a bunch of bananas, a chest of fruit carried by a woman dressed as a Central American peon, and even a live donkey, as a reminder of the origin of the fruit. A similar gag is repeated by Jerry Lewis in full drag and lip synching in the 1953 movie *Scared Stiff*, in which Miranda actually performs a song about enchiladas, quite out of place in the fictional Caribbean island where the movie is supposed to take place. The success of Miranda's look and style in comedy, cartoons, and drag performances reflects Hollywood's determination to pigeonhole the actress in very specific roles. Until the end of her career she was not able to act in less stereotyped characters, a situation that caused her to be critiqued as a sell-out in her native Brazil. The controversy became so intense that it inspired her 1940 song "Disseram que voltei americanizada" ("They Said I Have Come Back Americanized"), where she refers to traditional foods like *molho* (sauce) and *camarão ensopadinho com chuchu* (shrimp stew with chayote) as counterweighs to the bananas and the fruit that were constitutive elements in her Hollywood persona. Nevertheless, when she died in 1955 and her body was flown back to Rio de Janeiro, huge crowds gathered to honor her and the federal government declared national mourning.

Of course, by then, banana marketers had already taken notice of the popularity of the iconic Miranda. In 1944 United Fruit introduced the Miss Chiquita character, a banana wearing a supposedly tropical dress and a fruit hat. The identification of the exotic woman with the fruit was complete, for the enjoyment of all banana consumers. Miss Chiquita, turned into an advertising tool, was destined to a long life. In 1963 she appeared on the stickers that identify the United Fruit products, remaining an anthropomorphized banana until 1987 when she was transformed into a woman, albeit fictional, designed by artist Oscar Grillo. Finally in 2003 the character was given actual life by actress Jennifer Canales.

From her launch, Miss Chiquita was a hit, inspiring songs and a series of animated cartoons that followed her adventures. Released in 1945, the first cartoon shows Miss Chiquita—voiced by popular singer Monica Lewis—getting off a ship that has transported her from a tropical place to North America. Here she explains the use of bananas to a group of silent, formally dressed, and mostly overweight white men that supposedly compose the welcome committee for whom she is putting on her performance. After reminding viewers that they should not put bananas in the refrigerator, she goes on extolling the healthiness of the fruit, especially for children. Many of the bananas in the cartoon are actually moving and speaking characters, but it is Miss Chiquita that steals the scene with her fluttering eyes and long eyelashes. The tip of her head goes through her hat, replacing the bananas that were visible in Miranda's costume but reinforcing the identification between fruit and character. Her elongated form allows her sinuous movements, and her low-waisted dress shows most of her yellow body, building on the stereotype of the hot-blooded and sensual Latina all the way to her hip shake and her winking "*sí sí sí sí.*"

The Terry Twins recorded the Chiquita Banana song in 1946. The short film feature is a Latino equivalent of blackface performance, with two white female performers adopting clothing and moves that would be immediately identified by viewers as Tropical. The music and the rhythm alternate between Caribbean rhythms and swing music, although the dance moves lack the sensuality that Miss Chiquita flaunts in the cartoons. Also the singers' dresses do not have the same vivid colors as the fictional character, creating the impression of an overall pale impression of the original. In the following years, United Fruits banked on the popularity of Miss Chiquita to publish small cooking guides and other printed material that suggested various and original uses of the fruit, from cornflakes and banana to more complicated recipes. The goal was to push banana consumption in mainstream homes, highlighting the fruit's versatility and accessibility. Miss Chiquita became so iconic that her various avatars appeared on the stickers that mark all United Fruit and, later, Chiquita Brand products. Chiquita marketers also launched competitions for the most original banana-inspired stickers.

At the turn of the millennium, bananas and Chiquita still play a visible role in the way Americans relate to the Caribbean, Central America and, generally speaking, to their Southern neighbors. The iconic figure is still copied, made fun of, developed in all forms of popular culture, its longevity testifying to its continuing relevance. A Carmen Miranda / Miss Chiquita drag impersonator, for instance, was feature prominently in the 2000 movie by Fina Torres, *Woman on Top*. Its overall effect, as I have already mentioned, is to erase clear distinctions among different populations and cultures to create recognizable, pleasurable, and conveniently compounded exotic characters that do not require American consumers to engage with the dazzling variety of the Caribbean. The impact of this approach on the contemporary perceptions of Caribbean food in the U.S. deserves in-depth research focusing not only on domestic practices but also public eating establishments, private supper clubs, street food, carnivals like the Brooklyn Labor Day Parade, cookbooks, recipes, marketing and packaging, menus, as well as food in Caribbean resorts and cruises.

Before concluding, it is relevant to suggest a few methodological observations. First, it is crucial to maintain a distinction between the images and practices projected by popular culture, media, and commercial entities, in our case mainly based in the USA, and the realities of the everyday lives of people in all walks of life within the USA and in other parts of the world (cf. Hall 2005: 9). Although the two dimensions are certainly linked, and exert a reciprocal influence, those connections cannot be taken for granted, but rather should be examined in their historical, social, and psychological aspects, analyzing their development and assessing their effects. Popular culture is not a mere reflection of reality, but can play an ideological role in reinforcing power structures and cultural assumptions even when it appears to be critical of the present state of affairs. Under other circumstances, popular culture can provide subtle provocations and real attacks against the social status quo as viewers know and perceive it.

Representations can acquire special relevance when they are inscribed as norms, ideals, and expectations onto bodies that try to make sense of their daily lives in families, armies, factories, and kitchens. Representations of food, its production and consumption in popular culture can interact with the way individuals represent and experience their identities and even their own bodies. Anthropologist Arjun Appadurai noted in his 1996 *Modernity at Large* how imagination and fantasy have become a fundamental social practice, playing an important role in offering to many individuals and communities throughout the world new filters through which they can perceive and represent their daily lives, and interacting with other spheres of cultural, social, and political life (cf. Appadurai 1996). Popular culture is particularly relevant because it provides visual and aural elements, narrative components, and embodied practices that can be borrowed by individuals, subcultures, and whole communities to make sense of their everyday experiences. As a consequence, new narratives, changing identities, and possible practices reflected, created, and made visible by popular culture become part of a shared global patrimony that participates in the constitution of contemporary subjectivities.

However, as Stuart Hall (1980) argued, there are huge margins for disruption in communication processes between the encoding mechanisms on the side of the production and the decoding processes on the side of the final users of the message. In other words, media producers often find their message failing to get across to their audiences, when it is often either completely distorted or accepted quite selectively, depending on the audience' cultural, social, and political environment. In a similar way, film theorists Robers Stam and Louise Spence warned against rigid interpretations of audience understanding of the movies:

The film experience must inevitably be infected by the cultural awareness of the audience itself, constituted outside the text and traversed by sets of social relations such as race, class and gender. We must allow, therefore, for the possibility of aberrant readings, reading which goes against the grain of the discourse. Although fiction films are persuasive machines designed to produce specific impressions and emotions, they are not all-powerful; they might be read differently by different audiences. (Stam and Spence 1983: 19)

We need to keep in mind these caveats when proceedings with our analysis of food in popular culture. Only empirical research, through surveys and spectatorship analysis—well beyond the scope of this work—would be able to ascertain how this repository of images, sounds, and narrative elements transforms into actual projections, ideas, values, and practices in different parts of the world.

BIBLIOGRAPHY

Appadurai, Arjun, ed. 1986. *The Social Life of Things. Commodities in Cultural Perspective*. Cambridge: Cambridge University Press.
—. 1996. *Modernity at Large*. Minneapolis: University of Minnesota Press.
Banana Museum. [http://www.bananamuseum.com/ (retrieved 31 October 2013)].
Barthes, Roland 1986. *The Rustle of Language*. New York: Hill and Wang.

Burgoyne, Robert 2003. "Memory, History and Digital Imagery in Contemporary Film." *Memory and Popular Film*. Ed. Paul Grainge. Manchester: Manchester University Press, 220-236.
Carney, Judith and Richard Nicholas Rosomoff 2009. *In the Shadow of Slavery. Africa's Botanical Legacy in the Atlantic World*. Berkeley et al.: University of California Press.
Enloe, Cynthia 1990. *Bananas, Beaches and Bases. Making Feminist Sense of International Politics*. Berkeley et al.: University of California Press.
Fischler, Claude *1980*. "Food Habits, Social Change and the Nature / Culture Dilemma." *Social Science Information* 19.6: 937-953.
—. 1988. "Food, Self and Identity." *Social Science Information* 27.3: 275-292.
Foucault, Michel 1972. *Archaeology of Knowledge*. New York: Pantheon.
Grandin, Greg 2006. *Empires Workshop. Latin America, the United States, and the Rise of the New Imperialism*. New York: Metropolitan Books.
Hall, Matthew 2005. *Teaching Men and Film*. London: BFI Education.
Hall, Stuart 1980. "Encoding / Decoding." *Culture, Media, Language*. Eds. Stuart Hall, Dorothy Hobson, Andrew Lowe, and Paul Willis. London: Hutchinson, 128-138.
Harris, Jessica 2003. *Beyond* Gumbo. *Creole Fusion Food from the Atlantic Rim*. New York: Simon & Schuster.
Hunt, Lynn and Vanessa R. Schwartz 2010. "Capturing the Moment. Images and Eyewitnessing in History." *Journal of Visual Culture* 9.3: 259-271.
Jaakson, Reiner 2004. "Beyond the Tourist Bubble? Cruiseship Passengers in Port." *Annals of Tourism Research* 31.1: 44-60.
Jenkins, Virginia Scott 2000. *Bananas. An American History*. Washington: Smithsonian Institution Press.
Koeppel, Dan 2008. *Banana. The Fate of the Fruit that Changed the World*. New York: Hudson Street Press.
Kopytoff, Igor 1986. "The Cultural Biographies of Things. Commoditization as Process." *The Social Life of Things. Commodities in Cultural Perspective*. Ed. Arjun Appadurai. Cambridge: Cambridge University Press, 64-91.
Landsberg, Alison 2003. "Prosthetic Memory. The Ethics and Politics of Memory in the Age of Mass Culture." *Memory and Popular Film*. Ed. Paul Grainge. Manchester: Manchester University Press, 144-161.
Langdon, Robert 1993. "The Banana as a Key to Early American and Polynesian History." *The Journal of Pacific History* 28.1: 15-35.
Levenstein, Harvey 2012. *Fear of Food. A History of Why We Worry about What We Eat*. Chicago: University of Chicago Press.

Morgan, Jennifer 1997. "Some Could Suckle over their Shoulder. Male Travelers, Female Bodies, and Gendering of Racial Ideology, 1500-1770." *The William and Mary Quarterly*, Third Series 36.1: 167-92.

Schiebinger, Londa and Claudia Swan, eds. 2005. *Colonial Botany. Science, Commerce, and Politics in the Early Modern World*. Philadelphia: University of Pennsylvania Press.

Silverman, Kaja 1983. *The Subjects of Semiotics*. New York / Oxford: Oxford University Press.

Soluri, John 2003. "Banana Cultures. Linking the Production and Consumption of Export Bananas, 1800-1980." *Banana Wars. Power Production and History in the Americas*. Eds. Steve Striffler and Mark Moberg. Durham / London: Duke University Press, 48-79.

Stam, Robert and Louise Spence 1983. "Colonialism, Racism and Representation." *Screen* 24.2: 2-20.

Tompkins, Kyla Wazana 2012. *Racial Indigestions. Eating Bodies in the 19th Century*. New York: New York University Press.

Tucker, Richard 2000. *Insatiable Appetite. Banana Republics*. Berkeley et al.: University of California Press.

Wiley, James 2008. *The Banana. Empires, Trade Wars, and Globalization*. Lincoln: University of Nebraska Press.

Constructions of Authenticity

Cooking up a Storm
Residual Orality, Cross-Cultural Culinary Discourse, and the Construction of Tradition in the Cookery Writing of Levi Roots

SARAH LAWSON WELSH

Prelude

In November 2011, a story broke in the British press concerning contested claims to the original recipe for 'Reggae Reggae Sauce,' a commercial product introduced to the U.K. market by Jamaican born entrepreneur Levi Roots (Keith Valentine Graham) after winning £50,000 worth of investment some five years earlier on the BBC TV programme, *Dragons' Den*.[1] In 2007, Roots had appeared on the programme and pitched his business idea in an unusual format by performing it as a Reggae song, accompanying himself on guitar. After securing the investment from 'Dragon' investors, Peter Jones and Richard Farleigh, the *Reggae Reggae Sauce* brand was quickly adopted by one of the UK's major supermarkets, Sainsburys, and in a remarkably short period, Roots became a hugely successful millionaire businessman.

Reggae Reggae Sauce is now the flagship product in a hugely successful range of food products, TV appearances, websites, mobile phone apps and a series of recipe books introduced to the U.K. market by Roots. Roots was later sued by his former business partner, Tony Bailey, who claimed that Roots' recipe for *Reggae Reggae Sauce* was, in fact, his own, created by Bailey in Jamaica in 1984 but never written down. Bailey lost his case but not before Roots was called "a bare-faced liar" by Bailey's QC, Ian Glen, and forced to admit that his

---

1 "Levi Roots full *Dragons' Den* Appearance"
[http://www.youtube.com/watch?v=kQTzLJCUtjk (retrieved 12 August 2013)].

claim on TV and on his sauce bottles that the sauce recipe had been handed down to him by his Jamaican grandmother had been fabricated by Roots for marketing purposes.

The judge ruled that the sauce came from a basic, generic recipe and that Bailey and another associate, Sylvester Williams, had no rights in the brand or the business. This series of events might seem rather ephemeral were it not for their connection to some more enduring debates surrounding the role of food as a marker of cultural identity in a diasporic context and, in particular, the challenge to a politics of authenticity, enacted very publicly in this contemporary context.

Using this little case study as a starting point, I argue that Roots' published cookery writing reveals the complex and often problematic politics of popular cross-culinary discourse and the conflicted role of the cookery writer as 'ethnic advocate.' Using insights from Arjun Appadurai's (1988) writing on cross-cultural culinary discourse in an Indian context and from Ashley, Hollows and Taylor's examination of food writing and TV chefs (2004), Roots' first five cookery books, from *Reggae Reggae Cookbook* onward, are examined in terms of their early use of residually oral characteristics (proverbs, testimony and song lyrics) and their shift towards an increasingly orthodox and blandly Eurocentric format and style.[2] The latest and most stylised of these five, *Sweet* (2012) incorporates a 'retro' or 'vintage' styling which includes double page spread colour reproductions of European food labelling, food advertising and food miscellanea, including historical images of colonial food crops and food preparation from a

---

2   A sixth, *Grill It With Levi: 101 Reggae Recipes for Sunshine and Soul* has just been published by Ebury Publishing as this chapter goes to press. Its marketing copy summarizes Roots' commercially branded trajectory in the following excitable manner: "More than 100 sunshine-infused recipes for the barbecue or grill from our nation's best-loved West Indian chef. He's back and hotter than ever! Levi is getting back to his Roots with over 100 Caribbean- and sunshine-infused recipes for the barbecue and grill. From his first appearance—guitar in hand—in the *Dragons' Den*, Levi's winning personality and sunny food has brought a taste of Caribbean joy to our dinner plates. In this book, Levi gets back to his Jamaican influences with over 100 recipes to conjure up those lazy, hazy summer days. He cooks up feasts for the barbecue and grill with fresh, healthy ingredients that have been given his special West Indian twist—think Chicken with Molasses, Sugar and Lime; Calypso Burgers with Tropical Salsa; and Jamaican Snapper Parcels—all washed down with a Sunshine Smoothie. 'Grill it with Levi' brings together all Levi's passions: healthy, quick and flavourful food, cooking outside and eating with friends. All the recipes can be cooked on a barbecue—or, if the weather's not so sunny—you can bring the summer inside. Shake that Reggae Reggae Sauce and let's get some soul back into our food!"

variety of Caribbean and European sources (British, French, Spanish, Dutch). In including such visual texts, *Sweet*'s format opens up some interesting questions about food histories and food provenance in a Caribbean and diasporic context. However, in terms of its recipes and the nature of the written text, this latest publication is much more standardized and Europeanized than the early books. Indeed, I argue here that Roots' earliest cookery writing *deliberately* combines recipes with autobiography, photos and other paratextual elements as well as an apparently informal, but in fact carefully constructed, first person narrative voice in order to invoke a particular version of the cookery writer as 'authentic' transmitter of culturally specific culinary knowledge, the holder of 'tradition' as well as, on occasion, the purveyor of exotic 'otherness' to a non-Caribbean audience.[3]

---

3   I understand the term 'authentic' to mean, in this context, "[t]he idea of an authentic culture [...] [as] present in many recent debates about post-colonial cultural production" (Ashcroft, Griffiths, Tiffin 1998: 21). Its editors sum up the problematic nature of this much contested term by noting how: "the demand for rejection of the influence of the colonial period in programmes of decolonization [...] invoked the idea that certain forms and practices are 'inauthentic,' some decolonizing states arguing for a recuperation of authentic pre-colonial traditions and customs. The problem with such claims to cultural authenticity is that they often become entangled in an essentialist cultural position in which fixed practices become iconized as authentically indigenous [or as authentic markers of a certain imagined community or national collective] and others are excluded as hybridized or contaminated. This has as its corollary the danger of ignoring the possibility that cultures may develop and change as their conditions change" (ibid.). They go on to note the strategic advantages of assuming a culturally essentialist position, what Spivak terms 'strategic essentialism,' as: "clearly, certain kinds of practices are peculiar to one culture and not to others, and these may serve as important identifiers and become the means by which those cultures can resist oppression and oppose homogenization by global forces" (ibid.). However, they conclude "the emergence of certain fixed, stereotypical representations of culture remains a danger. The tendency to employ generic signifiers for cultures that may have many variations within them may override the real differences that exist within such cultures. Markers of cultural difference may well be perceived as authentic cultural signifiers, but that claim to authenticity can imply that these cultures are not subject to change" (ibid.). In this paper I argue that Roots adopts some of these markers of cultural difference, sometimes to an extreme and reductive level but that ultimately, his cookery writing gives way to a more creolized and thoroughly hybridized aesthetic. I show how his claims to authenticity are carefully constructed, rather than 'natural' givens, especially in a more distanced, diasporic context, but also how a more cross-cultural aesthetic emerges in his writing.

Ultimately, I argue, Roots' cookery writing is mired in contradiction, as may well be the plight of all those who write not only in a cross-cultural context but in our contemporary globalized economy of food and media presence: it promises specificity (Jamaicaness), but simultaneously reifies and homogenizes Caribbean cooking through the branding of both Roots and his sauce as marketable commodities. Similarly, Roots' invocation of a poetics of Caribbean exile, nostalgia and loss in his first book, *Reggae Reggae Cookbook*, is not only exposed as partly fabricated, but shown to be challenged by a contradicting imperative in Roots' later books to show Caribbean food as not only experiential but also emphatically transferable and adaptive in a British Caribbean diasporic context. That is to say, the nature of the recipes in consecutive books shifts from a showcasing of a version of Caribbean cooking as exotic 'other,' to an element of improvisational fusion or creolization, what Roots himself calls "dubbing it up," to a more superficial "spicing up" of familiar dishes to, in the latest book, a Caribbean "twist" on some British culinary stalwarts. What emerges is a complex, compromised, but nonetheless arresting culinary version of the Caribbean nation in the multi-cultural context of the U.K.

Introduction

In "From Fiction to Foodways: Working at the Intersections of African American Literary and Culinary Studies" (2007), African-American food scholar, Doris Witt outlines her:

two fundamental aims […] to explore what sorts of contributions people trained to analyze ideology and aesthetics rather than material culture might make to the study of African American foodways and, conversely, to explain why increased attention to food can benefit African American literary and cultural studies. (Witt 2007: 102)

Whilst Witt's research terrain is clearly not Caribbean, her methodology and commitment to working at the intersection of literary and food studies is one that can be usefully transferred to a Caribbean context and one which I adopt here.

This essay on the role of food and food writing in a Caribbean diasporic context derives from a larger series of projects centered on the representation of food and foodways in Caribbean writing and the ways in which food functions within and across a wide range of genres: fiction, poetry, testimonies, colonial and planter's accounts, autobiography and cookery writing (cf., for example, Lawson Welsh 2013). The *Reggae Reggae* court case raises some interesting issues regarding the construction of 'tradition' and performances of cultural authenticity in relation to the narration of a particular *culinary* version of the Caribbean nation in the diasporic context of the U.K. The case involves Jamaican-born, British-based entrepreneur, Levi Roots and the *Reggae Reggae Sauce* story.

ETHNIC ADVOCACY AND THE CONSTRUCTION OF A NATIONAL CUISINE

Long before this court case came to public attention, I had started working on Roots' cookery writing, fascinated by his unusual career trajectory from street food provider to high profile food entrepreneur. I was interested not so much in Roots' meteoric rise to fame and commercial success after his appearance on the BBC TV programme *Dragons' Den*—something which seems depressingly firmly located in our popular cultural zeitgeist in the U.K.—but in the fact that his promotion of Caribbean food was yoked with a strong commercial brand identity from the very outset. This profile afforded Roots the role of business entrepreneur but also allowed him to assume the mantle of what Arjun Appadurai terms the cook as a kind of "ethnic advocate" (Appadurai 2008: 300). Appadurai notes how the proliferation of regional and ethnic cookbooks in the post-1960s period in India had two effective functions: "like tourist art […] they begin to provide people from one region or place a systematic glimpse of the culinary traditions of another, and they also represent a growing body of food-based characteristics of the ethnic Other" (299). Against this trend towards diversification, Appadurai shows how the "textualization of culinary traditions" (297) was crucial in "constructing the idea of a national or 'Indian' cuisine" (301). He notes a "few standard devices" (302) in those modern-day cookbooks which attempt to construct a conception of an Indian national cuisine:

The first is simply to inflate and reify an historically special tradition and make it serve, metonymically, for the whole…Another strategy…is inductive rather than nominal: the author assembles a set of recipes in a more or less subjective manner and, then, in the introduction to the book, gropes for some theme that might unify them. In many books this theme is found, not surprisingly, in the spices and spice combinations […]. (ibid.)

How far might these "few standard devices" (ibid.) Appadurai notes in those modern-day Indian cookbooks be applied to Roots and the construction of a particular conception of a culinary nation in his cookery writing? Has the thorough branding of Roots and his flagship product, *Reggae Reggae Sauce*, opened up or closed down possibilities for a real understanding and wider adoption of Caribbean cuisine in Britain? How far has it acted to fix or homogenize our understanding of Caribbean cooking in Britain, much as the constructed term 'curry' both popularizes and obscures the rich and varied culinary traditions that contribute to what we (lazily and inaccurately) call 'Indian' food in the U.K.?

Against initial hopes that the *Reggae Reggae* phenomenon—the products, the books, the iPhone apps, the TV programmes—might raise the profile of Caribbean cooking in the U.K. in some positive ways, have been growing misgivings about a product which seemed to encourage a reductive version of 'Caribbean cooking-lite' (i.e. one adds it to chicken and hey-presto, it 'Caribbeanizes' your cooking) with all the problems of 'authenticity' and exoticizing the Caribbean this invokes. Graham's chosen soubriquet of 'Levi Roots,' his musical pitch to the Dragons, his naming of his brand '*Reggae Reggae*' and the use of the tagline "put some music in your food" were interesting, not only insofar as they signaled Roots' multiple affiliations as a Rastafarian, a reggae musician and a food entrepreneur via the operation of a series of metonymic links, joining together food, music, and a certain sort of reggae aesthetic in Jamaican cultural production,[4] but also as they began to operate as a metonym for Caribbean cooking more generally.

One factor in Roots' success, some might argue, has been the relatively low profile of Caribbean food in the U.K. to date and thus the 'novelty' value of his brand for many British cooks and consumers. Why has Caribbean food not enjoyed the popularity of South Asian food in the U.K.? There are a growing number of studies on South Asian food (cf. Collingham 2006; Taylor Sen 2009) which argue that the lengthy and close colonial association between Britain and India, and the emergence of a body of Anglo-Indians who brought 'Indian food' home with them, might be one explanation, but even this cannot account for the fact that most of what we call 'Indian' food in the U.K. is in fact Bangladeshi in origin, in line with those migrants who set up restaurants here in the 1950s and 60s, and has undergone its own creolization in the U.K. Indeed, the appropriation and assimilation of 'Indian food' in the U.K. has been so total that one might argue it is now marked as a truly British dish, an ubiquitous cuisine rather

---

4   In this respect, Roots embodies quite a few common stereotypes of Jamaican culture within Europe, what Ashcroft et al. call "markers of cultural difference" (Ashcroft et al. 1998: 21). See Mimi Sheller's *Consuming the Caribbean* for a more detailed discussion of "the myriad ways in which Western European and North American publics have unceasingly consumed the natural environments, commodities, human bodies, and cultures of the Caribbean over the past five hundred years" (Sheller 2003: 3).

than an exotic and minority taste. The transmission and reception of culinary traditions matter and arguably no more so than when those traditions have never enjoyed the high profile and mainstream culinary influence that, say, South Asian food does in Britain. Indeed, to date there have only been a handful of British TV cooks of Caribbean descent: Rusty Lee, Ainsley Harriott, Andi Oliver (of Antiguan descent), and Lorraine Pascale, and none of these have been particularly successful in raising the profile of Caribbean cooking in the U.K. This is why Roots' intervention into the culinary fold of U.K. cookery writing and TV food programmes was so striking and perhaps, adventitious.[5]

Indeed, at the end of his first book, *Reggae Reggae Cookbook*, which is part cookbook, part memoir, Roots writes: "Reggae-Reggae Sauce has changed my life... My mission now is to promote Caribbean food and make it as popular in Britain as Indian food is. We West Indians have a strong affinity with Britain and the food is great, so it's a match made in Heaven" (Roots 2008: 184). Here Roots' explicit advocacy of Caribbean cuisine invokes a seemingly straightforward narrative of culinary discovery and consumption, a culinary ethnic advocate openly sharing his Caribbean cultural capital with an appreciative and already cosmopolitan U.K. audience. However, I argue that his cookery writing and his TV programmes can be seen to tell a more complex story and reveal something of the often-problematic politics of popular cross-cultural culinary discourse and the conflicted role of the ethnic minority cookery writer as ethnic advocate.

---

[5] Very recently in the U.K., a rival to the Roots empire has emerged in the person of chef and restaurateur, Barrington Douglas. Born to Jamaican parents in Britain, and having worked with a number of high profile British chefs, Douglas is launching his own range of Caribbean-inspired pies and sauces. Douglas comments: "We know Indian, Chinese, Italian, Mexican and French food, for example, are well loved in Britain but African-Caribbean food is less well known. I'm surprised by that as Caribbean people have been here for 60 years. The new flavours coming through are exciting for everybody. For me putting a fresh spin on British classics, and by doing things a little differently, helps move contemporary Caribbean food forward." More pointedly, he differentiates himself from the highly branded Roots by saying: "If Levi Roots is No 1 in the Caribbean food market there is room for me...And I'm not a guitarist or a musician. I'm a chef with a passion for food...I am British with a Caribbean heritage and I innovate" (cf. [http://www.examiner.co.uk/news/west-yorkshire-news/huddersfield-chef-barrington-douglas-launches-5166843 (retrieved 29 July 2013)]). My thanks to Wiebke Beushausen for bringing this link to my attention.

ECONOMIC VERSUS CULINARY CULTURAL CAPITAL

Roots' high profile as a TV celebrity and the aggressively marketed visibility of his *Reggae Reggae* brand raise some pertinent questions about the tension between economic and cultural capital (cf. Bourdieu 1971, 1993) in his cookery writing. Often, as Ashley, Jones and Taylor note,

> the attempt by television chefs to dissociate themselves from both the medium in which they have achieved celebrity, and the economic profits they have gained from it, is an attempt to assert their cultural legitimacy within the culinary field [...] chefs are people who have invested heavily in the culinary field [...] in what Bell (2002) calls 'culinary cultural capital': their legitimacy as arbiters of culinary taste come from the cultural capital they possess within a specific field. However as [Pierre] Bourdieu (1971 and 1993) argues, cultural capital does not have the same stable value as economic capital and there is a pressure to convert culinary prestige into economic wealth. Yet at the same time, if the chef shows too much desire for economic profit [i.e. 'sells out'], this can lead to cultural delegitimization. (Ashley et al. 2004: 179)

This raises some interesting questions about his entire *Reggae Reggae* project: how, for example, is Roots' apparent ease with celebrity and his commercial success, as witnessed by the growing *Reggae Reggae* empire—to coin a deliberately provocative phrase—of products, books and TV appearances, to be squared with Roots' self-professed role as ethnic advocate, a prominent practitioner and spokesperson for Caribbean cuisine in Britain? What are we to make of the successful businessman who is valued firstly for his entrepreneurial spirit but also for his Caribbean culinary cultural capital?

I argue that Roots' promotion of Caribbean cooking foregrounds both Caribbean tradition and origins on the one hand but on the other, in common with many of his TV chef peers, simultaneously emphasizes Caribbean cooking's possibilities in a globalized / cross-cultural context as a leisure pursuit, or lifestyle choice, now largely freed from the link between cooking and repetitive or onerous labor, let alone the slave origins of some of his recipes.[6] We might argue

---

6   A good example is his "sunshine box" and his motto: "Put some sunshine in your food." However, in his latest book, *Sweet* (2012) there are some interesting exceptions, including detailed references to his ancestry in the preamble to a recipe for the dessert 'Caribbean Cranachan': "My real surname is Graham, a legacy of the Scottish slave masters in Jamaica who passed their name to their offspring. Cracahachn is a classic Scots pudding, but this version, like me, is a mixture of Scottish and Caribbe-

then that Roots' cookery writing is, then, both concerned and not concerned with origins, his writing freighted with a series of tensions and contradictions in the construction of a Caribbean cultural identity via culinary practices (cf. Witt 2008: 118). At times, especially in the later, glossy Mitchell Beazley-published cookbooks, the writing and presentation veer dangerously close to what Witt terms "culinary tourism," part of a rise of interest in food from other cultures facilitated "in virtual form via the Food Channel or as a result of the [...] middle class's increasing ability to travel widely" (ibid.). As Witt suggests, "such cookbooks are, paradoxically, both complicit with and resistant to the global traffic in the iconography of ethnic multiplicity that Paul Gilroy, among others, has identified as a distinguishing and problematic feature of the late-capitalist marketplace" (ibid.).

To return to Bourdieu and the tensions between economic and cultural capital, as an ethnic minority chef in Britain, Roots has never been purely and simply what Bourdieu terms the cultural intermediary, the "new intellectual" (Bourdieu 1984: 371). Bourdieu's theorizing fails to take into account these important variables and is, in this sense at least, culturally homogenizing. Using the insights of critics who write about food and cultural difference in a national, regional or cross-cultural context, such as Arjun Appadurai, is an important corrective here. Even then, the case of Roots does not quite 'fit' this critical framework; unlike other prominent ethnic minority TV chefs in Britain, say, Indian cookery writer, Madhur Jaffrey in the 1970s and 1980s, the basis of his culinary discourse has been primarily commercial and brand-orientated and not really interested in regional difference. Instead, just as the *Reggae Reggae* brand has become metonymic of Roots' whole enterprise, so might his largely Jamaican-based cookery writing be read provocatively as a metonymic representation of Caribbean cuisine, made accessible to an Anglophone and cross-cultural audience?

---

an, as it uses rum instead of whiskey" (Roots 2012: 102). Here the hybridity of the dish is linked to the hybridity of the cookery writer, an interesting twist on ethnic advocacy in action.

Residual Orality and the Construction of Caribbean Culinary 'Tradition'

As I suggested at the outset, Witt argues provocatively that literary scholars and critics working in food studies have much to learn from each other. Indeed, she goes as far as to suggest:

that literary scholars interested in foodways might do well to follow the lead of the compilers of the *Norton Anthology of African American Literature* by incorporating vernacular and musical traditions into their analyses...excerpts from cookbooks, including recipes, should [also] be included in texts such as the Norton Anthology. (Witt 2007: 104)

As she wittily notes: "Sermons make the cut, yet it is not hard to find evidence that in many black churches the post-sermon meal is no less an art form than the sermon itself" (104). We might productively think through the implications of this recommendation in a Caribbean context too. Consider, for example, the following, but with "African-American" replaced with "Caribbean":

Granted, for the editors of the Norton Anthology to include recipes as part of the vernacular tradition would raise several fascinating but vexed questions regarding the relationship of African American performative [i.e. oral] culture to written texts, question which have long been asked of efforts to transcribe oral renditions such as song lyrics. As feminist scholars have demonstrated, however, cookbooks and recipes are not just transcriptions of performative culture. They are complex rhetorical structures that can be decoded using the sorts of tools literary critics typically bring to say, a novel. (ibid.)

This paper takes up this challenge by discussing Roots' five cookery books to date in terms of the use in the early books of residually oral characteristics (proverbs, personal testimony, riddles and song lyrics) coupled with an arresting performative style both on the page and screen. This style is retained in the television and online performances where Roots maintains his persona as charismatic cook, musical performer and one-man-brand. However, in the cookery writing there is a more discernible shift as later texts appear to become more orthodox and blandly Eurocentric in format and style, compared to the earliest ones.[7] How do such oral and performative elements construct a version of Carib-

---

[7] The reasons for this shift seem mainly commercial, as a new Levi Roots cookery book has been published each year since by the mainstream 'lifestyle' publisher Mitchell Beazley. The orthodox and blandly European format and style includes features such

bean cultural 'tradition' and affect our reading of the cookbooks? Does the reduced prominence of residually oral characteristics in his later books constitute some kind of cultural dilution or does it, in fact, open up possibilities for different strategies and approaches to the subject of Caribbean cuisine? One possible reading of this shift is that, as the oral performative elements of Roots' cookery writing become more muted, his interest in cross-cultural culinary discourse develops in sophistication, until he is able to articulate a new 'dub-it-up' aesthetic, based partly on the Caribbean practice of 'making do' and partly on a kind of cross-cultural discourse of culinary cross-fertilization or fusion for his Caribbean cooking in his 2010 cookbook, *Spice It Up*.

REGGAE REGGAE COOKBOOK

Roots' earliest book, *Reggae Reggae Cookbook* (2008), might be most accurately termed a cookbook-memoir as it deliberately combines recipes with autobiography, photos and other paratextual elements. Roots' 'life-story' is threaded through the text in episodic fashion and draws on his Jamaican childhood and family, notably his mother and grandmother, and thereafter his experiences of school, prison, food, music, Rastafarianism and Carnival in Britain. This in itself is significant as it represents an interesting inversion of male-authored cookery books where the focus tends to be on the recipes and the public profile of the cook rather than the cook's personal life.[8] In this case, the discursiveness and memoir-driven narrative of his first book, *Reggae Reggae Cookbook*, is more reminiscent of a number of other male-authored Caribbean texts which integrate

---

as subtler and more unified page colours (mainly white compared to the bright Rasta / Jamaican national flag colours of *Reggae Reggae Cookbook*), the lack of paratextual elements, greater use of standardized page layouts and fonts and the predominant use of the classic double spread (one page colour photograph, one page of text). *Sweet* is a slight diversion in its adoption of a 'vintage' styled scrapbook feel, comprised of photographed fabric backgrounds and collages of food-related images but even this is highly constructed and falls very squarely within current Euro-American marketing and retail trends in glossy 'lifestyle' publications.

8 Witt notes this phenomenon in African-American cookery writing, noting for example in relation to the male-African-American authored cookery books of the early part of last century that "cookbooks of the era by black men [...] largely reflect the authors' experiences as cooks in the public domain" and "are reticent about personal information; the focal point is the recipes, not the cook" (Witt 2007: 108).

different genres of cookery writing such as Austin Clarke's *Pigtails n' Saltfish* (2000) or John Lyon's more recent publication *Cook up in a Trini Kitchen* (2009), all of which interestingly challenge expectations that it will be primarily female-authored writing which utilizes this approach.[9]

In *Reggae Reggae Cookbook,* bold colors and graphics vie for attention with colour photographs and large font Caribbean proverbs and song lyrics in a way that suggests an apparently spontaneous and informal register and a relaxed organizing principle. Most interesting perhaps, is the insistence on the dual careers of Roots as musician and cook—which was integral to his winning pitch on the *Dragons' Den* programme—and the permeability of discursive borders between different art forms and kinds of writing throughout. Whereas in his earliest book, this is manifest throughout in textual juxtapositions and visual motifs of guitars and musical notes, in Roots' 2010 book, *Spice It Up*, it is restricted to the introduction and reduced to a more formal textual statement:

I always say that cooking is like making a piece of music. You lay out the ingredients like an orchestra or a band. The choice that you make is down to what flavors work together and what will complement the main ingredients. The music vibe is the merging and the mixing of these spices. (Roots 2010: 8)

Also, in *Reggae Reggae Cookbook,* oral proverbs and creole make their way into recipes[10] and a number of recipes are prefaced with personal reflections on family members' methods of cooking the dish (cf. Roots 2008: 72). Many of these oral proverbs are food, consumption or cooking related in line with the oral life-

---

9 This is partly due to the historical association of women's writing in general with confessional, autobiographical and other related genres, partly to the gendering of food socialization and cooking as a largely—but by no means exclusively—female activity in the Caribbean (especially within the Indo-Caribbean tradition), and partly due to the cross-generic nature of much residually oral cookery writing by Caribbean women which combines multiple annotations, folk wisdom, recipes and instruction, as Doris Witt also notes, of a female African-American tradition. For more on the gendering of Caribbean cooking in a Guyanese context, cf. Gillian Richards-Greaves (2013).

10 For example, 'Fry big fish first, little one after' glossed as "take care of the important things first" appears under a recipe for Oxtail and Butterbean stew (Roots 2010: 51); 'Wha' sweet goat, a go work im belly' glossed as "The things that give you most pleasure may also harm you" appears under a recipe for Brown Stew Chicken and Yard-Style Gravy (53); 'Pot full, pot cover get some' glossed as "Good fortune spreads to those close to you" under a recipe for Stew Beef (111) and 'Empty bag can't stand up' glossed as "You can't work on an empty belly" (128).

world of their largely African-Caribbean origin but such signifiers of traditional wisdom and conviviality are also, importantly, the deliberately cultivated subtext of Roots' book. Interestingly, in the first instance when an oral proverb is included (cf. 22), no gloss is provided but all later proverbs are glossed in standard English suggesting a largely British / European rather than Caribbean audience for his book. Even the song lyrics for his investment-winning pitch are included (cf. 153), which contributes to the reggae aesthetic and 'performative' dimension of the text. Elsewhere, in this first book, especially when Roots writes about his stall at the Notting Hill Carnival and his music career, elements of grassroots and street discourse enter the text and marks a more recent and urbanized residual orality. Traditional oral proverbs and aphorisms are joined by the creation of new myths of personal success, narratives of overcoming adversity, now couched in ironically inflected terms of 'slaying dragons' rather than taking more Caribbean traditional forms, which might also be regarded as residually oral, part of 'street-talk.'

In this way, I suggest, markers of residual orality are introduced into the printed text and the formality and orthodoxy of the single-voiced Euro-American 'mainstream' cookbook disrupted.[11] Not only do these personal reminiscences break up the text and challenge certain gender expectations we may bring to the text, but they also introduce a multi-generic perspective and, by moving away from the monologic, singular voice, repeatedly remind us of the wider Caribbean oral communal world to which cooking and the transmission of culinary wisdom and lore fundamentally belong. To adapt the grandmother's adage in the prologue to another Caribbean text, "It takes more than one life to make a person": "It takes more than one person to make a meal" (Melville 1997: 2).[12]

Reggae Reggae Cookbook is dedicated to Roots' maternal grandmother and mother, and might be read positively in terms of its gender politics, in terms of seeking to reconnect Caribbean cooking in a British diasporic context to Caribbean female agency and creativity. The peculiar formal features of this cookery book act to "preserve [...] female [...] tradition" by the deliberate use of "orality, [mother-tongue] and the [oral] discursiveness of [the] writing" (Mehta 2009: 185). The inclusion of autobiographical texts interspersed with recipes suggests a kind of interpersonal, and perhaps even "intergenerational script" (187) based in the shared love of cooking and 'gastrophilia' of grandmother and grandson. Roots acknowledges this himself in his introduction to *Reggae Reggae Cookbook*:

---

11 For example, contemporary cookery writing by Jamie Oliver or Nigella Lawson in a U.K. context.
12 Pauline Melville, *The Ventriloquist's Tale* (1997).

My gran taught me the magic of cooking: how to mix Caribbean flavors and the subtleties of traditional herbs and spices. She loved cooking and I would watch, transfixed, happy to be with her and to help her. She never gave me proper instructions—that wasn't her style. I learned all that I know about the wonderful West Indian food I have been cooking and eating all my life just by observing her. She would be so happy to know that many of her recipes are now here for you in my cookbook. (Roots 2008: 8)

What is elided here, and crucially, is how the transmission from the grandmother's oral culture to Roots' written text alters or affects the content and frame for reading this culinary wisdom. Roots tells us that 'gran' never gave 'proper' instructions, but by the end of this selection, he calls them 'recipes.' This is one of the many locations in *Reggae Reggae Cookbook* where the residual orality of the text strains against the confines of the cookery book's written format. Aren't recipes *by definition* 'proper' instructions and at what point is the improvisational practice of simply 'cooking' (without a book to guide you, as 'gran' surely did in her mythic Caribbean kitchen in the sun) translated into the 'proper' rhetoric of the recipe, in which the text standardizes and coerces the reader into re/creating an 'original' or authentic, or proper dish? These too, are postcolonial questions which the literary critic is especially well placed to ask, given the related concerns with orality, literacy, the role of language, the figure of the ancestor, constructions of 'tradition' and issues of cultural authenticity which are staples in much postcolonial literary criticism.[13]

Roots' inscription of the grandmother figure in the *Reggae Reggae Cookbook* as connected to older, ancestral female traditions (including the figure of Nanny of the Maroons, cf. Roots 2008: 29) is fascinating. The intermittent references to wider aspects of Jamaican and Caribbean culture in this and his later cookbooks, might be read as cynically contrived, a nod to cultural exoticism for an overseas audience rather than a genuine raising of cultural awareness of Caribbean history, but here the reference achieves something quite different: however, clumsily executed. Despite the male-transmitting voice of Roots himself, the re-inscription of the grandmother figure through highly personal paratexts such as this—as well as the recipes themselves—reconnects Roots' cookery writing to a wider Caribbean oral communal world of which the grandmother is part, but also locates respect, power and agency in both female figures—familial and historical.

---

13 My thanks to Nasser Hussain for his insightful comments on this chapter in draft, which form the basis of this point.

LOST ORIGINS: THE GRANDPARENTS' HOUSE

Despite the many written tributes and colour photographs of family, friends and other inhabitants of Roots' home village of Content, Jamaica, there are no photographs of his grandmother in his cookery books. More intriguingly, early on in *Reggae Reggae Cookbook* we find a double spread colour photograph of a rural Jamaican scene with no people or habitation save a crudely superimposed white crayon outline of a simple one-storey house. The picture is entitled "my grandparents' house." It serves as a perfect illustration of one of the most contentious and thorny issues surrounding culinary ethnic advocacy: the construction of tradition and the perception of the authentic. In this picture, which is both photograph and graphic, we find a perfect metonym for lost origins and re-constructed tradition. The ghostly outline of the grandparents' house with its childlike simplicity and naïve styling suggest both absence and presence, nostalgia for something irrevocably lost and the construction of a new but artificial 'presence' upon the palimpsest of loss. The cartoon-like superimposition of both the graphic and word 'home' on the photograph also suggest different modes of representation and the complexities of 'home' in this cross-cultural context. Of course, the photo of the grandmother's house as flimsily built upon absence takes on another level of meaning and even greater pertinence given the outcome of the 2011 court case between Roots and Bailey.

Like the superimposed house in the photograph, the residual orality of the *Reggae Reggae Cookbook* is only ever a pared down and approximate version of the original. It is, at the end of the day, a *written* text and the residual orality of the text is deliberately recreated. Similarly, the carefully constructed first person narrative voice, which may well be in large part Roots' own, is ultimately a rhetorical device designed to invoke a particular version of the cookery writer as 'authentic' transmitter of culturally specific culinary knowledge, the holder of 'tradition' as well as, on occasion, the purveyor of exotic 'otherness' to a non-Caribbean audience. Cookery writing is, we are reminded, a commercial enterprise.

In his later cookery books, most of which are arguably so similar as to be virtually indistinguishable, the freshness and idiosyncrasies of *Reggae Reggae Cookbook* are lost with a change to a more mainstream 'lifestyle' publisher and as commercial pressures become more apparent. The invocation of a poetics of exile, nostalgia and loss which is relatively prominent in the earliest two books cannot be sustained in the next two books. Instead, what becomes increasingly important is the contrary imperative to show Caribbean food as emphatically transferable and adaptive in a cross-cultural context, to be experienced by the widest audience in a contemporary U.K. setting. Roots adapts other cooks' commercial recipes, includes an increasingly number of crossover recipes and the writing moves towards a more confident articulation of a cross-cultural aesthetic which Roots calls his 'dub-it-up' approach. Arguably, something is lost here but something too is gained.

CARIBBEAN FOOD MADE EASY

The introduction to Roots' second cookery book, *Caribbean Food Made Easy* (2009), published as a spinoff from the BBC TV series which saw Roots take to the great Jamaican outdoors as well as featuring Roots cooking for family and friends in his home community of Brixton, London, opens with a reminder of Caribbean oral tradition. It starts with the words: "Yu tan deh call' yu wuddah never get come!" (No matter how much you shout I ain't gonna come), the young Roots' response to his grandmother's call to him to go fetch something for her cooking and acknowledges her culinary skill and inspiration: "What she taught me I now want to bring to this book, and she's still watching me go" (Roots 2009: 10). Indeed, the entire introduction acts as a paean to the grandparents, especially the grandmother figure as authentic transmitter of culinary tradition and wider life-inspiration to Roots.

Yet beyond the highly autobiographical introduction, this is a very different book from *Reggae Reggae Cookbook*. For example, personal reflection still prefaces some recipes though the figures are usually more celebrity than familial. Residual oral forms, such as riddles, still make it into the recipes,[14] but there is much less discursiveness and inclusion of residual oral or performative techniques in this text. Concomitantly, the emphasis is much more on adapting Caribbean food in a new cross-cultural setting, although the rationale and methodologies for this shift are not yet fully explained or realized. In this second book, Roots seems much more at ease with his celebrity status and the writing is much more assured in its representation of himself as ethnic advocate for Jamaican cookery and wider culture. However, *Caribbean Food Made Easy* also seems much more driven by commercial concerns, primarily the need to expand his repertoire and potential audience beyond what might be construed as a rather narrow audience interested in exotically 'other' food.

---

14 One such example is the inclusion of the creole riddle: "How water walk to ah pumpkin belly?" Answer: "the long vine that leads to the pumpkin" as a prefatory note to a recipe for pumpkin rice (Roots 2009: 123).

FOOD FOR FRIENDS

It is only in his third book, *Food for Friends* (2010), that Roots starts to articulate, in his introduction to the book, a more sophisticated aesthetic for his cookery, drawing both on the characteristically Caribbean practice and cultural philosophy of 'making do' (cf. 2010: 8, 11-12) and suggesting a 'dub-it-up' approach to cooking as his style (12).[15] On 'making do,' he comments on his Jamaican childhood:

Everyone was really poor back then, so what we ate would depend on who had something to cook. If my grandfather had harvested that day—dug some yams, or got some callaloo and cabbages—we'd know we had food in abundance. And if you had too much, you'd give it away. People didn't have money to buy local food. It was just given. You'd put out what you couldn't eat and people would take it. (8)

The 'dub-it-up' approach he outlines here is a more developed and explicit explanation of something which has featured in all his cookery books, starting in very limited ways with recipes for Reggae spiced-up beans on toast or cheese on toast in *Reggae Reggae Cookbook*. In *Food for Friends*, Roots explains its origins:

[When touring as a musician] I'd be in the dressing room, cooking up whatever local food we could grab. I always carried my seasonings... *my Sunshine kit*...so even if we found a place where there was nothing but a sweet potato I could still nice-up the ingredients...This is how I developed my dub-it-up approach to cooking. Dub in music originated in Jamaica. You'd make a piece of music with ten musicians and instruments and the engineer would get it afterwards and start to work. He'd take the guitar out and bring it in later with a reverb put on it or add a bit of echo, creating a fusion of sounds that became a piece of music. And you can do the same with food. I can take a typical brunch recipe or Christmas dish that is traditionally done, say, in Italy or Britain and dub it up by adding something that turns it Caribbean. (12; my emphasis)

---

15 'Making do' has an important specific function within domestic economy as an efficient means of eking out available food ('making do') by adding to and boiling up, for example, a one-pot meal each day; this social phenomenon and characteristically Caribbean 'cultural philosophy of food,' born out of historical necessity rather than choice, has been documented by a number of sociologists and critics including Olive Senior (1993) and Lynn Marie Houston (2005: xxv- xxvii).

There is a much more explicitly cross-cultural appeal to the recipes in this book and an emphasis on cross-culinary fusion or hybridization.[16] However, one hesitates to term this truly creolized cookery writing as nothing truly new is being created in the mix.

SPICE IT UP

In *Spice It Up* (2011), the focus is on spices, Roots' spice cupboard in particular, which the dust jacket text declares excitedly—and with no trace of irony—that Roots "plunders [...] to create exciting new dishes with everyday ingredients" (np.). His cooking is, then, predicated on 'plunder,' an especially interesting metaphor when used in a Caribbean context, given its history of piracy and plunder of different kinds, colonial and otherwise. Spices are still, predictably, tropes of the exotic invoked and used to 'spice up' known and 'everyday' British dishes such as Shepherd's Pie (cf. Roots 2011: 9), pork chops (cf. 29-32) or Toad in the Hole (cf. 26). The gesture towards cross-culinary fusion which began in *Food For Friends* continues in *Spice It Up*, but arguably never quite moves beyond a rather superficial 'marrying' of ingredients. Roots describes this in the introduction to *Sweet* (2012) as an aim to "explore the typical flavors of the Caribbean and how they marry with those recipes and ingredients we know and love in the UK" (Roots 2012: 6).

The introduction to *Spice It Up* is fascinating in relation to the branding of the Levi Roots / *Reggae Reggae* food empire and its relation to Caribbean cuisine in Britain more generally. This branding reaches its apotheosis with Roots' incredible statement that, in terms of chilli, "if you want something that is 'Levi Spice'—it's best to use Scotch bonnet" (Roots 2011: 8). Here the use of the term "Levi Spice" connotes a multitude of things, conflating the qualities of the Scotch bonnet chilli pepper (potent, strong, authentic, the 'real-deal' of Caribbean cuisine) with the Roots brand. One might applaud such verbal playfulness were it not rooted quite so firmly in marketing discourse, another transparent example of the *Reggae Reggae* empire's promotional machinery; however, it is slightly disquieting that the placeholder term or substitution 'Levi Spice' is here invoked to represent a whole chain of referents which reduces the complexities of Caribbean food, from chilli, to spice, to Levi Spice. Here, metonymically at

---

16 Examples include the 'dubbed up, homemade version of the dish,' 'Levi's baked beans' (38) and 'Caribbean spiced shepherd's pie' (95).

least, Roots does not even have to use his moniker: he *is* Caribbean food in Britain.

Sweet

Sweet (2012) is something of a departure for Roots, since it focuses exclusively on cakes, puddings and desserts. In his introduction, appropriately enough, Roots riffs on the multiple meanings of the book's title for himself, as a cook of Caribbean origin and for his largely British-based audience, as well as "the many sources of sweetness in the Caribbean that I explore in the recipes in this book" (Roots 2012: 9).[17] As in his very first book, *Reggae Reggae Cookbook*, a sense of longing and nostalgia for 'back home' is conveyed through recognizable tropes such as the recollection of childhood memories,[18] the paratextual placing of touristic photographs, old postcards and retro style illustrations of Jamaica and Jamaican icons (prominently of course, Bob Marley) which convey a wider reconstructed 'vintage' provenance to his text.

Sweet is the most stylized of Roots' cookery books to date. It incorporates a 'retro' or 'vintage' visual styling which include: historical images of colonial food crops and food preparation from a variety of Caribbean and European sources (British, French, Spanish, Dutch); double-page colour spreads of old maps (106-7); engravings of Amerindians (106-7); recipe book covers (12-13); food marketing materials such as excerpts from an old Jamaican Information Service magazine (154-5); drink labels (60-1, 124-5, 128-9, 166-7, 197, 204-5); drink coasters (204-5); cigarette cards (12-13); illustrated playing cards (82-3, 166-7); and food related miscellanea such as swizzle sticks (106-7), printed sugar sacks (12-13), vintage cooking utensils and children's toys (12-13). Often, the focus in these double spreads is on particular colonial crops or food products associated with the Caribbean such as cocoa and chocolate (38-9), coffee (38-9,

---

17 This is something which Austin Clarke also discusses in his food memoir, *Pig Tails'n Breadfruit* (cf. 1999: 4-5).

18 These include memories of being shown how to harvest honey by his grandfather (cf. Roots 2012: 9) and the figure of "fudge Man, who sells ice cream and sweeties [and] drives around on a moped with a little refrigerator […]. The old-fashioned horn that heralds his arrival is still the same today as it was in my childhood" (8); this rather obvious invocation of 'tradition' is contrasted with his British equivalent, the ice-cream van, which connotes, conversely, modernity: "in Brixton, where I live, the ice-cream van plays hip-hop!" (8).

188-9), bananas (154-5), pineapples, rum (188-9, 197) and, of course, sugar (12-13) as well as other 'exotic' fruits (60-1, 82-3) and fruit drinks.

This, too, is a deliberate construction of 'tradition,' though one which aligns much more readily to current trends in retail and marketing design in the U.K. There is notably only one spread of colour photos of contemporary Jamaica, all snapshots of urban graffiti and brightly painted wooden and galvanize buildings (216-17). Significantly though, despite the scrapbook aesthetic of the book's design, which suggests 'found' scraps of recipes carefully presented and preserved for posterity, the register of Roots' written text is altogether more formal and less improvised than in his first book and more orthodox and Eurocentric in orientation. Roots' once-foregrounded cultural capital, his knowledge of Jamaican culture and culinary tradition, is here commodified even further, as it is represented in the historical context of a rich, but selective, archive of material cultural and visual artefacts which arguably speak more to current European tastes in 'lifestyle' publications than they do to any recognizably Caribbean aesthetic. The recipes too are overwhelmingly British with a Caribbean 'twist,' a "celebrat[ion] of Caribbean flavors" (8) as Roots puts it in his introduction, though he still insists on a Caribbean provenance for communal cooking and conviviality, claiming that "it's very Caribbean for everybody to get involved in making a meal...Food brings people together and give them a reason to want to come round and visit each other" (9). The role of the cook as ethnic advocate seems much less significant here.

CONCLUSION

My approach to Roots' cookery writing has been one which takes up Witt's challenge to read "cookbooks and recipes [as] not just transcriptions of performative culture [but as] complex rhetorical structures that can be decoded using the sorts of tools literary critics typically bring to say, a novel" (Witt 2007: 104). I have also sought to foreground in my analysis, postcolonial notions of 'authenticity' as a contested term, Bourdieu's concepts of "commercial and cultural capital" (1971, 1993) and, after Bourdieu, Bell's notion of "culinary cultural capital" (2002). We might conclude that ultimately, Roots' cookery writing is mired in contradiction, as may well be the plight of all those who write not only in a cross-cultural context but also in a globalized economy of food and mass media presence. It promises specificity (Jamaicaness) but simultaneously reifies and homogenizes Caribbean cooking through the branding of both Roots and his range as marketable commodities. His performances in his TV appearances and cookery writing, as well as the social media and wider online presence of his brand, have allowed him a kind of ascension to representative 'Caribbeanness' for many of his audience in the U.K.[19] In this, Roots is a performer and a metonym / performance of Caribbeanness. Arguably, this is problematic precisely because the performance is so singular, so commercially motivated and so non-heterogeneous, with most of the recipes drawing upon Jamaican dishes and culinary traditions rather than wider Caribbean ones and Caribbean microcuisines, for example, and his invocation of a kind of Reggae aesthetic similarly fails to take account of the wider diversity of musical traditions from and in the Caribbean. Yet, undoubtedly Roots has done more than any other Caribbean cook to raise the stakes and status of Caribbean cuisine in Britain.

BIBLIOGRAPHY

Appadurai, Arjun 2008 [1988]. "How to Make a National Cuisine." *Food and Culture*. Eds. Carolyn Counihan and Penny van Esterik. London / New York: Routledge, 289-307.

Ashcroft, Bill, Gareth Griffiths, and Helen Tiffin, eds. 1998. *Key Concepts in Post-Colonial Studies*. London / New York: Routledge.

Ashley, Bob, Steve Jones, and Ben Taylor 2004. *Food and Cultural Studies*. London / New York: Routledge.

Bell, David 2002. "From Writing at the Kitchen Table to TV Dinners. Food Media, Lifestylization and European Eating." Paper presented at 'East Drink and Be Merry?'. Cultural Meanings of Food in the 21st Century Conference, Amsterdam, June 2001 [http://cf.hum.uva.nl/research/asca/themediareader.html (retrieved 25 August 2012)].

Bourdieu, Pierre 1971. "Intellectual Field and Creative Project." *Knowledge and Control. New Directions for the Sociology of Education*. Ed. Michael F. D. Young. London: Collier-Macmillan.

—. 1984. *Distinction*. London: Routledge.

—. 1993. *The Field of Cultural Production*. Cambridge: Polity Press.

Clarke, Austin 2000. *Pigtails n' Saltfish. A Barbadian Memoir*. Kingston: Ian Randle Publishers.

Collingham, Lizzie 2006. *Curry*. London: Vintage.

---

[19] There is even a *Reggae Reggae* app for the iPhone which the dust jacket of *Spice It Up* declares: "topped the lifestyle bestseller chart and headed Apple's list of the hottest cooking apps of 2010."

Higman, Barry W. 2008. *Jamaican Food. History, Biology, Culture*. Mona: University of West Indies Press.

Houston, Lynn-Marie 2005. *Food Culture in the Caribbean*. Trenton: Greenwood Press.

Lawson Welsh, Sarah 2013. "'A Table of Plenty.' Representations of Food and Social Order in Caribbean Writing. Some Early Accounts, Caryl Phillip's *Cambridge* (1991) and Andrea Levy's *The Long Song* (2010)." *ENTERTEXT*, Special Issue on Caribbean Literature and Culture "Opening Out the Way(s) to the Future" 10: 73-89.

"Levi Roots full *Dragons' Den* Appearance," YouTube Video, 15:08, posted by OfficialLeviRoots, 23 April 2012 [http://www.youtube.com/watch?v=kQTzLJCUtjk (retrieved 12 August 2013)].

Lyon, John 2009. *Cook up in a Trini Kitchen*. Leeds: Peepal Tree.

Mehta, Brinda 2009. *Notions of Identity, Diaspora and Gender in Caribbean Women's Writing*. Houndmills: Palgrave Macmillan.

Melville, Pauline 1997. *The Ventriloquist's Tale*. London: Picador.

Richards-Greaves, Gillian 2013. "The Intersections of 'Guyanese Food' and Constructions of Gender, Race, and Nationhood." *Food and Identity in the Caribbean*. Ed. Hannah Garth. London: Bloomsbury, 75-94.

Roots, Levi 2008. *Reggae Reggae Cookbook*. London: Collins.

—. 2009. *Caribbean Food Made Easy*. London: Mitchell Beazley.

—. 2010. *Food For Friends*. London: Mitchell Beazley.

—. 2011. *Spice It Up*. London: Mitchell Beazley.

—. 2012. *Sweet*. London: Mitchell Beazley.

—. 2013. *Grill It With Levi. 101 Reggae Recipes for Sunshine and Soul*. London: Ebury Press.

Senior, Olive 1991. *Making Miracles. Women's Lives in the English-Speaking Caribbean*. London: James Currey / Bloomington: Indiana University Press.

Sheller, Mimi 2003. *Consuming the Caribbean*. London / New York: Routledge.

Taylor Sen, Colleen 2009. *Curry. A Global History*. London: Reaktion Books.

Witt, Doris 2007. "From Fiction to Foodways. Working at the Intersections of African American Literary and Culinary Studies." *African American Foodways. Explorations of History and Culture*. Ed. Anne L. Bower. Urbana / Chicago: University of Illinois Press, 101-125.

The Transnational *Ajiaco*
Food Identity in the Cuban Diaspora

IVAN DARIAS ALFONSO

INTRODUCTION

Cuban food stories have been integrated to the national imaginary space since the early quests for defining national identity (cf. Ortiz 1939). Food metaphors, for example, were used to define the Caribbean island, appealing to the historical periods resulting from the annihilation of the indigenous population, the Spanish colonial past—including the influx of African slaves—and after independence from Spain. Renowned ethnologist Fernando Ortiz (1939) used the word *ajiaco*, a traditional stew or broth found in the country's cuisine to define national culture. *Ajiaco*, originally a native dish, was adopted by the Spanish settlers and later by the slaves who contributed to it with their own ingredients.

Ismael Sarmiento Ramírez (2003) argues that *ajiaco* was considered a quintessential Cuban (*criollo*)[1] dish since colonial times. Examples found in travellers' literature of the period prove that many returning *criollos* favoured *ajiaco* over foreign recipes (cf. 2003: 200). It can be argued that attempts to define Cuban food after independence consciously dismissed the imports of other cultures, mainly those of African slaves and indentured workers from China. Examining cookbooks from before the Revolution, Christine Folch (2008) observes that this kind of literature provided a particular representation of food practices by showing the immigrants' contribution to the Cuban national menu in stereotypical and

---

1 The word *criollo* was the name given to Cuban-born people of European descent, primarily Spanish. Later it was used to identify everything commonly found on the island or appropriated by its inhabitants in a sort of collective claim to reinforce authenticity. The word is also used as a synonym for Cuban.

caricatured manners. The illustrations accompanying recipes portrayed black Cubans with "engorged lips and distorted features as to appear simian" and Chinese men with "wide grins and slit eyes" (Folch 2008: 218). Writing in 1956 for one of these cookbooks, in a well-known essay reprinted in 1966, Ortiz emphasized the African components of the Cuban diet. He traced the origins of many foodstuffs common on the island (for example, *fufú, funche* and *champola*, amongst others) incorporated into everyday meals back to Africa, praising the value of the slaves in shaping the idea of the national cuisine (cf. Ortiz 1966: 69).

Notions of what constituted 'national' food remained relatively unchanged in the Republican Period (1902-1959), or they were determined by social inequalities in the sense that upper and middle class families kept a more varied supply of ingredients and dishes whereas the working class families maintained more subsistence-based food practices. However, the Cuban Revolution produced a major change regarding the social divisions, which became more pronounced in the ensuing years when issues of food scarcity and food security signalled the pitfalls of revolutionary rule (cf. Alvarez 2004).

Three years into the Revolution, the new Cuban authorities were forced to ration food. Due to the increased purchasing power of the population and decreased food production, a rationing booklet (*la libreta*) was established (cf. Benjamin et al. 1986). Food consumption in every Cuban household was determined by the availability of products allocated by the distribution system. What followed then, were periods of relative food scarcity in the late 1960s until the early 1970s and times of better provision throughout the 1980s.

A direct result of the Revolution was the emergence of the Cuban-American diaspora. Geographical proximity and Cold War policies made it possible for many Cubans to settle in the United States. From the first wave of emigrants, mainly the country's upper class, to subsequent influxes (Freedom Flights, Mariel Boatlift, *Balsero* Crisis), the Cuban-American community grew in size and became very active in its opposition to the revolutionary government. Cuban-Americans also excelled at promoting national belonging or reinforcing *Cubanidad* or Cubanness (cf. Garcia 2007). They looked for strategies for remembering and celebrating the pre-revolutionary Cuba, in order to make it coincide with the myth of the ancestral homeland so common to many diasporas (cf. Safran 1991).

Over the decades, Cuban culture flourished north of the Florida Strait. Emigrants identified with a particular notion of Cubanness created outside the Caribbean island. In terms of food consumption, Cuban restaurants developed a taste for past meals recreated with ingredients found in the host country. Cuban-American mothers and grandmothers shared old recipes with their offspring in a process that Cuban scholar Víctor Fowler calls a pedagogical project: "an ordered and reasoned articulation of experiences to transmit a precise cultural heritage" (Fowler 2002: 11).

I would like to illustrate this with a recent example from the social media. As part of the press coverage for the London Olympic Games, American broadcaster NBC showed an interview with multimedalist swimmer Ryan Lochte's mother. Havana-born Ileana 'Ike' Lochte praised the Olympic poster boy's preference for Cuban food including *croquetas* cooked by his 90-year-old grandmother (cf. Nespral 2012). Shortly after the broadcast, a photomontage circulated on the web and was shared on the social media, stating that "behind every great man there was a Cuban grandmother making croquetas." The intersections of food and diaspora in the Cuban-American community had never seemed so relevant.

When talking about Cuban food, the main name that comes to mind is Nitza Villapol, the national cooking guru. She attained celebrity in the 1950s thanks to her book and television show *Cocina al minuto* (Cooking in one minute) that continued on Cuban national television until 1991. However, what is interesting is that her book, considered the bible of Cuban cuisine, was one of the possessions Cuban exiles took when they settled in the United States. Copies of it, reprinted without Villapol's permission, still circulated in Spanish-language bookstores in Dade County in the 1990s (cf. Santiago 1998).

On the island, food traditions were difficult to sustain, depending on the availability of resources, but many practices remained the same. Researchers from the Centre of Anthropology of the University of Havana discovered little variations in the way daily meals were ranked according to its importance. Despite periods of low food supply, Cubans tried to maintain breakfasts, lunches and dinners and consider the latter as the most important meal of the day (cf. Núñez González 1999). However, that changed radically after 1989 when imports from the socialist block fell by 90 per cent and Cubans had to endure a so-called Special Period (cf. Kapcia 2000). Fuel was reduced, which affected public transport; power cuts were a regular occurrence, but the most visible sign of the whole crisis was the shortage of food.[2]

In this context, restrictions to travel abroad were partially lifted and Cubans began to emigrate.[3] Some joined the Cuban-American community, others pre-

---

2   The assessment of the impact of the food scarcity on Cuban society has taken a long time to appear in the national debate. Cuban poet Arístides Vega Chapú edited in 2011 a collection of personal memories of Cuban authors who experienced the Special Period and narrations about food scarcity were predominant in the pages of the book.

3   Until very recently (January 2013) Cubans were not allowed to travel abroad freely. Cubans who wanted to leave needed a visa given by the destination country's authori-

ferred culturally similar places (Spain and Latin America), but an increasing number of educated professionals opted for travelling to previously considered exotic destinations such as Sweden, Norway and the U.K. Some emigrated when they met and married foreigners who had gone to the Caribbean island when the country overcame decades of isolation and promoted international tourism as a way to boost economic recovery.

The expansion of the tourist industry demanded a regular supply of cooking and food items. Therefore, agriculture was diversified to include special farming facilities that catered to the new and booming economic sector. Other measures included the creation of small private business for the sale of food products, which became known as *paladares*. Many of these food ventures targeted international tourists, so Cuban food also benefited from visitors who came and developed a taste for it and later shared their experiences. Cuban restaurants sprung up in many European cities. Their menus were sometimes based on Cuban recipes but so-called Cuban dishes also included ingredients and seasonings that were not traditional in the Cuban kitchens. Compared to regional cuisines like the Mexican and the Anglo-Caribbean, traditional Cuban food is neither diversified nor highly seasoned.

The Cuban diaspora in London appeared in the aftermath of the relaxation of national laws prohibiting Cubans to travel abroad. Unlike many compatriots' migratory trajectories ending in the U.S., Cuban-Londoners could only emigrate through legal means, in many cases, through marriages to British citizens. Others came on student visas and overstayed, while some others arrived through cultural exchange trips.

Data from the Office for National Statistics estimate the number of Cubans in Britain to be 2000 (cf. ONS, 2012). Unlike other diasporic communities in the country, they do not live in particular areas or form ethnic based communities. In this regard, they resemble other Cuban émigrés in Europe whose reluctance to form collective groups and geographical dispersion has been recently documented (cf. Wimmer 2001, Sánchez Fuárros 2008, Berg 2011).

This article is based on a series of qualitative interviews carried out in London, in 2006-2008. The research was conducted with a varied sample of interviewees comprising twenty males and twenty females. Most of them originally came from Havana (27), but I also managed to include participants from other provinces such as Villa Clara (4), Matanzas (3), Holguín (3), Pinar del Río (1), Guantánamo (1) and Sancti Spiritus (1). Their ages range from the early twenties

---

ties and an exit permit granted by Cuba's Interior Ministry (MININT), which was difficult to get if the reasons for travelling did not include education, sport or cultural events.

to 50 and older. However, 80 per cent of my participants (32) belonged in the 30-45 age group. As for their time in diaspora, the majority (24) have lived between five and ten years outside the homeland, 13 have spent between ten and twenty years in London and three interviewees have been living in the U.K. for more than twenty years. In terms of the sample's geography, seven participants reside in Central London, six in North West London, ten in North London, seven in South London, two in East London, two in West London, one in South West and three in South East London. I interviewed one participant who lived in Colchester, Essex. She gained a Chevening Scholarship, which was one of the ways to come to Britain from Cuba in the mid-1990s, so she was a member of that group of migrants who firstly came for study purposes and later married a British citizen. I also recruited one participant who lived in Brighton, East Sussex, but worked in London, so he could give me the experience of living in the city as a commuter.

FOOD AND DIASPORA, THEORETICAL APPROACHES

The impact of food in a diasporic context and its potential as an identity marker has been the focus of research about transnational communities since the emergence of Diaspora Studies. Food habits have been explored to illustrate strategies of identity construction because of the symbolic implications of food and commensality in telling us something about ourselves and our place in the world (cf. Bell and Valentine 1997).

Early theories on human dispersal (cf. Safran, 1991, Cohen 1997) identified the maintenance or restoration of the previous homeland as one of the key features of diaspora. The country of origin, recreated in the host country, idealized as a mythical land to return to, becomes an important centre from which notions of cultural identity originate and are subsequently shared by the members of a diasporic group. However, diasporas also become evident in the continuous interactions of everyday life (cf. Brah 1996).

In diaspora, food attains a vital importance in terms of cultural distinction because food and commensality are part of the extensive repertoire of cultural practices migrants carry with them. Food rituals and meal preparation, as well as the kitchen as a location, enable the creation of a particular space where identity markers can be comfortably acknowledged and ultimately shared. Diasporic citizens use food as a marker of difference with the added goal of asserting their identities. Such a practice exemplifies conceptualizations of the symbolic implications of foodstuff and meals and their potential as a means of communication, which has been a concern for anthropologists and social theorists (cf. Barthes 1961, Lévi-Strauss 1968, Douglas 1972, Bourdieu 1984, Mintz 1985). I am referring to an identity that can be understood as a process rather than as a concept (cf. Hall 1996). I can point out that identity formation is a process that does not conclude with a complete and unchallenged notion of identity. Individuals in society are constantly defining themselves in terms of identity and through exclusions based on their relationships with others. In diaspora, what one finds distinctive is that not only is the sense of an individual identity formed but a "collective" identity is created as well. I focus on those characteristics which allow individuals to identify themselves as members of a particular ethnic and national group and that also suggest a collective association. Since I look at diaspora as the main context to analyse how identities are formed, I am considering the potential implication of home and host country, the two major forces in channelling claims of belonging.

I also based my theorizations of identity on the idea that it is constituted through discursive practices (cf. Hall 1997). In the context of the Cuban Revolution, we must remember that issues of belonging and national identity were intensively redefined and shared on exclusive basis, where being Cuban was equated with being revolutionary, implying an unconditional loyalty to the communist government.[4] Ernesto Guevara's notion of "the new man" (*hombre nuevo*) was adopted as a template for collective social aspirations. It postulated the ideal of sacrifice as an ultimate goal and gave priority to a national identity based on revolutionary values, and on strict codes of racial, gender and sexual identification (cf. Guevara 1965).

Migrants and those wanting to leave the country were labelled *gusanos* (worms), and *escoria* (scum) in 1980 prior to the Mariel Crisis, in accordance with an official discourse that limited national sentiments and the idea of a homeland to the geographical boundaries of the Caribbean island. Therefore, those on the island remained "Cuban" whereas those in the diaspora were automatically dismissed as "anti-Cuban." It is worth mentioning that after the Special Period, this dichotomy was deemed irrelevant in the national debate about identity. Ariana Hernández-Reguant has noted a discursive turn in the way in which the Cuban authorities approached the subject of national identity. She argues that the idea of nation was redefined as an ethnic and cultural community, rather than as a political entity (cf. Hernández-Reguant 2009:70).

I also understand the diasporic experience as a generator of new understandings, which exceed any essentialist claim rooted in the homeland or in the host

---

4   For a discussion of national identity and the Cuban Revolution see Kapcia (2000), Behar and Suárez (2008), Hernández-Reguant (2009).

country. Rather than situating the diasporic space within the common tensions of "here" (host land) and "there" (homeland), I aim to explore further associations in line with Homi Bhabha's (1994) notion of the "third space,"[5] and I define diaspora as a fertile ground where new notions of cultural belonging can emerge. Based on these new associations migrants can not only locate themselves with respect to their country of origin, but also to the host country or, given the prevalence of multiple migratory flows in the current globalised world, to transitory destinations.

In such a varied compendium of stories of uprooting and displacement, settlement and difference, I argue that food continues to assert its importance as a signifier of both the past and the future. As a reference to the past (homeland) it traces the origins of a cultural attachment; as a link to the future, it ensures the on-going process of identification and self-categorization.

Studies of food and diaspora have shown that culinary practices are turned into markers of difference between emigrants and local populations. Hannah Bradby observed how Glaswegian women of Punjabi origin divided their daily food into "our food," which comprised foodstuff traditionally found in Punjabi cuisine and "their food" signalling every other import (cf. Bradby 1997: 231). This persistence in limiting food choices to appropriate values according to cultural tradition marks diasporas' attempts to remain distinctive, sometimes to their own detriment. Nassima Mannan and Barbara Boucher (2002) studied the Bangladeshis in London to conclude that dietary habits were maintained as a source of pride and identity despite the health risks involved.

Diasporic food practices can also impact on food habits in the homeland. The most notable case being Belize where, as Richard Wilk (1999) has demonstrated, the idea of national food was created in diaspora long before the country existed as a nation with its current name. Belizean restaurants in Los Angeles enabled a strong association between food consumed in those places with food customs common in the former British colony.

'Ethnicised' restaurants in particular have become a privileged space for the display of national identities traits. The main attraction for emigrants to frequent these places is not only to sample homeland food, but also to experience commensality in a way similar to that of their country of origin. Examining the ex-

---

5   I am referring to a third space which is not located here (the host country or London, in this case) nor there (the homeland). Bhabha argues that all cultural systems are constructed in a 'Third Space of Enunciation.' In accepting this argument, I stress that the inherent purity and originality of cultures are 'untenable.' By embracing the hybridised nature of cultures I can depart from the problematic binarisms that have shaped previous notions of culture and, in this case, national (Cuban) culture.

ample of Chinese restaurants, Sally Chang (2002) concluded that emigrants decorate social spaces, such as restaurants, with motifs from their places of origin in order to ensure co-ethnic solidarity. Following similar strategies, Colombian emigrants succeeded in creating an ethnicised space for a display of national symbols and Latin American identities in the Elephant and Castle Shopping Centre in London (cf. Roman-Velazquez 1999).

Research (cf. Narayan 1995, Kershen 2002) has also shown that 'ethnic' restaurants are the preferred places for migrants to socialize, when food stands out as a strong cultural export; however, not all emigrants share similar food traditions nor advocate a public display of them. According to Anne Kershen, migrants reserve their dietary culture for the private space (cf. Kershen 2002:7). Home kitchens then, become a more suitable space for the reproduction of homeland food and its ceremonies.

In her research on Cuban émigrés in Australia, Eurídice Charon Cardona (2004) noted that food practices have enabled a Cuban identity, which has remained confined to the domestic space. Kitchens constituted a distinctive setting where food habits are shared and homeland recipes are re-created using local ingredients or imported ones, similar to those found on the Caribbean island. Consequently, subject construction has become a more private concern, in contrast to other Cuban diasporic hotspots, such as Miami, where identity markers are more visible and collectively shared, permitting a public display of a more distinctive Cuban identity. One of the reasons for this more public profile appears very clearly related to the size of the population of diasporic Cubans in Miami, which exceeds one million. In contrast, the number of Cubans in Australia is much smaller, similar to the size of the diaspora in London.

TALKING ABOUT FOOD, TALKING ABOUT CUBA

The issue of food has always been problematic in the history of the Cuban Revolution, mainly because, even though it is an agriculture-based nation, Cuba never produced enough to feed its own people. In the 1990s, when the ingredients of the national diet became scarce, the Cuban media never acknowledged such food shortage.[6] The Cuban government tried to avoid recognition of problems such as malnourishment and a food crisis, mainly because these phenomena related to

---

6   A popular joke at the time suggested going grocery shopping on the eight o'clock news program, because national television was the only place where fruit and vegetables were shown.

less developed nations, which would result in a costly political defeat (cf. Alvarez 2004). After 30 years of claiming that Cuba was ahead of any other unindustrialized country, it would have been catastrophic to admit that a sign of underdevelopment as obvious as "hunger" was part of Cuban life.

When I asked the participants about their definition of Cuban food, I was always presented with a list of common dishes found in the island's popular cookbook. Many of these relate to the smells and tastes Judith Olson and James Olson (1995) defined as quintessentially Cuban in their analysis of the Cuban-American diaspora. Our interviewees described "national food" in terms of its nutritional value and about the health benefits or risks of its daily consumption. I believe this assessment of the national diet was mediated by their migratory experience because many compared Cuban food with the wide variety of diasporic cuisines available in London. Living abroad has enhanced their perception of dishes, and also ways, in which to prepare them, which suggests that food habits have changed, as I shall demonstrate. However, Cuban food still retains an important association with the homeland because of the way it was invoked by many participants. Expressions such as "lick one's fingers" or "feeling of being at home" reflect the influence food has to evoke memories of their homeland.

These examples suggest, as key themes in the anthropology of food have also demonstrated (cf. Douglas 1972), that food is imbued with meaning. Our participants also acknowledged the importance of food contexts, which also inscribed food practices with a distinctive characteristic; many then proceeded to identify the role of this context in shaping their previous food experiences on the island. For example:

Cuban food has deteriorated a lot with the Revolution, unfortunately. Cuban food can be [...], the dishes eaten in Cuba could be counted on the fingers of one hand. Because of the necessity, [...], you understand why the government has been forced to produce high yielding crops for a population in need of food; [...], it can't give up land to plant rare vegetables, but in Cuba you don't find traditional vegetables either. So the quality [of Cuban food] has suffered a lot. I have a cookbook from before the Revolution, and the amount of recipes and dishes that I hadn't even seen [is huge]. (Ruben)[7]

In the previous fragment Ruben locates the radical changes in Cuban food in the aftermath of the Revolution. The early agricultural policies of the revolutionary government impacted food production, distribution and conditioned food intake amongst the population, but it is difficult to claim that the participants could contrast this argument with the reality of pre-1959 Cuba, since the majority of them

---

7   All names used are pseudonyms.

were born and bred in the revolutionary years. Their understandings of previous decades can only be achieved by memory work through conversations with parents and grandparents or as in Ruben's case by cookbooks from that time.

Another opportunity for remembering past experiences related with food could have been a casual encounter with what Julio Ramón calls "the other Cuba," referring to Miami. In his case, he was able to encounter the forgotten flavours of his childhood in capitalist Cuba, in the U.S.A.:

Those who had lived for the past 49 years still don't know what the famous Cuban sandwich is, which is a mix of ham, cheese, gherkins, and what we used to call *medianoche* [lit. midnight], [...] and my children tasted it later and I used to tell them, you can't have this [in Cuba]; lots of people in Cuba don't know what a *buñuelo* is, or custard, or rice pudding because if you have rice, you're not going to use it to make dessert; that's a lie, rice pudding with cinnamon on top. All this you find it in the other Cuba that is Florida. And a cookbook is not the same. Written gastronomy theory is not the same as feeling the flavour of grandmother's cooking, or auntie's or mother's, cooking in the kitchen. Then, that memory is lost. (Julio Ramón)

Besides the importance of placing food and commensality in a specific context, that of revolutionary Cuba, I also encountered several participants who emphasized a certain essentialisation of Cuban food. I would argue that both context and essentialist versions are very much related when I analyse food and notions of identity. By acknowledging the importance of context, participants were able to identify those developments (food production, distribution), which affected food habits and customs throughout their life in revolutionary Cuba.

In diaspora, the participants can access different representations of national food, either through cookbooks or by visiting other diasporic enclaves. They can contrast their previous versions of Cuban food with these new discoveries and reflect on its importance for personal strategies of subject construction. In their own words, their notion of Cuban food has been limited to a list of recipes, which could be prepared depending on the availability of the ingredients.

–What is Cuban food for you?
–It's like Cuban music, what do you mean by that? See what I mean? I don't know if you saw the article from maybe three or four months ago, which appeared in the Travel supplement of *The Guardian*,[8] about Cuban food and the journalist said: Well, Cubans do not have a culinary tradition. I wrote [back] in fact, they never published the letter, but I don't know; people have a very strange idea of what Cuban food is and I think that we are to

---

8   *The Observer's Travel Supplement*, 30 April 2006.

blame too, because we are constantly reinforcing the idea that [Cuban food] is *congrí* [rice and black beans], pork, *tostones*, salads, and it is varied.
–Did you always have Cuban food in Cuba?
We ate what we could. Oh, we ate whatever was available, as simple as that: in the good times, we had good meals, do you understand? But the variety of a cuisine depends on the sense of adventure of the person who cooks. That's why I tell you that Cuban music and Cuban food go hand in hand, and that includes the elements of culture […] Zeus [a Cuban hard rock band] is as Cuban as Van Van, [a popular music group] do you understand? (Miguel)

Miguel found the definition of Cuban food problematic because, as he explained, certain elements have been over-represented as national cuisine. He argued for a broader notion of homeland food that would also include dishes that emerged in the revolutionary years. Miguel compared it with the example of the band Zeus, which remained underground during the 1980s when rock music was generally discouraged as not being representative of Cuban music and socialist values. However, as he explains, Zeus could also be a part of the homeland.

As Miguel puts it, "lack of creativity" was one of the reasons given to justify the recurrence of certain dishes in their everyday meals. Participants described, for example, how they were used to a basic diet of rice, beans and a *plato fuerte* (animal protein). Repetition was a direct consequence of the state distribution system, although I should consider other social factors. Class divisions, for instance, determined that those families with a higher income could "experiment" more. The importance of class in the Cuban context may appear counterproductive, considering that the Cuban authorities have always defended the classless nature of the island's society. However, many studies (cf. Martin 1996, Uriarte-Gaston 2004, Corrales 2004, Valdés Paz 2005, Domínguez 2008) have demonstrated that class divisions persisted during the Revolution or became more pronounced in the aftermath of the Special Period (cf. Espina Prieto 2005). To my participants, acknowledging the importance of class in assessing their experience on the homeland, is another direct consequence of living in diaspora and in Britain in particular, where discussions about class have dominated social and political discourse over decades.

One of the interviewees, Adrian, who had lived in a working class neighbourhood in Havana prior to migrating, explained to me that he had a specific Cuban meal on his most nostalgic days: rice, fried eggs on top and a banana. This version of a national meal, as some other participants called it, is packed with social meaning in our opinion. Rather than being a quintessentially Cuban recipe, it refers to a more urban version of an everyday meal. Its preparation was linked to the availability of the main ingredients, as rice, eggs and bananas were relatively easy to obtain, even in periods of acute food scarcity. It also reveals how food supplies varied depending on the household social status even when, allegedly, all families received an equivalent amount of groceries allocated in the ration booklet.

Many participants confirmed this assumption when they told us that they knew of households where meals and food habits were different, implying less varied or poorer diet habits.

I knew that in the majority of the houses around my house there weren't as many ingredients as in mine. (Camilo)

I did not pay much attention since I always ate whatever it was served. But as I began to know certain people, I used to dine in the houses of the main celebrities of Cuban culture and of course, they had more *poder adquisitivo* [purchasing power]. And you realized that there were other… spheres of Cuban food. (Ángel)

Both participants acknowledge a social context associated with previous food practices in the homeland, which helps them to reflect on the social inequalities of their Cuban menus. I would point out that their understandings of homeland food culture are now mediated by this reasoning; therefore I argue that participants evaluate their experiences with food in Cuba to incorporate them as part of their everyday life and as a distinctive feature of their identity. They differentiate national / traditional Cuban food from the more practical dishes and food choices they were compelled to live with.

COOKING WITH COOKBOOKS

References to cookbooks appeared frequently during interviews. Undoubtedly they are a useful resource to my respondents, either when they read about national food or prepare recipes, because cookbooks often include more than the procedure for cooking a dish. One can find information about the history, traditions and culture associated with a particular dish. In the Cuban context they date from colonial years and are useful to theorize about national identity. Panikos Panayi argues that cookbooks have the same role for culinary development as political ideology has for the evolution of states (cf. Panayi 2008: 214). Recently Folch (2008) has concluded that recipe books were used to promote a "whiter and European" representation of Cuba by trivializing and ignoring the contributions of Afro-Cubans. With the Revolution, cookbook content changed. For example, some of our participants mentioned cookbooks and specifically the Cuban food bible, *Cook in One Minute* by Nitza Villapol.

Yes, we had a book of Cuban recipes, and that famous one by Nitza Villapol, and she started very well, but when the crisis came she began to invent: let's eat fried flowers with tomato sauce, and people said, "What?" What is that flower called, is it *Marpacífico*? [...] And people began to say, "Oh-oh, *le está patinando el coco* [she is losing her mind]" or "*se le pasó la rosca* [she has a screw loose]" because at this point to eat flowers? And in reality, when you analyse [what she said] those plants had important nutritional value, but in the Cuban conscience what you get is rice, beans, pork, chicken, fried ripe plantain and that's it, and fish, that's it. There is nothing else. (Aldo)

Oh, Nitza Villapol recipes. I have read about that. [...] I read about that in a book I brought, written by a Cuban journalist who writes chronicles about Cuba and one of them was about Nitza Villapol. He reports on an interview he had with her after the Special Period. Because Nitza was a highly educated woman, she did a lot of research [to find out] what she could cook with what was available. For example, there was a time when there were only potatoes. She researched on what she could do with potatoes, and every week she presented a potato-based recipe, a new one, and it went like that until the program was suspended. (Ana)

These comments show the relevance of Nitza Villapol's cookbook to homeland cuisine. Perhaps her endeavours concentrated on stimulating a healthy and nutritious way of eating with what was available rather than promoting a national cuisine. Nevertheless, since many of our interviewees identified her book as their Cuban food guide, I believe it must help them in their process of identity formation.

Living in diaspora, our participants did not rely on just one homeland reference, a cookbook in this case. The advent of globalization and the marketing of ethnic food have also brought about a vast printed collection of recipes from all over the world, including Cuba and its diaspora. Many respondents have come across "unfamiliar" recipes for national food in so-called Cuban cookbooks. My participants were not familiar with these Cuban dishes because they did not know many of the ingredients needed for their preparation. I asked them about these "rare" Cuban food examples. Some respondents were particularly cautious about incorporating these recipes into their everyday cooking repertoire, but others welcomed the idea of experimenting with new versions of national food. I contend that food could contribute to gaining knowledge about the past. This idea represents a key point in the process leading to a new identity construction. The case of food is particularly important because it is closely related to the domestic setting. Certain food practices that practically disappeared in more public and shared locations were kept in smaller places, at household levels (cf. Núñez González 1999).

This section has demonstrated how Cuban food is contextualized. Emigrants are able to examine their previous ideas of "national diet" or of "typical meals," depending on the knowledge they have gained regarding the social constraints of food on the island. I argue that this examination affects their notion of identity because in London Cubans tended to accept that their everyday meals in Cuba were far from their common version of national food. Lunches and dinners in the homeland were the result of often chaotic attempts to provide basic nourishment at family levels rather than more elaborate cultural strategies of nutrition. They had more to do with "feeding" than with gastronomy (cf. Wilson 2009).[9] In diaspora, the availability of food allows our participants to use it as a collateral resource in their display of Cubanness. Food habits are rooted in their past; therefore any possible revision of that past reconsiders the impact of food. In addition, the emigrants discovered unfamiliar recipes of the homeland culinary heritage—mainly through cookbooks—, which inevitably led them to recognize and adopt unfamiliar representations of Cuba.

I would add that the term 'authentic' has been used in this section as a synonym for a social construction, because I reject any essentialist claim about what Cuban food signifies. I argue that the departure from those reduced versions of national food enables our participants to sustain a different strategy of subject construction. I made the parallel that the adjective *Cuban* in Cuban food is expanded in diaspora in order to conclude that it then becomes a powerful modifier to guide their notions of cultural identities. Our respondents dismissed the idea of a 'one and only' way to cook Cuban style, whether it was influenced by a deliberate approach like in Camilo's case or by a previous stint in diaspora (Julia). I have discussed traditional food and 'circumstantial' food throughout this section.

---

9   The reference is made in an attempt to explain how the lack of food ingredients and the exhausting process of gathering foodstuff leave little time for food preparation. In that sense, and especially in those households where domestic tasks are much divided along gender lines, Cubans are used to a daily ration of uncomplicated and quick meals.

FRIENDS, PARTIES AND SOCIAL EATING

In earlier sections of this article, I mentioned the importance of ethnicised restaurants for community building and the display and sharing of ethnic identity markers. However, in the case of my participants, very few preferred such places for gathering. Cubans in London are very dispersed geographically because they do not live in just one London area, and are almost invisible as a diasporic group. Unlike other diasporas in London's hyperdiverse landscape, they do not congregate on specific areas or around strong cultural and collective institutions.[10]

In this regard, I deemed their diasporic experience as an individual endeavour, although there are some instances where the group is noticeable, which give us an idea of the real number of Cubans in London. Íñigo Sánchez Fuárros has described a similar pattern of visibility in the Cubans in Barcelona. He argues that a sense of identity could only be observed in certain spaces, which were part of what he called the "social routes of Cubanness" (Sánchez Fuárros 2008:74). From his asseveration I can infer that a collective identity could not be comfortably asserted outside these limited settings. Sánchez Fuárros examined the ethnicised places in Barcelona (restaurants and clubs), but during our research I carried out participant observation in the now-defunct *Carnival de Cuba* (Cuban carnival) to arrive at the same conclusions.

Cuban restaurants in London were also not particularly favoured as meeting places. Many participants complained that the food was not Cuban, paralleling claims of authenticity common to many diasporic food venues. However, their reluctance may be just another reason to explain why Cuban food has been difficult to market for British and other foreign palates. Restaurants, for example, are decorated according to a visual aesthetic supported by a foreign gaze, the vision of the island by a visitor, a tourist. Bright colours, palm trees, beaches and anachronistic political symbols (UJC emblem, Che Guevara portraits, communist slogans) adorn walls and corners. Such a garish array of objects suggests a representation of the island gained through foreign eyes, which normally appreciate the touristic attractions first and then later on incorporate the political symbols without understanding how they really feature in Cuban society. In ad-

---

10 Since the early 2000s, the Cuban consulates in Europe have been very active in promoting meetings to group Cuban emigrants (*Encuentros de Cubanos Residentes en el Exterior*). Some of these events have been regularly held in London, along with others organised by the Martí-Maceo Cultural Society (*Sociedad Cultural Martí-Maceo*), which also aims to represent Cubans in the U.K. However, since the Cuban consular authorities host them, not all émigrés are willing to participate in these activities.

dition, menus appear as another re-interpretation of the island diet featuring exotic imports common to other, Anglo-Caribbean countries or even to other constructed multicultural food traditions now common in Britain such as chillies and curries.

Cuban-Londoners, nevertheless, create their own spaces for sharing previously learned food habits and the consumption of Cuban meals. They prefer the intimate spaces of their own kitchens. I mentioned earlier that the majority of my participants were married to British partners or to other European citizens. This and other practices I will comment on in the next section may have influenced many answers expressing that participants did not prepare Cuban meals every day. Instead Cuban food was reserved for special occasions, as some acknowledged:

Yes, I prepare Cuban food and I do my Cuban-themed afternoons, as I call them with a game of domino and Cuban music. I mean, a real Cuban party, which was another thing that shocked me [when he arrived]. We didn't go to a party, we went to an English party. So when we used to go [to dinner parties] there were wine bottles coming in and out and everybody chatting and [I said] hang on, where's the music. (César)

César's aim at creating a Cuban-themed party appears to be twofold. He is refusing to accommodate his socializing routines to the socially accepted norms in the host country. But, as he explains, this is achieved through a negotiation process. He told us that going to dinner parties with no music (or dancing) was something he had to adapt to, but that did not prevent him from creating his Cuban style dinner parties where the space was reproduced according to the way it was done in Cuba.

Another participant also came up with a similar idea to invite his Cuban or British friends.

When I arrived I used to cook Saturdays and weekends […]. It was like a *Sábado de la Rumba*[11] in our house. We took the drums out and played rumba, I did some rapping and that was it. We ate Cuban food, I used to do my little *ajiacos* and that was it, like a CDR[12] party at home. (Danilo)

---

11 A well-known cultural event held at the Havana venue of the *Conjunto Folclórico Nacional* (National Folklore Ensemble) since the early 1970s.

12 Founded in 1960 to confront counterrevolutionary activities, the *Comité de Defensa de la Revolución* (CDR) organises Cubans at street level.

Both participants identify the power of music as a cultural reference to create an environment suitable for asserting their identity. Cuban restaurants, and even those Latin-themed ones, regularly play the island's music; however, in César and Danilo's cases they also select the music in order to ensure a more "authentic" gathering. I would like to draw attention towards the fact that both participants, Afro-Cuban males from Havana's working class neighbourhoods of Centro Habana and Habana Vieja, were in charge of cooking. Research about gender issues on Cuba (cf. Holgado Fernandez 2001, Pertierra 2008, Krull and Davidson 2011) has stressed how Cuban kitchens have remained a women's domain. Racial stereotypes have also helped in constructing an idea of masculinity in a very limited way along the domestic division of labour. Some participants recognized this fact, some declared they never learned to cook, while some others, however, have overcome prejudices and negative associations as part of their personal strategies of identity formation.

I wanted to highlight new notions of masculinity relevant to their sense of Cubanness displayed and experienced in a semi-collective environment. Not all male participants knew how to cook and many had to learn when they came to London, depending on whether domestic chores were shared in their respective households. Others, although initially married to British women, came out as gay men years later and their new sexual identity had made them reconsider their previous domestic roles.[13]

Female participants did not exhibit a wider range of cooking skills either. Housing shortage has been recognized as one of the most critical problems in Cuban cities. Therefore, it is common to find up to three generations of the same family living under the same roof. In such a context, the kitchen has remained the realm of mothers and grandmothers, who do all the cooking and food preparation (cf. Krull and Davidson 2011).

To be honest, in Cuba I had nothing to do with the kitchen because my mum [didn't let me in]. No, no, that was *zona vedada* [forbidden zone]. (Emilio)

No [I did not cook in Cuba]. Because I lived with my mum and my grandma, so I did not have their authorization to enter that part of the house. But here, yes [I cook]. (Silvia)

---

13 Isabel Holgado Fernández (2001) argues that within the Cuban Revolution one can only be very macho or very mother; as though there is no room for chosen identities (cf. Holgado Fernández 2001: 320). She summarizes the dominant discourse of the society that assigns women and men very specific social roles: women as mothers; men as brave machos.

Both participants' comments reinforced this notion of kitchens as a particular space in the homeland in terms of the domestic division of labour. However, both have changed their level of interaction with that space in diaspora. In London, the kitchen is a more welcoming domain, especially when it comes to inviting fellow Cubans. As one of our participants (Julia) stated, food is just a pretext for a gathering because she always plans the cooking event as a special occasion to ensure conversation in Spanish, for example, which she normally does not do with her British husband.

A Quest for Homeland Taste, Revised Food Practices

Having explored what the respondents defined as "core" ingredients of the interviewees' idea of national food, I analyse how and if their everyday menus were noticeably Cuban. The characterizations of Cuban food I have presented in the previous sections of this article, might suggest that the emigrants maintain a diet similar to the one they had in the homeland, a diet notable for the prevalence of Cuban traditional recipes. This trend is similar in other migrant groups (cf. Bradby 1997, Kershen 2002, Charon Cardona 2004). However, interviewees' answers also reveal that their everyday practices did not necessarily involve the preparation of Cuban menus.

There are several reasons participants gave for eating non-Cuban foods, ranging from practical limitations to more abstract ones. Certain dishes of Cuban food require a considerable time in their preparation, which seems daunting to those with very busy lifestyles:

Black beans, for example, [take] three hours; I do not have three hours. I cook recipes that take less time. I mean, I cook, I am used to cooking, but I spend half an hour more or less cooking. (Alicia)

On the other hand, to some of our participants, their understanding of Cuban food denoted a "reduced" version of the national diet, the kind of food they used to have in their homes. As I explained, this varied depending on factors like social status and access to provisions outside the government distribution schemes. Therefore, for some of them, the experience of diaspora signifies an overcoming of their previous and limited diet and a way in which to identify themselves as more "open" in terms of their food choices. In addition, many of them, especially the male respondents, learned how to cook in London. This group arrived without any kitchen skills, because in their households a female family member, mainly mothers or grandmothers, always did the cooking.

I asked participants if their diet had been altered after coming to London. Six admitted to no change, but the rest (34) acknowledged modifications in their food habits and their diet. Some simply agreed (eight) but others provided evaluative responses such as "some changes" (four), "a lot of changes" (two) and "huge changes" (20).

In diaspora, interviewees had modified their food practices by transforming the routines of food preparation, but the most important modification has been the preference for healthier variants of food. This includes our interviewees' concern for introducing more vegetables into their diets, as well as organic products.

Normally [my diet] has changed in the sense that, for example, rice... I eat rice two or three times per week, but it has changed in a positive way because in Cuba you eat lots of things that are really bad for you. [...] But here I like to vary. I eat a lot of vegetables, salads, soups. Cubans are not "soup people", but I'm sorry, we do mix a lot. For example, I like Chinese food, and pasta. I mean, I always try to vary; I never eat [the same]... and what you would never see me eating is supermarket cans, never! Heating up canned food... I prefer to cook fresh food, I eat fresh food instead of anything that has been canned for five years, aged. (Mirtha)

I ate few vegetables, not because I did not have them in Cuba, because for example...eggplants were left to rot in the market stalls [because] people didn't pay attention to them, the same with broccoli and cabbages. I had learned to make sophisticated things with cabbage, but I didn't learn what to do with eggplants. I tried it once and I didn't like it. So my life here... since I love cooking and I have had friends from all over the world, well, then I take a bit from every nationality the way to prepare each vegetable and I incorporate it to my cooking. (Monica)

I had a very limited diet in Cuba. I didn't like to try. I ate almost no vegetables; I didn't eat fish because my experience of eating fish in Cuba was that of eating *merluza* [hake] with a lot of bones, see what I mean? And that's one of the things I have discovered that Cuba is an island with a poor consumption of fish. You go to any other Caribbean island and they eat a lot of fish, a lot of seafood, as a general rule. And here I eat more fish because it is healthier than meat and sometimes it is even cheaper because it is better. [So] my diet, yes, it is one of the things that has changed most since I came to London. (Felix)

These quotes suggest that Cubans have had a positive reaction to including more vegetables into their diets whilst also keeping some of their homeland food habits. This differs from the general assumption that ethnic minorities try to maintain their own cooking and eating patterns as long as possible (cf. Mennell et al. 1992, Mannan and Boucher 2002).

My respondents' choices of healthier food reflect their desire to overcome the food preconceptions of their previous diet in Cuba. Despite the standardized availability of food in the homeland, their idea of national food is also personalized in the sense that it depends on the food culture participants experienced at home. Therefore, their food prejudices can be explained by the impact their families had in creating and sharing a food culture.

In my house in Cuba you ate rice and beans, and sometimes spaghetti, but on very few occasions. However, my aunt in Santa Clara [...] she was the kind of person who liked to cook; she liked to experiment, so there was not always black beans in her place. I lived with her when I was in University, and she was the one who experimented [with food] more; sometimes it was okra stew that I couldn't eat [because of my] lack of culture, because okra is delicious and you know what Cubans are like: "Oh, no I don't eat that". And for instance, I never eat squash in Cuba, and here I love squash. (Yamilé)

I used to go to my aunts' houses, my aunts from my father's side and they used to make *gandinga*[14] and things like that, and I used to look at it there and never [ate it] and that's a stupid thing because now I don't know what it tastes like. Now if I go to a place where they make that, at least I would try it because the thing is since you don't know it and nobody has taught you how, you don't know it. So my change has been like, now I don't say that I don't like something if I haven't tried it, tasted it. (Hilda)

One of my interviewees was a vegetarian, quite remarkable for a Cuban. In the early 2000s, the Cuban government started a campaign to promote a wider intake of fruit and vegetables, but I was surprised not because of her food choice was made in London, where more provisions were available to sustain a diet like that, but by her revelation that she was already a vegetarian before coming to the United Kingdom:

–That must have being very rare in Cuba.
–Indeed. No, no, that gave me a lot of problems. Every time I was invited to dinner: rice, beans and pork meat [I had to say] Oh, I don't eat pork. "Oh, you don't eat pork, would

---

14 *Gandinga* is a stew made with the pork's heart, kidneys, and livers.

you like me to cook chicken?" It's just like I don't really like chicken. "No, no, it can't be, and what do you eat, *chica*, you are going to die!" (Ledis)

Unlike other participants, Ledis sees her experience in diaspora as a continuation of her lifestyle in Cuba and of a food choice that seemed vital to her identity. She has not changed her habits by aiming at a healthier diet because of the availability of fruit and vegetables in London. For other participants like Miguel, changes in diet had another reason:

I used to buy a lot of chips, I used to buy a lot of cans [canned food]; do you understand? Spam [laughs], black puddings, sausages, all of that; do you understand? And some time after my wife and I sat down to talk because she... at that time we had our son, and she wanted to start buying organic food, and we started to change; well, I started to change my diet. I used to buy a big bottle of Coca Cola every week, for example. I stopped it immediately. It's been like seven years that I don't drink that and it all happened because of my son, because our son once said, I want to be big [to grow up] like daddy to drink Coca Cola, because we didn't give him that. (Miguel)

This quote summarizes how a previously known food practice in the homeland is being revised and changed in diaspora. Miguel came from Cuba where he was accustomed to consuming certain products that might account for a non-healthy diet, when compared to the food standards he encountered in London. His main motivation to change was not the possible implications for his own health but that of the other members of his family. In his case the decision to change his diet came after a consensual discussion with his wife, although this was indirectly influenced by a widespread culture of organic food he was exposed to in the host country. In the interviews, I also noticed that the observance of local attitudes towards food, especially drinks, affected my respondents' perception of previously known food practices:

I learned to drink wine [in London] because I started to discover other things, yeah, a lot of things, like with food, with everything. You learn with the variants you find here and from that you start to form your own opinion of what you like, and of what you don't like, isn't it? The clearest preference occurs when you are left with a pint in front of you, and you think that it is too much, and that you'll never finish it, and as a general rule the first ones... In the first years you see that your friends have finished their fifth [pint] and you haven't started your second one, so you realize that, yes, it is a cultural shock. (Miguel)

In this section, I have shown how the participants engage in a revision of food practices learned in the homeland. In diaspora they have adopted a "healthier" approach towards food. However, that does not mean that they have abandoned traditional Cuban food because of health-related issues. On the contrary, they still consider homeland food healthy, based on the general assumption that in Cuba food is produced without chemicals.[15]

Conclusion

In summary, Cuban food has provided a sense of belonging for our participants. It is regarded as a marker of identity and personal identification and as a symbol of Cuban culture. In diaspora, national food retains its significance as a reference of home and family life, and it becomes a popular pretext for gatherings of friends and for family celebrations.

Cubans in London seem to reduce the notion of Cuban food to a list of basic ingredients or recipes that constitute their idea of the national diet, but they also included lots of other foods, even from before 1959. However, the experience of living in Britain has exposed them to manifold culinary customs and to a new realm of flavours and tastes that some of them have incorporated as part of their everyday life. The emigrants opt for healthier variants of food, although they do not reject recipes and dishes from Cuban cuisine, which can be considered "unhealthy" in diaspora.

Food practices in diaspora can also be used to sustain theorizations about gender and gendered spaces. While some practices reproduced the gender dynamics of Cuban households, others revealed a significant departure from traditional gender roles and the gender division of domestic labour. Male migrants, for example, negotiate certain aspects of their gender identity that challenge stereotypical versions of masculinity common in the homeland.

Having come to a global city with a varied offering of local and ethnic food, migrants are able to recreate Cuban food with locally sourced ingredients. This strategy, although not always successful, helps to mitigate the cravings for the tastes of the homeland even though at times it causes frustration because certain dishes are impossible to replicate in London.

---

15   When the Eastern Socialist bloc collapsed and Cuba lost all the supplies from the Soviet Union, fertilizers and pesticides became scarce. The Agricultural authorities promoted a greener agenda based on the use of organic alternatives to plant growth and pest control.

Food is also used to make meanings about the nation. The emigrants engage in a revision of the homeland's culinary practices. Cuban food is situated in a diaspora context where recipes and food habits are 'revised' either because of health and nutrition, or because of socio-political factors associated with food in Cuba. Uses of national food and food practices invite a wider questioning of what 'Cuba' is because personal stories of food in the homeland influence the process of subject construction. The incorporation of contextualized versions of national food result in narratives of belonging and pride and permeate the migrants' creation of a diasporic space, where national identity can be 'comfortably' asserted.

BIBLIOGRAPHY

Alvarez, José 2004. "Overview of Cuba's Food Rationing System." Department of Food and Resource Economics, Florida Cooperative Extension Service. Gainesville: University of Florida. [http://edis.ifas.ufl.edu/fe482 (retrieved 27 July 2010)].

Barthes, Roland 1997 [1961]. "Toward a Psychosociology of Contemporary Food Consumption." *Food and Culture. A Reader.* Eds. Carole Counihan and Penny van Esterik. London: Routledge, 20-27.

Behar, Ruth and Lucia Suárez, eds. 2008. *The Portable Island. Cubans At Home in the World.* New York: Palgrave Macmillan.

Bell, David and Gill Valentine 1997. *Consuming Geographies. We Are What We Eat.* London: Routledge.

Benjamin, Medea, Joseph Collins, and Michael Scott 1986. "How The Poor Got More." *The Cuba Reader. History, Culture, Politics.* Eds. Aviva Chomsky, Barry Carr, and Pamela Maria Smorkaloff. Durham / London: Duke University Press, 344-353.

Berg, Mette 2011. *Diasporic Generations. Memory, Politics and Nation Among Cubans in Spain.* Oxford: Berghahn Books.

Bhabha, Homi 1994. *The Location of Culture.* London: Routledge.

Bourdieu, Pierre 1984. *Distinction. A Social Critique of the Judgement of Taste.* Translated by Richard Nice. London: Routledge / Kegan Paul.

Bradby, Hannah 1997. "Health Eating and Heart Attack. Glasgowegian Punjabi Women's Thinking About Everyday Food." *Food, Health and Identity.* Ed. Pat Caplan. London: Routledge, 213-235.

Brah, Avtar 1996. *Cartographies of Diaspora. Contesting Identities.* London: Routledge.

Chang, Sally 2002. "Sweet and Sour. The Chinese Experience of Food." *Food in the Migrant Experience*. Ed. Anne Kershen. Aldershot: Ashgate, 172-195.

Charon Cardona, Eurídice 2004. "Re-Encountering Cuban Tastes in Australia." *The Australian Journal of Anthropology* 15.1: 40-53.

Cohen, Robin 1997. *Global Diasporas. An Introduction*. London: UCL Press.

Corrales, Javier 2004. "The Gatekeeper State. Limited Economic Reforms and Regime Survival in Cuba, 1989-2002." *Latin American Research Review* 39.2: 35-65.

De la Fuente, Alejandro 2001. *A Nation for All. Race, Inequality and Politics in Twentieth-Century Cuba*. Chapel Hill: University of North Carolina Press.

Domínguez, María Isabel 2008. "Cuban Youth. Aspirations, Social Perceptions, and Identity." *Reinventing the Revolution. A Contemporary Cuba Reader*. Eds. Phillip Brenner, Marguerite Rose Jimenez, John M. Kirk, and William M. Leogrande. Plymouth: Rowman and Littlefield, 292-297.

Douglas, Mary 1999 [1972]. "Deciphering a Meal." *Implicit Meanings. Selected Essays in Anthropology*. Ed. Mary Douglas. London: Routledge, 231-251.

Espina Prieto, Mayra 2005. "Structural Changes since the Nineties and New Research Topics on Cuban Society." *Changes in Cuban Society since the Nineties*. Eds. Joseph Tulchin, Lilian Bobea, Mayra Espina Prieto, and Rafael Hernández. Woodrow Wilson Center Report on the Americas 15. 81-102. [http://www.wilsoncenter.org/topics/pubs/Cuba.pdf (retrieved 25 May 2009)].

Folch, Christine 2008. "Fine Dining. Race in Pre-Revolution Cuban Cookbooks." *Latin American Research Review* 43.2: 205-223.

Fowler, Víctor 2002. "A Traveler's Album. Variations on *Cubanidad*." *boundary 2* 29.3: 105-119.

Garcia, Maria Cristina 2007. "The Cuban Population of the United States. An Introduction." *Cuba. Idea of a Nation Displaced*. Ed. Andrea O'Reilly Herrera. New York: State University of New York Press, 75-89.

Guevara, Ernesto 2007 [1965]. *El Socialismo y el Hombre en Cuba*. Reprint. Havana: Ocean Sur: Centro de Estudios Che Guevara.

Hall, Stuart 1996. "Introduction. Who Needs Identity?" *Questions of Cultural Identity*. Eds. Stuart Hall and Paul Du Gay. London: Sage, 1-17.

—. 1997. "The Work of Representation." *Representation. Cultural Representations and Signifying Practices*. Ed. Stuart Hall. London: Sage / Open University, 13-74.

Hernández-Reguant, Adriana 2009. "Multicubanidad." *Cuba in the Special Period. Culture and Ideology in the 1990s*. Ed. Adriana Hernández-Reguant. New York: Palgrave Macmillan, 69-88.

Holgado Fernandez, Isabel 2001. *¡No es Fácil! Mujeres Cubanas y la Crisis Revolucionaria*. Barcelona: Icaria Editorial.

Kapcia, Antoni 2000. *Cuba. Island of Dreams*. Oxford: Berg.

Kershen, Anne 2002. "Introduction. Food in the Migrant Experience." *Food in the Migrant Experience*. Ed. Anne Kershen. Aldershot: Ashgate, 1-16.

Lévi-Strauss, Claude 1997 [1968]. "The Culinary Triangle." *Food and Culture. A Reader*. Eds. Carole Counihan and Penny van Esterik. London: Routledge, 28-35.

Krull, Catherine and Mélanie Josée Davidson 2011. "Adapting to Cuba's Shifting Food Landscapes. Women's Strategies of Resistance." *Cuban Studies* 42: 59-77.

Mannan, Nassima and Barbara Boucher 2002. "The Bangladeshi Diaspora and its Dietary Profile in East London 1990-2000." *Food in the Migrant Experience*. Aldershot: Ashgate, 229-243.

Martin, Randy 1996. "Cuba and the Rest." *Social Text* 48: 133-137.

Mennell, Stephen, Anne Murcott, and Anneke van Otterloo 1992. *The Sociology of Food. Eating, Diet and Culture*. London: Sage.

Mintz, Sidney 1985. *Sweetness and Power. The Place of Sugar in Modern History*. New York: Viking Press.

Narayan, Uma 1995. "Eating Cultures. Incorporation, Identity and Indian Food." *Social Identities* 1.1: 63-87.

Nespral, Jackie. "Ryan Lochte's Mom on How He Became a Great Swimmer." NBCMiami 13 July 2012. [http://www.nbcmiami.com/news/sports/Ryan-Lochtes-Mom-on-How-He-Became-a-Great-Swimmer-and-Her-Fondest-Olympics-Memory-160924915.html (retrieved 20 February 2013)].

Núñez González, Niurka 1999. "Algunas Concepciones Alimentarias de los Cubanos." *Revista Cubana de Alimentación y Nutrición* 13.1: 46-50.

Office for National Statistics (ONS) 2012. *Population and Nationality by Country of Birth*. [http://www.ons.gov.uk/ons/taxonomy/search/index.html?pageSize=50&sortBy=none&sortDirection=none&newquery=Cuba&content-type=Reference+table&content-type=Dataset&nscl=Population+by+Nationality+and+Country+of+Birth (retrieved 20 February 2013)].

Olson, James and Judith Olson 1995. *Cuban Americans. From Trauma to Triumph*. New York: Twayne Publishers.

Ortiz, Fernando 1966. "La Cocina Afrocubana." *Casa de las Américas* 36-37: 63-69.

—. 1973 [1939]. "Los Factores Humanos de la Cubanidad." *Órbita de Fernando Ortiz*. Ed. UNEAC. Selección y Prólogo de Julio Le Riverend. Habana: UNEAC, 149-157.

Panayi, Panikos 2008. *Spicing up Britain. The Multicultural History of British Food*. London: Reaktion Books.
Pertierra, Ana Cristina 2008. "En Casa. Women and Households in Post-Soviet Cuba." *Journal of Latin American Studies* 40.4: 743-767.
Roman-Velazquez, Patria 1999. *The Making of Latin London. Salsa Music, Place and Identity*. Aldershot: Ashgate.
Safran, William 1991. "Diasporas in Modern Societies. Myths of Homeland and Return." *Diaspora* 1.1: 83-99.
Sánchez Fuárros, Íñigo 2008. *"¡Esto Parece Cuba!" Prácticas Musicales y Cubanía en la Diáspora Cubana de Barcelona*. PhD Thesis. University of Barcelona, Barcelona.
[http://digital.csic.es/bitstream/10261/10429/1/Tesis_ISanchez_2008.pdf (retrieved 20 March 2009)].
Santiago, Fabiola 1998. "Nitza Villapol, 74, Cuban Cooking Advisor." *Miami Herald*, 21 October, 4B.
Sarmiento Ramírez, Ismael 2003. "Alimentación y Relaciones Sociales en la Cuba Colonial." *Anales del Museo de América* 11: 197-226.
Uriarte-Gaston, Miren 2004. "Social Policy Responses to Cuba's Economic Crisis of the 1990s." *Cuban Studies* 35: 105–36.
Valdés Paz, Juan 2005. "Cuba in the 'Special Period.' From Equality to Equity." *Changes in Cuban Society since the Nineties*. Eds. Joseph Tulchin, Lilian Bobea, Mayra Espina Prieto, and Rafael Hernández, 103-124. [http://www.wilsoncenter.org/topics/pubs/Cuba.pdf (retrieved 25 March 2006)].
Vega Chapú, Arístides, ed. 2011. *No Hay que Llorar*. La Habana: Ediciones La Memoria-Centro Cultural Pablo de la Torriente Brau.
Wilk, Richard 1999. "'Real Belizean Food.' Building Local Identity in the Transnational Caribbean." *American Anthropologist* 101.2: 244-255.
Wilson, Marisa 2009. "Food as a Good versus Food as a Commodity. Contradictions between State and Market in Tuta, Cuba." *Journal of the Anthropological Society of Oxford* 1.1: 25–51.
Wimmer, Andreas 2001. "Zurich's Miami. Transethnic Relations of a Transnational Community." *Transnational Communities Programme, Working Paper Series*.
[http://www.transcomm.ox.ac.uk/working%20papers/wimmer.pdf (retrieved 28 November 2009)].

Reinventing Local Food Culture in an Afro-Caribbean Community in Costa Rica

MONA NIKOLIĆ

In accounts on the Costa Rican national culinary culture, the national cuisine has recently been portrayed as *cocina criolla costarricense*, with the term *criolla* (creole) used in Ulf Hannerz' sense of 'creolization' (cf. Hannerz 2000), pointing towards this culinary culture's emergence from the confluence of multiple and diverse culinary traditions. But whereas indigenous and European influences on the national cuisine are discussed in detail, Caribbean culinary influences are usually considered as less significant and as regionally limited to the province of Limón, which is home to the majority of Costa Rica's Afro-Caribbean population. Due to the fact that this province and its population have long been isolated from the rest of the country, for geographical as well as social reasons, local culture and cuisine that evolved in Limón are quite distinct from the rest of the country's cuisine. In Costa Rica, Caribbean cuisine therefore constitutes a marker of regional, as well as ethnic identity, distinguishing the Afro-Caribbean population culturally and culinarily from the rest of the country. In recent decades, however, Costa Rican food scholars have repeatedly articulated concerns about the *cocina afrolimonense*'s[1] disappearance and, in order to prevent this re-

---

1 I am here using the term *cocina afrolimonense* that is used to refer to the Caribbean food culture of the province of Limón in the academic context, to stress the local character of this cuisine in comparison to the Caribbean food culture. I prefer *cocina afrolimonense* over the also wide-spread term *cocina limonense* to underline that I am talking about the food culture of the Afro-Caribbean population, as there are a number of other food cultures in Limón, such as indigenous, Chinese, and Indian (cf. Ross de Cerdas 2002, for example) that, despite the fact that they have all impacted the local

gional cuisine from being lost, started to publish accounts and cookbooks (cf. Chang Vargas 1984: 46; Jiménez Acuña 2007: 15; Ross de Cerdas 2002:12-13).

The *cocina afrolimonense*'s decrease in importance in everyday life is opposed to an increase in its importance in the context of tourism. With the rise of international tourism from the late 1980s onwards, the sale of Caribbean food turned into a source of income for local Afro-Caribbean families living in popular tourist destinations. This was the case in Puerto Viejo de Talamanca, where I conducted fieldwork in 2011.

Referring to my fieldwork findings, my paper explores the negotiation of different ideas of Caribbean culture and cuisine, circulating in cookbooks, guidebooks, and on websites, in the context of tourist consumption. Giving special attention to the concept of 'authenticity,' I will show how these negotiations lead to a reinvention of an 'authentic' Caribbean culinary culture in the local context, thereby reinforcing among the local Afro-Caribbean population a sense of belonging and ties to a transnational Afro-Caribbean community. After a short introduction to Puerto Viejo de Talamanca, I will turn to the theoretical framework of the research.

PUERTO VIEJO DE TALAMANCA

The Talamancan region was first populated in the first half of the 19th century by Afro-Caribbean settlers immigrating from Bocas del Toro, Panama, as well as from the Columbian Island of San Andrés and the Nicaraguan Bluefields (cf. Palmer 2005: 21, 73). The history of the region's Afro-Caribbean settlement is therefore differing slightly from that of the rest of the province of Limón, where Afro-Caribbean immigration is usually regarded as starting with the construction of the Atlantic Railroad and the immigration of railroad-workers from the West Indies, predominantly Jamaica (cf. Ross de Cerdas 2002: 18-20). With a lack of roads connecting Talamanca with the Costa Rican capital San José or Limón's capital, Puerto Limón, Talamanca's Afro-Caribbean population was always oriented to Panama keeping up numerous familial and economic ties to the neighboring country (cf. Palmer 2005: 128). Aside from these relations to Panama, the early settlers maintained trade and social relations with the native indigenous population, which also influenced local food culture (cf. 71).

Afro-Caribbean population's culinary culture, should not be rendered invisible by using the term *cocina limonense* to describe the local Caribbean food culture.

Puerto Viejo de Talamanca, the village in which I conducted my fieldwork today is one of the most popular tourist destinations on the Atlantic Coast.[2] During the last ten years, in spite of significant out-migration of the local population for a lack of working opportunities, there has been a massive population increase, due to national and international immigration. The village's population can be estimated as some 2500 residents, 30% of which are outsiders from other parts of Costa Rica, America, Europe, and Asia, turning Puerto Viejo into a culturally diverse village (cf. *Caribbean Way* 2011: 33; Vandegrift 2007: 125). Since the late 1980s, tourism has become the main source of income for the local population, the main focus being on ecological and community-based tourism, with the NGO Asociación Talamanqueña de Ecoturismo y Conservación (ATEC) having established its 'headquarters' in the village. Apart from national parks and wildlife reserves, the place attracts tourists because of the 'Caribbean Flair' and the 'Caribbean Lifestyle' of its inhabitants (cf. Vandegrift 2007:125). Being such a popular tourist destination, Puerto Viejo counts with a fluctuating number of about 50 restaurants, selling all kinds of different cuisines. Even though only about ten restaurants are explicitly specialized in selling Caribbean food, a far greater number is selling at least some Caribbean dish. The menu of a restaurant offering international cuisine, run by Italians, shown in Photo 1, gives an idea of the competition that exists:

---

2 During my fieldwork stay in Puerto Viejo from March through May 2011, I focused on the local Afro-Caribbean population that was living on the preparation and selling of Caribbean food to tourists. I worked predominately with restaurant owners and staff, as well as two teachers that were giving Caribbean cooking classes to tourists. Apart from participant observation, I conducted semi-structured interviews both with the local Afro-Caribbean population and national and international tourists.

Photo 1: Restaurant Menu; Puerto Viejo de Talamanca

Source: Mona Nikolić, 2011.

As can be seen on the board, even restaurants that are specialized in different types of cuisines are offering Caribbean dishes like rice and beans, *patacones*, *pollo caribeño*, and *pescado caribeño*. In order to last in this highly competitive field, local Afro-Caribbeans engaged in the preparation and selling of Caribbean food are faced with the challenge to mark their own performance and range of dishes as different from that of others. Despite this need to highlight their own performance's uniqueness, the performances and the dishes offered have to be judged as 'authentic' and legitimately Caribbean both by tourists and local Afro-Caribbeans. This is linked to the importance of consumption and food as an identity marker and the relevance of 'authenticity' in the context of tourist consumption that I now turn to in the discussion of the theoretical framework of my research.

CONSUMPTION AS A MARKER OF IDENTITY

Following a social constructivist perspective, I use the term 'identity' to describe a process embedded in social and discursive practices, a continual project, that social actors are developing in relation to an 'Other.' As several authors have pointed out, within this process of identity construction external concepts can serve as important guidelines (cf. Cornell and Hartmann 2007: 84; Natter and Jones 1997: 146-8; Sandoval García 2004: 4-12). Another aspect of identity construction relevant to the topic of my research is the fact that identities are constructed, expressed, and incorporated (consciously as well as unconsciously) in a number of ways. One way of constructing and expressing identities is through consumption.

The relation of consumption habits and identity construction has been subject of numerous works within social and cultural studies (cf. Bell and Valentine 1997; Bourdieu 2007; Halter 2000; Lupton 1996; Warde 1997). Among consumption habits, eating habits and cuisine hold a special position, connecting the physical with the political, social, economic, and cultural sphere. A 'cuisine,' following Eva Barlösius, is a complex cultural code, which is containing instructions for the flavor, the combination of ingredients, and the way how to eat the food prepared (cf. Barlösius 1999: 123). These instructions guarantee the uniformity of a cuisine's flavor, which is why cuisines evoke feelings of sameness or difference and are therefore able to unite as well as to separate (cf. ibid.). The role of cuisines and eating habits as identity markers is linked to the function of taste as a criterion for distinction, discussed by Pierre Bourdieu in his theory of the *habitus*. Taste is the operator by which practices and goods are turned into distinctive signs and as such into expressions of social positions (cf. Bourdieu 2007: 284). It is therefore possible to discern social positions by looking at the social actors' preferences and eating habits (cf. 104). In a similar vein, commodities, as representations of a certain social status, obtain a communicative function in social competition. This is why authors like Pasi Falk accord them a decisive role in the construction and expression of identities: consuming commodities that represent a highly valued lifestyle, a consumer is able to construct and express his or her own identity as similar to those Others leading this esteemed life (cf. Falk 1994: 129). Food, according to Deborah Lupton is the "ultimate 'consumable' commodity" (Lupton 1996: 23), as eating is the highest degree of incorporation of external values into the body.

The *cocina afrolimonense* was not only ascribed importance as a marker of identity in national discourse, but also among the local Afro-Caribbean population, something which becomes evident from the following account in which

Johnny,[3] a tourist guide, who gives cooking classes on Caribbean cuisine, is talking about the preparation of the *rondón*:[4]

The authentic Caribbean women do the *rondón*, yeah, only authentic Caribbean women do the *rondón*. Why? Number one: The majority of the women don't know how to chip a coconut now. And the banana. It stains your finger, you don't wanna stain your finger, they wanna be painting now. And really pretty, you know? Brand new polishing, you know? - 'You mad? I just painted my nails today. Never!' (Johnny, April 2011)

He makes explicit the relation between Afro-Caribbean identity and Caribbean food: only by preparing 'authentic' Caribbean food—that is by using the traditional preparation techniques and ingredients—an Afro-Caribbean is an Afro-Caribbean; likewise, only Afro-Caribbeans are believed to be able to cook 'authentic' Caribbean food.[5] In this statement, Johnny is pointing towards the problem of the progressive disappearance of local dishes, because of a lack of knowledge and willingness among the local population to prepare them.[6] While this identity marker is thus in danger of disappearing, the Caribbean cuisine is at the same time gaining in importance in the context of tourist consumption. With regard to the impact of tourist consumption on the local culture, it is relevant to discuss the usage of the concept of authenticity in the context of tourism.

---

3 For reasons of identity protection, all the names of my interviewees have been changed.
4 *Rondón* is the local name for a dish similar to the Jamaican 'rundown.'
5 Cooking in this local context is not an activity actively taught, but rather learnt unconsciously. By growing up in the Afro-Caribbean community and witnessing others cook, cooking techniques are internalized and a sense for the 'right' flavors is developed. Cooking here can be understood as a form of incorporated knowledge and incorporated cultural capital which is expressed (unconsciously) through the cook's actions (cf. Bourdieu 2008: 135-6). Many of my interviewees thus characterized cooking Caribbean food as a natural skill of Afro-Caribbeans.
6 His talking about the female population here is also owed to the fact that the *rondón* is often prepared by men. Criticizing the loss of knowledge, he is not only focusing on women, however.

TOURISM AND 'AUTHENTIC' LOCAL CULTURES

While tourism and the commercialization of local cultures within its context are on the one hand criticized as a homogenizing and destructive influence threatening local cultures, they are on the other hand understood as a way for local people to transform their cultural capital into a source of living (cf. Howes 2000: 2, 12-13).

In tourism studies, the search for 'authenticity' has been considered one of the core motivations of tourists since Dean MacCannell introduced the concept in the 1970s, claiming that tourists are interested in experiencing "life as it really is lived" (MacCannell 1976: 94), that is, in getting to know 'authentic' or 'real' local cultures. As Ning Wang points out, in the realm of tourism studies, 'authenticity' is often used as it was originally used in the context of museums, where the criterion for 'authenticity' was the fact that a product was made by local actors, according to local traditions. Authenticity, in this sense, is the quintessence of the 'original' and the 'real' (cf. Wang 1999: 350-1). Johnny's statement above can be taken as an example of this point of view. From a constructionist perspective, on the other hand, rather than searching for the 'real,' tourists are searching for an 'authenticity' that is itself the result of social construction (cf. Wang 1999: 356). Here it is important to take John Urry's concept of the 'tourist gaze' into account. The tourist gaze, according to Urry, is a way of looking at things oriented towards the perception of the different, the unique, and the new. He distinguishes the 'collective' from the 'romantic' tourist gaze: the collective tourist gaze is often associated with mass-tourism, whereas tourists that are accorded the romantic tourist gaze are claimed to be searching for individual experiences of authentic local cultures (cf. Urry 1990: 27-33; 2002: 40-5). However, in order to be judged as an authentic and therefore valuable experience by tourists, cultural performances have to be in accordance with and enhancing the tourists' ideas about the particular culture they are visiting. This leads to the emergence of new 'authentic' local cultures in the course of the touristic development of places.

In Costa Rica, even though tourism is often mentioned as one of the reasons leading to the deterioration of local Caribbean food culture by Costa Rican scholars (cf. Chang Vargas 1984: 46; Jiménez Acuña 2007: 15; Ross de Cerdas 2002: 12-13), it is at the same time a factor contributing to the rise in consciousness of the importance of the local cuisine. As Marjorie Ross points out, foreigners discovered and appreciated the *cocina afrolimonense* before the Costa Rican population did:

Al vencer el muro natural con que caudalosos ríos y montañas han aislado al centro de la costa, Costa Rica ha ido descubriendo, más lentamente que los extranjeros, no solo el panorama selvático y la virginidad de la belleza intocada de los canales y la exuberancia de la costa, sino el picante sabor del crisol cultural limonense. (Ross de Cerdas 2002: 10)[7]

Today, this value given to the local cuisine by foreigners is very apparent in the tourist industries' descriptions of the Costa Rican cuisine, e.g. on websites and in guidebooks, where the Caribbean cuisine of Limón is usually presented as one of the highlights, as far as culinary experiences are concerned, as in this quote taken from the *Lonely Planet Costa Rica* (2006) which reads:

Perhaps the tastiest local cuisine is found on the Caribbean coast. Spicy coconut-milk stews (rondón), garlic potatoes, well-seasoned fish and chicken dishes are all lip-smacking good. Also, don't miss the savory 'rice and beans' (in English), red beans and rice cooked in coconut milk. (Vorhees and Firestone 2006: 81)

Apart from proving the value given to the *cocina afrolimonense*, the descriptions in guidebooks and on websites also help to spread and support a touristic image of this culinary culture, which is that of a cuisine reflecting the Jamaican origin of Limón's population:

Most folks in Costa Rica will tell you, the Caribbean coast of Costa Rica boasts a different flavor and feeling than the rest of the country. Heavily influenced by Jamaican culture, much of the food here is spicier with a more Caribbean flair. Rice and beans on this side of Costa Rica are often cooked with coconut milk, lending the concoction a much sweeter flavor. The cuisine on this coast also relies heavily on the many fish and shellfish that are caught daily, and the seafood here is truly divine. (Escapeartist, Inc. 2011)

A look at the local dishes listed in guidebooks and on websites, provides the following picture (see Figure 1): The dish most frequently named is the rice and beans, followed by the *rondón*. Among the pastries, *pan bon* and *patí* are repeatedly recommended. These four dishes are the ones considered characteristic for the *cocina afrolimonense* on a national level and they are the dishes and pastries

---

[7] "By overcoming the natural wall by which large rivers and mountains isolated the center from the coast, Costa Rica has come to experience, more slowly than the foreigners, not only the jungle panorama and the virginity of the untouched beauty of the canals and the exuberance of coast, but the spicy flavor of Limón's cultural melting pot" (my translation).

that national as well as international tourists travelling to Puerto Viejo most often ask for.

Figure 1: Description of the Cocina Afrolimonense *in Guidebooks*

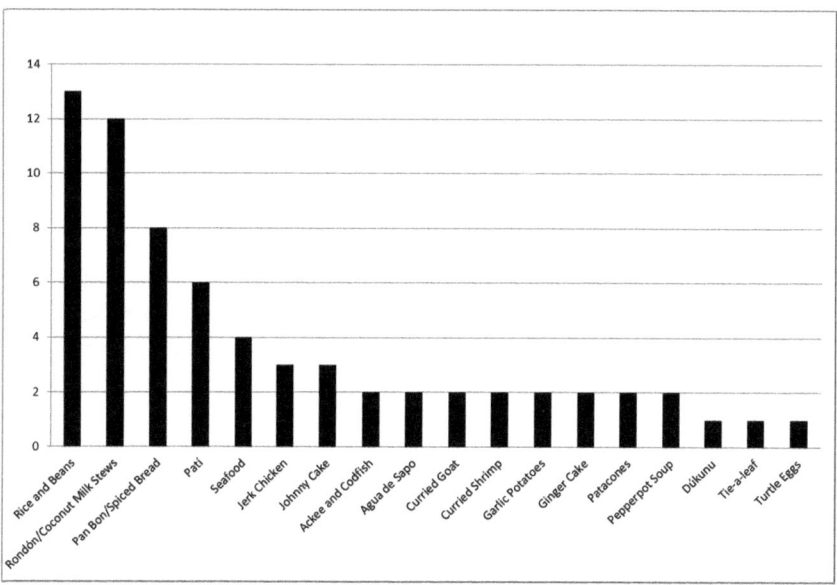

Source: Caribbean dishes and drinks recommended on 21 websites and in guidebooks; Mona Nikolić, 2013.

This touristic image of the local culture is not always congruent with local reality, as is indicated in the following statement: "I love jerk chicken, but it's so hard to find jerk chicken in Puerto Viejo. You get rice and beans, but it's nothing like Jamaican food" (Stephen, April 2011). Having expected a cuisine similar to the Jamaican, Stephen, a tourist from the United States expressed his disappointment about the difficulty to purchase a dish like jerk chicken in Puerto Viejo.

Given the importance of the fulfillment of the tourists' expectations for the success of the restaurant business, these recommendations influence the way the local Afro-Caribbean population presents and perceives their own local cuisine and identity. In order to meet tourists' expectations, on account of the loss of incorporated, culinary knowledge in the local context, people living on the preparation and selling of Caribbean food are increasingly turning to cookbooks and online publications of recipes of Caribbean dishes for information and inspiration. In order to understand the impact of the presentations in cookbooks, it is important to discuss the link between cookbooks and the 'authenticity' of local food cultures next.

COOKBOOKS AND 'AUTHENTIC' LOCAL CUISINES

The relevance of cookbooks in the emergence of a cuisine is usually stressed in studies on national cuisines (cf. Appadurai 2008; Ayora-Díaz 2010: 412-14; Goody 1996a; Parkhurst-Ferguson 2010: 102). Due to the selective incorporation of recipes, cookbooks serve as institutions, determining which dishes, flavors, and modes of preparation form part of a specific cuisine (cf. Parkhurst-Ferguson 2010: 102; Sutton 2001: 142). This importance of cookbooks is linked to the process of transforming oral tradition and practical knowledge into literature. With regard to the context of oral traditions, the concept of the original is not applicable: oral traditions are transformed in the context of performance and one performance is as correct and true as the other. When oral traditions are written down however, the fact that one version of a particular oral tradition is chosen to be recorded in written form changes the status of this version. Due to the importance given to this version by writing it down and to the fact that it is now the 'oldest' available version, the written down version can be and is used as reference to proof the correctness of other performances of this oral tradition (cf. Goody 1996b: 10, 154, 164-66, 175). The writing down of recipes thus produces ideal and 'authentic' versions of the dishes, and at the same time both demands and provides the means for their exact reproduction. While the recording of recipes in written form is therefore counteracting change, it may also present a basis for innovation, as Jack Goody points out (cf. 1996a: 129-31).

Cookbooks are sometimes referred to as literature of nostalgia since books on regional or national cuisines are often written with a focus on the past, by people interested in the conservation of the culinary traditions that are sometimes no longer living in the specific region or even foreigners (cf. Appadurai 2008: 302; Sutton 2001: 142-56). This is true for the most prominent books on the *cocina afrolimonense* written by Costa Rican scholars, none of them Afro-Caribbean and all of them motivated by the aim to prevent this regional food culture from disappearing. Instead of only presenting a description of the actual state of being, the scholarly portrayal of the *cocina afrolimonense* mirrors the national Costa Rican way of perceiving this cuisine, as can be seen in the enumeration of dishes and drinks presented in Figure 2:[8] Apart from taking up the aspects of the unfamiliar by mentioning dishes made from fruit and vegetables that are fairly unknown outside the region—such as akee or breadfruit—or by listing dishes made from turtle meat, the enumerations give a very clear picture of the dishes commonly attributed to this cuisine in national discourse, like rice and beans, *rondón*, akee and codfish, blue draws, the baked goods *patí*, *plantintá*, and *pan bon*, or the drinks *agua de sapo* and sorrel.

On my arriving in Puerto Viejo, the impact of these cookbooks was very apparent, not only for the great number of Costa Rican cookbooks sold in local souvenir stores, but also for the fact that my interviewees referred to some of these books to substantiate their answers to my questions. Kelley, a restaurant owner from Puerto Viejo, explained the local population's growing dependency upon these books:

Finding people who can cook the Caribbean meals, based on the grandpa times, these people becoming less and less likely, every year that goes by. I recently bought a book with recipes of the Caribbean. It's written by a Costa Rican woman, from San José. She likes the cooking so much that she has written a book. (Kelley, March 2011)

Apart from expressing his pride of his culinary culture, he is here emphasizing the importance of the cookbooks, against the background of the literal dying out of the local, incorporated culinary knowledge. With cookbooks being seen as a source of trustworthy information, the image of the *cocina afrolimonense* presented in the books deeply influenced the way my Afro-Caribbean informants perceived and depicted their own cuisine. Additionally, the image circulating in cookbooks corresponds in a great extent to the tourists' ideas on the *cocina afrolimonense* (see Figure 1) and was therefore in accordance with their tourist gaze. In the next section, I will show how the foreign concepts and the touristic demand impact the local culinary culture.

---

8   With exception of Carolina Jiménez Acuña's work, none of the books explicitly deals with the food culture of the Talamancan region, but rather with the *cocina afrolimonense* in general.

Figure 2: Description of the Cocina Afrolimonense *in Cookbooks*

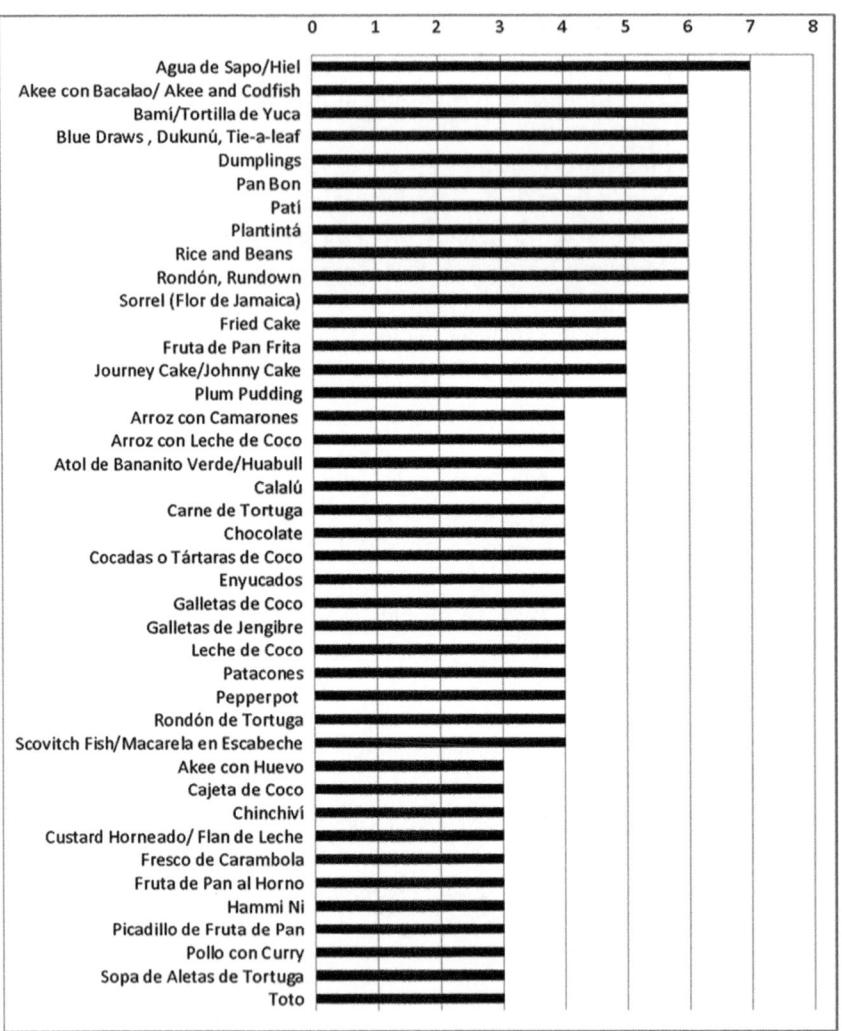

Sources: Afrolimonense dishes and drinks mentioned in the accounts and cookbooks published by Álvarez Masís (2007); Chang Vargas (1984); Chang Vargas et al. (2001); Jiménez Acuña (2007); Pardo Castro (2003); Ross de Cerdas (2002); Ross González (2001); Sedó Masís (2008); multiple enumerations; Mona Nikolić, 2013.

THE REINVENTION OF LOCAL FOOD CULTURE IN PUERTO VIEJO DE TALAMANCA

In Puerto Viejo, the touristic search for 'Caribbeanness' is acceded in a number of ways. For instance, restaurants and souvenir stores are usually set up in brightly-colored wooden houses, partly on stilts and with a veranda. Furthermore, it is not uncommon to see walls decorated with Jamaican flags, banners with the portrait of Bob Marley, flower arrangements, or paintings of exotic fruit and birds, and to hear reggae music playing. The 'Caribbeanness' is not only constructed by creating a 'Caribbean' atmosphere, but also in the restaurants' menus.

In what follows, taking *pan bon* and jerk chicken as examples, I will demonstrate the interconnectedness of the tourist gaze, cookbooks, and the process of constructing and expressing local culinary culture and identity as authentic Afro-Caribbean in Puerto Viejo de Talamanca.

TOURIST DEMAND, COOKBOOKS, AND THE (RE-)INTEGRATION OF THE *PAN BON* INTO LOCAL FOOD CULTURE

Pan bon is a fruit-bread made of yeast dough, candied fruit, raisins, and spices like nutmeg, vanilla, and cinnamon. It is one of the most popular Caribbean baked goods among Costa Ricans and it is one of the dishes most representative of the *cocina afrolimonense*. As such, it is usually one of the dishes sold when it comes to representing the province of Limón at celebrations such as on the *Día de las Culturas*.[9] Its recipe is normally published in the cookbooks on *cocina afrolimonense* (see Figure 2) and recommended in guidebooks (see Figure 1). Being so emblematic of the *afrolimonense* food culture, *pan bon* is what Costa Ricans and international tourists travelling to Limón are interested in tasting and it is what Costa Ricans travelling to Limón either take back home for personal consumption or are requested to carry back. Thus when I first went to Puerto Viejo on my research stay in Costa Rica in September 2010, friends of mine

---

9   The *Día de las Culturas* is celebrated on October 12th in remembrance of Columbus' arrival. The holiday is today a day to celebrate and commemorate the cultural diversity of Costa Rica. On this occasion, the provinces are represented by the particular dances, arts and crafts and foods and drinks considered emblematic of the particular provinces, marking their uniqueness.

from the Costa Rican Central Valley asked me to get them a loaf of *pan bon*. I was then planning to meet Carolina Jiménez Acuña, author of the book *Sazonando Recuerdos* (2007), a book on Puerto Viejo's Caribbean culinary culture. Carolina Jiménez Acuña had published a recipe of the *pan bon* in her book. So when I asked her, where I would be able to buy a *pan bon* in Puerto Viejo, I was surprised to be told: "Es que aquí no hay tradición de pan bon" (Carolina Jiménez Acuña, September 2010).[10] She had included the recipe anyways, although there were only a few women in Puerto Viejo who knew how to prepare *pan bon* at the time she wrote the book, of which one, Marla, was preparing it on demand. Like Carolina, George, who is the owner of a restaurant south of Puerto Viejo, complained about the fact that there was no one preparing *pan bon* in the southern Talamancan region: "Por ejemplo el pan bon, no puedes encontrar un pan bon por aquí. No sé si lo has buscado, pero cuesta. A mi, la gente me pregunta y yo no sé dónde mandarlos por el pan bon" (George, April 2011).[11] He usually sends his customers to Puerto Viejo, where Marla's *pan bon* is sometimes sold at her brother's restaurant.

Growing touristic demand and the fact that *pan bon* is such an unchallenged marker of Afro-Caribbean identity on a national level have led however to a rise in its importance in the local context as well. When I asked my Afro-Caribbean informants—those earning a living from selling Caribbean food to tourists—to list the dishes they considered part of the local Caribbean cuisine, if pastries were named, the *pan bon* was always among the first baked goods named (see Figure 3). Although it was not a bread my Afro-Caribbean informants would bake at home, it was not uncommon that they would order it from Marla once in a while. This way, instead of disappearing from the local context, *pan bon* consumption was slowly spreading among the local Afro-Caribbean population and even among families that had not traditionally baked it. What is more, when I returned to Puerto Viejo in August 2011, the *pan bon* supply was about to triple, as there were now two other women who had decided to put *pan bon* on their menu in order to sell it to tourists. External images of Caribbean cuisine had thus influenced local consumption as well as local preparation habits.

The integration of *pan bon* into the local eating habits and cuisine is an example of how local cuisine is changed and constructed in accordance with national, as well as international, tourist ideas about the *cocina afrolimonense*. By integrating a bread like *pan bon* into the local food culture—both into the con-

---

10 "It's that there is no *pan bon* tradition here" (my translation).
11 "The *pan bon* for example, you can't find a *pan bon* round here. I don't know if you've tried to, but it's difficult. People are asking me where to get *pan bon* and I don't know where to send them for the *pan bon*" (my translation).

cept and the eating habits—the Afro-Caribbean restaurant owners and families were presenting their food culture and themselves as Afro-Caribbean, enhancing the tourist gaze (cf. Urry 1990: 26-7). At the same time, by eating *pan bon*, a bread so emblematic of the *cocina afrolimonense*, they displayed their Afro-Caribbean identity and their belonging to the Costa Rican Afro-Caribbean community in Limón. This is possible because of the communicative function of food and the act of consumption. By consuming as well as offering food that is representative of the Costa Rican *afrolimonense* community, my Afro-Caribbean informants confirmed their own Caribbeanness and their sameness to other members of the *afrolimonense* community (cf. Barlösius 1999: 123; Falk 1994: 128-9). Instead of only using the *pan bon* to present their own 'Caribbeanness' to their customers, this bread was a dish my Afro-Caribbean informants identified with, as becomes obvious from the fact that they had incorporated it into their concept of their Caribbean food culture (see Figure 3). It had become a marker of their Afro-Caribbean identity.

The publication of the *pan bon* recipe in the cookbooks on the *cocina afrolimonense* supported this integration both by sustaining the food's importance as a marker of Afro-Caribbean identity in Costa Rica and making the recipe available to a larger number of people. My interviewees did not question the fact that the concept presented in cookbooks was an 'authentic' portrayal of the *cocina afrolimonense*. Their own unfamiliarity with some of the dishes appearing in the books was taken as an example for the loss of culinary knowledge that had taken place and even though some of my interviewees questioned the success of this way of transmitting culinary knowledge, they perceived the books as a way to save the local food culture. Marla, for instance, had contributed some of her recipes to Carolina's cookbook, although she did not believe that baking could be learnt by simply following the instructions in a book. Referring to her own struggle to learn how to make *pan bon*, she pointed out that this was a bread particularly difficult to prepare:

Ella era la que comenzó a vender repostería. Fue mi mamá. Y con el tiempo, ella lo pasó a mi, porque ella se enfermó, dejando el trabajo. Bueno lo más difícil para mi, a aprender era el pan bon. Porque yo nunca lo había mezclado y ahora, cuando me tocaba, mi mamá, - yo tenía miedo, entonces ella vino aquí y me enseñó como hacerlo y ya. (Marla, March 2011)[12]

---

12 "She was the one who started selling pastries. It was my mother. And by the time, she passed it to me, because she got sick and stopped working. Well, what was most difficult for me to learn was how to prepare the *pan bon*. Because I had never prepared the

Instead of fearing growing competition, Marla was afraid that her family tradition would be lost as her own daughters had not been interested in baking, and only one had learnt how to bake some cakes and pastries: "No quieren nada de eso. Hay una que ya está en San José que ya sabe hacer patí, sabe hacer unos de los queques, sabe hacer el cheesecake y todo eso. Menos el pan bon" (Marla, March 2011).[13] Despite her reservations about learning from books, she believed the publication of recipes in cookbooks to be a possible way to preserve the local food culture. But, as can be seen in the case of *pan bon*, it is at the same time promoting the approximation of the local food culture and the particular concept of the *cocina afrolimonense* circulating in these books.

Figure 3: Local Concept of the Cocina Afrolimonense

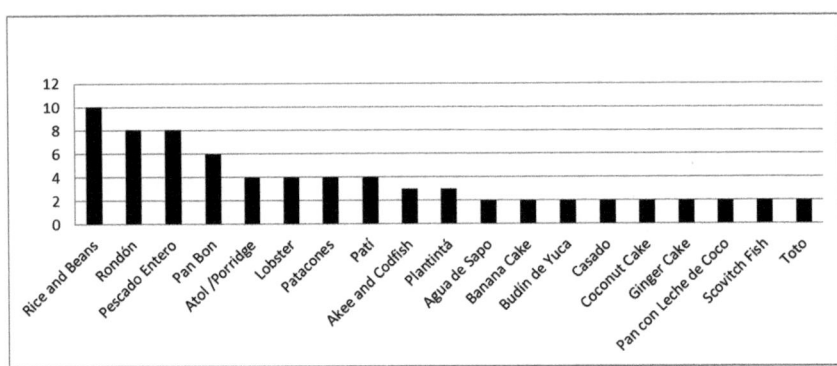

Source: Caribbean dishes and drinks named by my Afro-Caribbean informants working in the food selling and restaurant business in ten free-listing occasions; multiple enumerations; Mona Nikolić, 2013.

---

mixture and when it was my turn to do it, my mother—I was afraid, so she came here and showed me how to do it and that was it" (my translation).

13 "They don't want to have anything to do with this. There is one who is already living in San José, she knows how to prepare *patí*, she knows how to prepare some of the cakes, she knows how to make the cheesecake and everything; except for the *pan bon*" (my translation).

PRESENTING CARIBBEANNESS AND THE CHANGE FROM *POLLO CARIBEÑO* TO JERK CHICKEN

Pan bon represents an example of how the local culinary culture is brought into line with the image of the *cocina afrolimonense* in the context of tourist consumption. In order to present their culture and identity as Afro-Caribbean however, people living by selling Caribbean food in Puerto Viejo were not only drawing on cookbooks on the *cocina afrolimonense*, but were increasingly looking for Caribbean recipes on homepages and in books on Caribbean food culture. In other words, they oriented their performance towards a general and the international tourists' idea of the Caribbean food culture to act in accordance with the touristic demand. This leads to the integration of Caribbean dishes that had formerly not been part of the *cocina afrolimonense* and to a change in the preparation of local Caribbean dishes. One example is the jerk chicken already mentioned above. In Puerto Viejo, chicken is usually prepared as *pollo caribeño*, that is 'chicken in Caribbean sauce,' by placing chicken legs overnight in a marinade made from *Salsa Lizano*,[14] soya sauce, vinegar, and mixed spices, and then frying them until brown the next morning in a mixture made from oil, garlic, and sugar. The so-prepared chicken legs are then further cooked, adding sliced onions, bell peppers, tomatoes, and spices. In Puerto Viejo de Talamanca, the *pollo caribeño* is commonly served with the rice and beans. Despite its difference from the Jamaican jerk chicken, it is the latter that is recommended in some guidebooks (see Figure 1). Some restaurant owners, like Linda, have therefore started to offer it. When Linda talked about the changes in her menu, she did not mention the jerk chicken as one of the foreign dishes included. To her, it was rather an amplification that supported the Caribbeanness of her menu. This opinion was shared by my other interviewees. Johnny, talking about changes that occurred in the restaurant menus, referring to Linda's menu, summarizes this point of view: "Right now, my mom has started to do jerk chicken and put it on the menu, but that is Caribbean food" (Johnny, March 2011). As it is a dish representative of the Caribbean culinary culture, its integration into the menu does not change the fact that what is offered at the restaurant is Caribbean food. Instead of threatening the authenticity of the performance of Caribbeanness, it is rather seen as improving it: by integrating a dish like jerk chicken that is associated with Caribbean food culture on an international level, restaurant owners are providing their customers with the Caribbean food the latter are expecting. The performance of Caribbeanness in the restaurants is therefore judged as authentic

---

14 Local brand, similar to Worcestershire sauce.

by international tourists, but also the restaurant owners and staff themselves are perceived as authentic Afro-Caribbeans, their Afro-Caribbean identity unquestioned (cf. Urry 1990:26-7).

While jerk chicken has not yet replaced the *pollo caribeño* in everyday life, it is—as in the case of *pan bon*—becoming a dish that my interviewees identify with as a marker of their Afro-Caribbean identity. This identification with foreign Caribbean dishes also expresses their sense of belonging to a larger transnational Caribbean community.

The approximation to a general Caribbean cuisine in the context of tourist consumption impacts upon the local foodways in two contrasting ways. On the one hand, Caribbean dishes that are part of the *cocina afrolimonense* are preserved in the local context: dishes that had been bound to be lost are reintegrated and those that were uncommon are becoming part of the local food culture, as has been shown for *pan bon* and jerk chicken respectively. On the other hand, the catering to the tourists' taste also encourages the loss of dishes of the local food culture, as local dishes that are not characteristic of the Caribbean culture are driven out of the market and are likely to disappear from the local context. The commercialization of Caribbean food culture in the context of tourism therefore does not lead to a revival, but rather to a reinvention of local food culture and the understanding of the local Afro-Caribbean population of Puerto Viejo de Talamanca as belonging to a larger, transnational Caribbean community. Apart from a mere feeling of belonging to the transnational Caribbean community, at the background of the loss of local culinary knowledge that has taken place, the need to offer authentic Caribbean food to tourists leads to a strengthening of the relations with other Caribbean communities.

STRENGTHENING TIES TO NEIGHBORING CARIBBEAN COMMUNITIES

The sense of belonging to a larger Caribbean community and the self-positioning in a Caribbean cultural context were reinforced by the fact that local culture and identity are considered and constructed as Afro-Caribbean in the context of tourist consumption. Nonetheless, the need to perform their own Caribbeanness in this context, by providing a menu in accordance with foreign ideas about the Caribbean food culture, also favored a comparison of the local food culture with these foreign images and with other Caribbean communities and culinary cultures. This often resulted in a feeling of their own culinary culture as less Afro-

Caribbean and complaints about the obstacles those interested in keeping a Caribbean culinary culture alive in Costa Rica are facing:

> Nuestros abuelos Jamaiquinos, que llegaron acá, tienen platos, de ellos, de Jamaica, y muchos platos que no se pueden hacer, porque por ejemplo, muchos productos de materia prima, no son sembrados en Costa Rica. Yo por ejemplo, algunos solamente los conozco por recetas. Pero ahora, si tiene la receta, no puede hacerlo, porque no existe en el país: No lo siembran, no lo cultivan, tampoco lo comercializan. Nosotros, como tenemos el restaurante, tenemos que ir a comprarlas en Panamá, porque en Costa Rica no hay, no hay de estos. Entonces, le digo, es una cultura que está en este país, pero no es tan fácil conseguir las materias, para hacer, para elaborar todas estas. (George, April 2011)[15]

George's family is from Panama, not from Jamaica, but he is here talking about the Jamaican ancestry reaffirming his own and the local Afro-Caribbean people's belonging to Jamaica and the Caribbean culture. In comparison with other Caribbean food cultures, their own food culture seems less rich and less authentic, part of which, as George claims here, is due to the lack of ingredients needed for the preparation of Caribbean food. Thus, even with the recipes at hand, people are faced with the problem that some ingredients necessary to prepare an authentic Caribbean dish cannot easily be obtained, as they are no longer produced locally. Among those ingredients are salted pigtail and okra, both components of pepperpot, or salted codfish that is used to prepare codfish and akee, for example. And even though one can get salted fish imported from Norway in local supermarkets, which can be used and sometimes is used to replace the codfish, my interviewees pointed out the necessity to go to Panama to prepare the real, authentic dish.[16] Apart from the difficulty to obtain the authentic ingredients—that

---

15 "Our Jamaican grandfathers, who came here, have dishes of their own, and a lot of dishes that cannot be prepared here, because, for example, a lot of raw materials are not sown in Costa Rica. I know some of these only for the recipe. But now, if you do have the recipe, you cannot prepare the dish, as it does not exist in the country. They don't sow it, don't cultivate it and don't commercialize it. We, as we do have the restaurant have to go to buy it in Panama, as it does not exist in Costa Rica. So, I tell you, it is a culture existing in Costa Rica, but it is not so easy to get the material to prepare all these things" (my translation).

16 An alternative would be purchasing these ingredients in Puerto Limón, where they are usually brought from Panama by local traders and sold at the market. My interviewees, living closer to the Panamanian border than to Puerto Limón, preferred going to Panama. This crossing of borders was facilitated as most of them were holding a Panamanian ID-Card.

is ingredients prepared according to Caribbean tradition—that guarantee the right flavor of the dishes (and therefore their authenticity), this need to buy the ingredients in Panama can be explained with reference to Pasi Falk's theory, who holds that feelings of inferiority arising from the comparison with esteemed Others can be reduced through the consumption of the goods these Others are consuming (cf. Falk 1994: 121). By preparing the same dishes that are cooked in other Caribbean communities, using the same ingredients, my interviewees are reaffirming their own Afro-Caribbean identity at the same time as they are displaying it to tourists and meeting the tourists' expectations.

While it has been quite common for the local Caribbean population in the past to cross borders in order to buy some of the ingredients needed in Panama, those economic relations have become more important with the integration of these dishes in the restaurant menus and the locals' desire to serve authentic Caribbean food to their customers and present themselves as Afro-Caribbean. All the restaurant owners relied heavily on these relations to keep their restaurants going. Furthermore, it is not only ties to Panama that are strengthened. This is partly linked to Costa Rican conservation laws, as there are some ingredients that one is neither allowed to consume nor to bring to Costa Rica. With controls at the Costa Rican-Panamanian border tightened, people are increasingly evading those restrictions by (re-)establishing ties to other Caribbean communities, such as San Andrés, asking personal acquaintances there to send the ingredients one cannot bring from Panama anymore. The already existing transnational relations are strengthened at the same time as the transnational network is enlarged. Apart from perceiving themselves as Afro-Caribbean and as belonging to a transnational Caribbean cultural context and community, the local Afro-Caribbean population of Puerto Viejo de Talamanca, engaged in the selling of Caribbean food, was actively participating in this transnational Caribbean community.

Conclusion

In Puerto Viejo de Talamanca, at a time when local food culture is in danger of disappearing, tourist demand and external appreciation have created awareness for the value of the Caribbean food culture among the local Afro-Caribbean population. The need to present their own identity and culture as 'authentic' Caribbean in accordance with tourists' expectations has—apart from a reintegration of some local Caribbean dishes—promoted the integration of dishes emblematic both of the *cocina afrolimonense* and the Caribbean food culture into the local eating habits and concept of Caribbean cuisine. This integration was enhanced by the publication of recipes in cookbooks and on websites that did not only contribute to the determination and circulation of a concept of 'authentic' Caribbean food culture, but also helped local restaurant owners to cook Caribbean meals in accordance with these ideals by making available the instructions on how to prepare the dishes.

Rather than a mere revival of the local Caribbean food culture, local food culture is reinvented through a negotiation of local and foreign concepts of Caribbean food culture. Through this reinvented food culture, people engaged in the preparation and selling of Caribbean food are presenting themselves as Afro-Caribbean, not only as a performance of Caribbeanness under the 'tourist gaze,' but also as reinforcing of a sense of belonging to the transnational Caribbean community among the local population.

On the other hand, this self-positioning within the Caribbean cultural context promotes the comparison with other Caribbean food cultures, which then causes a sense of their own food culture as less 'authentically' Caribbean, due largely to the fact that the local food culture has disappeared from everyday life and ingredients needed to prepare Caribbean dishes are no longer available. The challenge to present an 'authentic' Caribbean culinary culture has led to an increase in the relevance of transnational relations to neighboring Caribbean communities, primarily driven by the need to obtain the ingredients necessary to create this 'authentic' Caribbean food. These relationships have become vital both for the performance of Caribbeanness in the context of tourist consumption and for holding on to a Caribbean food culture as a marker of their own Afro-Caribbean identity in everyday life. In summary, it is therefore through the need to (re-)create a sense of cultural identity through the production, sale, and consumption of authentic Caribbean food, the local Afro-Caribbean population of Puerto Viejo de Talamanca is actively involved in a transnational Afro-Caribbean network, upholding existing relations to Afro-Caribbeans living in neighboring countries and constructing new ones.

BIBLIOGRAPHY

Álvarez Masis, Yanori 2007. *Cocina Tradicional Costarricense 2. Heredia y Limón.* San José: Centro de Investigación y Conservación del Patrimonio.

Appadurai, Arjun 2008. "How to Make a National Cuisine. Cookbooks in Contemporary India." *Food and Culture. A Reader.* Eds. Carole Counihan and Penny van Esterik. New York: Routledge, 289-307.

Ayora-Díaz, Steffan Igor 2010. "Regionalism and the Institution of the Yucatecan Gastronomic Field." *Food, Culture and Society* 13.3: 397-420.
Barlösius, Eva 1999. *Soziologie des Essens. Eine sozial- und kulturwissenschaftliche Einführung in die Ernährungsforschung.* München: Juventa.
Bell, David and Gill Valentine 1997. *Consuming Geographies. We Are Where We Eat.* London et al.: Routledge.
Bourdieu, Pierre 2007. *Die feinen Unterschiede. Kritik der gesellschaftlichen Urteilskraft.* Frankfurt a. M.: Suhrkamp Taschenbuch Verlag.
—. 2008. *Sozialer Sinn. Kritik der theoretischen Vernunft.* Frankfurt a. M.: Suhrkamp Taschenbuch Verlag.
Anonymous 2011. *Caribbean Way* 35: 33.
Chang Vargas, Giselle 1984. *Remedios Caseros y Comidas Tradicionales Afrolimonenses.* San José: Editorial Ministerio de Educación Pública.
Chang Vargas, Giselle et al., eds. 2001. *Nuestras Comidas.* San José: CECC.
Cornell, Stephen Elicott and Douglas Hartmann 2007. *Ethnicity and Race. Making Identities in a Changing World.* Thousand Oaks et al.: Pine Forge Press.
Escapeartist, Inc. 2011. "Costa Rican Cuisine." *Escapeartist Costa Rica* Web [http://costarica.escapeartist.com/costa-rican-cuisine/ (retrieved 10 February 2013)].
Falk, Pasi 1994. *The Consuming Body.* London et al.: Sage Publications.
Goody, Jack 1996a. *Cooking, Cuisine and Class. A Study in Comparative Sociology.* Cambridge et al.: Cambridge University Press.
—. 1996b. *The Logic of Writing and the Organization of Society.* Cambridge et al.: Cambridge University Press.
Halter, Marilyn 2000. *Shopping for Identity. The Marketing of Ethnicity.* New York: Schocken Books.
Hannerz, Ulf 2000. *Transnational Connections. Culture, People, Places.* New York: Routledge.
Howes, David 2000. "Introduction. Commodities and Cultural Borders." *Cross-Cultural Consumption. Global Markets, Local Realities.* Ed. David Howes. London et al.: Routledge, 1-16.
Jiménez Acuña, Carolina 2007. *Sazonando Recuerdos Anécdotas, Historia y Recetas de Cocina de Puerto Viejo de Talamanca.* San José: EUNED.
Lupton, Deborah 1996. *Food, the Body and the Self.* London et al.: Sage Publications.
MacCannell, Dean 1976. *The Tourist.* New York: Schocken Books.
Natter, Wolfgang and John Paul Jones III 1997. "Identity, Space and Other Uncertainties." *Space and Social Theory. Interpreting Modernity and Post-*

modernity. Eds. Georges Benko and Ulf Strohmayer. Oxford / Malden: Blackwell, 141-161.

Palmer, Paula 2005. *"What Happen." A Folk-History of Costa Rica's Talamancan Coast*. Miami: Distribuidores Zona Tropical, S.A.

Pardo Castro, Elena 2003. *Limón y su Cocina. Recetas de Cocina Recopilados por la Dra. Elena Pardo C*. San José: Editorial de la Universidad de Costa Rica.

Parkhurst-Ferguson, Priscilla 2010. "Culinary Nationalism." *Gastronomics* 10.1: 102-109.

Ross de Cerdas, Marjorie 2002. *La Magia de la Cocina Limonense. Rice and Beans y Calalú*. San José: Editorial de la Universidad de Costa Rica.

Ross Gonzalez, Marjorie 2001. *Entre el Comal y la Olla. Fundamentos de la Gastronomía Costarricense*. San José: EUNED.

Sandoval García, Carlos 2004. *Threatening Others. Nicaraguans and the Formation of National Identities in Costa Rica*. Athens: Ohio University Press.

Sedó Masís, Patricia 2008. *Comidas y Tradiciones de Costa Rica*. San José: Escuela de Nutrición, UCR. [CD-ROM].

Sutton, David E. 2001. *Remembrance of Repasts. An Anthropology of Food and Memory*. Oxford et al.: Berg.

Urry, John 1990. "The 'Consumption' of Tourism." *Sociology* 24.1: 23-35.

—. 2002. *The Tourist Gaze*. London et al.: Sage Publications.

Vandegrift, Darcie 2007. "Global Tourism and Citizenship Claims. Citizen-Subjects and the State in Costa Rica." *Race / Ethnicity. Multidisciplinary Global Perspectives* 1.1: 121-143.

Vorhees, Mara and Matthew Firestone 2006. *Lonely Planet Costa Rica*. Victoria: Lonely Planet Publications.

Wang, Ning 1999. "Rethinking Authenticity in Tourism Experience." *Annals of Tourism Research* 26.2: 349-370.

Warde, Alan 1997. *Consumption, Food and Taste. Culinary Antinomies and Commodity Culture*. London et al.: Sage Publications.

Consumption and Communities

Barrels of Love
A Study of the Soft Goods Remittance Practices of Transnational Jamaican Households

DWAINE PLAZA

INTRODUCTION

For the past twenty years I have sent barrels from Toronto to Falmouth where my family lives. My family is very poor and I am fortunate to have left Jamaica as a domestic worker. I send my barrel of love around Christmas and when school starts back in September. I try to send the essentials like: corned beef, sardines, peanut butter, ketchup, mayonnaise, flour, rice, cooking oil, macaroni, laundry powder, school supplies, clothes and shoes. You know the items that are very dear in Jamaica. I feel a sense of obligation to help out my sister and brother's children who did not get the same opportunity that I got from loving God. Living in Toronto was not easy as a domestic but over the years I have done better and I continue to care deeply for those left behind in Jamaica...so I do what I can. (Janet, a 55-year-old Jamaican-Canadian)[1]

The contemporary Jamaican diaspora living in Canada, Britain, and the United States is the product of a 'culture of migration' that developed as a survival strategy in the context of a long secular decline in sugar production and plantation agriculture starting in the early 1800s (cf. Marshall 1982). Most Jamaicans like Janet migrated to Canada since the late 1960s because they saw this as a step towards finding more opportunities for better pay and a wider range of goods

---

1   All names used in the paper are pseudonymous. The identities of the interviewee respondents are changed so as to protect anonymity and confidentiality. See Table 3 for an overview of the characteristics of each interviewee.

and services. International migration for many Jamaicans continues to be a mobility strategy to gain access to better opportunities for sending back money and resources to further uplift the lives of those who could not migrate because of age, lack of necessary skills, or immigration policy preferences. The remittances sent back to Jamaica for family, kin, and fictive kin includes soft goods,[2] money transfers, and the direct payment for intangibles like cellular phone bills, electricity bills, school tuition, and various fees. The available data on the exact amount of remittances being sent to Jamaica each year is limited because it is very difficult to track the transfer of soft goods. Soft goods sent in a barrel or cash put into a card and mailed back to Jamaica are completely below the radar in terms of how much impact they have on the Jamaican family or the economy as a whole.

What we do know much more about is the impact of remittance via official channels like banks, postal money order transfers, or remittance companies. In 2005, monetary remittances became the largest source of foreign exchange in Jamaica. Remittances accounted for U.S. $1,204 million, compared to U.S. $770 million for bauxite and alumina, U.S. $389 million for tourism, U.S. $60.2 million for sugar, and U.S. $35.5 million for rum (cf. World Bank 2005). Even more interesting according to the 2005 World Bank *Time for Action Report*, remittances to Jamaica are more than 100% greater than foreign direct investment when measured as a percentage of gross domestic product (GDP). In 2008, there was a twelve per cent decline in remittances to Jamaica, in part due to the global recession that lasted until 2010. In 2011, the World Bank noted that remittances to the Caribbean grew by two per cent. These figures confirm that monetary remittances are the mainstay of the external Jamaican economy both in terms of their contribution to the balance of payments and in providing disposable income for local household expenditure.

There is currently little research that has examined the socio-cultural nature of remittance practices of the approximately 200,000 Jamaicans who live in the province of Ontario, Canada. Most of the research that has been done on remittance practices focuses mainly on the magnitude and impact of remittances on households and communities in other developing countries (cf. Itzigsohn 1995; Levitt 2001; Orozco 2002, 2004). The large numbers of empirical studies in this area have been summarized in several overview papers (cf. Rubenstein 1983; Massey and Parrado 1994; McElroy and De Alberquerque 1988). Policy initia-

---

2   Soft goods (consumables) may be defined either as goods that are immediately consumed in one use or ones that have a lifespan of less than three years. Examples of nondurable goods include food, clothing, footwear, personal products, medications, cosmetics, cigarettes, office supplies, and textiles.

tives to enhance the development impact of remittance flows have also been the subject of a number of policy reviews by international agencies (cf. Orozco 2002, 2004). However, much less is known about the volume, frequency, or cultural practices related to the sending of soft goods by Jamaican-Canadian migrants to their family, kin, and fictive kin who live in Jamaica. The existing remittance studies fall short of examining how sent barrels, boxes, and suitcases provide multi-directional caring for families based in Jamaica.

METHODS AND PROCEDURES

This article is based on data collected in 2006 from two Canadian International Development Agency (CIDA) funded research projects. The research was undertaken through the Centre for Research on Latin America and the Caribbean (CERLAC), York University, Toronto, with the collaboration of the Centre D'Études Ethniques des Universités Montréalaises (CEETUM) and the Département de Démographie of the Université de Montréal. The 2005 data was collected by the Canadian Foundation for the Americas (FOCAL).[3]

The survey designed by CERLAC and CEETUM involved a non-random sample of (n=138) individuals who were: born in Jamaica, living in Canada for at least a year, 18 years of age or over, and involved in major decisions in the household in which they lived. The survey covered various measures of the amount, frequency, and purpose of remittances sent by household members. It also covered who in the household sent remittances, to whom the remittances were sent, how they were sent, the costs of sending, and household income, as well as rough measures of identity and perceptions of racism in Canadian society. The survey design sought to ensure diversity of background, particularly in terms of length of residence in Canada, schooling, gender, and age / generation.

The survey designed by FOCAL was based on one designed by Manuel Orozco at the Inter-American Development Bank (IDB) and the United States Agency for International Development (USAID). As such the results of the FOCAL Jamaican survey fits with the wider work done on the Caribbean. The FOCAL survey involved purposive, non-random face-to-face interviews with a sample of (n=766) Jamaicans who receive remittances. All of the participants had to be over 18 years, Jamaican, and have family and relatives who live in

---

3   The Canadian Foundation for the Americas (FOCAL) commissioned Market Research Services Ltd. (MRSL) in 2005 to carry out a survey of Jamaicans who receive remittances from Canada, the United States, and the United Kingdom.

Canada, the United States, or Great Britain and who send money or goods to them.

This paper also uses qualitative data collected from a series of in-depth (n=20) individual interviews with Jamaican-Canadians and (n=5) focus group meetings in Toronto. Table 3 in the appendices provides an overview of the socio-demographic characteristics of the individuals interviewed for this study. All of the interviews and focus group meetings were audiotaped and lasted between one and two hours. The interviews were transcribed and analysed using a "constant comparative method of analysis," a strategy of data analysis that calls for continuously "making comparisons" and "asking questions" (Strauss and Corbin 1998: 47). Interviews and focus group meetings were coded and sorted according to emerging themes. These themes were then compared for generalizability. Essentially, as Strauss and Corbin (1998) note, this type of analysis involves identifying categories, patterns, and themes in one's data through one's interaction with the data. After this analysis, similarities and differences were documented based on our personal understanding, professional knowledge, and the literature.

These three data sources allowed for an examination of the 'gifts' that Jamaican-Canadian immigrants and their families in the diaspora send to relatives at home in the form of barrels of food, soft goods, clothing, luxury items, and electronics. On the Jamaican side, the data allows for tracking the volume and frequency of barrels received. These data sources provide a clearer picture of the remittance practices of transnational Jamaican families (See Tables 1 and 2 for an indication of the items sent in barrels from Canada to Jamaica).

The use of multiple research methods for studying the culture of barrel remittance practices has allowed for an examination of the symbolic expression of affection, reciprocity, and cultural identity Jamaican-Canadians derive from sending barrels to their relatives. The practice of sending barrels plays the role of maintaining and solidifying linkages of obligation and caring to family, kin, and fictive kin. The case study approach for the sending of barrels as it applies to Jamaicans has implications for the other countries that make up the English-speaking Caribbean whose diaspora populations have similar practices of sending barrels of food, clothing, medicine, luxury goods, and other items to maintain long-term caring for family members.

BACKGROUND TO CARIBBEAN MIGRATION TO CANADA

Dramatic changes in Canadian immigration policy in the mid to late 1960s led to the formation of a large Caribbean community in Canada. Prior to the 1960s, Canada selected immigrants through a nation-of-origin preference system that favored Europeans and virtually excluded immigration from other regions of the world, including the Caribbean. After 1967, immigrant selection was based on individual attributes such as occupational skills, schooling, language skills, and age. Country of origin, as an indirect indicator of ethnicity and race, was no longer relevant for immigrant selection. As a result of the policy shift to a points-based system, in the late 1960s through the mid-1970s, some 8,000 to 12,000 immigrants arrived in Canada from the Caribbean annually (cf. Plaza 2001). Various factors contributed to the size of this flow, including high unemployment and low wages in the Caribbean relative to Canada and the existing culture of migration in the Caribbean.

According to the 2006 Canadian census, there are 578,695 persons of former British, Dutch, and French Caribbean origin living in Canada. There are also 102,430 persons of Haitian origin who are now living in Quebec and 4,780 persons from the Spanish-speaking Caribbean residing in the rest of Canada. A better estimate of the total population of Caribbean-origin people living in Canada is between 600,000 and 700,000 persons (cf. Simmons and Plaza 2006: 133). Jamaica is by far the major source of Caribbean immigrants to Canada since the mid-1960s. Also according to the 2006 census, there are 231,110 Jamaican origin people living in Canada, or about 38.5 per cent of all Caribbean immigrants. Guyana is the next highest source country with 25 per cent, Trinidad and Tobago accounts for 21 per cent, and Barbados for four per cent. The Eastern Caribbean, which constitutes the "rest of the Caribbean territories" (ibid.) supplies approximately eight per cent of the total immigrants.

In Toronto, Caribbean migrants have faced a variety of problems in the labor and housing markets. For many Caribbean immigrants, unemployment and labor market segmentation have contributed to relatively low housing ownership and lower median incomes for some Caribbean groups (cf. Henry 1994).

THEORETICAL FRAMEWORK

Transnational families are families in which individual members live in two or more different countries (cf. Dreby 2006). Their strategy of survival relies on the ability to maximize earnings by sending one or more of their core members to work abroad while some or all dependents stay in the home country (cf. Burawoy 1976). It is only recently that attention has been given to the 'double-wellbeing' role that many Caribbean migrants have sustained. It is now clear that large proportions of Caribbean immigrants regularly send funds home to their relatives and overseas communities (cf. Henry 1994).

Various studies observe that Caribbean migrants in general, and Jamaicans in particular, do not forget their home communities nor lose contact with families, community organizations, and political movements in their countries of origin as they become part of a new society (cf. Ho 1993; Fog Olwig 2002), rather Caribbean migrants take advantage of new opportunities, through travel and inexpensive telecommunications, to be simultaneously part of their home society and the society to which they have moved (cf. Glick Schiller et al. 1992; Portes 1996; Vertovec 2001). The home and migrant new settlement societies are simultaneously transformed by these transnational links. This can include infusions of new types of food, music, dances, and festivals that celebrate the diverse contributions of these new immigrant groups into the host societies (cf. Vertovec 2001).

Schlossberg (1989) refers to the concepts of 'marginality' and 'mattering,' which encompass these variables, and the connection that we desire as human beings. The feeling of marginality is a result of the perception of not belonging or fitting in within a certain group or community. This feeling may be permanent, especially if an individual feels that they are trapped between two worlds and must identify by paralleling two cultures. Mattering may promote successful transitions through connection and support that may encourage feelings of personal worth. Feelings of mattering also promote better coping skills with the many transitions and events associated with immigration and settling into a foreign culture. Those who feel that they matter will have a better chance of success, implying that feelings of mattering may lead to the ability to transition more positively to a new situation (cf. Schlossberg 1989).

Caribbean migrants have been found to be engaged in the construction of transnational social fields (cf. Basch et al. 1994). Though migrants invest socially, economically, and politically in their new diaspora locations, they have continued to participate in the daily life of the society from which they emigrated but did not abandon (cf. Glick Schiller 1998). The transnational activities in which Caribbean-origin migrants engage may encompass work, business, politics, or various social endeavors. Specifically, this might involve their participation in high school alumni associations, fund raising for disaster relief, joining a diaspora association, engaging in organized Caribbean sports clubs (cricket and soccer), or attending church services where the worshipers are predominantly of Caribbean origin.

As a direct result of exposure to systemic and institutionalized racism, many Caribbean migrants living in metropolitan countries have experienced a sense of 'cultural mourning.' The idea of cultural mourning has its origins in the theories of object loss as conceptualized by Sigmund Freud. According to Freud, the loss felt by the infant at the initial break from the mother, compels the infant to repeatedly attempt to "fill the gap" (cf. Freud 1939: 29). The act of 'filling a gap' takes many forms and might ultimately result in a perpetual attachment to the mother (cf. Ainslie 1998). Severe object loss can be devastating and lead to a psychological imbalance with feelings of extreme sadness, guilt, or an "impairment of the capacity to function right" (Frankiel 1994: 72).

In most cases of object loss however, mourning does not result in derangement. According to Volkan the mourner eventually finds "linking phenomena" that provide "a locus to externalize contact between aspects of the mourner's self-representation and aspects of the representation of the deceased" (Volkan 1981: 55). Linking objects play a role in mourning in that they create "a symbolic bridge" (56) that allows the mourner to reconcile their grief. Linking objects might include eating authentic 'back home' food, listening to Soca or Reggae music, belief in the myths and folklore of Caribbean culture, and code switching in the use of language (cf. ibid.).

Ainslie elaborates on the theory of cultural mourning to help explain the transition that often takes place with immigrant groups like Caribbean people who find themselves living in a hostile foreign land. He notes:

When an immigrant leaves loved ones at home, he or she also leaves the cultural enclosures that have organized and sustained experience. The immigrant simultaneously must come to terms with the loss of family and friends on the one hand, and cultural forms (food, music, art, for example) that have given the immigrant's native world a distinct and highly personal character on the other hand. It is not only the people who are mourned but the culture itself, which is inseparable from the loved ones whom it holds. (Ainslie 1998: 118)

Ainslie draws on Winnicott's theory which suggests that immigrants living abroad often find a space to engage in activities "that bridge the emotional gaps" (91) created by their feelings of dislocation and loss. This space allows first generation immigrants and their children to restore the object loss they feel. This might include the engagement in activities that create the "illusion of restoration of what was lost" (92), such as regularly consuming 'back home' food, Skyping family members, posting photographs on Facebook, or attending a visiting Reggae artist show. Ainslie further notes that immigrants tend to fill this potential "empty" (95) space with activities, objects, or artifacts that keep alive a continuity with their homeland. In this regard, the potential space serves as a platform where immigrants can begin to negotiate their adaptation to the new environment.

Individual remittance-sending practices take place within the context of family. Specifically, these sums represent a sense of obligation between family members and often the expression of profound emotional bonds between relatives separated by geography. Feminist scholars have differentiated between two forms of family obligations that provide a useful starting point for understanding Caribbean transnational family care. The two forms are caring about family and caring for family (cf. Ackers 1998). Caring about family encompasses contact and emotional support and refers to emotional functions connected with sociability, advice, comfort, and self-validation. Activities which express caring about family include communication by social media, telephone, letters, and email, return visits, participation in family decision making, and sending of remittances, whereas caring for family refers to concrete, hands-on caregiving. An example of the latter is sending for elderly relatives to live in the metropolitan countries so that they can be eligible to receive good healthcare (cf. Finch and Mason 1990).

A moral obligation dimension is crucial to understanding the caring about and caring for kin relationships within transnational Caribbean family and kinship networks in general. Finch and Mason (1990) advocate the concept of 'kinship morality' to suggest that a set of moral discourses inform the behavior of individuals toward their kin in the Caribbean. Similarly, Williams suggests that people negotiate their transnational familial relationships within these moral guidelines, and act as moral agents involved in negotiating "the proper thing to do" (Williams 2004: 18) in and through their commitments to others. These caring commitments may cross the boundaries of blood, marriage, residence, culture, and country (cf. Reynolds 2006).

Caring about family members and kin seems to assume a crucial relevance in the context of migration and geographically dispersed families. The very existence of transnational families rests on the vitality and durability of kin ties in spite of great distances and prolonged separations (cf. Reynolds 2004). Reynolds (2005) adopts the term 'cultural remittance' to advance the theory of transnational caring about relationships. She notes that cultural remittance represents emotional attachments and the way in which migrants abroad utilize their family links to maintain cultural connections to their place of origin (cf. Levitt 2001). Other forms of cultural remittance include owning and building property back home, the celebration of cultural rituals and national events in the new country of residence, and keeping abreast of news back home through the internet and newspapers (cf. Horst and Miller 2006). Cultural remittance reinforces ethnic identity and is viewed as a sign of continued commitment to the kin left behind, as well as a commitment to keeping kin together.

Multi-directional caring-for practices, obligations, and responsibilities continue to operate within the family networks of Caribbean diaspora families. Their accounts of daily activities and family relationships provide a wealth and range of examples of transnational care provision between family members. Most common is care between siblings, grandparents and grandchildren, parents and children, and affluent and less wealthy family members.

FINDINGS FROM THE SURVEY DATA

The 2006 survey conducted by CERLAC of (n=138) individuals provided a very interesting look at the trends in barrel-sending in terms of the amount, frequency, and purpose of sending to Jamaica by family and kin in Canada (see Table 2 for barrel-sending trends). The survey conducted by FOCAL of (n=766) Jamaicans who all had relatives who live in Canada, the United States, or Great Britain provided a very interesting look at the trends in barrel-receiving in Jamaica (see Table 1 for barrel-receiving trends). The combination of these two data sets allow for a detailed picture of the macro trends in barrel-sending and -receiving within the Jamaican diaspora community.

Focusing first on the barrel-senders from Canada (see Table 2), it is important to note that the majority were women between the age of 25 and 54 years old who had completed secondary school or higher. Not surprisingly, the older and younger Jamaican-Canadians were not engaged in sending barrels back to family and kin in Jamaica. The young were more likely to have less feelings of obligation while the older cohorts avoided the bureaucracy and trouble of packing a barrel. It would be much easier to send money to family. Most of the barrel-senders in Canada had migrated six or more years prior to the interview. What is interesting is that the Jamaican-Canadians continue sending barrels even if they have lived in Canada twenty or more years. This trend suggests continuity with Reynolds (2004) theory of long-term multi-directional caring practices. The respondents who sent barrels estimated that the content of the barrel packed helped eleven or more family members. The barrels that were sent contained a great deal of non-perishable basic food items, medical supplies, and clothing. These items suggest that families in Canada were attempting to help their families in Jamaica to find temporary respite from the ravages of poverty and structural adjustment policies. Barrel sending fulfills the obligation of transnational caring that is part of the Jamaican culture of migration. The exchange of a barrel of food involves intricate negotiation of obligations. In this two-way relationship there is an expectation that the immigrant will continue to send monetary or soft goods in order to help family left behind. Family in Jamaica, on the other hand, provides a psychological sense of mattering and belonging (cf. Schlossberg 1989). They also provide a long-term insurance policy in case the immigrant felt a need to return to Jamaica to live or even make a holiday visit. This is particularly important in the hostile racist climate of Canada where Jamaican immigrants have been considered as 'outsiders' despite the length of time they have been there (cf. Plaza 2007).

Focusing next on the barrels received in Jamaica (see Table 1), it is important to note that the majority of barrel-receivers reported being unmarried women between the ages of 18 and 44 with three or more people living in their household. The barrel-receivers worked full time and had at least completed high school. Despite this relatively high level of schooling, most of the barrel-receivers rated their home as being poor or working class. The frequency of barrels arriving in Jamaica varied from at least one per year to as many as three. The majority of the barrels arrived at Christmas time or during the start of the school year. The soft goods packed in a barrel are usually used by four or more people in Jamaica. The average estimated value of the goods contained in barrel was U.S. $455. For this survey, no question was asked about the content of the barrel. These trends in receiving barrels in Jamaica suggest that poor and working class Jamaicans are dependent on barrels sent from abroad by family. The barrels of soft goods sent by family in the diaspora supplement the diet and nutritional needs of poor families (cf. Levitt 2001). Without these supplements, it is likely that there would be more starvation and hunger among the poor and working classes in Jamaica.

Although the survey data provides a general picture of the macro trends in barrel-sending and -receiving, the qualitative data allows for a better understanding of the logic and rational for sending barrels from Canada. The barrel-sending process from Jamaican-Canadians seems to be best understood using Reynolds' (2005) theory of transnational caring about relationships. Barrel-sending seems to be a sign of continued commitment to family and kin left behind.

TRANSNATIONAL LINKS IN BARREL SENDING

Virtually all of our interviewees had a similar story about their motivations for sending barrels of food and other soft goods to Jamaica. The main motivation seems to be satisfying a feeling of obligation to help out those who still live in Jamaica. This was a feeling that continued despite the length of time individuals lived in Canada. The more communication individuals maintained with family and kin living in Jamaica the greater the feeling of obligation seems to have been. This communication most often came in the form of regular telephone calls, mobile phones, social media like Facebook, email communication, or return visits to Jamaica. The more individuals knew about the circumstance of their family, kin, or friends back in Jamaica, the greater the likelihood their sense of obligation compelled them to take some sort of action. This was certainly the case for Elizabeth, who tells us:

I have been sending to Jamaica since I first arrived in Canada in 1975. I come to Canada to do domestic work. I left behind a son so I was sending money to his granny to take care of him. Over time I started packing a barrel at Christmas and Easter to send for my mom and Glen my son. My barrel was always packed with rice, cooking oil, flour, you know the basics that can last a long time. I did not see my son again for ten years but when he got to Canada he told me how much he and my mom depended on the content of the barrel along with the money I was sending back. So today I continue to send a barrel each Christmas to my half sister who still lives in Jamaica. She has seven children, she works as a domestic in Kingston which does not pay much. I also feel sorry for her because none of the men she had the children with are reliable in supporting them own pickney. (Elizabeth, a 63-year-old Jamaican-Canadian)

We also heard about the pressure and stress for sending food and goods had on some Jamaican families in Canada. The desire to send was also generational and often depended on particular individuals within families who felt a burden to continue sending despite migrating from Jamaica many years ago. Not surprisingly, we heard that the first generation tended to be highly involved in maintaining transnational linkages with family and friends; by the second generation however, there seems to be a waning sense of responsibility for those still living in Jamaica. Part of this decline in obligation by the second generation might be explained by the fact that many of them only know their family and kin in Jamaica from holiday visits or through secondhand knowledge provided by parent(s). This link is often not solid enough to sustain a long-term feeling of obligation and responsibility for those still living in Jamaica. This was certainly happening in Grace' family in Toronto. Her children have become acculturated to Canadian values of a nuclear family and caring only for those who are closest. Grace on the other hand continued to give long distance transnational caring to her mother and brother. She also was very concerned that once she is gone, her family in Jamaica will suffer because no one will feel compelled to send barrels or money to them. Grace tells us:

My generation still feels very obligated to help out those left in Jamaica. I moved to Canada in 1976 and since then I have always sent to my mother and brother who live there. I supported them through the bad times under Manley when it was hard to find food on the grocery store shelves. My children who have only visited Jamaica two times in their life feel less of a sense of obligation to help out their cousins who live in Jamaica. When I am packing a barrel for my nieces and nephews in Jamaica my children question my actions and often laugh at me. They see their cousins as ungrateful and demanding of my hard work. My children are different than me they are more Canadianized and so I don't see them continuing my sense of obligation to my relatives. Once I am gone their tie to Jamaica will be mainly as a memory not somewhere they feel a pull and a desire to live. (Grace, a 72-year-old Jamaican-Canadian)

SOCIO-CULTURAL PATTERNS IN SENDING BARRELS

In the next section, we examine the sociocultural patterns of barrel-sending from Canada. This includes the ritual of packing the barrels in Canada and the intentional selection of family members in Jamaica who are deserving of help through receiving a barrel or specific material content. From the interviews and focus group data, it became evident that women and men had very specific roles and responsibilities in the sending of barrels. There were also very interesting rituals of collecting food and other soft goods that would go into the barrels by each gender. The following accounts by Clarence and Emily make this very evident.

My mother and sister are always in charge of buying the barrel contents when it's on sale. Ma and sis spend a month or two buying up flour, rice, pasta, 'bully beef,' flour, sugar, cooking oil, and other basics to put in the barrel. They can also add in clothing and shoes when there is a request. Once everything is assembled in our apartment that's when I come in to pack the barrel with them. We pack it then unpack it and then repack it maximizing all the airspace in the barrel. It's like a giant jigsaw puzzle to assemble a barrel that is packed to the max. Our objective is to get as much in as possible because a barrel costs the same to ship no matter what the weight. Once the barrel is ready I call the shipping company and they pick it up and in a month or so it's in Kingston. (Clarence, a 26-year-old Jamaican-Canadian)

Normally my brother in Clarendon sends me a list of items the family will need. The list contains food items, clothing, and shoes for each of his children. I do my best over about a one-month period to find these items on sale at No Frills, Costco, The Bay, Walmart, or the Dollar Store. Once I have the items assembled then I call to have a barrel delivered to my house. My sister who also lives in Toronto will come over with some items she has bought and we will commence packing the barrel. It's a labor of love that eventually involves my son who comes into the picture to move the barrel to the front of the house so it can be pickup and shipped. (Emily, a 68-year-old Jamaican-Canadian)

Clarence and Emily's reflection about the process of barrel-packing in their family was quite typical of the other interviewees. Clarence' quote suggests that the packing of barrels with food and clothing was a family ritual that gave satisfaction to everyone because it fulfilled an obligation to help and stay in touch with transnational family and kin (cf. Reynolds 2004). Clarence and Emily's family members each had gendered roles in the packing of the barrel, something that was typical of the other interviewees. The ritual involved women as the key players who dedicated an extended period of time shopping for just the right food and clothing to be packed into the barrel. Clarence' mother and sister sought to find items of food and clothing that were on sale or deemed to be vital for the long-term care and welfare of individuals back in Jamaica. The role for the male in the barrel process also seemed to be fairly typical. Clarence' role was to help pack the food and clothing items into the barrel. Men were also relied upon to coordinate the logistics of the barrel being moved to Jamaica. This role might require strength to move the barrel from one location to another in the home.

At no time was the barrel-packing process described as being haphazard or unplanned. The basic food items in most barrels shipped to Jamaica included: pasta, rice, flour, and cooking oil. Each of these intentionally selected food items satisfied two purposes. First, the items could be used as a basic ingredient in most recipes. Secondly, the basic goods tended to be very high in carbohydrates. These items when consumed would give the feeling of being full.

The data suggests that Jamaicans sending barrels from Canada are very selective in terms of which family members they chose to send help to. Not all family members in Jamaica were deemed to be equally worthy of help. We heard numerous reports of individual senders having elaborate lists of who was 'deserving' and who was not. The barrel or money that was sent to Jamaica was targeted to particular families or family members within the extended family networks. Individuals seem to have developed their own checklist of who was worthy and deserving of help. They also had lists of family members who were deemed as lazy, unscrupulous, or wasteful and therefore unworthy of getting anything sent to them. Margaret, for example, had very specific criteria to rank her family members. She tells us:

I send to my sister in Jamaica but not my brother. My sister and her children are so humble and deserving whereas my brother and his children are ungrateful and demanding. My brother also is a drinker who does not try and help anyone but himself. So when I send a barrel it's just to my sister and her children. Yes I do put something in for my brother but it's never the same as my sister Rhonda who works so hard and tries to make something of herself and her family. I see this every time I visit Jamaica. So for me I am willing to help out Rhonda and her kids the best that I can. (Margaret, a 58-year-old Jamaican-Canadian)

The selective process was counter-intuitive because individuals were not sending only on the basis of family need but rather sending was based on pragmatic choices based on family history, relationships, and subjective assessment of each family member. This family 'politics' has not been considered in the work of Reynolds (2004) and Levitt (2001) in terms of multi-directional transnational caring practices.

Many of the individuals interviewed for this study reported that they continued to support family, kin, and fictive kin in Jamaica despite having lived in Canada more than ten years. The individuals who continued to feel a sense of obligation and responsibility to help out in Jamaica seemed to be this way because of their personality and for some their religious convictions. Some of the interviewees had grown up in poor rural districts of Jamaica and so they had experienced poverty and suffering firsthand. This encouraged them to feel a sense of commitment to the poor and less fortunate. Others had a strong religious ideology that compelled them to help their neighbors even if they were not wealthy themselves. This ultimately resulted in some individuals sending back barrels and money over the years to people who may not have been blood relatives. Sometimes the person who they were sending for passed away or migrated to Canada. Despite this change some individuals would refocus their giving to someone in Jamaica they felt was deserving of help; Daphney, who had had a mother pass away, continued to send money and barrels back to the next-door neighbor in Jamaica. Daphney felt that while she was growing up in Jamaica, the neighbor acted as a surrogate parent for her. Daphney tells us:

It's funny my mother passed away three years ago but I still send money and barrels back to our next-door neighbor Miss Ivy. She was my mother's best friend and I also knew her as an aunt while I was growing up. She took care of me and taught me so many life lessons. So even though she is not my blood relative I feel sorry for her since her own children who live in Miami don't send her anything. I pack a barrel at Christmas and send it to her. You cannot imagine how happy and grateful she is on the phone when I tell her the barrel is on the way. (Daphney, 43-year-old Jamaican-Canadian)

SOCIAL CLASS OF BARREL SENDERS AND RECEIVERS

The social class of families in Jamaica, not surprisingly, made a difference in terms of who was sending barrels and who was receiving them. Respondents who came from self-identified upper middle-class families often felt less obligation to send barrels or money to their Jamaican family and kin because more often than not they did not need help from abroad. There were many upper class families living in Jamaica who could afford to buy imported and local food in any quantity they needed in Jamaica. As a result, we discovered that successful Jamaican-Canadians in these circumstances reported sending money and barrels to charities, orphanages, and non-family who they identified as deserving in Jamaica. Many of these individuals sent back goods and money because they felt a sense of obligation to help out poor people in order to 'pay back' for all the economic advantages and opportunities they had in Jamaica. Roger, who came to Canada in 1982 from an upper middle-class family in Jamaica, had a first degree before migrating to Canada and, as a result, he had very little difficulty in securing a good job. Members of his immediate family in Jamaica did not need money or food sent to them because of their social class status. Over the years, Roger felt nationalistic, nostalgic, and somewhat guilty for all that he had grown up with. As part of the privileged group in Jamaica, Roger reported that he never felt any economic pressures of not having enough. Over the years, Roger figured out how to satisfy his feelings of guilt and nationalism by selecting a few worthy charity groups in Jamaica to help out by sending them money and barrels. Roger tells us:

I came to Canada with my university degree already in hand in 1982. Since then I have moved around to a few jobs but mostly white-collar positions. My family in Jamaica lives in Stony Hill and so I grew up upper middle class. We were never wanting for anything while I was growing up but my mother always had a sense of helping out those not as fortunate. I continue that tradition today by helping out an orphanage in Kingston. I send money twice a year and for Christmas I pack a barrel with food and clothing and send it to them. I full the barrel with flour, rice and oil, corn beef, mackerel, you know the basics that I know the children will benefit from. I don't send to my parents or my sisters who are still living there because they can afford these items. So for me I am motivated by the decline in Jamaica and my feeling of sympathy for those less fortunate than me, just like my mother. (Roger, a 66-year-old Jamaican-Canadian)

ARRIVAL OF BARRELS IN JAMAICA

On the receiving end in Jamaica, we also heard a gendered story with regard to the barrels' arrival and processing. The barrel would arrive at one of the two main ports, Kingston or Montego Bay. On arrival, a customs broker would alert the family that it had reached the port. It was up to the family to organize the logistics of getting the barrel off of the port and then transported to their home. This role more often seemed to have been handled by a male in the household. This process could often take an entire day working with a customs broker. By the time the barrel came off the port, it might have incurred a few hundred Jamaican dollars in duties and possible bribes. There was also the organizing of transport of the barrel back to the family home, possibly at great cost depending on the distance to the family home. The barrel was most often addressed to a female family member in Jamaica. It was then her job to check through the barrel and make a phone call to the family member in Canada to report the arrival of the barrel. Glen-Roy was one of many interviewees who stopped sending barrels because of the logistics and cost in Jamaica involved in getting the barrel from the port to their familial home. He says:

I prefer to send money to my mother in Jamaica over a barrel. In the past I would send a barrel at Christmas but the problem is the logistics of clearing and transporting the barrel from Kingston where it drops down to my mother's home in Manchester. My mother in her seventies had to hire someone to do this for her. The tout would go up pay the customs duty on the barrel, get it off the wharf by hiring a large van and then drive back to Mom's home in the country. Then she would have to pay him a fee on top of having to give him something from inside the barrel. I did the math and it's better for her to get the money by Western Union and she can go to the grocery store in Manchester and buy what she needs. It's more practical and it saves on aggravation. (Glen-Roy, a 46-year-old Jamaican-Canadian)

BARREL CHILDREN IN JAMAICA

One group that received barrels on a regular basis was that comprised of Jamaican children left behind by mothers who had migrated to seek better opportunities.[4] Quite regularly Jamaican children were left in the care of grandmothers while their own parent(s) sought out mobility and better opportunities by moving to work in far off locations. These children have been referred to in the academic literature as 'barrel children.'[5] The symbiotic relationship between mothers and daughters ensured that the young Jamaican women could move North and live in Canada with the knowledge that their children were being raised in loving and trustworthy households. In return for providing a good home, grandmothers in Jamaica were regularly sent money and often a barrel of soft goods. Enough resources were sent that the mother could take care of the children as well as themselves. Both money and barrels were intended to help family members survive in conditions of scarceness. Ultimately, when the Jamaican mothers in Canada found themselves more stable and in better economic circumstances they would then send for their child(ren) left behind in Jamaica. The children might have been separated for many years but moving to Canada gave them access to more opportunities like schooling, better healthcare, and better housing conditions. Despite Jamaican women having their children with them in Canada, many would still continue to support their mothers and other family members in Jamaica. This feeling of debt to relatives is evocative of what Reynolds (2004) refers to as a culture of obligation that transnational Jamaican-Canadian migrants feel about relatives remaining behind. Calbert who arrived in Canada as a twelve-year-old knew very little about his mother other than the fact that she sent his grandmother a barrel full of food, clothing, and other soft goods while he was

---

4 Claudette Crawford-Brown (1994) described the phenomenon of "barrel children." She notes that these are children who, while waiting in the Caribbean to migrate to their parents in the metropoles of North America and the United Kingdom, receive material resources in the form of food and clothing in lieu of direct care.

5 The term 'barrel children' is accepted throughout the Caribbean in reference to children whose parents migrate leaving them in the care of siblings, relatives, or friends, and who are provided for through barrels sent with non-perishable items and through remittances sent home regularly. Recent studies have also shown that, despite the inflow of foreign capital and the presence of relatives, 'barrel children' in Jamaica have a harder time coping without their parent(s), and often have suicidal thoughts (cf. Crawford-Brown 1994).

growing up; while he did meet her on two return holiday visits, it was never long enough to develop a close relationship. Calbert tells us:

I did not know my mother until I was twelve years old. Prior to that, my mother went to Canada to work as a domestic. She never forgot about me and my grandmother. Mummy always sent money or barrels to help granny who was taking care of six grandchildren from three sisters. I recall before every Christmas a big barrel would come into the yard and it was full of toys, candies, cookies, mackerel, crackers, flour, rice, cooking oil, macaroni, clothes, and shoes for each of us. Grandma would divide it up equally among us. Actually my mother put labels on each item so that each child knew something was coming to them from within the barrel. It was a happy time even though we were very poor—I knew that I had a mom in Canada who did not forget me. I think the term used now to describe children like me is barrel children. (Calbert, a 38-year-old Jamaican-Canadian)

Many rural families in Jamaica survived the lean times by using the food and other goods sent from the diaspora Jamaican community. These care packages were often the only lifeline that young people had to keep them from falling into various states of malnutrition and starvation in Jamaica. This was certainly the experience of Michelle who recalls the ritual of receiving barrels while growing up in Jamaica:

When the barrel arrived at home I can remember it was like Christmas Day because we all gathered around as the lid was pried off. We all knew it was coming because my mother would call and tell my grandmother ahead of time. Once granny opened the barrel, my cousins and I would watch her pull out cans of corned beef and sardines, cookies, bags of rice, cooking oil, macaroni, school supplies, clothes, and new shoes. Each item of clothing and shoes in the barrel had a specific name pined to them so that there was no question as to who was getting what. We also knew that night and for the first week or so granny would be preparing meals with the tasty foreign food in the barrel. After that, she would ration out the food so that it lasted until the next barrel would arrive. (Michelle, a 33-year-old Jamaican-Canadian)

The barrels sent to Jamaica allowed both the children and the older grandmother or caregiver to survive the conditions of poverty. The soft goods sent in barrels on a regular basis allowed barrel children to supplement their nutrition and also to survive the many years of separation between themselves and their biological mothers. When mothers and children are eventually reunited in Canada the fact that they stayed in contact via the regular barrels being sent means that the children may feel less psychologically abandoned. The adjustment to Canada is that much easier for barrel children if they arrive feeling less abandoned by their mothers.

DISCUSSION OF THE QUANTITATIVE AND QUALITATIVE DATA

The qualitative and quantitative data in this study provide a better insight into the practices of barrel-sending and -receiving. First, the data suggests that Jamaican women in both Canada and Jamaica are much more likely than men to be imbedded in transnational caring-for family networks. The women in our study expressed a greater feeling of obligation for taking long-term responsibility for those less fortunate in their family network. This could be a reflection of the different socialization between men and women in general. It might also be explained by the work of Finch and Mason (1990) or Reynolds (2005) who note that there is a moral obligation dimension in the caring about and caring for kin relationships within transnational Caribbean family and kinship networks that is shouldered more by women. That is not to say that Jamaican men are not doing anything in terms of caring for family; Jamaican men are more likely from this research to send monetary types of remittance. This is likely to take the form of money sent via a transfer company like Western Union or via a hand transfer of money sent with a friend. Jamaican men seem less likely to hand pack a barrel and then ship it down on their own. The men will be more likely to be part of a group sending a barrel. In that group, the men seem to be more likely to buy the items that go into the barrel, arrange for the shipping company to pick up the barrel, and help to make sure that the logistics of the barrel shipping were completed.

Not surprisingly, members of the second and third generation of Jamaican-Canadians are less likely to be engaged in transnational caring for family and kin still living in Jamaica. The second generation reported seeing this responsibility as something that their mothers and grandmothers were more deeply responsible for. If the second generation did participate in the barrel-sending process it might come in the form of pooling a fixed amount of money to be used for the purchase of soft goods, or they might provide a set of lightly worn or used clothes for relatives back in Jamaica. There was not an example to be found where a second or third generation interviewee was organizing or participating in a barrel transfer on their own.

A final observation from the data was the long-term continuity of sending. Despite living in Canada for more than 20 years, many respondents continued to send remittances in the form of money or the occasional barrel to family and kin. Some like Elizabeth, Lucy, Janet, Lisa, Roger, Laura, Angie, Emily, Margaret, and Barbara—who had all lived in Canada more than 25 years—had all continued to send money and barrels back to Jamaica. The trends in Table 3 show evidence that despite being away from their place of birth for decades, older first generation migrants from Jamaica continue to stay in close touch with those family, kin, and friends who are still back 'home.' They seem to feel a sense of obligation to help and to provide long distance transnational caring. This pattern seems to agree with the theoretical work of Ackers (1998) and Reynolds (2004, 2005).

Conclusion

The main motivation for the long-term sending of barrels of food and soft goods to Jamaica seems to be satisfying a feeling of obligation to help out those who still live in Jamaica. This was a feeling that continued despite the length of time away from Jamaica. Jamaican-Canadians send barrels of food stuff, soft goods, and other consumer items as a way to convey their love, affection, and caring to their family, kin, and friends in Jamaica.

The barrels that arrive in Jamaica are often full of items that were purchased in Canada because they represented the basic food that would help family and kin maintain short-term nutrition and sustainability in an economy that has fewer opportunities and an increasing cost of living.

Both Jamaican-Canadian women and men are engaged in ritualized behavior when it comes to barrel sending. There seem to be gendered roles in terms of purchasing, preparing, and shipping barrels of soft goods and food from Canada to Jamaica. Ultimately, when the barrel arrived in Jamaica, there was another gendered, ritualized process in terms of receiving and distributing the contents of the barrel. The barrel sending and receiving suggests that there is a symbolic expression of affection, reciprocity, and cultural identity that Jamaican-Canadians derive from sending barrels full of soft goods to their relatives in Jamaica.

The practice of sending barrels plays the role of maintaining and solidifying linkages of obligation and caring to family, kin, and fictive kin. What is interesting is that transnational families have particular ways of conveying to family that they will not abandon them despite the many years that they may have migrated.

Future research is needed in terms of the rituals of the packing, shipping, and receiving of the barrels. Also more data is needed on the impact that these barrels have on family nutrition levels in various parts of Jamaica. How does the content of these barrels supplement the diet of families and individuals? What role do these barrels play in terms of changing the taste for local foods on the Jamaican families? How do these foreign foods affect the local merchants and higglers trying to sell their goods in the market?

Table 1. Socio-Demographic Characteristics of Individuals in Jamaica Who Reported Receiving a Barrel in 2005

Gender of Barrel Recipient	
Female	67.8
Male	33.2
Age of Barrel Recipient	
18-34	65.8
35-44	22.8
45 and Over	11.5
Social Class of Barrel Recipient	
Wealthy/Professional	20.6
Working	48.1
Poor	31.3
Marital Status of Barrel Recipient	
Single, never married	59.8
Married	22.5
Other	17.7
Employment Status of Barrel Recipient	
Employed	55.4
Temporarily unemployed	15.8
Student	16.2
Other	12.2
Education Level of Barrel Recipient	
Primary/Prep School	6.6
Secondary/High School	44.3
Diploma/Certificate	25.3
College/University	21.6
Number of People in House Where Barrel Arrives	
1-2 persons	17.1
3-4 persons	44.1
5 or more persons	37.2

Frequency of Receiving Barrels in Jamaica	
Once a month	1.9
2-3 times a year	34.5
Once a year	58.9
Other times	4.3
Number of People in Jamaica Who Benefit from Barrel	
One	3.2
Two-Three	36.7
Four-Six	45.3
Seven or More	13.2
Estimated Value of the Barrel Content Received	
Mean Value U.S dollars	$445
Median Value U.S dollars	$200
Percent of Families Sharing the Content of Barrel	50.9

Source: FOCAL 2005 non-random sample of 766 Jamaicans who receive remittances and are over 18 years old.

Table 2. Socio-Demographic Characteristics of Barrel Senders from Canada 2005

Gender of Jamaican-Canadian Barrel Senders	
Female	61.5
Male	38.5
Age of Jamaican-Canadian Barrel Senders	
18-34 years	32.4
35-44 years	29.3
45 and Over	37.8
Number of Years Living in Canada	
1-10 years	15.6
11-20 years	44.6
21 or more years	39.8
Number of Barrels Sent over 5 Years	
1-2 Barrels	33.3
3-4 Barrels	23.6
5-6 Barrels	20.9
7 or More Barrels	22.2
Content of Barrels	
Clothing	57.6
Basic Food/ Cans	56.8
Medical Health	32.1
Books School Supplies	39.2
Tools	24.8
Irons Radios	41.6
Candies Cookies	44.8
Goods Sell Commercial	8.8
Family Business	7.2
Car Parts	4.8
Other Items	4.1

How is Barrel Sent	
Barrel Sent Alone	79.4
Barrel Shared	20.5
Estimated Number Who Benefit from Barrel	
1- 5 People in Jamaica	13.4
6- 10 people in Jamaica	13.4
11 or more people in Jamaica	73.2

Source: 2005 CERLAC non-random sample of (n=138) Jamaican born immigrants living in Canada over 18 years old.

Table 3. Characteristics of Interviewees[6]

Interviewee Pseudonyms	Age	Generation	Gender Self Identified	Citizenship Status	Social Class	Occupation	Country of Birth	Length of Time in Canada	No. Family Living in Jamaica	No. Family Living in Canada	Type of Remittance	Frequency of Remittance
Elizabeth	63	first	Female	Can/Jam	Middle	Social Worker	Jamaica	35 years	70	45	Money/barrel	Infrequent
Lucy	56	first	Female	Canadian	Lower middle	Pastor of Church	Jamaica	27 years	60	40	Money/barrel	Occassionally
Calbert	38	first	Male	Canadian	Middle	Mechanic	Jamaica	11 years	50	60	Money	Occassionally
Glen-Roy	46	second	Male	Canadian	Working	Factory Worker	Jamaica	35 years	30	45	Money	Occassionally
Janet	55	first	Female	Can/Jam	Lower	Retail Sales	Jamaica	28 years	60	35	Money/barrel	Frequently
Steadman	26	second	Male	Canadian	Lower	Chef	Canada	26 years	Not Sure	Many	Never	Never
Michelle	33	second	Female	Canadian	Middle	Lawyer	Jamaica	27 years	60	45	Money	Infrequent
Lisa	47	first	Female	Canadian	Working	Factory Worker	Jamaica	25 years	45	40	Money/barrel	Occassionally
Roger	66	first	Male	Can/Jam	Upper	Insurance Sales	Jamaica	25 years	50	66	Money/barrel	Infrequent
Vanessa	26	second	Female	Canadian	Middle	Real Estate	Canada	26 years	Not Sure	50	Never	Never
Rhonda	43	first	Female	Canadian	Lower	Unemployed	Jamaica	20 years	60	80	Never	Never
Imani	22	second	Female	Canadian	Middle	University Student	Canada	22 Years	50	90	Never	Never
Laura	50	first	Female	Canadian	Middle	Teacher	Jamaica	35 years	40	55	Money/barrel	Occassionally
Angela	49	first	Female	Canadian	Lower middle	Bank Teller	Jamaica	38 years	30	25	Money/barrel	Frequently
Oscar	36	first	Male	Canadian	Upper	Marketing/Sales	Jamaica	22 Years	Not Sure	42	Money	Rarely
Emily	68	first	Female	Canadian	Lower middle	Retired	Jamaica	47 years	38	30	Money/barrel	Ocassionally
Clarence	26	second	Male	Canadian	Working	Social Worker	Canada	26 years	35	25	Money	Rarely
Grace	72	first	Female	Canadian	Lower middle	Retired	Jamaica	51 years	35	55	Money	Infrequent
Daphney	43	first	Female	Can/Jam	Middle	Secretary	Jamaica	22 Years	55	60	Money	Occassionally
Margaret	58	first	Female	Canadian	Middle	Nurse	Jamaica	31 Years	60	40	Money/barrel	Frequently
Barbara	55	first	Female	Canadian	Middle	Nurse	Jamaica	28 Years	55	66	Money/barrel	Frequently

6   Note: All names used above are pseudonyms. We have tried to keep the interviewees anonymous when constructing the matrix. All first generation interviewees are born in the Caribbean and migrated to Canada after age twelve. All second generation were born in Canada of Caribbean parent(s) or arrived in Canada before age twelve.

BIBLIOGRAPHY

Ackers, Louise 1998. "Caring at a Distance. Women, Mobility and Autonomy in the European Union." *Revista Critica de Ciencias Sociais* 31.50: 121-151.

Ainslie, Ricardo 1998. "Cultural Mourning, Immigration, and Engagement. Vignettes From the Mexican Experience." *Crossings. Mexican Immigration in Interdisciplinary Perspectives.* Ed. Marcelo Suarez-Orozco. Cambridge, MA: Harvard University Press.

Basch, Linda, Nina Schiller, and Christine Blanc 1994. *Nations Unbound.* Langhorne, PA: Gordon and Breach.

Burawoy, Michael 1976. "The Functions and Reproduction of Migrant Labor. Comparative Material from Southern Africa and the United States." *American Journal of Sociology* 81.5: 1050-1087.

Crawford-Brown, Claudette 1994. *The 'Barrel Children' of the Caribbean. The Socio-Cultural Context of the Migrant Caribbean Family.* Dept. of Sociology and Social Work, UWI, Mona, Jamaica: ISER.

Dreby, Joanna 2006. "Honor and Virtue. Mexican Parenting in the Transnational Context." *Gender and Society* 20.1: 32-59.

Finch, Janet and Jennifer Mason 1990. "Filial Obligations and Kin Support for Elderly People." *Ageing and Society* 10.2: 151-175.

Fog Olwig, Karen 2002. "A Wedding in the Family. Home Making in a Global Kin Network." *Global Networks* 2.3: 205-218.

Frankiel, Rita 1994. *Essential Papers on Object Loss.* New York: New York University Press.

Freud, Sigmund 1939. *Civilization, War and Death. Selections from Three Works by Sigmund Freud.* Ed. John Rickman. London: Hogarth Press.

Glick Schiller, Nina 1998. "The Situation of Transnational Studies." *Global Studies in Culture and Power* 4.2: 155-166.

Glick Schiller, Nina, Linda Basch, and Christina Blanc-Szanton 1992. *Transnational Perspective on Migration. Race, Class, Ethnicity, and Nationalism Reconsidered.* Annals of the New York Academy of Sciences 645. New York: The New York Academy of Sciences.

Henry, Francis 1994. *The Caribbean Diaspora in Toronto. Learning to Live with Racism.* Toronto: University of Toronto Press.

Ho, Christine 1993. "The Internationalization of Kinship and the Feminization of Caribbean Migration. The Case of Afro-Trinidadians in Los Angeles." *Human Organization* 52.1: 32-40.

Horst, Heather and David Miller 2006. *The Cell Phone. An Anthropology of Communication.* London: Berg Publishing.

Itzigsohn, Jose 1995. "Migrant Remittances, Labor Markets and Household Strategies. A Comparative Analysis of Low Income Household Strategies in the Caribbean Basin." *Social Forces* 74.2: 633-655.

Levitt, Peggy 2001. "Transnational Migration. Taking Stock and Future Directions." *Global Networks* 1.3: 195-216.

Marshall, Dawn 1982. "The History of Caribbean Migrations." *Caribbean Review* 11.1: 6-9.

Massey, Douglas and Emilo Parrado 1994. "Migradollars. The Remittances and Savings of Mexican Migrants to the USA." *Population Research and Policy Review* 13.1: 3-30.

McElroy, Jerome and Klaus de Albuquerque 1988. "Transition in Small Northern and Eastern Caribbean States." *International Migration Review* 27.3: 30-58.

Orozco, Manuel 2002. "Globalization and Migration. The Impact of Family Remittances in Latin America." *Latin American Politics and Society* 44.2: 41-66.

—. 2004. *Distant But Close. Guyanese Transnational Communities and Their Remittances from the United States.* Diálogo Interamericano, Informe Encomendado por la Agencia para el Desarrollo Internacional de EEUU, AID. Washington, DC.

Plaza, Dwaine 2001. "A Socio-Historic Examination of Caribbean Migration to Canada. Moving to the Beat of Changes in Immigration Policy." *Wadabagei. Journal of Diaspora Studies* 4.1: 39-80.

—. 2007. "An Examination of Transnational Remittance Practices of Jamaican Canadian Families." *Global Development Studies* 4.3-4: 217-250.

Portes, Alejandro 1996. "Global Villagers. The Rise of Transnational Communities." *The American Prospect* 25: 74-77.

Reynolds, Tracey 2004. *Families, Social Capital and Caribbean Young People's Diasporic Identities.* Families and Social Capital ESRC Research Group, Working Paper Series 11. London: South Bank University.

—. 2005. *Caribbean Mothers. Identity and Experience in the UK.* London: Tufnell Press.

—. 2006. *A Comparative Study of Care and Provision Across Caribbean and Italian Transnational Families.* Families and Social Capital ESRC Research Group, Working Paper Series 16. London: South Bank University.

Rubenstein, Hymie 1983. "Caribbean Family and Household Organization. Some Conceptual Clarifications." *Journal of Comparative Family Studies* 14: 283-298.

Schlossberg, Nancy 1989. "Marginality and Mattering. Key Issues in Building Community." *Designing Campus Activities to Foster a Sense of Community.* Ed. Dennis C. Roberts. San Francisco: Jossey-Bass, 5-15.

Simmons, Alan and Dwaine Plaza 2006. "The Caribbean Community in Canada. Transnational Connections and Transformation." *Negotiating Borders and Belonging. Transnational Identities and Practices in Canada.* Eds. Lloyd Wong and Vic Satzewich. Vancouver: University of British Columbia Press, 130-149.

Strauss, Anselm and Juliet Corbin 1998. *Basics of Qualitative Research. Techniques and Procedures for Developing Grounded Theory.* California: Sage Thousand Oaks.

Vertovec, Steven 2001. "Transnationalism and Identity." *Journal of Ethnic and Migration Studies* 27.4: 573-582.

Volkan, Vamik 1981. *Linking Objects and Linking Phenomena. A Study of the Forms, Symptoms, Metapsychology, and Therapy of Complicated Mourning.* New York: International Universities Press.

Williams, Fiona 2004. "Rethinking Care in Social Policy." *Janus* 12.1: 6-24.

World Bank 2005. *World Bank Time for Action Report.* Washington D.C.: World Bank.

Hindu Ritual Food in Suriname

Women as Gatekeepers of Hindu Identity?

Elizabeth den Boer

Religious Practice: Cooking for the Gods

Food possesses no intrinsically religious significance, nor does any other object. However, as with any object, food may become imbued with sacredness and thus gain religious and ritual meaning. Sacredness is a realm of psychological content, not psychological function or structure (cf. Beit-Hallahmi 1989: 13). Food evidently becomes imbued with substantial religious, social, and cultural connotations as shown in rituals and celebrations (cf. Douglas 1972, 1981; Firth 1973). The links between the domains of food and religion remain poorly defined, possibly due to the fact that relations between these domains are mainly mediated by women (cf. van Esterik 1998).

In Suriname as well as India, only men act as cooks when food is prepared in a makeshift open kitchen to feed large public congregations, such as weddings and offerings (*jag*). Women are only involved in the preparation of ritual food that takes place in the secluded area of the kitchen, for example, during death rituals. Cooking and eating are activities that cut across the opposition of secular and sacral. It has been suggested that a study of how women perceive religious action will offer a more comprehensive analysis of the religious field than when research focuses exclusively on the much more visible role of the males (cf. van Esterik 1998).

This paper will primarily focus on the ritual food prepared for the daily domestic worship (*pujá*) and 'fasts and vows' (*vrata*), as well as the occasional communal *jags*, birth (*muran*) and funerary (*marani*) rituals. Moreover, due to the limited space available, the preparation, offering, and distribution of food in temples will be glossed over here. A distinction should furthermore be made between consecrated food (*prasád*), which is first offered to the deities, but is then returned to the devotee, and that which is offered directly to the guests at a funeral rite in which effectively the ancestors and the deceased are fed through the sumptuous meals 'offered' to specific priests or guests. Even though both types of food are strictly vegetarian,[1] the manner of their preparation is very different: the former is 'pure' (sectarian), mostly *satvik* (prepared without onion and garlic), whereas the latter is 'impure' (secular)—some families allow ingredients such as fried onion and garlic.

The study of ritual food not only deals with the issues mentioned, but also with the means of expressing the ambiguity and the contradiction implicit in religious practice. On the one hand, (knowledge of) ritual is a form of control, on the other, particularly in times of (rapid) change, it constitutes a particular dynamic of social empowerment (cf. Bell 1992). 'Ritual food' offers women this means, hence this article also focuses on the issue of whether women have a sufficient understanding of orthodox Hinduism in order to prepare the culturally and ritually appropriate food offerings, and whether they use this knowledge to strengthen their position in the socio-religious domain. More significantly, how do they deal with the required interpretation and reinterpretation of principles and meanings, some of which touch on significant controversies in the *Sanátana Dharma* (in Suriname also referred to as orthodox Hinduism).[2] Among many ethnic groups of Suriname, food is encoded with numerous social messages: through food, one can convey trust and equality if the food offered is accepted, or impose distance (and ethnic or caste distinction) through refusal (cf. Khan 1994: 249 f.). In such a society, food is imbued with general social connotations. In Hindu practice, this extends to the religious and ritual realm; to the Hindustani community gender may also play a major role.[3] As for Surinamese Hindustanis, there exist some prejudices, such as for example the idea that Hindustani women, and women of the *Sanátana Dharma* in particular, are more submissive than the women of other ethnic groups. Also, the idea that women in general and these women in particular are seen as purveyors and transmitters of culture requires a closer look. Interestingly, the proportionate number of Hindustani women migrants during the first years of indentured labor was quite low, i.e. 26.7%

---

1 Note that Hindu vegetarians usually eschew eggs.
2 It is the term used for the form of Hinduism that was allegedly brought from India. Furthermore, Hindu reform movements such as the *Arya Samaj* were also promoted in the Caribbean, including Suriname, in the beginning of the 20th century.
3 Hindustani (in Dutch *Hindostaan*) is the term used in Suriname and the Netherlands for the descendants of the British Indian indentured laborers, i.e. used as a term to distinguish ethnicity, not to be confused with 'Hindus.'

(cf. de Klerk 1998 [1951]:103), which raises the question as to how the position of women as purveyors of culture should be approached. This important issue deserves greater attention since in the literature the primary focus has usually been on the male migrants.

THE HINDUSTANI COMMUNITY IN SURINAME

After the abolition of slavery in the West Indies between 1834 and 1863, colonial sugarcane planters desperately sought new sources of cheap labor. A stream of indentured laborers from India to the West Indies commenced in 1838 when the first Indian immigrants arrived in British Guiana (today's Guyana), in 1845 in Trinidad, and in 1873 in Suriname (cf. van der Veer and Vertovec 1991:149). Thus, the present-day East Indian communities in the Caribbean are the descendants of those indentured laborers.[4] By 1917, when the system of indentureship ended in Suriname, about 34,000 Indians had arrived there. Around 82% of these were Hindus, of which probably the majority belonged to the caste of *Ahirs* (caste of cow-herders) or similar;[5] about 17% were Muslims (de Klerk 1998 [1953] II: 99, 103); and less than 1% were Christians. Historically and culturally, Suriname is part of the Caribbean—however with its national language of Dutch, and its past and present ties with the Netherlands, it is linguistically isolated from the Caribbean and Latin America (Manuel 2000: III). In 2004, Suriname had a population of 492,829, of which the Hindustanis formed the largest group with 135,117 people (see Table 1), with 70.2% Hindu, 11.6% Muslim, 6.5% be-

---

4   The term East Indian is still used in the Caribbean for the descendants from the indentured laborers from India, mainly the provinces Bihar and Uttar Pradesh (formerly known as United Provinces).

5   The castes were stated by the laborers themselves; some may have concealed their caste as there was a strong preference for this caste, for being farmers, in the plantation system. Majumder notes: "It is however interesting to note that the coolies of Calcutta did not always belong to the lower castes for whom manual labour was not taboo according to cast rules. The members of upper castes would also often avail of the anonymity of a large city, considerably far from their village home where chances of recognition were negligible, to adopt a profession not sanctioned by cast rules" (Majumder 2010: 58). See also for Fiji: "Similarly, other Brahmins, Ksatriyas and Punjabis, to avoid being rejected for recruitment, registered themselves as belonging to a different cast" (Rajendra 2004: 47).

longing to one of the Christian denominations and the rest either claiming to be non-religious or registering no religious preference (see Table 2).

Most Surinamese live in the coastal area, concentrated in the capital Paramaribo and its vicinity, and in the district of Nickerie with its relatively large Hindustani community. Geographically, we can roughly divide the capital into three sectors: the center and the north, where the relatively well-off segment of the population is situated; and the southern part of the city, which is populated primarily by people from the middle class. In the outskirt areas, people are often laborers or agriculturists. Notably, the higher and middle class of Paramaribo's north and center were influenced by 'Western' culture, with a preference for speaking Dutch and Sranan Tongo, the lingua franca of Suriname. The Hindustanis reluctantly speak their language, Sarnami Hindi, of which only a few have any active knowledge.[6] Dutch is gaining more and more prestige,[7] although some of the Creole officials try hard to propagate Sranan Tongo and push it towards the status of a national language. Hindustanis living in the outskirts of the city, in the districts, and the district of Nickerie in particular, are considered by themselves and others to be conservative and showing a more comprehensive knowledge of what they conceive as their culture, religious traditions, and language.

---

6   They demonstrate their integration into Caribbean culture and as stakeholders in the Surinamese community by, at least in public, not appearing to cling to their ethnic and cultural heritage. The dynamics of cultural belonging demands ongoing research as this position seems to be changing again.
7   Dutch was for long perceived and therefore despised as the language of the colonial rulers, only of use for those wanting a career in the civil service and education. With the increase in appreciation for a good education and opportunities in a non-agricultural career Dutch started to gain more prestige.

Table 1: Population of Suriname by Ethnicity

	Population		%
Ethnicity	**1972**	**2004**	**2004**
Creole	119,009	87,202	17.7
Hindustani	**142,917**	**135,117**	**27.4**
Javanese	57,688	71,879	14.6
Mixed[8]	-	61,524	12.5
Maroon	35,838	75,553	15.3
Other	24,155	31,975	6.4
Unknown	-	32,579	6.6
Total	379,607	492,829	100

Source: ABS report 2005:18, table H1.

Table 2: Religious Affiliation of the Hindustani Community

Religion	Male	Female	Unknown[9]	Total	%
Christian	4,052	4,700	2	**8,754**	6.48
Hindu	48,565	46,234	1	**94,800**	70.16
Muslim	8,039	7,597	13	**15,649**	11.58
Traditional[10]	125	129		**254**	0.19
Other	220	226	1	**447**	0.33
No religion	187	153		**340**	0.25
Does not know	7,703	6,985	68	**14,756**	10.92
No Answer	57	60		**117**	0.09
Total	68,948	66,084	85	**135,117**	100

Source: ABS report 2005: 33, table 7

---

8   These categories are not strictly comparable since in 1972 'Mixed' was also classified under 'Other' and many 'mixed' people categorized themselves as Creole.
9   The statistics do not clarify the term 'unknown.'
10 The term 'traditional' was not explained in the interviews, hence also used by individuals as to follow the 'traditional religion' of their family, which could be Hindu, Muslim, Christian, etc.

Hinduism in Suriname

It is evident that the new situation of the first Indian indentured laborers was completely different and in a way hostile to what they were used to in their homeland. The social, cultural, and economical patterns in Suriname had partially already been established with a Creole imprint. The newly-arrived Indians had to establish their own place in the plantation-based structure. By language, religion, culture, and customs they were alien from all layers of this Caribbean society. The forms of religiosity they brought along had to be adapted to the new environment, a process in which their culture and religion developed largely independently from the Indian subcontinent. After arriving in Suriname, the Hindustani community was permitted a certain degree of freedom to preserve and practice their own customs. To the present day, the Hindustanis have established numerous religious, social, educational, and political institutions. As this study focuses on Hindu food practices, emphasis is given to Hindu Surinamese in the following.

A notable feature in the entire Caribbean is that the dwellings of most *Sanátana Dharma* Hindus are marked by *jhandis* (colored religious flags) in their front yard.[11] For reasons of cultural and religious visibility, as explained above, a number of followers of *Sanátana Dharma* living in the center and north of Paramaribo do not follow this tradition. The *jhandis* are, of course, a religious symbol, but they also function as an identity marker especially against neighboring Christians or even *Arya Samaji*. Almost every Surinamese recognizes these as 'Hindu houses.'[12]

Particularly in the early decades of indentured labor, there was not much interaction with the religious leaders in India, except for the western part of Suriname where the proximity to the Guyanese border facilitated the exchange with Hindus from Guyana and Trinidad. The residents of Nickerie benefitted from the closer contact of the Guyanese with India since in the British colonies there was regular contact with Indian religious teachers and leaders. Hence, we may say

---

11 *Jhandis* are a tradition brought from the rural areas of Uttar Pradesh and Bihar, where the traditional use of these flags is still in practice (observations by N. Mohkamsing in 2006). The dwellings of the devotees of Kabir Panth (a small community of around 150 people) can also be identified by their white flags.

12 With the increase of Hindu immigrants from Guyana, there has been a notable intensification of the *jhandi* cult in Suriname, obviously fuelled by the 'Tamil' background of some of the Guyanese who also worship Kali Mai, i.e. Goddess Kali, characterized by the black flags, showing a clear distinction between the Surinamese *jhandis*.

that religious developments in Suriname have been influenced by the forms of Hinduism and Islam already present in the Caribbean among indentured laborers in former British Guiana from an earlier date, i.e. from 1838. As for their self-designation, Hindus use the term *Sanātana Dharma* which means 'Eternal Law / Religion.' It is the term used for the form of Hinduism that was brought from India. Furthermore, Hindu reform movements such as the *Arya Samaj* were also promoted in the Caribbean, including Suriname, in the beginning of the 20th century.

Since the first indentured laborers arrived, the culture of the Hindu community has seen various changes in areas such as religion, rituals, ritual food, its preparation, and the role women play in all these areas. A notable transformation is that the Hindus in Suriname are as a rule non-vegetarians. On arrival, most of the Hindus were not vegetarian or had already lost their vegetarianism while in the depot in Calcutta, as attested by Munshi Rahman Khan,[13] when many started eating meat, if they had been vegetarian at all. On the consumption of food, Rahman Khan writes for instance:

Sunday came. We would have mutton and *roti*. Goats and sheep were killed and cooked. ... Everyone ran for the canteen. Raghunandan, the head supervisor, declared that the vegetarians would be served separately. Only then I noticed that there were only 10-20 Hindus who did not eat meat. (Khan 2003: 133)

This account is from the depot before setting sail to Suriname. On the food served during the journey, he writes:

Every fifteenth day we had fresh mutton and *roti*. Daily we had *dal*, *roti*, tamarind chutney, canned meat and lemon juice. Everybody, Hindu or Muslim, had to eat whatever was served. If someone refused, he had to fast. On board of the ship there was no difference between high or low caste, between Hindu or Muslim or any other race. (135)

It needs to be highlighted that he possibly downplays the implications of this diet for Muslims, for it is certain that the meat the Muslims ate was not *halal*. During my fieldwork, I asked women what they knew about the eating habits of their grandparents during the voyage, and indeed, their stories about grandparents' cooking mutton and goat on the ship seemed no exception.

---

13 Munshi Rahman Khan came to Suriname as an indentured laborer when he was 24 years old. He never returned to India. He wrote about his experiences in a diary, a unique document as he was one of the few well-educated among the indentured laborers. His diary was published only in 2003.

OBSESSION WITH FOOD?

During my research in Suriname I encountered a number of generalizing and prejudicial statements about Hindus and their alleged obsession with food. There are a range of prejudices and stereotypes of this 'obsession' which may be part of the dynamics of a multi-ethnic, multicultural, and multi-religious society such as Suriname. In the Hindu community of Suriname there exists a vivid culture of food, both socially and ritually. This is connected with and derived from their ancestral heritage where the preparation and consumption of food plays an important role in both daily life and Hindu rituals and ceremonies from India. Generally, it seems impossible to enter any Hindustani home without being offered food and drinks, regardless whether its residents are Christian, Hindu, or Muslim. Refusing food is equal to refusing the hospitality offered. A refusal may be taken as an insult. When visiting Hindustani friends in Suriname or the Netherlands (or for the same matter in India), I still have difficulties not to overeat at dinners because of having problems with turning down more food offered at the end of a meal. While this may be stereotypically interpreted as obsession with food by some, it may also emphasize the significance of sharing food as a practice to reestablish relationships and communities in the form of communal meals.

Within the orthodox Hindu communities, food—in general and, more specifically, ritual food—plays a significant role in expressing religious and social identity. The latter is expressed, for example, when saying 'we like our *dál-bhát* (lentils and rice).' Thereby, people state that, as conservative Hindustanis, they stick to *their* simple but authentic food. With this, they mean food that is prepared with the ingredients they believe their parents and grandparents used, the spices that remind them of their Indian roots as passed down in the diaspora; food that is now known as traditional Surinamese Hindustani food, such as lentils and rice, roti with chicken, all prepared with the typical Surinamese *massala* (mix of spices), and not to be confused with the food and spices from India. Food in all its simplicity can only be prepared by experienced women with knowledge of the traditional kitchen, in the way it has been handed down through generations as a traditionally inherited wisdom in cookery. It is the hand of the cook that flavors the dish as authentic to Hindustani Suriname. Through the study of the role Hindu women play in keeping their religious vows and observance (*vrata*) and preparing ritual food, this article will show how these ideas have emerged and to what extent they are relevant, and, if correct, what has caused this socio-cultural behavior.

Whereas Hindu belief systems in South Asia have stimulated a wide range of studies on Indian food symbolism (e.g., Khare 1992, Appadurai 1988, Babb 1970, Marriott 1968), there does not exist significant literature on eating habits and their ritual connotations in Surinamese Hinduism outside of C. J. M. de Klerk's cursory remarks in his study of orthodox Hinduism in Suriname (1951). In the past two decades, the Hindustani community in Suriname and the Netherlands has attracted some scholarly attention (van der Burg, Damsteegt, Ramsoedh, van der Veer, Mungra, etc.), however none specifically on ritual food, religious observances, gender, or identity formation.

VRATA AND PART-TIME VEGETARIANISM

The eating of ritually prescribed food often marks the termination of a service, fast, or vow in Hinduism. The communal consumption of consecrated food (*prasád / bhog / bhojan*) during temple services, weddings, and funerals, or private consumption of fruit (*phaláhár*), milk, sweets, particular vegetables, and spices, during daily worship at home, religious fasts (*upavása*), vows (*vrata*), etc., are closely connected to each other. All these rituals, ceremonies, observances, and festivals prescribe their particular kinds of food, ingredients, and preparation, as well as when, with what, and how one should consume them. Apart from the preparation of food for large public congregations, such as weddings and large religious gatherings, ritual food is prepared by women. Consequently, the focus is on women as they are the main performers in this field, some of whom, in particular during important rites, guard the ritual purity of their kitchens ferociously.

The question that presents itself with respect to the changing situation of the orthodox Hindus in Suriname in particular is how and to what extent they adapt what they believe to be original prescriptions to their very different situations and environment.[14] My interviews and experience in daily life interaction with women show that their knowledge of the original Hindu codes of conduct is limited or non-existent. Also my question regarding the rationale behind the original Hindu ritual codes of conduct were answered or dismissed, as follows: "This is

---

14 These rules concern mainly references to not only scriptures but also prescriptions for the way rituals are to be performed, ingredients to be used, and their assumed traditional order and hierarchy in executing rituals. Hence, this not only concerns general rituals but also specific instructions for the preparation of food both for the gods and for family consumption.

our tradition, we don't know, it is tradition and that's why we keep it." This does not imply that, since arrival, information and knowledge were not available. While in the early days of diaspora only a few were literate and books were very scarce, over time pamphlets and books were ordered and pandits and gurus came from India. Initially, not many women had access, but times changed and girls also received opportunities for education. While the older generation of women depended on the words of the pandit, the era of the internet and social media has reached the very young. Young women and girls are becoming more and more active to find their 'own' truth and follow rules they believe to be the source of their Hindu faith, shaping their own *vrata*.[15]

When the preparation and consumption of ritual food is considered in the context of orthodox Hinduism, one of the first things that comes to mind is not the food itself, but the paradoxical abstention from it, usually indicated by terms such as *upavāsa* (fast) and *vrata* (vow). In Suriname, however, the term *vrata* is used for both fast as well as vow. Mackenzie-Pearson observed in India that a "*vrata* is usually understood to be a rite that is performed on a regular basis to achieve particular objectives, following rules that have been transmitted from one generation to the next" (Mackenzie-Pearson 1996: 2). As she further observed, many Hindus "immediately think of women in connection to *vratas*" (ibid.). Thus it seems that *vratas* are predominantly something women do and have done for generations. *Vrata* refers to the notion of a particular religious observance which involves fasting, worship (*pujā*), the listening to a recitation of a narrative (*kathā*) about the efficacy of the rite, and the giving of gifts (*dān*) of money and items of food and clothing to another person, usually a Brahman.

In Suriname we find different *vratas* with a particular wish in mind. Most of them require that only vegetarian food is eaten on particular days and festivals. For instance, many orthodox Hindus observe vegetarianism on Monday and Tuesday (or Tuesday and Thursday), depending on the deity or deities worshiped by the particular devotee. Some also abstain from onions, garlic, and salt on those days. Many individuals, however, observe their fasts and vows without any specific knowledge of the religious notions that originally inspired them. Priests and the educated (with special interest in their heritage), know that the Monday *vrata* is for Shiva, the Tuesday for Vishnu, and the Thursday for Durga, the latter mostly observed by women.

This idea of what I call part-time vegetarianism is a recent development in Surinamese Hinduism.[16] Only a very small minority (around 5%)[17] continued to

---

15 Many travel to India in search of their roots and new gurus.
16 Traditionally, not many Hindus in Suriname are vegetarians. Even among the Brahmins only a few are strict vegetarians. On the other hand, vegetarianism has now

maintain their vegetarian traditions after signing their contracts in India. The form of vegetarianism we find in Suriname, i.e. as a *vrata* for one or two days a week, arose around 30 to 40 years ago, generally on instigation of a pandit as a vow to get a wish fulfilled or after the wish was fulfilled.[18] Up until then, the majority of Hindus were omnivorous and only a small percentage (around 10%)[19] would abstain completely from meat, fish and eggs. Also, among the caste of the Brahmins,[20] vegetarianism did and does not occur more often, nor did or do pandits abstain from meat, fish and eggs. Only weddings and death rituals constituted vegetarian occasions, in addition to a number of Hindu festivals and rituals, such as *Mahashivratri*, *Navratri*, and *Durga pujá*.

PURITY AND IMPURITY

The opposition of purity and impurity is traditionally central to the social relations between Hindu groups and individuals, as well as to the relations between gods and humans (cf. van der Burg and van der Veer 1986: 516). We may extend the notions of purity and impurity further to the pair *juthá* (touched > polluted > impure) and *a-juthá* (untouched > unpolluted > pure). It is of interest to investi-

---

again been introduced by the International Society for Krishna Consciousness (ISKCON); people 'converted' to Krishna devotion become strict vegetarians and generally eat *satvik* food. Also other Hindus become vegetarians for religious as well as non-religious reasons.

17 There are no records of the food habits of the indentured laborers. The number of around 5% is the conclusion of interviews with Hindustanis conducted during 2004-2006.

18 After interviewing about one hundred people and asking them about their own food habits and that of their family, in-laws, neighbors, and other acquaintances, I came to the conclusion that vegetarianism on particular days, as described above, is of recent origin, starting between 30 and 40 years ago. Families with a vegetarian tradition from indentureship contract times are extremely rare, and full-time vegetarianism is a relatively new phenomenon in Suriname. All the women I interviewed underscored that they all started their fasting and vegetarian days on the advice of a pandit.

19 This is the conclusion of interviews during fieldwork I carried out in the period 2004-2006 in Suriname among the Hindustani community.

20 Although the caste system disappeared in Suriname, the caste of the Brahmins still exists. The majority of the elderly generations (second and third generation after indentured labor) have knowledge of the caste to which their ancestors belonged.

gate the extent to which Hindu women in the Caribbean abide by these basic principles of Hinduism, especially when one realizes that women take the food observances more seriously than men do. While van der Burg and van der Veer downplay "the key notion of purity" as something that "has become a mere sentiment in Surinamese Hinduism" (van der Burg and van der Veer 1986: 516)—viewing it as simply "colouring but not determining religious practices and discourses" (ibid.)—other scholars arrive at the opposite conclusion. Aisha Khan, for instance, states that in Trinidad "the concept of pollution exists within the structure of class and ethnic relations" (Khan 1994: 253). This controversy underlines that the debate is still open. In fact, a closer study of the problem shows that in Suriname the notion of 'pollution' is not only a focus of discussion but also of religious practice. For instance, in Suriname menstruating women are banned from the preparation and distribution process of ritual food. The removal of shoes before entering a temple or a private home also refers to the notion of pollution. People entering Hindu temples are also supposed not to have eaten any meat, fish or eggs on that particular day. Worshippers, who are alerted, sometimes ask certain individuals *"bisáhin khaile hai?"*, that is, whether he or she has consumed non-vegetarian food. In this regard, the term *bisáhin* (Hindi *bisáyandh*), 'smelly' or non-vegetarian, is used as an adjective qualifying food as 'polluted' (= non-vegetarian) food.

A more general and simple way to recognize the notion of *juthá* as touched, soiled, and therefore polluted, is via the observation that many Hindus do not eat or drink food or drinks touched by others; for instance, they will not drink from a cup or bottle if another person drank directly from it before them. This idea of 'unhygienic pollution' is avoided by most Hindustani people in Suriname, independent from their religious convictions. Apart from the socio-cultural implications of this practice, it also has sacral and ritual dimensions.

In *Purity and Danger* (1966), Mary Douglas suggests that purity and impurity are social constructs, and shows how the physical body can act as a symbol of group identity. The boundaries of the human body are the metaphor for the boundaries of the group. Acceptance and non-acceptance of food establishes boundaries. In the multi-ethnic Caribbean societies, this acceptance and non-acceptance, as well as the preparation and contribution of ritual food, become markers of Hindu identity. However, there probably is a strong process of negotiation and (re-)definition since not all orthodox Hindus follow the fasts and vows on food, yet consider themselves undoubtedly orthodox Hindu, in particular in the political sense of opposition to other ethnic groups. On the other hand, how are these individuals or groups considered by the faithful who do observe their *vratas*? Do people also identify themselves through ritual food? To non-

Hindus it seems clear that most Hindus eat only vegetarian food on certain days of the week, and are very attached to their *dál-bhát*. However, within the Hindustani group (regardless of their religion) there seems to exist an ambivalent attitude towards those who do not care for their traditions. On the one hand, there is no attitude of considering their negligence of *vratas* as sin (*páp*). On the other hand, it is a way of marking the boundaries of the ethnic group and a symbol of identity.

GENDER AND IDENTITY

In India, Hindus generally associate women with ritual food and *vrata*. Behind the famous ethical injunctions to Hindu women to "Be like Sita!" or "Be a Second Sita!" lies the ideal of the perfect wife (*pativratá*). In the *Rámáyana*, a classical Sanskrit epic, Sita is presented as the devoted and faithful wife of Rama, her husband. The paradigm of the *pativratá* most certainly includes the performance of one of the wife's chief traditional duties: cooking for her husband as well as for family, guests, and the gods.[21] However, in the *Rámáyana*, which defines her as the *pativratá*, as the quintessential perfect wife, Sita actually never cooks. According to the text, the only thing the ideal wife did, in her particular situation, was to gather nuts and fruit from the forest (cf. Herman 1998).

Hindu women in Suriname are also admonished 'to be like Sita.' These religious and social gender concepts play a major role in the personal, religious and social identity formation of Surinamese Hindu women and men. From childhood on, in particular in more conservative circles, women have been taught to model their subordinate role as woman and wife after Sita's role. Generally speaking this submissive role manifests in, among other things, most women obediently following the religion of their husband after marriage, with occasional exceptions.

To what extent do women in Suriname follow the ideal image of womanhood and observe, for instance, female fasts such as *karváchaut* (for the husband's long and healthy life after the model of Savitri)? One of my friends, named Karuna, attested that, until recently, some women in Nickerie observed *karváchaut*; she noted that "they are influenced by the women of the neighboring country Guyana and of course women of Guyana married to Surinamese men

---

21 Note that in Hindu marriage, the husband equals a god for the wife who ought to be 'worshiped' by her as a devotee would serve her favorite deity.

continue the practice after moving to Suriname." While talking about this topic she sighed:

> I'd like to go to Nickerie during *karváchaut* and meet and watch women who perform this *vrata*. Then I will follow myself because it looks so beautiful and romantic in the movies. You know, in the evening looking at the moon through the sieve, having your fast broken when your husband puts the first bite in your mouth. So romantic. (Karuna)

It seems that Karuna idealized the practice of *karváchaut* in India in the hope that this religious practice would not only benefit her husband's health and well-being, but at the same time give a romantic boost to her marriage. Karuna seemed to be exemplary for all the women I met, who lived with the idea that the romantic Bollywood images are a reflection of daily life practice in India. Nevertheless, young women more and more reject these idealistic notions to express their independence and emancipation, thereby also rejecting the 'Sita syndrome.'[22] Hence the question arises: 'why do women observe *vratas*?' The first impression is they follow solely for the benefit of others, such as their husband and children or the family. They also observe these *vratas* for social, physical, psychological, and spiritual benefits. Thus they provide an avenue for the expression of profound spiritual yearning or, for some, to gain a measure of control over their lives.

WOMEN AS GATEKEEPERS: RITUAL COOKING AND VEGETARIANISM

During my stay in Suriname in the period from 2004 to 2006, I spoke with many women about culture, religion, and particularly about food and cooking. I came across women with a variety of different reasons and motives for (changing) their religious food habits. In the following paragraphs, I will give examples of those motives, such as coping with an unfaithful husband, health, and fertility. It will indicate that themes such as empowerment, gatekeeping, and subversion of the 'Sita syndrome' (cf. Bhatt 2008) may often be accounted for in terms of respect just because of old age or traumatic experiences.

Years before my research started, I had participated in a funerary ritual after the death of a Hindu cousin, and had been involved in ritual cooking (cf.

---

22 Karuna appeared to me like a textbook case of the so-called 'Sita syndrome' (cf. Bhatt 2008).

Mohkamsing-den Boer and Zock 2004). On this occasion, we were cooking for the spirits of the dead. For the purpose of preparing the food women and men were separated; the kitchen became female territory; men were banned and would be chased away if they dared to even glance into it. The kitchen was also supposed to be pure, so menstruating women were banned as well. The cooking itself seemed complex, not just vegetarian food, but also *satvik* and specific vegetables had to be cooked. I remember that I had never seen so many different vegetables being prepared for one occasion. Also, the method of preparation was different from everyday cooking. What struck me most was the role of the grandmother in the family. That she was giving instructions in the kitchen seemed natural to me. However, I had not expected that it was she, who was called time and again into the room where the rituals were performed to give advice and instructions to the pandit who was executing the rituals. She spoke with a powerful assuredness, both in the kitchen to the women cooking and to the priest performing the ritual. A sweet old lady was transformed from shy and seemingly unobtrusive into an authority. No one questioned her knowledge. Clearly, for everyone present, she was a gatekeeper of Hindu rites. Her age and knowledge enabled her to speak authoritatively, no longer confined to the submissive role women are supposed to assume. As a gatekeeper she ensured that the ritual was to be performed correctly, being at the same time generous and precise in transmitting her knowledge to the younger generations, both for the food preparation and execution of the rites.

Do women get the same appreciation when cooking at home? Domestic cooking always involves ritual cooking as well. Early morning, after *pujá*, *prasád* is served, mostly a small sweet dish such as *halva* or *kheer*. Always cooked by the lady of the house, this dish is first offered to the deities and then offered to the family, a ritual practice that is applied to every meal. This is the main reason why Hindu women will never taste the food while cooking: it has to remain pure, untouched (*a-juthá*) otherwise it cannot be offered to the deities. Religiously, it is of utmost importance for a man to be married to a traditional woman, who is able to observe and perform the religious duties, many of which are connected with food and its preparation. How deeply this is imbedded in the mind of women, is shown by the following example:

I first met Mrs. Kumar by chance during a search for Indian herbs, a good opportunity to meet women and talk with them about food, ritual food, and *vratas*. Mrs. Kumar is a well-educated and religious woman, economically well off. She is a lively lady and very pleased to talk with me about her spirituality. She was around 55 when we first met. A few years before, she had divorced her husband, a diplomat: "My husband had several extramarital affairs. I had done everything to keep our marriage going and tried to be like Sita. However, at a certain point I could no longer bear his affairs and decided to divorce him." After the separation she retreated in her own house in Paramaribo and turned to a more spiritually oriented life. She recounts:

A few years ago, around the year 2000, I gave up meat and became a full-time vegetarian. I also began to study the holy scriptures such as the Ramayana and Mahabharata more regularly. I changed my life, my rhythm, everything. Early morning at three o'clock I wake up for my daily *pujá* and meditation. On Monday, Tuesday and Thursday I observe more specific food restrictions. (Mrs. Kumar)[23]

She elaborates how she dedicates Monday to Shiva, Tuesday to Ganesha and Thursday to Vishnu. The restrictions involve *satvik* food (prepared without onion and garlic). She wants to live her life as pure as possible. And while talking, she pulls me to her veranda where she had made a big poster with her own translation and interpretation of the *Gayatri mantra*.[24] It should be noted here that the recitation of this mantra is traditionally restricted to Brahmin males, therefore this act may be interpreted as a demonstration of her independence.

She had also changed her house into a shelter for abused Hindustani women. She felt that she should do something particularly for her own community; people should become aware of the richness of their own culture, and, in her own words "the superiority of Hinduism that can bring peace and balance to the country." Restoring balance was a recurring theme during our conversations.

When asked, she told me that her parents and grandparents did not observe any food restrictions, beside abstinence from beef; they also did not observe any vegetarian days. Mrs. Kumar states that she has returned to the roots of her Hindu heritage, showing her purity as a good and religious wife through food and the kitchen, the place where women are appreciated and honored and as such

---

23 Apart from the special *vratas* and *upvaas*, many Hindus also fast on a particular day in a week. Each day of a week is dedicated to a particular god. Though the designated days may vary from region to region and community to community (both in India and Suriname), the general dedication of the days is Sunday to Surya (sun god); Monday to Shiva; Tuesday to Ganesha, Durga, Kali, and Hanuman; Wednesday to Saraswati and Krishna; Thursday to Vishnu and his incarnations, and, for some regions, Lakshmi; Friday is to Mother Goddess—Mahalakshmi, Santoshi Ma, Annapuraneshwari, and Durga; and Saturday to alleviating the bad influence of Shani.

24 The *Gayatri Mantra* is a highly revered mantra from the *Rigveda* (3.62.10), although reserved for Brahmin males, through modern Hindu reform movements the practice spread to women and all castes.

showing her ex-husband how he has forsaken a good traditional Hindu woman. Although her story and life show many contradictions, she still tries her utmost to be like Sita, while on the other hand trying to protect women suffering the betrayal of the ideal of the perfect wife.

Years before I moved to Suriname, I met an elderly Hindustani woman in the Netherlands, known as Aunty Rose; it was only later in Suriname that I also met her twin sister. After independence they had lived for some years in the Netherlands, but returned when they retired. One of them is a widow, the other divorced after a marriage full of abuse. They built their houses next to one another. Both sisters are Hindus and observe vegetarianism on Monday and Tuesday, on which days they do not use onion, garlic, and salt. They only eat plain rice, vegetables, and fruit. Both rise in the morning around 6 o'clock to do their *pujá*, each under the *jhandi* in their own front yard. When asked why they keep their vegetarian days, and why on these particular days, they replied, "We don't know, but we do so in honor for Vishnu and Shiva. It's our tradition." Also to the question why they abstain from onion and garlic these days, I received a similar reply, "We don't know, it is our tradition" and "On those days it just doesn't taste right." They started to observe these *vratas* at different moments in their lives. After further questioning, the reason behind their ritual observances became clear. Aunty Rose recalls:

About 30 years ago, my son was 15 years old and he became very ill. The doctors were of no help, they couldn't give medicines, they just didn't know. So I went to the pandit. He told me to start with a *vrata* on Monday and Tuesday. Those days I should abstain from eating meat, fish, eggs, salt, onion and garlic. Then, Moona, my son, recovered soon. Until today I continue this *vrata*. It is good for the health and wellbeing of your family. Some years later my sister joined me in the *vrata*. This is what happens when you're twins. (Rose)

She took a pause and then continued, "Our parents and grandparents did not know these things. Only on special occasions such as weddings and burials they abstained from meat and fish."[25] Once a year, they have a *Durga pujá* and renew the *jandhis* in the front yard. They observe all the holidays with their *vratas* and *pujas*. On special occasions they visit a nearby *Sanátana Dharma* temple.

Chandra is a civil servant, working for the Department of Cultural Studies in Paramaribo. She is a deeply religious woman. When asked, she told me that she follows the *Sanátana Dharma*. In her second marriage by then, she had divorced her first husband after many years of domestic abuse and violence. Now, Chan-

---

25 It took until the 1960s before the Hindus were allowed to cremate their dead.

dra lives with her in-laws, but complains almost constantly about the ill treatment she gets from her mother-in-law. Even after giving birth to a healthy baby girl, this did not change:

You know, I thought that I was infertile so I went to the *pandit*. He recommended observing fasts and special daily *pujas*. And here, look at my daughter! She was born because of my efforts. You understand that I have to keep to my *vratas* for the wellbeing of my child! (Chandra)

Chandra enjoys telling this story again and again, often followed by one of her most favorite stories about her daughter, "She greets the deities, you know, already from the beginning. Now one and a half years old, she always greets the *devtas* (gods) with folded hands and this without anybody showing her before how to do this *namaskar*." Chandra follows the same pattern as others: on Monday, Tuesday, and Thursday, she only takes vegetarian meals without onion and garlic, mostly fruit, sweets, plain rice, and vegetables. It seems that she adjusts her fasts increasingly to taking only sweets and fruits on these days. She tells me that she is in the process of becoming vegetarian. She keeps these days for the blessings of respectively Shiva, Durga, and Krishna.

Once a year she performs a *Durga pujá* at home, the time when new *jhandis* are placed in the front yard. Lately, she has started to notice 'appearances' of Ganesha on the walls of her garden. She keeps all the different Hindu holy days along with their respective *pujas* and *vratas* and regularly goes to a nearby *mandir* (temple). Chandra also tells me that her parents and grandparents were not used to this kind of vegetarianism; they only followed the vegetarian diet on ritual occasions such as *Maha Sivaratri*, *Navratas*, and *Durga pujá*. Her in-laws, and their ancestors, too, followed this pattern.

CONCLUSION

In migration situations, the way to prepare food, the ingredients, the smell and taste remind people of their homeland, or of the sentiments of 'better days' from the past. Ritual food, too, may serve this function. It provides a sense of belonging, the adherence to one's own ethnic and religious group, where the rules of ritual food are observed strictly. Daily food, and ritual food in particular, are culturally determined by many different and often unwritten rules. Who are the ones to safeguard these rules and pass them on?

For most Hindu women the preparation and consumption of food, both ritual and non-ritual, is a superficial indicator of their submissive role in society: they adjust their religious and cultural traditions to their husband's and in-laws'. For either big or small rituals, only women prepare the ritual food, which means time-consuming cooking for big gatherings of people. Women are usually busy preparing food when the rite or service has already started; hence they are only partly involved in the rite. In the *Sanātana Dharma*, the priests are male and there is a strict division between women and men in religious and social duties in public. This makes their role one of service: serving the gods and serving men.

I have posed the question whether women are true bearers of Hindu culture in a society where they are bound to follow the religion and traditions of their husband and in-laws. Although a complete answer requires further research, I can tentatively conclude that a lot of women not only take the role as gatekeepers of Hindu identity and ritual very seriously, but their ritual role exceeds the limits of the realms prescribed by the rules of gender segregation.[26] This became very clear when a ritual 'cooking for the gods' was transformed into an instructional session for the pandit, conducted by a very experienced grandmother. Obviously the priest was supposed to have complete knowledge, but reality showed that in this complicated case of the death of a very young woman, the experience of women was needed. Could this role be fulfilled by a man as well? At this stage of research, my answer is 'no.' Only women are allowed in the kitchen to cook ritual food for the gods, hence they only know what, how, and when food is to be prepared. By practice they learn the sequence of the food to be offered and through the years they learn the rationale behind it as well. In this case, the ritual could not have been completed without a woman's knowledge.

Throughout my research and daily life experience in Suriname (and among the Hindustani community in the Netherlands), it is mostly women that take up *vratas* for different reasons and purposes. In Suriname, as in India, women may generally be associated with ritual food and *vratas*. Their daily life practice inspires other women to follow suit. It is an ongoing tradition that is changing with the dynamics of modern life. In the current situation, religious women take responsibility in passing on the living, dynamic tradition of their Hindu faith, at least when it comes to the complex role of food in their social and ritual life.

---

26 Hindus in Suriname identify themselves through (ritual) food, in many ways, which are, however, too numerous to expand on within the limits of this article.

Bibliography

Algemeen Bureau voor Statistiek (Office for Statistics) 2005. *ABS report Census 2004*. Paramaribo: Algemeen Bureau voor Statistiek in Suriname.

Appadurai, Arjun 1988. "Cookbooks and Cultural Change. The Indian Case." *Comparative Studies in Society and History* 30: 3-24.

Babb, Lawrence A. 1970. "The Food for the Gods in Chhattisgarh. Some Structural Features of Hindu Ritual." *Southwestern Journal of Anthropology* 26: 287-304.

Beit-Hallahmi, Benjamin 1989. *Prolegomena to the Psychological Study of Religion*. London / Toronto: Associated University Press.

Bell, Catherine 1992. *Ritual Theory, Ritual Practice*. New York: Oxford University Press.

Bhatt, Archana Pathak 2008. "The Sita Syndrome. Examining the Communicative Aspects of Domestic Violence from a South Asian Perspective." *Journal of International Women's Studies* 9.3: 155-173.

van der Burg, Corstiaan, Theo Damsteegt, and Krishna Autar, eds. 1990. *Hindostanen in Nederland*. Leuven / Apeldoorn: Garant.

van der Burg, Corstiaan and Peter van der Veer 1986. "Pandits, Power and Profit. Religious Organization and the Construction of Identity among Surinamese Hindus." *Ethnic and Racial Studies* 9.4: 514-528.

Douglas, Mary 1972. "Deciphering a Meal." *Daedalus* 101: 61-81.

—. 1981, "Food and Culture. Meaning the Intricacy of Rule Systems." *Social Science Information* 20: 1-35.

—. 2002 [1966]. *Purity and Danger. An Analysis of Concept of Pollution and Taboo*. London / New York: Routledge.

Esterik, Penny van 1998. "Feeding their Faith. Recipe Knowledge Among Buddhist Women." *Food and Gender. Identity and Power*. Eds. Carole M. Counihan and Steven L. Kaplan. Amsterdam: Harwood Academic Publishers, 45-81.

Firth, Raymond 1973. *Symbols. Public and Private*. London: Allen and Unwin.

Herman, Phyllis K. 1998. *Sita in the Kitchen. The Pativrata and Ramarajya*. Paper Presented at the 1998 Sita Symposium, Colombia University.

Khan, Aisha 1994. "*Juthaa* in Trinidad. Food, Pollution, and Hierarchy in a Caribbean Diaspora Community." *American Ethnologist* 21.2: 245-269.

Khan, Munshi Rahman 2003. *Autobiography of an Indian Indentured Labourer. Munshi Rahman Khan (1874-1972)*. Delhi: Shipra Publications.

Khare, Ravindra S., ed. 1992. *Eternal Food. Gastronomic Ideas and Experiences of Hindus and Buddhists*. New York: State University of New York Press.

de Klerk, C. J. M. 1998 [1951]. *Cultus en Ritueel van het Orthodoxe Hindoeïsme in Suriname*. Amsterdam: De Klerk.
Mackenzie-Pearson, Anne 1996. *Because It Gives Me Peace of Mind*. New York: New York State University Press.
Majumder, Mousumi 2010. *Kahe Gaile Bides, Why Did You Go Overseas? On Bhojpuri Migration Since the 1870s and Contemporary Culture in Uttar Pradesh and Bihar, Suriname and the Netherlands*. Allahabad: G.B. Pant Social Science Institute.
Manuel, Peter 2000. "The Construction of a Diasporic Tradition. Indo-Caribbean 'Local Classical Music'." *Ethnomusicology* 44.1: 97-119.
Marriott, McKim 2007 [1968]. "Caste Ranking and Food Transactions. A Matrix Analysis." 133-172. *Structure and Change in Indian Society*. Eds. Milton Singer and Bernard S. Cohn. Chicago: Aldine Transaction.
Mohkamsing-den Boer, Elizabeth and Hetty Zock 2004. "Dreams of Passage. An Object-Relational Perspective on a Case of Hindu Death Ritual." *Religion* 34: 1-14.
Rajendra, Prasad 2004. *Tears in Paradise. A Personal and Historical Journey, 1879-2004*. Auckland: Glade Publishers.
Ramsoedh, Hans and Lucie Bloemberg 1995. *The Institutionalization of Hinduism in Suriname and Guyana*. Paramaribo: Surinaamse Verkenningen.
van der Veer, Peter 1984. "Hoe Bestendig is 'De eeuwige religie?' Enkele Vragen rond de Organisatie van het Surinaams Hindoeïsme." *Bonoeman, Rasta's en Andere Surinamers. Onderzoek naar Etnische Groepen in Nederland* 11: 1-124.
van der Veer, Peter and Steven Vertovec 1991. "Brahmanism Abroad. On Caribbean Hinduism as an Ethnic Religion." *Ethnology* 30.2: 149-166.
Vertovec, Steven 1991. "East Indians and Anthropologists. A Critical Review." *Social and Economic Studies* 40.1: 133-169.
Vertovec, Steven 1992. *Hindu Trinidad. Religion, Ethnicity and Socio-Economic Change*. London: Macmillan Caribbean.

"De fuud dem produus me naa go iit it!"
Rastafarian 'Culinary Identity'[1]

Annika McPherson

Tracing Rastafari Dietary Practices

In Yasus Afari's version of the Rastafarian food pyramid—which can vary according to different groups or individual interpretation—a daily basis of cereal grains, root vegetables, and tubers, as well as derived products is supplemented by fruits, legumes, and vegetables in a variety of forms including juices, as well as water, punches, herbal and roots-based drinks, plus oil. Milk products and certain fish are to be consumed moderately or not at all, while the dietary intake is to be complemented by "consistent meditation, physical work, and exercise in clean fresh air" (Afari 2007: 155).

Early studies of Rastafari, commonly dated to have emerged in the 1930s in West Kingston, Jamaica, do not pay much attention to such dietary practices, which seem to have been gradually formulated and continue to be subject to considerable variation. The U.S. American anthropologist and sociologist George Eaton Simpson is generally referenced as the earliest academic researcher on the movement based on his five fieldwork trips to Jamaica between 1946 and 1971, although his main interest had been the syncretistic religious cult of Revival Zion (cf. Simpson 1998: 218). In Simpson's recollection (unlike in Sheila Kitzinger's mid- and late-1960s studies), ganja "was not smoked during Rastafari meetings, and beards and dreadlocks were a less prominent feature of the move-

---

[1] The title quote is derived from Anthony B's track "Where Is The Black Man Rights" from the album *Rise Up* (2009). I thank Michael Westphal for the suggested transcription according to Cassidy and LePage (2002, 1976). The term "culinary identity" is borrowed from Afari (2007: 144).

ment than they became later" (Simpson 1985: 287). The 1958 report *The Rastafarian Movement in Kingston, Jamaica* (reprinted in Augier and Salter 2010) in its description of "The Creed of a Ras Tafari Man [sic]" merely mentions that

> [a]lcohol is forbidden, together [w]ith gambling. Wine may be drunk in small quantities. It is forbidden to cooperate with any Government except that of Ethiopia. Current Jamaican beliefs in obeah, magic and witchcraft are nonsense – these have no empirical validity. Revivalism, whether Pocomania or Zion, is deliberate propagation of Babylonian error through which the mental slavery of the black man is maintained. Pork is forbidden (Leviticus II). The 'herb' (ganja) is a gift of God, who enjoined us to smoke it in Genesis 8, Psalm 18 and Rev. 22. (Augier and Salter 2010: 24)

The observed dietary rules are interspersed with other summarized "doctrines and orientations," and only the "taboo on pork (Deuteronomy 16)" is singled out as "common to all" Rastafari (25). Taking into consideration the few studies that are available on the formative years from 1930 to 1950, Simpson's initial comparative religious approach and socio-political contextualization of the movement probably account for the absence of detailed references to dietary practices in the early phase.[2] Based on oral history sources, John Homiak in the mid-1990s reassessed the emergence of Ital[3] food and rules of the Livity as well as the spread of dreadlocks within the Rastafari movement as a result of the intervention of the ascetic Higes Knots of East Kingston rather than the purging of the traces of Revivalism by the House of Youth Black Faith of West Kingston, as Barry Chevannes and others have argued, or as a distinction of Leonard P.

---

2   I here follow Maureen Rowe's distinction of three phases of the movement into "the formative years (1930-1950), the early years (1951-1971) and the later years (1972 to the present)" (Rowe 1998: 74). For a study of the formative phase of the movement in the wider context of Ethiopianism, see Hill (2001). A notable exception to the general neglect of detailed considerations of dietary practices in Rastafari is Mandy G. Dickerson's Master's Thesis *I-tal Foodways. Nourishing Rastafarian Bodies* (Louisiana State University, 2004).

3   Variant spellings such as Ital, I-tal, and ital, as well as the discrepant (non-)capitalization of Livity and similar terms in the literature on Rastafari are indicative of contentious transcriptions of I-yaric or Dread Talk (cf. Pollard 2000) versioning based on spoken interaction and thus have been maintained as used in the respective sources. While Ital is commonly regarded as an I-talk version of 'vital,' other synonyms in the examples below similarly point to the variety of choices in active language transformation processes that are aimed at countering attempts at standardization.

Howell's guardsmen at his Pinnacle commune (cf. Malloch 1985 in Edmonds 2003: 59). The Higes Knots—who walked barefoot along the streets, wore crocus bags (knots) and carried a staff or rod as a marker of their rejection of Babylon—are thus now frequently credited to have introduced the foodways and lifestyle associated with the Ital (cf. Chevannes 1994: 169; Homiak 1995: 151-6). Both versions, however, point to gradual transitions within the early movement through the formulation and negotiation of distinct Rastafarian practices, which allowed for a differentiation, for example, from initial similarities to Revivalist practices (cf. Chevannes 1994: 169; 1995).

With the increasingly global spread of Rastafari, identity formation became a more important research topic and parts of the discussion shifted from sociological to cultural questions. In Dennis Forsythe's cultural analysis, "Rastafarianism [sic] is the first mass movement among West Indians preoccupied with the task of looking into themselves and asking the fundamental question, Who Am I? or What Am I?" in "a desperate call for an alternative counterculture more suitable to the needs of black people in these times" (Forsythe 1980: 62). Forsythe points out that "people are asking and are still waiting for a definition of Rasta" and categorizes Rastafari as "a Black Power movement that is struggling to assert itself" (63-4). The extent to which dietary practices form part of this process of self-assertion is outlined in the following in order to demonstrate that a persisting problem is not so much *how* precisely to define Rastafari, but rather the very attempt at categorization itself.

Even when they do not receive much attention, following the traces that dietary practices have left in many studies on Rastafari allows for an elaboration of their significance within the wider cultural context.[4] As mainly the linguistic practices of "I and I talk" (Afari 2007: 114) are emphasized when illustrating Rastafari philosophy or notions of subjectivity, it is important to note that these are also applied to food, e.g. when "inanimate objects such as fruits are also reaffirmed with the *I* sound," e.g. in the observation that "*Banana* includes a negative sound *ban* and is changed to *Iana, Jahana,* or *freebana*" based on the belief "that a word can kill or cure and that every word carries a vibration" (Simpson 1985: 288–9). The increasing emphasis within the movement on the concept of nature as observed by Simpson points to the "ideal [...] of a nonindustrial society, one in which only natural, unprocessed foods with no additives are eaten, hair and beards are uncut, ganja as the 'holy herb' is consumed in various ways, and life is unhurried" (290). Aside from denouncing the eating of pork, by the mid-

---

4   While I am aware of a number of publications dealing with Ital food and lifestyle in nutritional anthropology and Caribbean food studies, I here examine their relevance or neglect only in more general studies on Rastafari.

1970s "Rastafarians had spread the word about *Ital* (pure) food, condemning the preservatives used in food processing and urging self-sufficiency," which resonates with an assessment of Rastafari as an "individual and collective movement" whose aim is "to regain the sense of personal worth and dignity which society has denied" (ibid., emphasis in original). Dietary aspects thus need to be placed alongside other forms of cultural expression such as music, poetry, and visual arts. To Forsythe, Ital food and the general

> stress on 'physical body culture,' their herbal culture with the practice of inhaling herbal smoke through the water of the chillum or chalice pipe, their taboo on pork, all attest to the Brethren's Universal awareness and strivings for the maximum of Ever-Living Life and a soulful existence. (Forsythe 1980: 79)

This is to be recovered from the legacy of enslavement. Rastafari, then, is a culture in the sense of "an adaptive mechanism" across the entire realm of social significance, i.e. an "all encompassing [...] prism for those people wanting to know themselves individually and collectively" (65). Although Forsythe does not specify dietary practices in his list of characteristics, they form an intrinsic part of what he calls the "search for energy, for power, for 'Ever-Living-Life'" (70), which also extends to other practices relating to the body:

> As the Rastaman [sic] experiments with herbs, using the prism of his own being and senses as the major judge in his experimental movements forward, he learns to define the Good for the 'I' and thereby comes to know that 'I.' He works this new consciousness into his physical structure. New dimensions and original vibrations of his being become stimulated back into action and natural circulation is restored. It provides a real foundation for the heightening of consciousness to the heights of understanding some of the intricacies of the mind in interaction with the body. (80)[5]

Seen through this "prism" of *being* Rastafari, consciousness and physical structure cannot be separated. Given such a notion of the unity of mind and body, the

---

5   In his masculine-encoded notion of Rastafari, Forsythe connects the "sub-conscious layer of primeval energy and creativity which links the 'I' to Africa and to the Universe," and which also finds expression in Rastafarian art, explicitly to the "basic struggle aimed at regaining that sense of Manhood and dignity which the society has historically robbed, distorted or denied" (Forsythe 1980: 80). His 1983 study *Rastafari. For the Healing of the Nation* furthermore points to the frequent intersection of academic studies and more personal quests for meaning creation concerning Rastafarian ways of being.

neglect of dietary practices in many general studies of Rastafari seems to again be an effect of the lens of the sociology and anthropology of religion through which the movement has been and continues to be studied.

Based on mid-1960s fieldwork, Leonard Barrett discusses Rastafari food in the anthropological tradition of Claude Lévi-Strauss and others as an "index in assessing social groups" (Barrett 1997: 140), according to which dietary practices are seen to symbolize social and religious ideas. Quoting his interlocutors— including the well-known elder Sam Brown's Rastafarian code: "We are vegetarians, making scant use of certain animal flesh yet outlawing the use of swine's flesh in any form, shell fishes [sic], scaleless fishes, snails, etc."(ibid.)—in Barrett's account even pork could be consumed when necessity dictated:[6]

> The diet of the Rastafarians is very rigid; for example, meat as a whole is considered injurious to the body. When it comes to meats they do eat, pork is not one of them. They refer to pork as "that thing." The author was told, however, that when a Rastafarian is hungry and can find nothing but the gift of a piece of pork, he will change the name to "Arnold, and then partake of it." Here we can observe a typical Jamaican folk rationality, the typical "trickster" mentality. The significance of this is the old Rastafarian theology which states: "There is nothing neither good or bad, but thinking makes it so." Ras "H" explained that one of the reasons for rejecting meat is that it leaves worms in the human body, and that when these worms defecate in the stomach it gives one a sickly feeling. (ibid.)

In the groups of Barrett's study small-sized scaled fish and especially 'sprat' are considered one of the "prime staples" (141) while

> larger fish are predators and represent the establishment—Babylon—where men eat men. But the food of the greatest worth to the cultists [sic] is vegetables of almost every kind. Like ganja, the earth brings forth all good things. Food is cooked with no salt, no processed shortening, and few condiments except in its I-tal form. If they need oil, they will make use of the dried coconut in which the richest oil is found. The word "I-tal" is another Rastafarian word that is fast becoming part of Jamaican speech. It means the essence of things, things that are in their natural states. So, the Rastafarian food is now known as I-tal food. There may be great commercial possibility for this word in a short while. Many of

---

6 Barrett authored several studies on Rastafari between 1968 and 1988, of which *The Rastafarians* (1997 [1988]) has since been republished and remains in circulation as a 'classic' on the movement. Ras Sam Brown called for Rastafarian participation in politics and was the first Rastafari to run a political campaign in the Jamaican election of 1961. Barrett, who interviewed him in the mid-1960s, also quotes his "Twenty-One Points" campaign (cf. Barrett 1997: 148-50).

the Jamaican foods are now renamed; for example, one of the vegetables known all over the island as Callalu [sic] is now called *Illalu* to sound like I-tal. As we have already indicated, the Rastafarians will not drink liquor of any kind, nor milk or coffee, but they will drink herbal tea and anything made from natural herbs and roots. They will not use patent medicines but will use any herbal concoctions used in the folk tradition. (ibid.)[7]

These observations both establish a link between Rastafari practices and more general 'folk traditions' and exemplify the linguistic and dietary influence of Rastafari on the wider society through Ital food. The indicated "commercial possibility" by now has materialized at least in so far as Barrett's prediction that "creative personalities will emerge such as restaurateurs specializing in Ital foods similar to the kosher foods of other religions" (259) by now have spread not only across the Caribbean but can also be found in all sizeable global Rastafari communities as well as in other markets for vegetarian and vegan food and products. Barrett places this economic potential within the group of "functional Rastas," i.e. those not organized into a "church" or other groups with a predominantly religious focus (cf. 257-8), which also includes sculptors, painters, poets, musicians, and artists, and is seen as indicative of the movement's wider contribution to Jamaican society. Yet, the economic gains derived from these commercial activities rarely flow back into the community, a tendency which is furthered by the problem of an increasing commodification of Ital in the cultural marketplace (cf. Jaffke 2010). Barrett furthermore points out that

[t]he Rastafarians are also careful about the preparation of their food, and in some cases exhibit a kosher precaution. Hence they are not in the habit of eating food of unknown sources. They have strict rules even among their women folk [sic]. Their wives may not cook for them during their menstrual periods as this is forbidden in their scriptures. The Rastafarians also prefer to eat foods from their own plantations [sic]. For this reason, one of the most coveted items among the cultists is land on which they can live and cultivate their own foods. A Montego Bay 'dread' put it this way: 'We need lands on which we can pitch the tents of Jacob.' (Barrett 1997: 142)

Here the comparative religious framework within which Ital food is mainly understood in Barrett's study comes to the fore again, as does the tendency to generalize in spite of the many different group and individual variations of dietary and other rules. What becomes clear, however, is that dietary practices in general

---

7   Barrett also describes a "test" by one of his interviewees about whether he would consume the bitter Cirassee tea and the Ital food placed in front of him as testing his "sincerity" and acceptance of Rastafarian hospitality (Barrett 1997: 141-2).

constitute a bridge between more 'religious' and 'functional' Rastafari (cf. 257), and from both into the wider society.

While Barrett mentions that salt is not used in the preparation of food, he does not explain this habit or its symbolic function. In *Rastafari. Roots and Ideology*, Barry Chevannes links the avoidance of salt to similar practices and traditions across the Caribbean, including "a belief from the slave period 'that slaves who had not eaten salt were able to fly back to Guinea'" (Warner-Lewis 1990: 15, cited in Chevannes 1994: 35). These traditions link "salt with exile and the avoidance of salt with repatriation" (Chevannes 1994: 35), and more generally associate salt "with the loss of spiritual force" (Schuler 1980: 96, cited in Chevannes 1994: 35).[8] According to Chevannes, "Rastafari salt avoidance, under the Ital rubric, is probably linked to ideas of spiritual force and repatriation prevailing from the time the earliest Africans were forced across the middle passage into bondage" (Chevannes 1994: 35), although a similar link between salt and the spirit world exists in many European cultures as well. If the consumption of salt was linked to the impossibility to return to Africa, the diet of salted fish and pork that was imported for the enslaved and the post-emancipation workforces (cf. 34) constitutes a palpable form of oppression. While Chevannes reads the later adoption of salt fish and ackee as a national dish as "indicative of the extent to which most Jamaicans have become reconciled to adopting the island as their land" (35), Rastafarian salt avoidance can in contrast be seen as an act of resistance to this oppressive legacy.

Even though, with regards to the historicization of Jamaican culture at large, Mervyn Alleyne has argued that the application of resistance theory can be problematic, Rastafari dietary and other practices are commonly interpreted as acts of cultural resistance (cf. Alleyne 1988: 20).[9] Horace Campbell, in *Rasta and Re-*

---

8   By reference to Monica Schuler's social history of the indentured BaKongo who came to Jamaica after emancipation, Chevannes points out that "according to BaKongo cosmology a barrier of water called *kalunga* separates the living from the dead, and the BaKongo identified *kalunga* with the Atlantic ocean after their contact with the European slave traders. America, therefore, was to them the land of the dead. Once taken there, there was no way that any but the exceptional could return except through salt-free diet." Hence, in Schuler's words, "in Jamaica to resist eating salt may have been a metaphor for resistance to foreign ways [...]. Thus, only those who were faithful to African ways were worthy to return to Africa" (Schuler 1980: 96, cited in Chevannes 1994: 34-5), which resonates with Rastafari aims of repatriation.

9   Resistance theory according to Alleyne is inadequate for conceptualizing Jamaican culture because "[f]irst, it either ignores or fails to deal satisfactorily with the apparent contradiction between the view of slavery as a brutal, oppressive, and degrading insti-

sistance, comments on the rise of "the culture of resistance, called reggae" and the concomitant "shift in emphasis of the movement from the preoccupation with Haile Selassie and Ethiopia to the battles for liberation in Southern Africa" (Campbell 2007: 6):

> The Rastafari song—reggae—was the highest form of self-expression, an expression which was simultaneously an act of social commentary and a manifestation of deep racial memory. This memory had been kept alive by the attempt of the Rasta to build upon the foundations of the Jamaican language with their own contribution, called Rasta talk. The question of cultural resistance could not be examined simply within the context of music, since the food policy—called ital food—the language, and efforts at communal practices were as much a part of the rasta culture as the songs of mobilisation which said "Get Up, Stand Up, Stand Up For Your Rights." (ibid.)[10]

While some Rastafari might object to the suggested shift in emphasis or the role attributed to Reggae in general, both the religious and the cultural interpretive lenses outlined so far place dietary practices alongside other practices, which together inform the culture, or rather the Livity, of Rastafari.

---

tution and the view that slaves were able to develop their own positive cultures. Second, it presents the development of this culture in too many ways as a reaction to Whites and to slavery. [...] Third, it presents slave culture as a development of the period of slavery" (Alleyne 1988: 20). Rather than linking it to previous cultural influences, a generalized emphasis on resistance can thus create a "cultural void" that keeps the culture of enslaved Africans within the orbit of slavery and oppression (cf. ibid.). For a more general notion of acts of resistance, cf., e.g., Sharp (2000). Cultural resistance arguably functions as political resistance, even though it is frequently seen as curtailed by utopian elements and visions of ideal society (cf. Duncombe 2002).

10 One recent example for invocations of Itality in Reggae can be found in Anthony B's "Where Is The Black Man Rights" (2009). The song places Ital dietary practices in the context of the Black nation, the legacy of enslavement, the Black Holocaust, and continuous exploitation, exposing the hypocrisy of exclusionary Western notions of and appeals to 'humanity.' Echoing Garveyite philosophy through its word, sound, and power practices and evoking positivity, the track furthermore points out the literal as well as the spiritual effects of the global food crisis.

Itality and Rastafari Livity as Identity Work

Like Ital, Livity has various descriptions ranging from "a code of relationships with God, nature, and society" (Chevannes 1994: 169) to a consciousness or "living according to the strict principles of Rastafari" (Edmonds 2003: 60), i.e. a life that is "essentially a re-definition of culture along moral perspectives" (Afari 2007: 72). The "livet" or diet of Rastafari in turn is "a cultural and social indicator that clearly represents and reflects the RASTAFARIAN world view and natural way of life as seen through the eyes of food and nutrition" (155, emphasis in original). The connection of these aspects becomes clear in Andwele's formulation:

Ital represents the organically undefiled preparation of food, which is also a counter to the Western way of life that was introduced to the African in the New World. Through the eating of Ital, Rastas were countering the Western way of preparing and eating food. In doing so, the statement was being made that the Western eating habits were unhealthy, unhygienic, anti-Creation and anti-God.
Ital made Rastas see the oneness between a natural way of living and a natural way of eating and their unity with Jah (God). It stressed that this dead food they were socialized and culturally moulded to eat was responsible for the domination and for the many sicknesses of the body and the mind that Black people were experiencing. The word that was recreated for this food was 'deaders,' which led to what the word means and that is 'death.' But this death for the Rastafari was not just physical. It was also spiritual. (Andwele 2000: 18)

Hence, organic and natural dietary practices serve to counteract "Babylon's plan to destroy the minds of black people" and Ital living includes spiritual components such as the practice of "herbal healing," which connects the use of ganja to the wider belief "that the entire universe is organically related and that the key to health, both physical and social, is to live in accordance with organic principles, as opposed to the artificiality that characterizes modern technological society" (Edmonds 2003: 60).[11] Food as "the staff of life" is inextricably entwined with the notion of healing and medicine in the dictum "let your food be your medicine and your medicine be your food" (Afari 2007: 142). Herbal healing thus "plays a

---

11 Such "herbal healing" also permeates the cinematic representation of Rastafari, e.g. in Ted Bafaloukos' *Rockers* (1978), in which the protagonist Horsemouth retreats to the 'original' Rasta in the mountains for healing and guidance, or in Dickie Jobson's film *Countryman* (1982), where Countryman's wisdom and guidance are suffused with magical powers that are inextricably linked to his 'naturalness.'

major role in the de-alienation and decolonization of the African mind" (Edmonds 2003: 61), while the conjunction of the bodily, stylistic, linguistic, as well as dietary practices of Rastafari Livity "are encoded with symbolic significance, the essence of which is a rejection of the Babylonian character of Jamaican society and a commitment to the struggle for selfhood and dignity through the development of an African-centered cultural identity" (73). Although he questions "intellectual Rasta" Leahcim Semaj's theorization of a development of Rastafari from religion to a popular (in the sense of indigenous) culture to a national (i.e. collective social) culture aiming at universal (humanistic) culture (cf. 137-8), Edmonds firmly places Rastafari as "culture bearers," which again emphasizes cultural over socio-religious factors and also points to the global spread of the movement.[12]

In the global context, Florian Kroll expands the discussion of Ital Livity to a group of "Bushdoctors [sic]" (Kroll 2006: 234) of the South African Cape region. They describe their "gradual awakening to Rastafari through the association with symbols and rituals, often accelerated by reasonings with elder Rastas" (ibid.) as well as a general "anti-materialist culture [which] embodies the concept of the original rootsman identity" relating to "the natural or God-given order of things" (ibid.):

Ital livity demands an everyday commitment to the pure, natural, vital and organic. A Bushdoctor practising a 'strictly ital' lifestyle expresses his relationship to Jah and His Creation in the smallest details of everyday life. In its relationship to material culture, it means that things should be used in their original, natural, and organic state. This is particularly manifested in the dietary code observed by Bushdoctors which again is symbolic purification. Accordingly, the Bushdoctors eat vegetarian and largely unprocessed food. (ibid.)

This "ital ethos" also finds expression in dreadlocks and other bodily practices, attire, naming, language, and rituals, so that "on a symbolic level, their focus on herbalism is not only an expression of ital livity as formulated by Jamaican Rastafari, but it is also a way of reconnecting with their regionally unique Khoisan heritage and a distant, idealized precolonial past" (ibid.). Here, localized variations of Ital Livity emerge. Whereas Barrett's study lacks a comparative vocabulary other than the religiously connoted "kosher," the "ital ethos" places Itality within the wider spectrum of cultural practices adopted from Jamaican Rastafari, while localizing it within the Khoisan context. What is shared, howev-

---

12 For a discussion of the global spread of Rastafari, cf. Savishinsky 1994 and Boxill 2008.

er, is the "struggle for *I-nity*—transcendence of the Babylon-Zion duality in each person to uncover the original divine nature of humanity" (235), which emphasizes the psychological aspect of consciousness formation through Ital Livity's acts of identity work across the entire spectrum of cultural signification: The divine potential in "perception, consciousness, words, habits and deeds" in McFarlane's phrasing relates to the "ability to command the self" and the creation of "a new identity and meaning" (McFarlane, cited in Kroll 2006: 235). As opposed to the duality of selfhood as flesh and spirit, the practices of Ital Livity aim at a "return to an original state of Oneness with Jah and His Creation" (Kroll 2006: 235).

In the context of Ital Livity, it is important to note articulations of some Rastafari women's 'disenchantment' with Livity in the sense of a strict Rastafarian lifestyle, as well as their rejection or challenge of Ital practices, for example those relating to sexuality, as Imani M. Tafari-Ama has pointed out:

On the one hand, the livity of Rastafari is designed to ensure a healthier way of living because of the emphasis placed on things natural, or "ital." On the other hand, encouragement of natural practices in spheres such as that of sexuality raises challenges: procreation may not be desired every time one is fertile, and as one informant, Nefertiti, suggested, the protection from risks—for example, venereal diseases—is critically important to woman. Sistren also pose the question of whether the Judaic principles from which much of Rastafari's patriarchal ideology derives are currently proving inappropriate for the self-definition and independence of females. (Tafari-Ama 1998: 91)

Maureen Rowe's theorization of a "gray area" in Jamaican cultural space informed by "a European ideal and theory and a retained African behavior" (cf. Rowe 1998: 73-4), however, emphasizes that notions of both the male role and of patriarchy cannot simply be transferred into this space from without but need to be examined from within and have to be contextualized with great care.[13] Keeping in mind this intervention regarding the potential tension surrounding notions of Itality within the context of the Livity and the concomitant question of how to describe or distinguish Rastafari patriarchy within the wider social context, it has become clear that the significance of dietary Itality exceeds bodily sustenance and includes spiritual and mental codes:

---

13 Rowe provides a general assessment of the role of Rastafari women, while Tafari-Ama (1998) explores the "rebel woman tradition" and other gender aspects in the movement, and Collins (2000) provides a global comparative perspective on Rastafari women. Yawney ("Moving with the Dawtas of Rastafari," 1994) in turn has argued for an intersectional approach to understanding gender relations among Rastafari.

Man [sic] is spiritual, mental and physical. Therefore, the spiritual vibrations that we absorb, feed our spirit-soul, while the intangible / mental substance and intellectual knowledge that we ingest, feed our minds, and the physical substances that we eat, feed our physical structure. The food we eat, therefore, can be seen as the fuel that we use to operate the human vehicle, which is called the body (goody). This human goody houses the mental and spiritual faculties that together constitute the living man. It is therefore logical to conclude that we can consciously cultivate the beings whom we are and (will) become. (Afari 2007: 142)

Since H.I.M. Haile Selassie is also referred to as a "living man" in Rastafari, this notion of embodiment of godliness, or the inseparability of divinity and humanity, resounds with the "original man" concept of Rastafari, whose "purpose is to restore and sustain the Ancient original order of life and creation" through Livity in the sense of the above-mentioned "re-definition of culture along moral perspectives" (71-72). The harmonization of the secular and the spiritual is invoked in the dietary practices of "vege-fruitarian livet / diet which is in natural harmony with the ecological balance and the overall (w)holistic view of life and creation" (143) as well as the notion of the human body as a "temple" (72, 81). Food, dietary practices, and environmental as well as spiritual consciousness thus form an entity:

[T]he "food revolution" of The RASTAFARIANS speaks to the revolution of the mind and the cultural and social engineering and re-engineering that is an integral part of the Livity of Rastafari. Therefore, the state of mind of the people can be calibrated and regulated by the culinary identity and taste, so as to harmonize with their heritage, cultural focus, collective aspirations and national identity. (157, emphasis in original)

As in this logic "mankind can cultivate his [sic] physical, mental and spiritual state, by the corresponding choices made in the different areas of his life," Rastafari 'culinary identity' is consistent with the primary mandate of self-determination—"to cultivate and create one's own destiny"—and food is seen as "a social indicator as well as an instrument for social re-engineering and social change" (158-9). As to their global impact, Afari specifically credits the Jamaican Rastafari with the increase not only of a global "culinary consciousness," but also the Livity's other cultural expressions "propagated through the creative works of art, music, literature and philosophy" (159).[14]

---

14 Literary representations of Ital Livity include Roger Mais' *Brother Man* (1954), Orlando Patterson's *The Children of Sisyphus* (1964), Zindika's *A Daughter's Grace* (1992), and Masani Montague's *Dread Culture. A Rasta Woman's Story* (1994), in

Such individual and societal transformation through cultural practices allows for an understanding of dietary practices as empowering acts of identity work. As Charles Price has shown in his ethnographic study of Rastafari,

> [i]dentity transformation involves identity and cultural work. Identity work entails the activities involved in creating and managing one's self-concept and its reference points. These activities are simultaneously cultural work because people use symbols and give them meaning, learn from other people, and interpret cultural materials [...]. Finally, they participate in ritualistic and routine interactions that fuel (but not necessarily nourish) their identities. My interlocutors explained that becoming Rastafari involved making connections among various dimensions of their experience: an acute awareness of oppression; a recognition of belonging to a denigrated group; a realization that there exists a longstanding tradition of positive understandings of Blackness; a discovery that one's cultural heritage has been hidden; that White cultural hegemony has distorted one's self-understanding. (Price 2009: 10)[15]

Although Price does not specify them in his acts-of-identity work in the sense of "the activities attendant to creating and internalizing a new identity" (168), the above examples have shown dietary practices to be an intricate part of Rastafarian Livity both on an individual and a collective level. Along the lines of John W. Pulis' assessment of "the ongoing and open-ended relation between religion, cultural expression, and everyday life" (Pulis 1999: 2-3), in the remaining section I thus link Ital Livity to a decolonial reading of Rastafari identity transformation beyond the dominant religious and countercultural frameworks for understanding and categorizing Rastafari.

THE DECOLONIALITY OF RASTAFARIAN ITAL LIVITY

As outlined above, Campbell's *Rasta and Resistance* (2007 [1985]), like many other studies, places Rastafari in the context of a culture of resistance—a link that is maintained to a great extent by way of Reggae's contribution to the spread of Rastafari linguistic and other cultural practices. With regards to their origins,

---

which it is variously linked to sociocultural differentiation, gradual awakening to Rastafari consciousness, and self-transformation, but also to some characters' disenchantment with the Livity. For a reading of Zindika's and Montague's novels, see Collins Klobah (2008: 179-89).

15 I thank Anastasia Wakengut for guiding me to this source.

such practices of resistance have to be placed in the wider context of anti-colonial struggles.[16] In a variety of ways they contribute to "the de-alienation and decolonization of the African mind" (Edmonds 2003: 61), which resonates with Frantz Fanon's (2008 [1952]; 2004 [1963]) foundational anti-colonial critique that positions the struggle for liberation in the psychological and cultural as much as in the political realm.

Based on the various Ethiopianist, Pan-Africanist, and Garveyite influences as well as drawing from Walter Rodney's *The Groundings with My Brothers* (2001 [1969]), Campbell places Rastafari in the context of "the people's right to their own history," in which national liberation is linked to "racial expressions [as] a *possibility* of assisting the region to free itself from foreign domination" (Campbell 2007: 6-7, emphasis in original). The practices of cultural and / or identity work of Rastafari thus are informed by, and in turn inform, the wider notion and project of cultural *as part of* political liberation. For the conceptualization of such cultural liberation, Campbell refers to Amilcar Cabral's observations on Portuguese colonialism in Western Africa:

The value of culture as an element of *resistance* to foreign domination lies in the fact that culture is the vigorous manifestation of the ideological plane of the physical and historical reality of the society that is dominated or to be dominated. Culture is simultaneously the fruit of a people's history, by the positive or negative influence which it exerts on the evolution of the relationship between man [sic] and his environment, among men or groups of men within a society, as well as different societies. (Cabral 1972 cited in Campbell 2007: 4, emphasis in original)[17]

Rodney contributed significantly to the positioning of Rastafari in the wider American and Pan-African Black Liberation struggle in general and Black Power in particular, and mobilized African history as a revolutionary tool. He emphatically asserts Rastafarian self-empowerment:

Now not only have we survived as a people but the Black Brothers in Kingston, Jamaica in particular, these are brothers who, up to now, are every day performing a miracle. It is a miracle how these fellows live. They live and they are physically fit, they have a vitality of mind, they have a tremendous sense of humour, they have depth. How do they do that

---

16 For a more general contextualization of decoloniality in relation to the emergence of Rastafari, cf. McPherson, "Rastafari and/as Decoloniality" (2014).

17 James offers a reading of Rastafari as a liberation movement in the context of Paolo Freire's "Pedagogy of the Oppressed" based on their shared "commitments to the construction of a new world order from the bottom up" (James 2008: 138).

in the midst of the existing conditions? And they create, they are always saying things. You know that some of the best painters and writers are coming out of the Rastafari environment. The black people in the West Indies have produced all the culture that we have, whether it be steelband or folk music. Black bourgeoisie and white people in the West Indies have produced nothing! Black people who have suffered all these years create. That is amazing. (Rodney 2001 [1969]: 68)

With this statement, Rodney not only renounces V.S. Naipaul's much-cited assessment that "nothing was created in the British West Indies, no civilization as in Spanish America, no great revolution as in Haiti or the American colonies. There were only plantations, prosperity, decline, neglect; the size of the islands called for nothing else" (Naipaul 1962: 27), but also the underlying notion that the "history of the islands can never be satisfactorily told. Brutality is not the only difficulty. History is built around achievement and creation; and nothing was created in the West Indies" (29). Contrary to such notions of non-creativity and non-achievement, a decolonial perspective emphasizes the empowerment inherent in the cultural practices of Rastafari as well as its challenges to the colonial conceptualizations of history embodied therein. Ital Livity, as outlined above, arguably forms an intricate part of such empowerment and identity transformation processes.

Anthony Bogues has placed both Rodney's and Fanon's "politics of postcoloniality" in the context of local and global anti-colonial struggles, decolonization, as well as theories of neocolonialism and of revolution, and links their interventions to revised notions of history, shared "modes of being" and quests for self-emancipation (cf. Bogues 2003: 148-50). Similar quests inform Bogues' notion of "dread history" as "an attempt both to grapple with the lived experiences of the Afro-Caribbean masses and to link these experiences to quests for emancipation and philosophies of hope" (179). 'Dread history' is not synonymous with but "draws from elements of the Rastafari worldview, to which it has a semantic relationship" in that it turns "the bourgeois colonial world [...] upside down" (ibid.). It is informed by "radical desire," emphasizes "historical silences" and constitutes "a radical ontological claim" as to both self-knowledge and historical knowledge in the sense of "how narrative and collective memory function" (ibid.):

Dread history is a general stance, a view of history, that I suggest is rooted in critical dimensions of the Jamaican subaltern's worldview. It is from within this perspective that native rebellious forms emerge in politics, music or culture. From the religious practices of Alexander Bedward to the contemporary lyrics of Bounty Killer, there is a remembering, a particular form of historicality, that can be discerned [...] Dread history emplots a narrative that carries the meanings of past events forward into the present. (180-2)

Such notions, I argue, inform not only the political, musical or cultural practices implied in this elaboration of 'dread history,' but specifically also Rastafari 'culinary identity,' especially given its linking of embodiment and consciousness.

As Walter Mignolo outlines in his genealogy of decolonial thought, "geo-historical and bio-graphical" (i.e. relating to the body-politics of knowledge, Mignolo 2011: xxi) aspects such as the ones articulated in Fanon's much-cited invocation "O my body, make of me always a man who questions!" (Fanon 2008: 232), stand "at the very inception of decolonial thinking" and constitute a "radical challenge" (Mignolo 2011: xxiii):

If you take Fanon's request, then you may not feel comfortable analyzing Fanon from an epistemic perspective in which your body doesn't call your mind into question. What are the connections between your body, bio-graphically and geo-historically located in the colonial matrix of power, and the issues you investigate? (ibid.)

Rastafari dietary and other bodily practices and worldviews acknowledge and in many ways contribute to the "delinking" from the "colonial matrix of power," which in Anibal Quijano's formulation can be described "as four interrelated domains: control of the economy, of authority, of gender and sexuality, and of knowledge and subjectivity" (8). Given their position vis-à-vis all of these colonially inflected relations of power, Rastafarian notions of Livity and Itality, as outlined above, thus place the movement firmly in a genealogy not only of decolonial *thought*, but furthermore of decolonial *practice*. Since the decolonial "originated [...] from the experience of decolonization in the Third World and in the works of Afro [sic] and Afro-Caribbean intellectuals and activists" (55), Rastafari 'culinary identity' as traced above can be placed in a decolonial framework of enactment of knowledge and understanding.

Finally, Ital Livity poses an epistemic challenge also insofar as it necessitates a thinking beyond and outside of the dominant comparative religious vocabulary which aims to describe and categorize Rastafari. As William Hart has shown, such comparisons often imply what he calls the "imperial / colonial model of religion," i.e. an "evolutionary / hierarchical model" that follows a schemata "from simple to complex religion, from primitive to civilized, from religions of the South to those of the North, from religions of the East to those of the West, from the religions of Africa, aboriginal Australia, and native America to the religions of Europe" (Hart 2002: 554). As the example of dietary and related cultural practices has shown, in order to avoid an easy subsuming of Rastafari under such an "imperial / colonial model of religion," one has to think of Rastafari mainly in its own terms, such as that of the Livity. The wider decolonial perspective suggested here thus aims to resist the urge to categorize Rastafari through any singular or dominant label and category, but rather encourages an understanding of categories like "religion" or "culture" as what James Clifford has called "translation terms" in the sense of "word[s] of apparently general application used for comparison in a strategic and contingent way" which, when "used in global comparisons [...] get us some distance *and* fall apart" (Clifford 1997: 39).

BIBLIOGRAPHY

Afari, Yasus 2007. *Overstanding Rastafari. 'Jamaica's Gift to the World.'* Kingston: Senya-Cum.

Alleyne, Mervyn C. 1988. *Roots of Jamaican Culture*. London: Pluto Press.

Augier, Roy and Veronica Salter, eds. 2010. *Rastafari. The Reports. 1958-1962. Caribbean Quarterly.* Cultural Studies Initiative. Kingston: University of the West Indies Press.

Andwele, Adisa 2006. "The Contribution of Rastafarianism to the Decolonization of the Caribbean." *Rastafari. A Universal Philosophy in the Third Millenium.* Ed. Werner Zips. Kingston / Miami: Ian Randle Publishers, 7-20.

B, Anthony 2009. "Where Is The Black Man Rights." *Rise Up.* Greensleeves.

Barrett, Leonard E. 1997 [1988]. *The Rastafarians*. Boston: Beacon.

Bogues, Anthony 2003. *Black Heretics, Black Prophets. Radical Political Intellectuals.* New York: Routledge.

Boxill, Ian, ed. 2008. *The Globalization of Rastafari.* Ideaz 7. Kingston, Jamaica: Arawak.

Campbell, Horace 2007 [1985]. *Rasta and Resistance. From Marcus Garvey to Walter Rodney.* London / Hertfordshire: Hansib.

Cassidy, Frederic Gomes and Robert B. Le Page, eds. 2002 [1967]. *Dictionary of Jamaican English.* Barbados et al.: University of the West Indies Press.

Chevannes, Barry 1994. *Rastafari. Roots and Ideology.* New York: Syracuse University Press.

—. ed. 1995. *Rastafari and Other African-Caribbean Worldviews.* New Brunswick: Rutgers University Press.

Clifford, James 1997. "Traveling Cultures." *Routes. Travel and Translation in the Late Twentieth Century.* Cambridge, MA: Harvard University Press, 17-46.

Collins, Loretta 2000. "Daughters of Jah. The Impact of Rastafarian Womanhood in the Caribbean, the United States, Britain, and Canada." *Religion, Culture, and Tradition in the Caribbean.* Eds. Hemchand Gossai and Nathaniel Samuel Murrell. New York: St. Martin's Press, 227-55.

Collins Klobah, Loretta 2008. "Journeying Towards Mount Zion. Changing Representations of Womanhood in Popular Music, Performance Poetry, and Novels by Rastafarian Women." *The Globalization of Rastafari.* Ed. Ian Boxill. Ideaz 7. Kingston: Arawak, 158-96.

Duncombe, Stephen 2002. "Introduction." *Cultural Resistance Reader.* Ed. Stephen Duncombe. London / New York: Verso, 1-15.

Edmonds, Ennis Barrington 2003. *Rastafari. From Outcasts to Culture Bearers.* Oxford / New York: Oxford University Press.

Fanon, Frantz 2004 [1961]. *The Wretched of the Earth.* Transl. Richard Philcox. New York: Grove Press.

—. 2008 [1952]. *Black Skin, White Masks.* Transl. Richard Philcox. New York: Grove Press.

Forsythe, Dennis 1980. "West Indian Culture Through the Prism of Rastafarianism." *Caribbean Quarterly* 26.4: 62-81.

—. 1999 [1983]. *Rastafari. For the Healing of the Nation.* New York: One Drop Books.

Hart, William D. 2002. "Slavoj Zizek and the Imperial / Colonial Model of Religion." *Nepantla. Views from South* 3.3: 553-78.

Hill, Robert A. 2001 [1981]. *Dread History. Leonard P. Howell and Millenarian Visions in the Early Rastafarian Religion.* Kingston et al.: Research Associates / School Times Publications and Miguel Lorne.

Homiak, John 1995. "Dub History. Soundings of Rastafari Livity and Language." *Rastafari and Other African-Caribbean Worldviews.* Ed. Barry Chevannes. New Brunswick: Rutgers University Press, 127-81.

Jaffke, Rivke 2010. "Ital Chic. Rastafari, Resistance, and the Politics of Consumption in Jamaica." *Small Axe* 31, 14.1: 30-45.

James, Leslie 2008. "Rastafari and Paulo Freire. Religion, Democracy, and the New World Order." *The Globalization of Rastafari.* Ed. Ian Boxill. Ideaz 7. Kingston: Arawak, 138-57.

Kitzinger, Sheila 1966. "The Rastafarian Brethren of Jamaica." *Comparative Studies in Society and History* 9.1: 33-9.

Kroll, Florian 2006 "Roots and Culture. Rasta Bushdoctors of the Cape, SA." *Rastafari. A Universal Philosophy in the Third Millenium.* Ed. Werner Zips. Kingston / Miami: Ian Randle Publishers, 215-55.

McPherson, Annika 2014. "Rastafari and/as Decoloniality." *Postcoloniality – Decoloniality – Black Critique. Joints and Fissures*. Eds. Sabine Broeck and Carsten Junker. Frankfurt / New York: Campus, forthcoming.

Mignolo, Walter 2011. *The Darker Side of Western Modernity. Global Futures, Decolonial Options*. Durham: Duke University Press.

Murrell, Nathaniel Samuel, William David Spencer, and Adrian Anthony McFarlane, eds. 1998. *Chanting Down Babylon. The Rastafari Reader*. Philadelphia: Temple University Press.

Naipaul, V.S. 1962. *The Middle Passage*. London: André Deutsch.

Pollard, Velma 2000. *Dread Talk. The Language of Rastafari*. Montreal: McGill-Queen's University Press / Kingston: Canoe Press.

Price, Charles 2009. *Becoming Rasta. Origins of Rastafari Identity in Jamaica*. New York / London: New York University Press.

Pulis, John W. 1999. "Religion, Diaspora, and Cultural Identity. An Introduction." *Religion, Diaspora, and Cultural Identity. A Reader in the Anglophone Caribbean*. Ed. John W. Pulis. Amsterdam et al.: Gordon and Breach, 1-12.

Rodney, Walter 2001 [1969]. *The Groundings With My Brothers*. Kingston: Miguel Lorne.

Rowe, Maureen 1998. "Gender and Family Relations in Rastafari. A Personal Perspective." *Chanting Down Babylon. The Rastafari Reader*. Eds. Nathaniel Samuel Murrell, William David Spencer, and Adrian Anthony McFarlane. Philadelphia: Temple University Press, 72-88.

Savishinski, Neil J. 1994. "Rastafari in the Promised Land. The Spread of a Jamaican Socioreligious Movement among the Youth of West Africa." *African Studies Review* 37.3: 19-50.

Sharp, Joanne P. et al. 2000. "Entanglements of Power. Geographies of Dominance / Resistance." *Entanglements of Power. Geographies of Dominance / Resistance*. Eds. Joanne P. Sharp et al. London / New York: Routledge, 1-42.

Simpson, George Eaton 1985. "Religion and Justice. Some Reflections on the Rastafari Movement." *Phylon* 46.4: 286–91.

—. 1998. "Personal Reflections on Rastafari in West Kingston in the Early 1950s." *Chanting Down Babylon. The Rastafari Reader*. Eds. Nathaniel Samuel Murrell, William David Spencer, and Adrian Anthony McFarlane. Philadelphia: Temple University Press, 217-28.

Tafari-Ama, Imani M. 1998. "Rastawoman as Rebel. Case Studies in Jamaica." *Chanting Down Babylon. The Rastafari Reader*. Eds. Nathaniel Samuel Murrell, William David Spencer, and Adrian Anthony McFarlane. Philadelphia: Temple University Press, 89-106.

Yawney, Carole D. 1994. "Moving with the Dawtas of Rastafari. From Myth to Reality." *Arise Ye Mighty People! Gender, Class and Race in Popular Struggles*. Ed. Terisa E. Turner. Trenton: Africa World Press, 65-73.

—. 1994. "Rasta Mek a Trod. Symbolic Ambiguity in a Globalizing Religion." *Arise Ye Mighty People! Gender, Class and Race in Popular Struggles*. Ed. Terisa E. Turner. Trenton: Africa World Press, 75-83.

Notes on Contributors

Berti, Ilaria is a PhD candidate in History at the University of Genoa, Italy. Her main research interests concern Food Studies, Atlantic History, History of Medicine, Cultural History, History of Travel, and Gender Studies. One of her forthcoming publications is entitled "'Feeding the sick upon stewed fish and pork, highly seasoned, produces the very best effects possible.' Slaves' Health and Food in a Jamaican Sugar Cane Plantation Hospital," in *Food and History* (2014).

Beushausen, Wiebke is a research associate in the junior research group "From the Caribbean to North America and Back" and a PhD candidate at the Neuphilologische Fakultät at Heidelberg University. Her thesis investigates the coming-of-age genre by Caribbean women writers in the diaspora locations Canada and the United States. In 2012, she was visiting researcher at the Centre for Research on Latin America and the Caribbean, York University, Toronto. She was a teacher in Jamaican literature, popular culture, and history at the English Department, University of Heidelberg.

den Boer, Elizabeth is affiliated with the University of Leiden and holds a a PhD from Radboud University in Nijmegen. Her research made a shift in focus from the study on the transitional function of dreams of the indigenous people of Suriname and Australia to culture and religion of the descendants of the British Indian contract laborers in Suriname and the Netherlands. She is particularly interested in modernity of Hinduism and Buddhism in the Netherlands, and the meaning of food in modern society. She is author of "Spirit conception. Dreams in Aboriginal Australia" in *Dreaming* (2012), "Kastenbewustzijn in Suriname" in *OSO, Tijdschrift voor Surinamistiek* (2009), and "Indian Religions in the Netherlands" in *Changing Images; Lasting Visions* (2008), edited by Neelam D. Sabharwal.

Brüske, Anne is head of the junior research group "From the Caribbean to North America and Back" at Heidelberg University. She holds a PhD in Romance Literature from Heidelberg University (2008) and has taught in Basel, Lyon, and Heidelberg. Her current book project focuses on the construction of social space and meta/intertextuality in narrative texts by U.S. Dominican, mainland Puerto Rican, Cuban American, and Haitian American authors. She has co-edited the volume *Dialogues transculturels à Montréal et à New York / Diálogos transculturales en Montreal y Nueva York* (2013) with Herle-Christin Jessen.

Commichau, Ana-Sofia is a research associate in the junior research group "From the Caribbean to North America and Back" and a PhD candidate at the Neuphilologische Fakultät of Heidelberg University. In her dissertation she focuses on identity constructions in contemporary Cuban-American autobiographies. In 2011 and 2013, she was visiting scholar at the Hermanos Saiz Montes de Oca University of Pinar del Rio, Cuba and at the Cuban Research Institute at the Florida International University in Miami, Florida. Her research interests are Cuban(-American) (autobiographical) literature and weblogs, transcultural identity, and communication.

Darias Alfonso, Ivan holds a PhD from Birkbeck, University of London and a Masters from Cardiff University's School of Journalism, Media and Cultural Studies. His research focuses on Cuban émigrés in Western Europe and constructions of identity. From 1994 to 2004 he worked on Cuban media (print, broadcast, and online) as a journalist and editor. He is also an award-winning fiction writer and is currently working on a book project on Cultural Memory in the Cuban diaspora.

Graziadei, Daniel is a lecturer at the Institute for Romance Philology at Ludwig Maximilian University of Munich, a literary translator, a blogger, and a poet. In 2013, he finished his doctoral thesis on islands in the archipelago of contemporary Anglo-, Franco-, and Hispanophone Caribbean literatures. His MA thesis on literary neo-avant-garde in the Americas has been published in 2008. He further published "Geopoetics of the Island," in *Tra paesaggio e geopoetica* (2011), edited by Marco Mastronunzio and Federico Italiano.

Helber, Patrick is a research assistant in the junior research group "From the Caribbean to North America and Back" and PhD student in Contemporary History at Heidelberg University. His thesis analyses the controversy on homophobic Dancehall music in the Jamaican press. In 2011, he was a visiting researcher at the University of the West Indies, Mona, Jamaica. He published the essay "'Ah My Brownin' Dat.' A Visual Discourse Analysis of the Performance of Vybz Kartel's Masculinity in the Cartoons of the Jamaica Observer," in *Caribbean Quarterly* (2012). His research interests are Postcolonial, Gender, and Critical Whiteness Studies.

Huber, Sebastian is a member of the PhD program ProLit and pursues a joint degree from Ludwig Maximilian University, Munich and the University of Alberta, Edmonton in 2014. In his doctoral thesis, entitled "Subject of the Event. Reagency in the American Novel after 2000," he deals with Thomas Pynchon's *Against the Day,* and Cormac McCarthy's *The Road,* amongst others, in conjunction with Alain Badiou's notion of subjective creations. He has published articles on Pynchon, Mark Z. Danielewski, Badiou, and Nelson Goodman. He loves sushi.

Kloß, Sinah is a research associate in the junior research group "From the Caribbean to North America and Back" and a PhD candidate in Social Anthropology at Heidelberg University. In her dissertation she focuses on the consumption and exchange of clothing among Guyanese Hindus in the context of migration to North America. In 2011-12, she was visiting researcher at the Department of Language and Cultural Studies, University of Guyana. She conducted fieldwork in Guyana and New York City. Her research interests are Material Culture Studies, Caribbean Hinduism, and Transnational Migration.

Lawson Welsh, Sarah has a PhD in Caribbean Studies from the Centre for Caribbean Studies, Warwick University, U.K. She is currently Associate Professor and Reader in English and Postcolonial Literatures at York St John University, U.K. She co-edited *Rerouting the Postcolonial. New Directions for a New Millennium* (2010) and *The Routledge Reader in Caribbean Literature* (1996). Her monograph, *Grace Nichols,* the first book-length study of Nichols, appeared in the British Council 'Writers and their Work' series in 2007. She is Associate Editor of *Journal of Postcolonial Writing* (formerly *World Literature Written in English*), published by Taylor & Francis.

De Maeseneer, Rita is Professor of Spanish American Literature and Culture at the University of Antwerp, Belgium, since 1998. She is specialized in literature from the Hispanic Caribbean and its diaspora. She has published *El festín de Alejo Carpentier. Una lectura culinario-intertexual* (2003), *Encuentro con la narrativa dominicana contemporánea* (2006), and *Devorando a lo cubano. Una* *aproximación gastrocrítica a textos relacionados con el siglo XIX y el Período Especial* (2012).

McPherson, Annika teaches British and Global Anglophone Literary and Cultural Studies at Carl von Ossietzky University, Oldenburg. Her research areas include Postcolonial Studies, Caribbean and South African Literatures in English, Black British Literature, Rastafari, Pan-Africanism, as well as theories and policies of diversity in comparative perspective. Her dissertation on white women authors in relation to postcolonial discourse was published as *White – Female – Postcolonial? Towards a 'Trans-cultural' Reading of Marina Warner's* Indigo *and Barbara Kingsolver's* The Poisonwood Bible (2011).

Nikolić, Mona is a PhD candidate in Social Anthropology at the Institute for Latin American Studies of the Free University of Berlin. In her dissertation project, she investigates the impact of cultural globalization on foodways and cuisine as identity markers in Costa Rica. In 2010-11, she did fieldwork as a research intern at the Escuela de Antropología, University of Costa Rica, holding a DAAD scholarship. Her research interests include the Anthropology of Central America, Culinary Anthropology, and Transnational Studies.

Parasecoli, Fabio is Associate Professor and Coordinator of the Food Studies Program, The New School, New York. His work explores the intersections among food, media, and politics, particularly in popular culture. He is author of *Bite Me! Food in Popular Culture* (2008) and *Al Dente. A History of Food in Italy* (2014). He is co-editor of the six-volume *Cultural History of Food* (2012).

Plaza, Dwaine is a Professor of Sociology in the School of Public Policy at Oregon State University. He has written extensively on the topic of Caribbean migration within the international diaspora. His publications focus on: return migration; remittance practices; hybridity and segmented assimilation among the second generation; new internet communication technology (Skype, Facebook, and e-mail); Canadian immigration policy; sexuality and identity issues among the second generation. His current research looks at transnational caregiving among Caribbean people.

Söllner, Louisa studied Comparative Literature at Göttingen, Perugia, and Munich, and also holds an M.Phil in Latin American Studies from the University of Cambridge. She completed her PhD dissertation *Missing Pictures. Photography, History, and Nostalgia in Cuban-American Literature* in 2012. Her research interests include cultural intersections between U.S. American and Latin American art and literature as well conceptualizations of writing space in modernist literature.